CHENG & TSUI
"Bringing Asia to the World"™

中文听说读写 · 中文聽說讀寫

INTEGRATED CHINESE

Simplified and Traditional Characters

4

Textbook

4th Edition

Yuehua Liu and Tao-chung Yao
Yaohua Shi, Liangyan Ge, Nyan-Ping Bi

Original Edition by Yuehua Liu and Tao-chung Yao
Yaohua Shi and Nyan-Ping Bi

CHENG & TSUI

"Bringing Asia to the World"™

Copyright © 2019, 2010, 2006, 1997 by
Cheng & Tsui Company, Inc.

Fourth Edition

5th Printing, 2021

25 24 23 22 21   5 6 7 8

ISBN 978-1-62291-150-9
[Fourth Edition, Simplified and Traditional
Characters, Hardcover]

ISBN 978-1-62291-151-6
[Fourth Edition, Simplified and Traditional
Characters, Paperback]

Library of Congress
Cataloging-in-Publication
Data [Third Edition]

Integrated Chinese = [Zhong wen ting shuo
du xie]. Level 2, part 2 / Yuehua Liu . . . [et al.]
– 3rd ed.
        p. cm.

Chinese and English.

Includes indexes.

Parallel title in Chinese characters.

ISBN 978-0-88727-689-7 (hbk.)
– ISBN 978-0-88727-688-0 (pbk.)
1. Chinese language –Textbooks for foreign
speakers–English. I. Liu, Yuehua. II. Title:
Zhong wen ting shuo du xie.

PL1129.E5I683 2009

495.1–dc22

Printed in the United States of America

The *Integrated Chinese* series encompasses
textbooks, workbooks, character workbooks,
teacher's resources, audio, video, and more.
Content is available in a variety of formats,
including print and online via the ChengTsui
Web App™. Visit chengtsui.com for more
information on the other components of
Integrated Chinese.

Publisher
JILL CHENG

Editors
MIKE YONG, RANDY TELFER,
and LEI WANG

Creative Director
CHRISTIAN SABOGAL

Illustrators/Designers
KATE PAPADAKI and LIZ YATES

Photographs
© Adobe Stock
© Cheng & Tsui
© Shutterstock*

Cheng & Tsui Company, Inc.
25 West Street
Boston, MA 02111-1213 USA
chengtsui.co
Phone (617) 988-2400 / (800) 554-1963
Fax (617) 426-3669

Photo Credits are listed on p. xxi.

This Fourth Edition of *Integrated Chinese* is dedicated to the memory of our dearest colleague and friend Professor Tao-chung (Ted) Yao.

Publisher's Note

When *Integrated Chinese* was first published in 1997, it set a new standard with its focus on the development and integration of the four language skills (listening, speaking, reading, and writing). Today, to further enrich the learning experience of the many users of *Integrated Chinese* worldwide, Cheng & Tsui is pleased to offer this revised and updated Fourth Edition of *Integrated Chinese*. We would like to thank the many teachers and students who, by offering their valuable insights and suggestions, have helped *Integrated Chinese* evolve and keep pace with the many positive changes in the field of Chinese language instruction. *Integrated Chinese* continues to offer comprehensive language instruction, with many new features, including the **ChengTsui Web App™**, as detailed in the Preface.

The Cheng & Tsui Chinese language program is designed to publish and widely distribute quality language learning materials created by leading instructors from around the world. We welcome readers' comments and suggestions concerning the publications in this series. Please contact the following members of our Editorial Board, in care of our Editorial Department (email: editor@chengtsui.co).

Contents

Preface

The *Integrated Chinese* (IC) series is an internationally acclaimed Mandarin Chinese language course that delivers a cohesive system of print and digital resources for highly effective teaching and learning. First published in 1997, it is now the leading series of Chinese language learning resources in the United States and beyond. Through its holistic focus on the language skills of listening, speaking, reading, and writing, IC teaches novice and intermediate students the skills they need to function in Chinese.

What's New

It has been over eight years since the publication of the Third Edition of IC. We are deeply grateful for all the positive feedback, as well as constructive suggestions for improvement, from IC users. In the meantime, China and the world have seen significant transformations in electronic communications, commerce, and media. Additionally, the technology available to us is transforming the way teachers and students interact with content. The teaching of Chinese as a second language needs to keep pace with these exciting developments. Therefore, the time seems right to update IC across delivery formats.

In developing this latest edition of IC, we have consulted the American Council on the Teaching of Foreign Languages (ACTFL) *21st Century Skills Map for World Languages*. The national standards for foreign language learning in the 21st century focus on goals in five areas—communication, cultures, connections, comparisons, and communities. In addition to classifying the applicable Language Practice activities by communication mode (interpersonal, interpretive, and presentational), we have added a host of materials that address the 5 Cs. The delivery of IC via the new **ChengTsui Web App™** elevates the teaching and learning experience by presenting multimedia and interactive content in a truly blended and integrated way.

New, visually rich supplementary modules that recur in each lesson have been introduced. These can be taught in any sequence to serve as prompts for classroom discussion and student reflection:

- Get Real with Chinese draws on realia to situate language learning in real-life contexts. Students are required to analyze, predict, and synthesize before coming to conclusions about embedded linguistic and cultural meaning. Photos and questions connect the classroom to authentic Chinese experiences. To familiarize students with both character sets, students are exposed to realia in simplified characters or realia in traditional characters.

- Chinese Chat provides opportunities for language practice in the digital environment. Realistic texting, microblogging, and social media scenarios show students how the younger generation has adapted Chinese to new communication technologies.

- Characterize It! encourages students to approach Chinese characters analytically. Additional activities are provided on the ChengTsui Web App.

- How About You? has been revamped for the first two volumes and newly introduced in Volumes 3 and 4. This module encourages students to personalize their study of vocabulary and learn words and phrases that relate to their own interests and background. Visual cues, which prompt possible answers, promote vocabulary expansion and retention. In Volumes 3 and 4, questions appear in Chinese only, and encourage students to answer in a full sentence or short paragraph.

- In A Way with Words, students will find in the example sentence new words and phrases that, although unstudied, bear a cognate relationship to a word or phrase that they have just learned in the current lesson. Based on the provided context, students are encouraged to guess at the meaning of these new words or phrases. The exercise is designed to raise students' awareness of the latent semantic interconnections among different vocabulary items and to foster their ability to expand their vocabulary on their own.

While not new to the Fourth Edition, Words & Phrases is new to Volumes 3 and 4 of IC. This is because as students move up proficiency levels the number of new syntactic structures decreases while the study of semantics becomes more and more important. Unlike Language Notes, which sheds light on lexical nuances and idiomatic usage, Words & Phrases elaborates on versatile words and phrases with multiple examples and should be given the same weight as Grammar.

Moreover, per ACTFL guidelines, we have included Compare & Contrast activities in the Cultural Literacy (formerly Culture Highlights) section in order to promote students' awareness of cultural diversity in a world of rapid globalization. This section as a whole has been given a lavishly illustrated, magazine-style treatment to better engage students.

In Volumes 3 and 4, the Text has been updated for additional visual interest, including with icons of the characters. The Before You Study, When You Study, and After You Study segments have been revised to include questions in Chinese. View & Explore, meanwhile, encourages students to make use of short, supplemental video clips available through the ChengTsui Web App.

The Vocabulary list, as well the Indexes, now provides simplified and traditional characters in full for each item in Volumes 3 and 4.

Bringing It Together (formerly Let's Review) continues to help students review language forms and language functions previously introduced.

Finally, the new Lesson Wrap-Up section includes context-based wrap-up projects, developed in line with ACTFL standards. These projects encourage students to become active learners by requiring them to engage in research beyond the textbook, and additional projects for this section are available through the ChengTsui Web App. The ability to speak and write cohesively is a key attribute of advanced learners; building on Make It Flow! in IC1 and IC2, we have created a new segment, Keep It Flowing, to help students develop and apply strategies for coherently and cohesively organizing information in written and spoken discourse. The Lesson Wrap-Up activities can be used as assessment instruments for the Can-Do Checklist, which encourages students to measure their progress at the end of the lesson.

As previous users of IC will note, we have renamed the four-volume series. The new sequencing of Volumes 1 to 4 better reflects the flexibility of the materials and the diversity of our user groups and their instructional environments. However, we also recognize that Volumes 1 and 2 are often used together in the first year of language instruction, and Volumes 3 and 4 in the second. Thus, for ease of reference, we have retained the sequencing of the lessons from 1 to 20 in each half of the series.

We have also relabeled complex grammatical structures. Users will now find continuous Roman numerals applied across the four IC volumes. Students and teachers can now easily see that five segments are devoted to the particle 了 , three to directional complements, and so on. Grammatical structures that are recycled for review purposes are marked "revisited," to allow teachers to decide how much time to spend on them. We hope that this new system brings greater organizational clarity and makes for easier cross-referencing.

As with the Third Edition, the Fourth Edition of IC features both traditional- and simplified-character versions of the Volume 1 and 2 textbooks and workbooks, and a combination of traditional and simplified characters in the Volume 3 and 4 textbooks and workbooks. However, in response to user feedback, we have updated the traditional characters to ensure they match the standard set used in Taiwan. For reference, we have consulted the Taiwan Ministry of Education's online *Revised Chinese Dictionary*. To reflect the predominance of simplified characters in Chinese language instruction, we have listed simplified characters first in the new edition of Volumes 3 and 4.

The most significant change in the Fourth Edition is the incorporation of innovative educational technology. Users of the print edition have access to audio (at chengtsui.co/resources), while subscribers to the ChengTsui Web App have access to audio plus additional, interactive content.

Users who choose to purchase the **Basic Edition** of the ChengTsui Web App will have access to:

- Audio (Textbook and Workbook)
- View & Explore video clips based on each lesson's theme
- Vocabulary flashcards
- Additional character practice
- Additional Lesson Wrap-Up projects

Users who choose to purchase the **Essential Edition** of the ChengTsui Web App will, in addition to the above, have access to the Workbook with automatic feedback for students and printable Character Workbook sheets for handwriting and stroke order practice.

In addition to the student editions, the ChengTsui Web App is available in an **Educator Edition**. The *Educator Edition* web-application overlay suggests teaching tips and strategies and conveniently makes connections between the Textbook and the additional resources provided in the Teacher's Resources, such as video activity worksheets, quizzes, and answer keys.

A key feature of the ChengTsui Web App is coherence. The innovative instructional design provides an integrated user experience. Learners can move seamlessly between the transmission, practice, application, and evaluation stages, navigating the content to suit their particular learning needs and styles. For more information about the Web App, please visit chengtsui.co.

Both in its print and digital versions, the new IC features a contemporary layout that adds clarity and rigor to our instructional design. Rich new visuals complement the text's revised, user-friendly language and up-to-date cultural content. We hope that students and teachers find the many changes and new features timely and meaningful.

Organizational Principles

In the higher education setting, the IC series often covers two years of instruction, with the first two volumes usually used in the first year of study, and the final two volumes in the second. The lessons first cover topics from everyday life, then gradually move to more abstract subject matter. The materials do not follow one pedagogical methodology, but instead blend several effective teaching approaches. Used in conjunction with the ChengTsui Web App, incorporating differentiated instruction, blended learning, and the flipped classroom is even easier. Here are some of the features of IC that distinguish it from other Chinese language resources:

Integrating Pedagogy and Authenticity

We believe that students should be taught authentic materials even in the beginning stage of language learning. Therefore, authentic materials (produced by native Chinese speakers for native Chinese speakers) are included in every lesson.

Integrating Traditional and Simplified Characters

We believe that students should learn both traditional and simplified Chinese characters. However, we also realize that teaching students both forms from day one could be overwhelming. Our solution is for students to focus on one form during their first year of study, and to acquire the other during their second. Therefore, the first two volumes of IC are available in separate traditional- and simplified-character versions, with the texts presented in the alternative character form in the Appendix.

By their second year of study, we believe that all students should be exposed to both forms of written Chinese. Accordingly, the final two volumes of IC include both traditional and simplified characters. Students in second-year Chinese language classes come from different backgrounds, and should be allowed to write in their preferred form. However, it is important that the learner write in one form only, and not a mix of both. In keeping with the differing conventions for the punctuation of traditional and simplified characters, punctuation marks for simplified characters have been set at the baseline and close to the preceding character, while punctuation marks for traditional characters have been set at the median and centered within the following space.

Integrating Teaching Approaches

Because no single teaching method can adequately train a student in all language skills, we employ a variety of approaches in IC. In addition to the communicative approach, we also use traditional methods such as grammar-translation and the direct method.

Users of the ChengTsui Web App can employ additional teaching approaches, such as differentiated learning and blended learning. Students can engage in self-paced learning, a very powerful study strategy. The product also facilitates breaking down direct instruction into more engaging "bites" of learning, which improves student engagement. Moreover, the ChengTsui Web App allows students to interact with the content at home and practice and apply their learning in the classroom with corrective teacher feedback, which has the potential to improve student outcomes. Additionally, teachers and learners do not need to follow the instructional flow of the underlying book. They can navigate using multiple pathways in flexible and customized ways and at varying paces for true individualized learning.

Acknowledgments

We would like to thank users around the world for believing in IC. We owe much of the continued success of IC to their invaluable feedback. Likewise, we would be remiss if we did not acknowledge the University of Notre Dame for sponsoring and inviting us to a one-day workshop on IC on April 9, 2016. Leading Chinese-language specialists from across the country shared their experiences with the IC authors. We are especially indebted to Professor Yongping Zhu, Chair of the Department of East Asian Languages and Cultures at Notre Dame, and his colleagues and staff for organizing the workshop.

Professors Fangpei Cai and Meng Li of the University of Chicago took time out from their busy teaching schedules to compile a detailed list of comments and suggestions. We are profoundly touched by their generosity. In completing this Fourth Edition, we have taken into consideration their and other users' recommendations for revision. Indeed, many of the changes are in response to user feedback. The authors are naturally responsible for any remaining shortcomings and oversights.

For two summers in a row, Professor Liangyan Ge's wife, Ms. Yongqing Pan, warmly invited the IC team to their home to complete the bulk of the work of revising the IC series. Words are inadequate to express our thanks to Ms. Pan for her gracious hospitality and her superb cooking day in and day out.

We are deeply grateful to our publisher Cheng & Tsui Company and to Jill Cheng in particular for her unswerving support for IC over the years. We would also like to express our heartfelt appreciation to our editors Mike Yong, Lei Wang, and the rest of the editorial team for their meticulous attention to every aspect of this new edition.

As we look back on the evolution of IC, one person is never far from our thoughts. Without Professor Tao-chung Yao's commitment from its inception, IC would not have been possible. Sadly, Professor Yao passed away in September 2015. Throughout the summer, Professor Yao remained in close contact with the rest of the team, going over each draft of IC 1 with an eagle eye, providing us with the benefit of his wisdom by phone and email. This Fourth Edition of IC is a living tribute to his vision and guidance.

Note: Prefaces to the previous editions of IC are available at chengtsui.co.

Series Structure

The IC series has been carefully conceptualized and developed to facilitate flexible delivery options that meet the needs of different instructional environments.

Component per Volume	Description	Print/Other Formats	ChengTsui Web App™
Textbook	• Ten engaging lessons per volume, each with readings, grammar explanations, communicative exercises, and culture notes	• Paperback or Hardcover • Simplified or Traditional Characters (Volumes 1 and 2) • Simplified and Traditional Characters (Volumes 3 and 4)	• *Basic, Essential*, and *Educator Editions*
Workbook	• Wide range of integrated activities covering the three modes of communication (interpersonal, interpretive, and presentational)	• Paperback • Simplified or Traditional Characters (Volumes 1 and 2) • Simplified and Traditional Characters (Volumes 3 and 4)	• *Essential* and *Educator Editions*
Character Workbook	• Radical- and character-writing and stroke order practice	• Paperback • Simplified and Traditional Characters	• *Essential* and *Educator Editions*
Audio	• Audio for Textbook vocabulary and lesson texts, and in Volume 1, pronunciation exercises • Audio for Workbook listening exercises, and in Volume 1, pronunciation exercises	• Audio available to print users at chengtsui.co/resources	• *Basic, Essential*, and *Educator Editions*
Video	• Volumes 1 and 2: acted dialogues and narratives presented in the Textbooks; also includes theme-related Culture Minutes sections in authentic settings • Volumes 3 and 4: documentary-style episodes correlating to the lesson themes in authentic settings	• One DVD per volume	• *Basic, Essential*, and *Educator Editions* • Streaming video
Teacher's Resources	• Comprehensive implementation support, teaching tips, sample syllabi, tests and quizzes, answer keys to the workbook exercises, and supplementary resources	• Downloadable resources that include core lesson guides along with ancillary materials previously on the companion website	• *Educator Edition*

Volume 4 Lesson Structure

All components of IC (Textbooks, Workbooks, and Teacher's Resources) are considered core and are designed to be used together to enhance teaching and learning. Recurrent lesson subsections are highlighted in the Textbook Elements column. Note that Supplementary Modules do not compose a separate section, but are rather discrete entities that appear throughout each lesson.

Section	Textbook Elements	Interactive Content	Workbooks	Teacher's Resources
Lesson Opener	· Learning Objectives state what students will be able to do by the end of the lesson · Relate & Get Ready helps students reflect on similarities and differences between Chinese culture and their own		· Opportunity for students to revisit learning objectives and self-assess	· Overview of language functions, vocabulary, grammar, pronunciation, and characters taught in the lesson · Sequencing recommendations and teaching aids
Text	· Chinese Text in each lesson demonstrates practical vocabulary and grammar usage · Before You Study includes lesson-related questions for teachers to use as warm-up activities · When You Study provides reading comprehension questions that students can answer after listening to and scanning the Text · After You Study includes summative questions that encourage students to produce discrete sentences · Language Notes shed light on semantic nuances and idiomatic usage · *Pinyin* version at the end of the lesson provides pronunciation support	· Audio builds receptive skills	· Listening comprehension and speaking exercises based on the dialogues · Reading comprehension	· Strategies for teaching the Text, plus question prompts

Section	Textbook Elements	Interactive Content	Workbooks	Teacher's Resources
Vocabulary	· Vocabulary lists define and categorize new words from the Text (proper nouns are listed last)	· Audio models proper pronunciation · Flashcards assist with vocabulary acquisition	· Handwriting and stroke order practice is provided in the Character Workbook · All exercises use lesson vocabulary to support acquisition	· Explanations, pronunciation tips, usage notes, and phrasal combinations
Grammar	· Grammar points, which correspond to numbered references in the readings, explain and model language forms		· Writing and grammar exercises based on grammar introduced in the lesson	· Explanations, pattern practice, and additional grammar notes
Words & Phrases	· Words & Phrases elaborates on useful words and phrases, highlighted in green in the lesson text, with multiple examples			
Language Practice	· Role-plays, pair activities, contextualized drills, and visual cues prompt students to produce language		· Exercises and activities spanning the three modes of communication (interpersonal, interpretive, and presentational), plus *pinyin* and tone practice, to build communication and performance skills	
Cultural Literacy	· Culture notes provide snapshots of contemporary and traditional Chinese-speaking cultures · Compare & Contrast draws connections between cultures		· Authentic materials develop predictive skills	· Background notes expand on the section and provide additional cultural information

Section	Textbook Elements	Interactive Content	Workbooks	Teacher's Resources
Lesson Wrap-Up	· Projects encourage review and recycling of lesson materials through different text types · Keep It Flowing develops students' ability to produce smooth discourse · Can-Do Checklist allows students to assess their fulfillment of the learning objectives	· Additional projects encourage students to produce written discourse	· Translation exercises provide opportunities to examine students' overall control of language forms and language functions in context	· Teaching tips for implementing self-diagnostic activities, answer keys for Keep It Flowing, and additional sample quizzes and tests
Supplementary Modules	· How About You? encourages students to personalize their vocabulary · Get Real with Chinese teaches students to predict meaning from context · Characterize It! explores the structure of Chinese characters · Chinese Chat demonstrates how language is used in text messaging and social media · A Way with Words raises students' awareness of the latent semantic interconnections among different vocabulary items	· Video, highlighted in the View & Explore segment, provides insight into non-verbal cues and communication plus context through authentic settings · Additional Characterize It! exercises increase understanding of characters	· Pattern exercises build radical and character recognition	· Teaching tips and strategies for fully exploiting and implementing these new elements

Scope & Sequence

Lesson	Learning Objectives	Grammar	Words & Phrases	Cultural Literacy
11 中国的 节日/ 中國的 節日 **China's Holidays**	· Name major Chinese holidays, give their dates, and identify foods with which they are associated · Express Chinese New Year wishes · Describe Chinese New Year customs · Wish others success or good health	1. Adjective/verb + 着/著 + verb 2. The preposition 以 3. The particle 嘛 4. The pattern（先）…再…	A. Verb + 起来/起來 B. 传统/傳統 (tradition; traditional) C. 热闹/熱鬧 (lively, buzzing with excitement, bustling with activity)	· New Year celebrations · The Lantern Festival · The Dragon Boat Festival · The Qingming Festival · The Mid-Autumn Festival
12 中国的 变化/ 中國的 變化 **Changes in China**	· Describe ways in which a place has or hasn't changed · Indicate that something is different from what you expected · Express concern about the consequences of a persistent state · Compare a place with what it used to be like	1. The modal particle 啊 2. 以 X 为/為 Y 3. 一 + reduplicated measure word	A. 要不是 (if it were not for; but for) B. 从来/從來 (from past till present, always, at all times) C. 看起来/看起來 (it seems) D. 尽可能/儘可能 (as much as possible, to do one's utmost)	· Nanjing and the Sun Yat-sen Mausoleum · Architectural preservation and Liang Sicheng · Temples of Confucius
13 去云南 旅游/ 去雲南 旅遊 **A Trip to Yunnan**	· Describe what costs a package tour may cover · Explain the differences between "soft" and "hard" sleeper cars · Describe Yunnan's natural and cultural attractions · Discuss high and low points of a trip	1. Numbers in idioms 2. Nouns with multiple attributives	A. 印象/印象 (impression) B. 分享 (to share joy, happiness, benefit, or something pleasant or positive) C. 只好 (have no choice but) D. 千万/千萬 (by all means, absolutely must) E. 不过/不過 (however, no more than)	· The Stone Forest · The Three Pagodas of Dali · The Old City of Lijiang

Lesson	Learning Objectives	Grammar	Words & Phrases	Cultural Literacy
14 生活与 健康/ 生活與 健康 Lifestyle and Health	· Talk about various types of exercise · Outline some healthy eating habits · Compare exercise habits in China and the U.S. · Point out the importance of a balanced diet · Describe habits that could age people prematurely or harm their health	1. Monosyllabic forms of disyllabic words 2. The conjunction and preposition 与/與 3. 只要···就··· 4. 即使···也···	A. 有的···, 有的··· B. 重视/重視 (to attach importance to, to think highly of) C. 等于/等於 (to equal, to be equivalent to, to amount to) D. 随便/隨便 (casual, careless, as one pleases)	· Cultivating vitality · Therapeutic practices · Smoking
15 男女平等 Gender Equality	· Talk about equal treatment in relationships · Discuss gender equality in the workplace · Summarize the changes in Chinese women's social status since 1950 · Describe how couples share household chores	1. Sentences with 是···的 (II) 2. 过来/過來 as a complement	A. 逐渐/逐漸 (gradually, little by little) B. 提高 (to improve, to raise; improvement) C. ···以来/···以來 (since) D. 拿···来说/ 拿···來說 (take . . . for example) E. 只有···才··· (only if) F. 表现/表現 (to show, to display, to manifest; performance, manifestation) G. 由 (by)	· Women in the workforce · Gender terms · Women's script
Bringing It Together (L11–L15)	· Review of L11–L15			

Lesson	Learning Objectives	Grammar	Words & Phrases	Cultural Literacy
16 环境保护与节约能源/ 環境保護與節約能源 **Environmental Protection and Energy Conservation**	· Describe how to get close to and relax in nature · Talk about indicators of a clean environment · Discuss green and renewable energy · Explain what government can do to reduce pollution · Identify what individuals can do to protect the environment	1. Verb 1 的 verb 1, verb 2 的 verb 2 2. Adjective reduplication (II) 3. Suggesting multiple alternatives with …吧，…吧 4. （有益）于/（有益）於 5. Adjective + 于/於	A. 想出（来）/想出（來）(to come up with) vs. 想起（来）/想起（來）(to recall) B. Four-character phrases C. 可不是吗/可不是嗎 (Isn't that so? How true!) D. 造成 (to cause, to give rise to) E. 从…做起/從…做起 (to start with)	· Green initiatives · Endangered species · Sustainability in ancient thought
17 理财与投资/ 理財與投資 **Wealth Management and Investing**	· Discuss whether you're a saver or a spender · Identify ways to invest money · List ways to purchase a big-ticket item · Describe your spending habits · Recount in basic terms the ups and downs of the stock market	1. Review of the 把 construction (I) 2. Verb reduplication (II)	A. 引起/引起 (to give rise to, to lead to) B. 算（是）(to count as, to be considered as) C. 合 (to combine, to join) D. 突然 (sudden, unexpected)	· The housing market · Stock exchanges · Saving · Income inequality
18 中国历史/ 中國歷史 **China's History**	· Narrate the general timeline of Chinese history · Describe the historical significance of major Chinese dynasties · Talk about important Chinese material and cultural artifacts · Discuss the contributions of key Chinese historical figures	1. 之一 2. 其中	A. 参观/參觀 (to visit, to look around) vs. 游览/遊覽 (to go sightseeing, to tour; excursion) B. 在…方面 (in terms of, in the area of) C. X 跟 Y 有关（系）/ X 跟 Y 有關（係）(related to, having to do with) D. 再也没…了/再也没…了，再也不…了 (no more, not anymore)	· The Imperial Era · A brief chronology of Chinese dynasties · Sun Yat-sen, father of modern China · Zhang Qian, Ban Chao, and the Silk Road · Innovation and exchange

Lesson	Learning Objectives	Grammar	Words & Phrases	Cultural Literacy
19 面试/ 面試 Job Interview	· Explain why China has been able to attract talent and corporations from overseas · Describe overseas returnees and their nickname · Recount a nerve-racking interview · Handle typical job interview questions	1. The structure 越 X 越 Y 2. The conjunction 既然 3. Verb 着 verb 着…/Verb 著 verb 著…	A. 叫做 (to be called, to be known as) B. 好在 (fortunately, luckily) C. 善于/善於 (to be good at, to be adept in) D. 往往 (more often than not) vs. 常常 (often)	· Multinational companies · Repatriated students · Interviews
20 世界变小了/ 世界變小了 The World Is Getting Smaller	· Explain the purpose of a gathering · Request and offer help · Discuss adjusting to life in a new country · Describe how the world is getting smaller	1. Summary of word order in Chinese 2. Review of the 把 construction (II)	A. 接受 (to accept, to take on, to undertake) B. 我说/我說 (I was wondering why) C. 而已 (and no more) D. 在…下 (under) E. 你说呢？/你說呢？ (What do you say?; What do you think?)	· Foreign students and teachers · Welcomes and goodbyes · Long-term expats · Yiwu: China's laboratory of multiculturalism
Bringing It Together (L16–L20)	· Review of L16–L20			

Abbreviations of Grammatical Terms

adj	adjective	pr	pronoun
adv	adverb	prefix	prefix
conj	conjunction	prep	preposition
interj	interjection	qp	question particle
m	measure word	qpr	question pronoun
mv	modal verb	t	time word
n	noun	v	verb
nu	numeral	vc	verb plus complement
p	particle	vo	verb plus object (for
pn	proper noun		detachable compounds)

Legend of Digital Icons

The icons listed below refer to interactive content. Audio is available at chengtsui.co/resources to readers who have purchased the print edition. All other digital content is available exclusively to ChengTsui Web App subscribers.

Audio — **Text, Vocabulary**

Video — **View & Explore**

Flashcards — **Vocabulary**

More characters — **Characterize It!**

More exercises — **Lesson Wrap-Up**

Photo Credits

Cast of Characters

Zhang Tianming
张天明/張天明

An American college freshman whose parents immigrated to the United States from Nanjing, China. He's obsessed with sports and computers. Although he's outgoing and has many friends, his girlfriend thinks he spends too much time online. He and his girlfriend Lisha are spending a semester in China.

Ke Lin
柯林

Al Collins, a graduate student and Lin Xuemei's boyfriend. He is very warm and loves to help others. This year he is studying in Beijing.

Li Zhe
李哲

Zack Ruiz, a senior and a good friend of Zhang Tianming's. On Tianming's suggestion, he is interning with a multinational company in China.

Zhang Tianming's older cousin
张天明的表哥/
張天明的表哥

In his early thirties, he lives in Nanjing and is passionate about the history and traditions of his hometown.

Make
马克/馬克

Markus Meyer, is a part-time model, actor, language tutor, and translator who lives in China and is originally from Germany. His non-German friends in Beijing call him Mark.

Lisha
丽莎/麗莎

Lisa Cohen, an American college freshman. She and Zhang Tianming were high school sweethearts. Lisha loves music and is interested in all things Chinese. She is also into fitness and especially enjoys yoga.

Lin Xuemei
林雪梅

A graduate student four or five years older than Zhang Tianming and Lisha. Lin Xuemei and Lisha quickly became good friends. She is now back in China looking for a job.

Lin Xuemei's uncle and aunt
林雪梅的舅舅、舅妈/
林雪梅的舅舅、舅媽

Both in their mid-forties, he is a lawyer, and she is a college professor. They are very dedicated to their careers.

Li Wen
李文

In her mid-twenties, she works as a museum guide. She is Lisha's language partner and aspires to go to graduate school. She lives in Beijing with her parents, who are in their early sixties and enjoy practicing tai chi in their retirement.

中国的节日

中國的節日

CHINA'S HOLIDAYS

Learning Objectives

In this lesson, you will learn to:

- Name major Chinese holidays, give their dates, and identify foods with which they are associated
- Express Chinese New Year wishes
- Describe Chinese New Year customs
- Wish others success or good health

Relate and Get Ready

In your own culture/community:

- What are the major traditional holidays?
- How do people celebrate these holidays?
- What do people customarily eat during these holidays?
- Which holidays are most associated with family?

课文

Text

Audio

Before You Study

Answer the following questions in Chinese to prepare for the reading.

1 学生一般在学期的什么时候申请出国留学？

2 你过什么节一定回家？

When You Study

Listen to the audio recording and scan the text; then answer the following questions in Chinese.

1 雪梅舅舅、舅妈住的环境怎么样？

2 中国有哪些重要的传统节日？

3 中国的什么节有点儿像美国的感恩节？为什么？

开始放寒假了，柯林决定到北京学中文，而林雪梅想在北京实习和找工作。他们一起来到了北京雪梅的舅舅家。

雪梅的舅舅是律师，舅妈是大学教授。他们住的小区[a]*环境很好，房子是一套三室两厅两卫[b]的公寓，家具都很新、很漂亮，每个房间都很干净，住起来很舒服。

今天是除夕，也就是春节的前一天。舅妈正在忙着[1]做年夜饭，舅舅在旁边帮忙。

柯林看见墙上贴着一张不大的红纸，纸上写着一个汉字，他认识，那是"幸福"的"福"字，可是贴倒了。

奇怪，雪梅，这个"福"字怎么贴错了，"福"字倒了。

没贴错。"福倒了"，"福到了"[c]，你想意思多好啊！

我懂了，懂了，真有意思！

雪梅，柯林，来、来、来，快坐下，吃饭了……大家都不喝酒，来，我们以[2]茶代酒，举起杯来，欢迎你们来北京！

課文

Audio

開始放寒假了，柯林決定到北京學中文，而林雪梅想在北京實習和找工作。他們一起來到了北京雪梅的舅舅家。

雪梅的舅舅是律師，舅媽是大學教授。他們住的小區[a]*環境很好。房子是一套三室兩廳兩衛[b]的公寓，傢俱都很新、很漂亮，每個房間都很乾淨，住起來很舒服。

今天是除夕，也就是春節的前一天。舅媽正在忙著[1]做年夜飯，舅舅在旁邊幫忙。

柯林看見牆上貼著一張不大的紅紙，紙上寫著一個漢字，他認識，那是"幸福"的"福"字，可是貼倒了。

奇怪，雪梅，這個"福"字怎麼貼錯了，"福"字倒了。

沒貼錯。"福倒了"，"福到了"[c]，你想意思多好啊！

我懂了，懂了，真有意思！

雪梅，柯林，來、來、來，快坐下，吃飯了……大家都不喝酒，來，我們以[2]茶代酒，舉起杯來，歡迎你們來北京！

Before You Study

Answer the following questions in Chinese to prepare for the reading.

1 學生一般在學期的什麼時候申請出國留學？

2 你過什麼節一定回家？

When You Study

Listen to the audio recording and scan the text; then answer the following questions in Chinese.

1 雪梅舅舅、舅媽住的環境怎麼樣？

2 中國有哪些重要的傳統節日？

3 中國的什麼節有點兒像美國的感恩節？為什麼？

---

* Here and throughout the book, red lesson text and letters correspond to explanations in the Language Notes; blue lesson text and numbers correspond to explanations in the Grammar section; and green lesson text corresponds to explanations in the Words & Phrases section.

为你们在新的一年里找工作顺利、学习进步干杯！

为舅舅、舅妈的事业成功干杯！

为舅舅、舅妈的身体健康干杯！

看，电视上春节晚会[d]开始了！我们一边吃饭一边看吧。

柯林，现在很多很多中国家庭都像我们一样，一边吃年夜饭，一边看春节晚会。

是吗？有好看的电视，又有好吃的菜，太棒了！舅妈做的清蒸鱼又嫩又香，真好吃。

柯林，你知道吗？年夜饭一定要有鱼，而且不能都吃了，要剩下一些。

为什么？那不是浪费吗？

"年年有鱼，年年有余"呀。"鱼"跟"余"发音一样，"余"有"剩下"的意思。

"年年有鱼，年年有余"，是"剩下钱"吗？中文真有意思。哎，中国还有好几个传统节日，吃的东西都不一样，对吧？

对。农历五月初五端午节……

吃粽子！

Top to bottom:
Firecrackers,
and *jiaozi*

為你們在新的一年裡找工作順利、學習進步乾杯！

為舅舅、舅媽的事業成功乾杯！

為舅舅、舅媽的身體健康乾杯！

看，電視上春節晚會[d]開始了！我們一邊吃飯一邊看吧。

柯林，現在很多很多中國家庭都像我們一樣，一邊吃年夜飯，一邊看春節晚會。

是嗎？有好看的電視，又有好吃的菜，太棒了！舅媽做的清蒸魚又嫩又香，真好吃。

柯林，你知道嗎？年夜飯一定要有魚，而且不能都吃了，要剩下一些。

為什麼？那不是浪費嗎？

"年年有魚，年年有餘"呀。"魚"跟"餘"發音一樣，"餘"有"剩下"的意思。

"年年有魚，年年有餘"，是"剩下錢"嗎？中文真有意思。哎，中國還有好幾個傳統節日，吃的東西都不一樣，對吧？

對。農曆五月初五端午節……

吃粽子！

Top to bottom:
Steamed fish
and *zongzi*

八月十五中秋节……

吃月饼。

中秋节有点像美国的感恩节，是一家人团圆的节日。还有正月十五元宵节……

吃那个圆圆、白白的东西……

元宵节，吃元宵嘛[3]！

对了，对了，我想起来了，元宵。

你们看，电视里在倒计时了，"十、九、八、七、六、五、四、三、二、一。"十二点了，新的一年开始了！

舅舅、舅妈，我们给你们拜年了！

大家过年好！

舅舅、舅妈过年好！恭喜发财！

发财、发财，大家发财。过年了，舅舅、舅妈给你们红包。

谢谢！谢谢！……外边怎么这么热闹？

过春节要放鞭炮。我们也买了很多，出去放吧。

雪梅，你给天明他们发个短信拜年吧。

Top to bottom:
A *hongbao*
and moon cakes

八月十五中秋節……

吃月餅。

中秋節有點像美國的感恩節，是一家人團圓的節日。還有正月十五元宵節……

吃那個圓圓、白白的東西……

元宵節，吃元宵嘛[3]！

對了，對了，我想起來了，元宵。

你們看，電視裡在倒計時了，"十、九、八、七、六、五、四、三、二、一。"十二點了，新的一年開始了！

舅舅、舅媽，我們給你們拜年了！

大家過年好！

舅舅、舅媽過年好！恭喜發財！

發財、發財，大家發財。過年了，舅舅、舅媽給你們紅包。

謝謝！謝謝！……外邊怎麼這麼熱鬧？

過春節要放鞭炮。我們也買了很多，出去放吧。

雪梅，你給天明他們發個短信拜年吧。

Top to bottom:
A lion dance
and *yuanxiao*

好。不过，我想先给爸爸妈妈打手机拜年，再⁴给天明、丽莎发微信拜年。

好吧。舅舅，舅妈，我们一起去放鞭炮吧！

柯林，你和舅舅去吧。我准备准备，等你们回来吃饺子。

什么？还吃？

View & Explore

Video

For deeper language immersion and more cultural information, watch "Lantern Festival," a short, supplemental video clip by Cheng & Tsui on this lesson's theme.

好。不過，我想先給爸爸媽媽打手機拜年，再⁴給天明、麗莎發微信拜年。

好吧。舅舅，舅媽，我們一起去放鞭炮吧！

柯林，你和舅舅去吧。我準備準備，等你們回來吃餃子。

什麼？還吃？

After You Study

Answer the following questions in Chinese.

1 中國人怎麼準備過年？除夕晚上做什麼？

2 中國人年夜飯吃些什麼？

3 中國人給人拜年時說些什麼？

Language Notes

a 小区/小區

小区/小區 (lit. small district) are planned residential developments in urban areas, often gated and composed of multistoried buildings. Many offer various facilities for residents' convenience, such as grocery stores and even beauty salons. Residents are charged a maintenance fee. In upscale 小区/小區, there is often a clubhouse with a restaurant and a fitness center. In Taiwan, the term 社区/社區 is preferred.

b 三室两厅两卫/三室兩廳兩衛

三室两厅两卫/三室兩廳兩衛 means "three bedrooms, a living room, a dining room, and two bathrooms." 三房两厅两卫/三房兩廳兩衛 is another way of saying the same thing.

c 福倒了，福到了

福倒了 (福 is upside down) is pronounced the same as 福到了 (福 has arrived). Many Chinese speakers are careful about using homophones or near-homophones. For instance, the number four (四) (sì) is often taboo because it sounds similar to 死 (sǐ), or "death." Consequently, in some places where Chinese is spoken, you may not find a fourth floor in a multi-story building. Similarly, many people like to have the number eight (八) in their phone and license-plate numbers because 八 (bā) rhymes with 发/發 (fā) (to prosper, to strike fortune). In the same vein, some couples avoid eating a pear (梨) together, because "to share a pear" (分梨) sounds the same as 分离/分離, meaning "to separate" or "to part ways."

d 春节晚会/春節晚會

春节晚会/春節晚會, colloquially shortened to 春晚, is a hugely popular, eagerly anticipated five-hour-long variety program broadcast on Chinese New Year's Eve. It airs on China's national TV station, China Central Television (CCTV).

Vocabulary

No.	Simplified	Traditional	Pinyin	Part of Speech*	Definition
1	节日	節日	jiérì	n	holiday, festival
2	舅舅	舅舅	jiùjiu	n	uncle (mother's brother)
3	舅妈	舅媽	jiùmā	n	aunt (mother's brother's wife)
4	小区	小區	xiǎoqū	n	residential development, residential complex
5	环境	環境	huánjìng	n	environment, surroundings
6	除夕	除夕	chúxī	n	Chinese New Year's Eve
7	年夜饭	年夜飯	niányèfàn	n	Chinese New Year's Eve dinner
8	墙	牆	qiáng	n	wall
9	贴	貼	tiē	v	to paste, to glue
10	福	福	fú	n	blessing, good fortune
11	倒	倒	dào	v	to turn upside down, to go backwards
12	奇怪	奇怪	qíguài	adj	strange, weird
13	意思	意思	yìsi	n	meaning
14	以	以	yǐ	prep	with [See Grammar 2.]
15	代	代	dài	v	to replace, to substitute
16	酒	酒	jiǔ	n	alcohol, liquor
17	举	舉	jǔ	v	to lift, to raise
18	顺利	順利	shùnlì	adj	smooth, successful, without a hitch
19	进步	進步	jìnbù	v/adj	to make progress; progressive
20	干杯	乾杯	gān bēi	vo	to drink a toast (lit. to dry the cup)
21	成功	成功	chénggōng	v/adj	to succeed; successful
22	晚会	晚會	wǎnhuì	n	evening gathering, soiree
23	剩（下）	剩（下）	shèng (xia)	v(c)	to leave a surplus, to be left (over)

* Parts of speech are indicated for most vocabulary items. Four-character phrases, idiomatic expressions, and other phrases that cannot be categorized by part of speech are left unmarked.

No.	Simplified	Traditional	Pinyin	Part of Speech	Definition
24	浪费	浪費	*làngfèi*	v/adj	to waste, to squander; wasteful
25	余	餘	*yú*	n/v	surplus; to have a surplus
26	传统	傳統	*chuántǒng*	n/adj	tradition; traditional
27	农历	農曆	*nónglì*	n	traditional Chinese lunar calendar (lit. agricultural calendar)
28	初	初	*chū*		first, early part of
29	粽子	粽子	*zòngzi*	n	sticky-rice dumpling wrapped in bamboo or reed leaves
30	月饼	月餅	*yuèbǐng*	n	moon cake
31	团圆	團圓	*tuányuán*	v	to reunite (as a family)
32	正月	正月	*zhēngyuè*	n	first month of the lunar year
33	元宵	元宵	*yuánxiāo*	n	night of the fifteenth of the first lunar month, sweet dumplings made of sticky-rice flour

"Guessing riddles" (猜谜/猜謎) (*cāi mí*) is a popular pastime during the Lantern Festival. These two "lantern riddles" (灯谜/燈謎) (*dēngmí*) have to do with Chinese characters. Can you figure out the answer to each riddle?

GET Real WITH CHINESE

No.	Simplified	Traditional	Pinyin	Part of Speech	Definition
34	嘛	嘛	*ma*	p	(particle used to emphasize the obvious) [See Grammar 3.]
35	计时	計時	*jì shí*	vo	to count time
36	拜年	拜年	*bài nián*	vo	to wish somebody a happy Chinese New Year, to pay a Chinese New Year call
37	恭喜	恭喜	*gōngxǐ*	v	to congratulate
38	发财	發財	*fā cái*	vo	to get rich, to make a fortune
39	红包	紅包	*hóngbāo*	n	red envelope containing gift money
40	热闹	熱鬧	*rènao*	adj	lively, buzzing with excitement, bustling with activity (of a place or scene)
41	鞭炮	鞭炮	*biānpào*	n	firecracker
42	春节	春節	*Chūnjié*	pn	Spring Festival, Chinese New Year
43	端午节	端午節	*Duānwǔjié*	pn	Dragon Boat Festival
44	中秋节	中秋節	*Zhōngqiūjié*	pn	Mid-Autumn Festival, Moon Festival
45	感恩节	感恩節	*Gǎn'ēnjié*	pn	Thanksgiving
46	元宵节	元宵節	*Yuánxiāojié*	pn	Lantern Festival

在中国，春节和中秋节是一家人团圆的节日。在你们国家呢？

在中國，春節和中秋節是一家人團圓的節日。在你們國家呢？

How About You?

Grammar

<u>1</u> | Adjective/verb + 着/著 + verb

In this structure, the second verb phrase indicates the reason for the first action or state:

A

快放寒假了，小王正忙着准备考试。

快放寒假了，小王正忙著準備考試。

It's almost winter break. Little Wang's busy preparing for exams.
(Little Wang is busy because he's preparing for his final exams.)

B

他急着去见朋友，没吃晚饭就走了。

他急著去見朋友，沒吃晚飯就走了。

He was in a rush to see a friend, so he left without having dinner.
(He was in a hurry because he needed to see a friend.)

C

妹妹哭着要哥哥陪她玩电脑游戏。

妹妹哭著要哥哥陪她玩電腦遊戲。

The younger sister burst into tears asking her older brother to play a computer game with her.
(The younger sister cried because she wanted her older brother to play a computer game with her.)

<u>2</u> | The preposition 以

以, which originates from classical Chinese, is used in modern Chinese as a preposition. Though it has many meanings, 以 can sometimes be translated as "to use" or "with." In the Text, 以茶代酒/以茶代酒 means "to use tea to replace alcohol." Let's look at some other examples of this usage:

A

他选课，只以兴趣做标准，不考虑将来是不是
容易找工作。

他選課，只以興趣做標準，不考慮將來是不是
容易找工作。

He chooses his classes with his interests as his only criteria. He doesn't consider whether [the classes he chooses] will make it easier to find a job.

13

老师以自己的生活经验教育学生。

老師以自己的生活經驗教育學生。

The teacher uses his/her life experience to educate his/her students.

---

3 | **The particle 嘛**

嘛 is a modal particle often used in casual conversation to suggest that the reasoning behind a statement is obvious and requires no further elaboration.

A

你不喜欢他，不想让他天天来找你，就告诉他嘛。

你不喜歡他，不想讓他天天來找你，就告訴他嘛。

If you don't like him and don't want him to come looking for you every day, then why don't you just tell him?

B

你说这个英文问题不难，那你翻译出来给我看看嘛。

你說這個英文問題不難，那你翻譯出來給我看看嘛。

You say that this English question is not difficult. Then translate it and prove it to me.

C Person A

我最不愿意跟数字打交道，可是妈妈非让我学金融不可。

我最不願意跟數字打交道，可是媽媽非讓我學金融不可。

There's nothing I dislike more than dealing with numbers, but my mom insists that I study finance.

Person B

你跟妈妈说清楚嘛，还是选自己有兴趣的专业好些。

你跟媽媽說清楚嘛，還是選自己有興趣的專業好些。

Then just tell your mom clearly. It's better to choose a major that you're interested in.

The pattern （先）…再…

The （先）…再… pattern can be translated as "(first)…then…" Like 才, 再 can link two clauses. However, unlike 才, 再 indicates that the action described in the first clause is a desired condition for the action in the second clause. In other words, the speaker would like to postpone the second action until the first action has occurred.

A   Q: 我们今年去云南旅游，怎么样？

　　我們今年去雲南旅遊，怎麼樣？

Let's take a trip to Yunnan this year. How about it?

　A: 我今年不想去，想等明年拿到硕士学位以后再去。

　　我今年不想去，想等明年拿到碩士學位以後再去。

I don't want to go this year. I'd like to wait until I receive my master's degree next year.

B   明年暑假我想先待在这儿打工挣点钱，然后再回纽约看父母。

明年暑假我想先待在這兒打工掙點錢，然後再回纽約看父母。

Next year over summer break, I'll stay here to make a little money working part-time. Then I'll go back to New York to see my parents.

C   这个问题我们应该先好好儿讨论讨论再做决定。

這個問題我們應該先好好兒討論討論再做決定。

We should discuss this question thoroughly before we make a decision.

Words & Phrases

Verb + 起来/起來

The structure "Verb + 起来/起來" indicates that the speaker is looking at, discussing, or commenting on something in terms of the action indicated by the verb. For example:

1 这个手机用起来很方便。

這個手機用起來很方便。

This cell phone is very convenient to use.
(In terms of using it, this cell phone is very convenient.)

2 饺子吃起来好吃，做起来不太容易。

餃子吃起來好吃，做起來不太容易。

Dumplings are delicious to eat, but not easy to make.
(In terms of eating, dumplings are delicious, but making them is not so easy.)

3 这把椅子搬起来很重。

這把椅子搬起來很重。

This chair is very heavy to lift.
(In terms of lifting it, this chair is very heavy.)

A WAY WITH WORDS

奇怪

王先生的家外边儿看起来很奇特，很像一条船。

现在连小孩都用手机，手机不再是新奇的东西了。

Using the word/phrase in orange as a clue, try to figure out the meaning of the words/phrases in blue; consult a dictionary if necessary. Consider how the literal and extended senses are related in each case.

奇怪

王先生的家外邊兒看起來很奇特，很像一條船。

現在連小孩都用手機，手機不再是新奇的東西了。

传统/傳統 (tradition; traditional)

传统/傳統 can be used as an adjective, as in (1) and (2):

1

我们在中国历史课里学了不少中国的传统文化。

我們在中國歷史課裡學了不少中國的傳統文化。

We learned a lot about traditional Chinese culture in our Chinese history class. [attributive]

2

他这个人很传统，不会做这样的事情。

他這個人很傳統，不會做這樣的事情。

He is a very traditional man. He wouldn't do such a thing. [predicate]

In addition, 传统/傳統 appears as an adjective in phrases such as 传统方法/傳統方法 (traditional method), 传统思想/傳統思想 (traditional thinking), 传统道德/傳統道德 (*chuántǒng dàodé*) (traditional morality), and 传统制度/傳統制度 (*chuántǒng zhìdù*) (traditional system).

传统/傳統 can also be used as a noun, as in (3) and (4):

3

这个学校有什么传统?

這個學校有什麼傳統？

What traditions does this school have? [noun]

4

不浪费是这个家庭的好传统。

不浪費是這個家庭的好傳統。

Not being wasteful is a good tradition in this family. [noun]

热闹/熱鬧 (lively, buzzing with excitement, bustling with activity)

热闹/熱鬧 is an adjective. It can be used as a predicate or as an attributive.

1 开学了，宿舍里来了很多新同学，大家都在忙着搬家，很热闹。

開學了，宿舍裡來了很多新同學，大家都在忙著搬家，很熱鬧。

School has started. Many new students have arrived at the dorm and everyone is busy moving in. There's a buzz of excitement. *[predicate]*

2 今天小李过生日，晚上大家开个舞会，热闹一下。

今天小李過生日，晚上大家開個舞會，熱鬧一下。

Today is Little Li's birthday. We are going to have a party this evening and have a great time. *[predicate]*

3 我一到热闹的地方就头疼。

我一到熱鬧的地方就頭疼。

Whenever I'm in a loud, bustling place, I get a headache. *[attributive]*

Language Practice

A | **A shift in perspective** | PRESENTATIONAL

In pairs, take turns completing the following statements:

1 粽子吃起来容易，做起来_____。

粽子吃起來容易，做起來_____。

2 这套公寓很大，住起来很舒服，但是打扫起来很_____。

這套公寓很大，住起來很舒服，但是打掃起來很_____。

3 毛笔字看起来很美，但是写起来很_____。

毛筆字看起來很美，但是寫起來很_____。

B | **Just making sure** | INTERPERSONAL

Imagine that it's your first day as an apprentice at a Chinese restaurant. You're taking directions from your supervisor, e.g.:

make the dumplings	cook the rice

Q: 我应该先做饺子还是先做米饭？
我應該先做餃子還是先做米飯？

A: 你应该先做饺子，再做米饭。
你應該先做餃子，再做米飯。

1	add sugar	add vinegar
2	make hot-and-sour soup	make home-style tofu
3	learn to make *zongzi*	learn to make moon cakes
4	prepare fruit	wash dishes

Name the date

Practice how to say the following dates on the Chinese lunar calendar. Don't forget to include 正 *(zhēng)* and 初 when appropriate.

1 first day of the first month

2 fifteenth day of the first month

3 tenth day of the second month

4 fifth day of the fifth month

5 seventh day of the seventh month

6 fifteenth day of the eighth month

D INTERPRETIVE **Nothing says the holidays like eating** PRESENTATIONAL

Match each of the holidays on the left with the name of the food that holiday is most associated with; then connect the name of that food with the appropriate image on the right.

感恩节／感恩節   月饼／月餅

春节／春節   饺子／餃子

元宵节／元宵節   火鸡／火雞

端午节／端午節   粽子

中秋节／中秋節   元宵

Report your answers to your partner.

Happy Chinese New Year!

What do Chinese people do to celebrate Chinese New Year? Take turns describing Chinese New Year customs based on the visual prompts, e.g.:

中国人过春节的时候把"福"字倒着贴。

中國人過春節的時候把"福"字倒著貼。

 1

 2

 3

 4

 5

A WAY WITH WORDS

顺利

你下午去买日用品的时候，能不能顺便帮我买点洗衣粉？

小张来学校一个月了，老师和同学们都对他非常好，他觉得什么事情都很顺心。

Using the word/phrase in orange as a clue, try to figure out the meaning of the words/phrases in blue; consult a dictionary if necessary. Consider how the literal and extended senses are related in each case.

順利

你下午去買日用品的時候，能不能順便幫我買點洗衣粉？

小張來學校一個月了，老師和同學們都對他非常好，他覺得什麼事情都很順心。

Well-wishes

Wish someone well on these occasions, e.g.:

During Chinese New Year

恭喜发财！/恭喜發財！

or 过年好！/過年好！

or 祝你春节快乐！/祝你春節快樂！

1 Your friend is celebrating his/her birthday

2 Your grandfather is celebrating his eightieth birthday

3 Your friend is wondering if he'll find a good job without too much difficulty

4 Your classmate is going to study in China and wonders if his/her studies will go smoothly

5 Your colleague is going to open a business and wonders if the business will be a success

Characterize it!

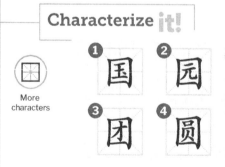

More characters

| What do the characters mean? |
| What is the common radical? |
| What does the radical mean? |
| How does the radical relate to the overall meaning of the characters? |

Don't miss out!

To ensure you don't miss out on anything during Chinese New Year when you visit China, make a list of the activities that people in China engage in. Be sure to list each activity under the correct day.

除夕

1 _____

2 _____

3 _____

4 _____

正月初一

1 _____

2 _____

3 _____

4 _____

Based on your list, work in pairs to describe Chinese New Year festivities.

Chinese Chat

Lin Xuemei just posted this on Facebook. What comment would you leave for her?

 林雪梅
6 minutes ago

给大家拜年了！我和柯林正在舅舅家吃年夜饭、看春晚，12点一到，就去外边儿放鞭炮！😊

3 people like this

 高成
好幸福呀！我已经好几年没回中国过年了！
4 minutes ago

 白小南
雪梅，祝你新年快乐，年年有余。🌹
4 minutes ago

  　　　　3 likes　2 comments

林雪梅：
給大家拜年了！我和柯林正在舅舅家吃年夜飯、看春晚，12點一到，就去外邊兒放鞭炮！😊

高成：
好幸福呀！我已經好幾年沒回中國過年了！

白小南：
雪梅，祝你新年快樂，年年有餘。🌹

New Year Celebrations

Before China became a republic in 1911, New Year celebrations in China began on the first day of the first month of the lunar calendar, usually falling in late January or early February. After 1911, China began observing the New Year, 元旦 (Yuándàn), on January 1, and Chinese Lunar New Year became known as the Spring Festival, 春节/春節. It remains the most important holiday in China, and people still refer to the activities surrounding the Spring Festival as 过年/過年 or "celebrating the New Year."

One of the most widely told legends about the origin of the Spring Festival describes a fierce beast called 年 that preyed on people and domesticated animals every New Year's Eve. One year, an old beggar appeared at a house offering to chase the beast away in exchange for a night's lodging. Dressed in red, the beggar illuminated the home with bright torches and decorated the front door with red paper. When the beast showed up around midnight, it was scared off by the sound of firecrackers and bright red decorations.

Since then, families have decorated the front door of their homes with auspicious couplets on red paper and lighting firecrackers. Relatives gather to share a New Year's feast, which typically includes 饺子/餃子 in northern China, and 年糕 (niángāo) (glutinous rice cakes) in the south. Children often receive cash gifts wrapped in red envelopes. On New Year's Day, people go out to visit relatives and friends and wish one another a happy new year.

Traditionally, the Spring Festival lasted from the first to the fifteenth day of the first month of the lunar calendar. Today, people in cities typically have

The Lantern Festival

The Lantern Festival, 元宵节/元宵節, falls on the fifteenth day of the first month of the lunar calendar. Its origin can be traced to the Han dynasty (202 BCE–220 CE). 元宵, which literally means "first night," marks the first full moon of the lunar new year. Colorful lanterns are lit at night; hence, the holiday's name in English. Today, almost every Chinese city puts on extravagant displays of lanterns in parks and historic areas, attracting tens of thousands of spectators. Many streets are decorated with colorful paper lanterns, some with riddles written on them. At night, people go out to admire the lanterns and guess the riddles. Exuberant dragon and lion dances also add to the festive mood of the holiday season. ◆

three work days off. Combined with the preceding and following weekends, the holiday break can last up to seven or eight days. While people customarily exchanged New Year's greetings by paying a brief visit in person, it is increasingly common to send New Year's wishes by text message.

Many of China's minority peoples have their own distinct New Year's traditions. Mongols, for instance, celebrate Tsagaan Sar (lit. White Moon) to mark the beginning of the lunar calendar. Turkic minorities such as the Uighurs, Kazakhs, and Kyrgyz, as well as the Farsi-speaking Tajiks, observe Nowruz or Persian New Year. Nowruz coincides with the vernal equinox, which falls around March 21. The Dai people in Yunnan, on the other hand, usher in the New Year in mid-April with the Water Splashing Festival. ◆

A display of lanterns with auspicious couplets

The Dragon Boat Festival

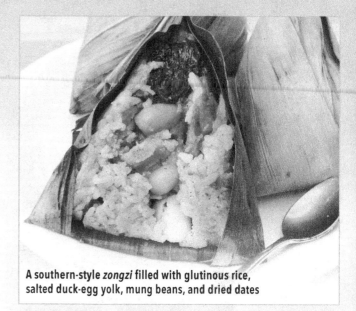

A southern-style *zongzi* filled with glutinous rice, salted duck-egg yolk, mung beans, and dried dates

The fifth day of the fifth month of the lunar calendar (usually in June) is the Dragon Boat Festival, 端午节/端午節. According to popular legend, the holiday started as a commemoration of the famous poet 屈原 (*Qū Yuán*, ca. 340–278 BCE), who drowned himself in the Miluo River (汨罗江/汨羅江) (*Mìluójiāng*). Devastated to learn the fate of this revered figure, people rushed out in boats to recover Qu Yuan's body. Some even threw 粽子, glutinous rice dumplings wrapped in bamboo leaves, into the water to prevent fish from feeding on his body. To commemorate Qu Yuan every year, boat races are held all over China during the festival. Each dragon-shaped boat features a drummer to keep the rowers in sync. People also eat 粽子 during the holiday. ◆

A dragon-boat competition in Foshan, Guangdong Province

The Qingming Festival

Traditionally, the Qingming Festival, 清明节/清明節, fell on the first two weeks after the vernal equinox. Today, the holiday is observed on April 5, when people all over China make offerings to their deceased relatives. Roads to cemeteries are often clogged for miles with traffic. In rural areas, there are elaborate ceremonies of ancestral veneration. Because the holiday is associated with warmer weather, some people go on day trips or fly kites. ◆

The Mid-Autumn Festival

The fifteenth day of the eighth month of the lunar calendar, which falls in September or early October, marks the Mid-Autumn Festival. It is a day for family reunion, which is symbolized by the full moon. While admiring the fullness of the bright moon, people enjoy moon cakes, which come in many regional styles. They are usually baked with sweet fillings including nuts or preserved fruit, or even with salted duck-egg yolks. In Suzhou and Shanghai, fresh and hot moon cakes with minced pork are also very popular. ◆

Some moon cakes have intricate designs; this moon cake features the Jade Rabbit, a companion of the moon goddess Chang'e

COMPARE & CONTRAST

Though holidays may appear timeless, their meaning and how they are celebrated are often the result of a negotiation between past and present. Seeking to navigate technological, social, and cultural change, people and communities often transform traditions in ways that their original celebrants could not have predicted. In 2017, people in China sent forty-six billion electronic *hongbao* (红包/紅包). Senders could opt to determine the total amount of money to give out among all receivers and let the delivery system divide the money randomly among designated receivers. While electronic *hongbao* are conceptually similar to paper *hongbao*, it is undeniable that they provide a different experience, and perhaps even have a different meaning. Do you engage in any holiday traditions that have borne the impact of technological, social, and cultural change? What aspects of how you celebrate those traditions do you think someone from the past would find hard to grasp? ◆

Lesson Wrap-Up

Project

The Chinese Student Association on your campus has invited you to give a slide presentation on public holidays in your country. Begin with an overview: How many are there? Does the number vary among different states/provinces? How many holidays does your home state/province observe? Describe in detail two traditional holidays in your country—Thanksgiving and Halloween, for instance, if you are in the U.S. Be sure to address the following questions:

· When do your chosen holidays take place?

· How do people celebrate them?

· What do people usually say to one another?

· What do people usually eat on the holidays?

· Why are these two holidays important to you and your family?

Keep It Flowing

Study the following example; pay particular attention to how the highlighted parts help the sentences flow smoothly from one to the next. Notice how:

· key words (中国春节/中國春節, 除夕的年夜饭/除夕的年夜饭) are positioned at the beginning of the sentence to outline the theme or topic

· time phrases (前一天, 中国人过春节的时候/中國人過春節的時候, 看完以后/看完以後, 放完鞭炮以后/放完鞭炮以後) help connect sentences

· certain statements (意思是, 舅妈说/舅媽說) introduce explanations and speeches

· certain conjunctions (而且) signify addition

林雪梅和柯林在舅舅家过春节

中国春节是农历正月初一，前一天是除夕。
林雪梅和柯林今年春节是在雪梅的舅舅家过的。
中国人过春节的时候，每家都喜欢贴"福"字，而且要倒着贴，意思是"福到了"。除夕的年夜饭一定要有鱼，而且要剩下一些，意思是"年年有余"，这一年的钱会剩下。雪梅他们一边吃饭一边看春节晚会。看完以后，他们出去放鞭炮。舅妈说，放完鞭炮以后，还要吃饺子。

林雪梅和柯林在舅舅家過春節

中國春節是農曆正月初一，前一天是除夕。林雪梅和柯林今年春節是在雪梅的舅舅家過的。中國人過春節的時候，每家都喜歡貼"福"字，而且要倒著貼，意思是"福到了"。除夕的年夜飯一定要有魚，而且要剩下一些，意思是"年年有餘"，這一年的錢會剩下。雪梅他們一邊吃飯一邊看春節晚會。看完以後，他們出去放鞭炮。舅媽說，放完鞭炮以後，還要吃餃子。

Describe how you celebrated Thanksgiving, Christmas, or the New Year last year. Study the cohesive devices highlighted in the example above. Use as many as possible to string together a response, based on the prompts:

。这个节日是在什么时候？

這個節日是在什麼時候？

。你去年是回家还是在学校过的节？

你去年是回家還是在學校過的節？

。如果回家了，说一下旅行怎么样。如果没回家，说一下为什么。

如果回家了，說一下旅行怎麼樣。如果沒回家，說一下為什麼。

○ 过节的时候，在房间里面和外面要放什么特别的
东西吗？家里人都会回来吗？

過節的時候，在房間裡面和外面要放什麼特別的
東西嗎？家裡人都會回來嗎？

○ 这个节日要吃什么特别的东西吗？

這個節日要吃什麼特別的東西嗎？

○ 有什么不能做的事或不能说的话没有？

有什麼不能做的事或不能說的話沒有？

**Can-Do
Check
List** ✔

I can

Before proceeding to Lesson 12, make sure you can complete the
following tasks in Chinese:

- ☐ Name traditional Chinese holidays, give their
  dates, and identify foods with which they are
  associated
- ☐ Express Chinese New Year wishes
- ☐ Describe Chinese New Year customs
- ☐ Wish others success or good health

Kāishǐ fàng hánjià le, Kē Lín juédìng dào Běijīng xué Zhōngwén, ér Lín Xuěméi xiǎng zài Běijīng shíxí hé zhǎo gōngzuò. Tāmen yìqǐ lái dào le Běijīng Xuěméi de jiùjiu jiā.

Xuěméi de jiùjiu shì lǜshī, jiùmā shì dàxué jiàoshòu. Tāmen zhù de xiǎoqū^a huánjìng hěn hǎo. Fángzi shì yí tào *sān shì liǎng tīng liǎng wèi*^b de gōngyù, jiājù dōu hěn xīn, hěn piàoliang, měi ge fángjiān dōu hěn gānjìng, *zhù qǐ lai* hěn shūfu.

Jīntiān shì chúxī, yě jiù shì Chūnjié de qián yì tiān. Jiùmā zhèngzài *máng zhe*^{1} zuò niányèfàn, jiùjiu zài pángbiān bāng máng.

Kē Lín kàn jiàn qiáng shang tiē zhe yì zhāng bú dà de hóng zhǐ, zhǐ shang xiě zhe yí ge Hànzì, tā rènshi, nà shì "xìngfú" de "fú" zì, kěshì tiē dào le.

 Qíguài, Xuěméi, zhè ge "fú" zì zěnme tiē cuò le, "fú" zì dào le.

 Méi tiē cuò. "Fú dào le", "fú dào le"^c, nǐ xiǎng yìsi duō hǎo a!

 Wǒ dǒng le, dǒng le, zhēn yǒu yìsi!

 Xuěméi, Kē Lín, lái, lái, lái, kuài zuò xia, chī fàn le . . . Dàjiā dōu bù hē jiǔ, lái, wǒmen yǐ^2 chá dài jiǔ, jǔ qǐ bēi lai, huānyíng nǐmen lái Běijīng!

 Wèi nǐmen zài xīn de yì nián li zhǎo gōngzuò shùnlì, xuéxí jìnbù gān bēi!

 Wèi jiùjiu, jiùmā de shìyè chénggōng gān bēi!

 Wèi jiùjiu, jiùmā de shēntǐ jiànkāng gān bēi!

 Kàn, diànshì shang *Chūnjié Wǎnhuì*^d kāishǐ le! Wǒmen yìbiān chī fàn yìbiān kàn ba.

 Kē Lín, xiànzài hěn duō hěn duō Zhōngguó jiātíng dōu xiàng wǒmen yíyàng, yìbiān chī niányèfàn, yìbiān kàn Chūnjié Wǎnhuì.

 Shì ma? Yǒu hǎokàn de diànshì, yòu yǒu hǎochī de cài, tài bàng le! Jiùmā zuò de qīngzhēngyú yòu nèn yòu xiāng, zhēn hǎochī.

 Kē Lín, nǐ zhīdào ma? Niányèfàn yídìng yào yǒu yú, érqiě bù néng dōu chī le, yào shèng xia yì xiē.

 Wèishénme? Nà bú shì làngfèi ma?

 "Nián nián yǒu yú, nián nián yǒu yú" ya. "Yú" gēn "yú" fāyīn yíyàng, "yú" yǒu "shèng xia" de yìsi.

"Nián nián yǒu yú, nián nián yǒu yú", shì "shèng xia qián" ma? Zhōngwén zhēn yǒu yìsi. Āi, Zhōngguó hái yǒu hǎo jǐ ge chuántǒng jiérì, chī de dōngxi dōu bù yíyàng, duì ba?

Duì. Nónglì wǔ yuè chū wǔ Duānwǔjié . . .

Chī zòngzi!

Bā yuè shí wǔ Zhōngqiūjié . . .

Chī yuèbǐng . . .

Zhōngqiūjié yǒu diǎn xiàng Měiguó de Gǎn'ēnjié, shì yì jiā rén tuányuán de jiérì. Hái yǒu zhēngyuè shí wǔ Yuánxiāojié . . .

Chī nà ge yuán yuán, bái bái de dōngxi . . .

Yuánxiāojié, chī yuánxiāo ma^3!

Duì le, duì le, wǒ xiǎng qi lai le, yuánxiāo.

Nǐmen kàn, diànshì li zài dào jì shí le, "shí, jiǔ, bā, qī, liù, wǔ, sì, sān, èr, yī." Shí èr diǎn le, xīn de yì nián kāishǐ le!

Jiùjiu, jiùmā, wǒmen gěi nǐmen bài nián le!

Dàjiā guò nián hǎo!

Jiùjiu, jiùmā guò nián hǎo! Gōngxǐ fā cái!

Fā cái, fā cái, dàjiā fā cái. Guò nián le, jiùjiu, jiùmā gěi nǐmen hóngbāo.

Xièxie! Xièxie! . . . Wàibian zěnme zhème rènao?

Guò Chūnjié yào fàng biānpào. Wǒmen yě mǎi le hěn duō, chū qu fàng ba.

Xuěméi, nǐ gěi Tiānmíng tāmen fā ge duǎnxìn bài nián ba.

Hǎo. Búguò, wǒ xiǎng xiān gěi bàba māma dǎ shǒujī bài nián, zài^4 gěi Tiānmíng, Lìshā fā Wēixìn bài nián.

Hǎo ba. Jiùjiu, jiùmā, wǒmen yìqǐ qu fàng biānpào ba!

Kē Lín, nǐ hé jiùjiu qù ba. Wǒ zhǔnbei zhǔnbei, děng nǐmen huí lai chī jiǎozi.

Shénme? Hái chī?

中国的变化

中國的變化

CHANGES IN CHINA

Learning Objectives

In this lesson, you will learn to:

- Describe ways in which a place has or hasn't changed
- Indicate that something is different from what you expected
- Express concern about the consequences of a persistent state
- Compare a place with what it used to be like

Relate and Get Ready

In your own culture/community:

- Has new development caused significant change over the past few years?
- Do any features draw tourists from other parts of the country and around the world?
- What are people's attitudes toward changing versus preserving places of significance?
- Are there any places that are viewed with a strong sense of nostalgia?

课文

Before You Study

Answer the following questions in Chinese to prepare for the reading.

1 你的家乡在哪儿？是个大城市吗？

2 你的家乡有什么景点或者名胜古迹？

When You Study

Listen to the audio recording and skim the text; then answer the following questions in Chinese.

1 张天明的父亲记得的南京是一个什么样的城市？

2 丽莎担心什么？

3 夫子庙有什么特别的地方？

张天明和丽莎上个学期末申请到中国学中文，原来以为时间会来不及，没想到学校很快就同意了。两个人可以在中国学习、生活三、四个月，这让他们非常高兴。

张天明和丽莎先到上海，然后坐高铁去南京。车很快，一个多小时就到了。天明的表哥[a]开车来接他们。表哥见到他们很高兴，说愿意当导游，带他们在街上走走，让他们好好儿看看南京。

爸爸常常说南京是个很安静的城市，没想到这么热闹！你看，大街上到处都是新盖的高楼，到处都是汽车。

这些年南京的变化是很大，我以前骑自行车上班，现在也开起车来了。

这跟我以前想像的中国完全不一样。在上海的时候，要不是到处都是中文，我还以为是在美国呢。

我爸爸说，他小时候在南京很少看到外国人，可是现在，你看，到处都有外国游客啊[1]！

我们不也是两个"老外"吗？哈哈！你看马路对面，美国快餐店，日本银行，法国服装店……

課文

Audio

張天明和麗莎上個學期末申請到中國學中文，原來以為時間會來不及，沒想到學校很快就同意了。兩個人可以在中國學習、生活三、四個月，這讓他們非常高興。

張天明和麗莎先到上海，然後坐高鐵去南京。車很快，一個多小時就到了。天明的表哥[a]開車來接他們。表哥見到他們很高興，說願意當導遊，帶他們在街上走走，讓他們好好兒看看南京。

爸爸常常說南京是個很安靜的城市，沒想到這麼熱鬧！你看，大街上到處都是新蓋的高樓，到處都是汽車。

這些年南京的變化是很大，我以前騎自行車上班，現在也開起車來了。

這跟我以前想像的中國完全不一樣。在上海的時候，要不是到處都是中文，我還以為是在美國呢。

我爸爸說，他小時候在南京很少看到外國人，可是現在，你看，到處都有外國遊客啊[1]！

我們不也是兩個"老外"嗎？哈哈！你看馬路對面，美國快餐店，日本銀行，法國服裝店……

Before You Study

Answer the following questions in Chinese to prepare for the reading.

1 你的家鄉在哪兒？是個大城市嗎？

2 你的家鄉有什麼景點或者名勝古蹟？

When You Study

Listen to the audio recording and skim the text; then answer the following questions in Chinese.

1 張天明的父親記得的南京是一個什麼樣的城市？

2 麗莎擔心什麼？

3 夫子廟有什麼特別的地方？

中国其他地方也这样，变化真的很大。

中国融入世界了，这是件好事。

可是我担心，这样下去[b]，有中国特色的东西会不会越来越少呢？

不会的。南京还是保留了很多有中国特色的东西。比方说建筑，南京最有中国特色的是夫子庙，那儿还有吃的、喝的、玩儿的……

那我们现在就去夫子庙，尝尝南京小吃[c]吧。

好啊！不管中国怎么变[d]，南京怎么变，肚子饿了要吃没变。你们听说过"民以食为天"[e2]这句话吧？

啊？什么？从来没听说过。

这句话的意思，简单地说就是，"吃"是老百姓生活中最重要的事儿。

哎，天明，你看，那是什么地方？人那么多，旁边好像还卖吃的、玩儿的，五颜六色，真好看，真热闹！

那就是夫子庙啊。

看起来，南京人真的是想尽可能保留老南京的特色、老南京的传统啊。

南京一边是一栋栋高楼大厦，一边是一座座[3]传统建筑，站在这儿，我好像听到了一种声音。

Top to bottom:
The Temple of Confucius;
a *xiaochi* takeout window;
and the Qinhuai, the Mother
River of Nanjing

中國其他地方也這樣，變化真的很大。

中國融入世界了，這是件好事。

可是我擔心，這樣下去[b]，有中國特色的東西會不會越來越少呢？

不會的。南京還是保留了很多有中國特色的東西。比方說建築，南京最有中國特色的是夫子廟，那兒還有吃的、喝的、玩兒的……

那我們現在就去夫子廟，嚐嚐南京小吃[c]吧。

好啊！不管中國怎麼變[d]，南京怎麼變，肚子餓了要吃沒變。你們聽說過"民以食為天"[e2]這句話吧？

啊？什麼？從來沒聽說過。

這句話的意思，簡單地說就是，"吃"是老百姓生活中最重要的事兒。

哎，天明，你看，那是什麼地方？人那麼多，旁邊好像還賣吃的、玩兒的，五顏六色，真好看，真熱鬧！

那就是夫子廟啊。

看起來，南京人真的是想盡可能保留老南京的特色、老南京的傳統啊。

南京一邊是一棟棟高樓大廈，一邊是一座座[3]傳統建築，站在這兒，我好像聽到了一種聲音。

Top to bottom:
A *bixie* (lit. "avoid evil"), a mythological symbol of Nanjing; the Medicine Buddha Pagoda and Zifeng Tower; and the Nanjing Yangtze River Bridge

什么声音?

历史的脚步声。来中国以前爸爸让我找他上的那个中学。一会儿我给他发微信, 告诉他南京变化太大, 那个中学已经找不到了, 再把今天拍的照片发给他看看。

哎, 我也听到了一种声音。

什么声音?

肚子咕噜咕噜叫的声音。走了这么多路, 你们好像不累不饿, 可是我这个导游又渴又饿。别忘了, "民以食为天"啊! 走, 吃饭去!

View & Explore

Video

For deeper language immersion and more cultural information, watch "Old and New Beijing," a short, supplemental video clip by Cheng & Tsui on this lesson's theme.

什麼聲音？

歷史的腳步聲。來中國以前爸爸讓我找他上的那個中學。一會兒我給他發微信，告訴他南京變化太大，那個中學已經找不到了，再把今天拍的照片發給他看看。

哎，我也聽到了一種聲音。

什麼聲音？

肚子咕嚕咕嚕叫的聲音。走了這麼多路，你們好像不累不餓，可是我這個導遊又渴又餓。別忘了，"民以食為天"啊！走，吃飯去！

After You Study

Answer the following questions in Chinese.

1 現在的南京和以前的南京有什麼不同？

2 南京的變化很大，但什麼沒變？

3 "民以食為天"到底是什麼意思？

Language Notes

<u>a</u> 表哥

表 (lit. external) here denotes a cousin whose father is not a brother of one's own father. For other terms for cousins and kin, see pp. 301-304, IC2.

<u>b</u> 下去

As we have learned previously, when placed after a verb, 下去 suggests an ongoing action or state. 这样下去/這樣下去 means "if this [state] persists."

<u>c</u> 小吃

小吃 (lit. small eats) refers to an entire class of snacks, typically not made at home but sold in specialized restaurants or by street vendors, and eaten almost anytime. 小吃 vary by region: Shanghai is famous for soup and pan-fried dumplings, 小笼包/小籠包 (xiǎolóngbāo) and 生煎包 (shēngjiānbāo); Sichuan for dandan noodles (担担面/擔擔麵) (dàndànmiàn) and wontons in red (chili) oil (红油抄手/紅油抄手) (hóngyóu chāoshǒu); and Xi'an for pork flatbread sandwich (肉夹馍/肉夾饃) (ròujiāmó) and broken flatbread in lamb broth (羊肉泡馍/羊肉泡饃) (yángròu pàomó).

<u>d</u> 变/變

变/變 is a transitive verb, so it can take a direct object, as in 水变颜色了/水變顏色了 (The water changed color). It's often followed by the complement 成: 那个中学变成了一个购物中心/那個中學變成了一個購物中心 (That middle school turned into a shopping center). By contrast, 变化/變化 is used on its own as a predicate: 天气变化得很快/天氣變化得很快 (The weather changed abruptly). 变化/變化 can also be a noun: 天气有变化/天氣有變化 (There has been a change in the weather).

<u>e</u> 民以食为天/民以食為天

民以食为天/民以食為天 is the second half of a famous saying from a Han dynasty (202 BCE–220 CE) text, which states: 王者以民为天，而民以食为天/王者以民為天，而民以食為天 (Those who rule consider ordinary people [as important] as heaven; ordinary people consider food [as important] as heaven).

Vocabulary

Audio

Flashcards

No.	Simplified	Traditional	Pinyin	Part of Speech	Definition
1	变化	變化	*biànhuà*	v/n	to change; change
2	末	末	*mò*	n	end
3	来不及	來不及	*lái bu jí*	vc	to not have enough time to do something, to be too late to do something
4	高（速）铁（路）	高（速）鐵（路）	*gāo(sù) tiě(lù)*	n	high-speed rail
5	表哥	表哥	*biǎogē*	n	older male cousin with a different surname
6	街	街	*jiē*	n	street
7	盖	蓋	*gài*	v	to build, to construct
8	骑	騎	*qí*	v	to ride
9	自行车	自行車	*zìxíngchē*	n	bicycle
10	上班	上班	*shàng bān*	vo	to go to work, to start work, to be on duty
11	想像	想像	*xiǎngxiàng*	v/n	to imagine, to visualize; imagination
12	要不是	要不是	*yàobúshì*	conj	if it were not for, but for
13	游客	遊客	*yóukè*	n	tourist
14	老外	老外	*lǎowài*	n	foreigner (slang)
15	哈	哈	*hā*	ono	(sound of laughter)
16	对面	對面	*duìmiàn*	n	opposite side
17	快餐	快餐	*kuàicān*	n	fast food
18	服装	服裝	*fúzhuāng*	n	clothing, apparel
19	融入	融入	*róngrù*	v	to merge into, to meld into
20	特色	特色	*tèsè*	n	distinguishing feature or quality, characteristic

No.	Simplified	Traditional	Pinyin	Part of Speech	Definition
21	保留	保留	*bǎoliú*	v	to remain as before, to retain
22	建筑	建築	*jiànzhù*	n/v	architecture; to build
23	尝	嚐	*cháng*	v	to taste
24	小吃	小吃	*xiǎochī*	n	small and inexpensive dishes, snacks
25	不管	不管	*bùguǎn*	conj	no matter, regardless of
26	变	變	*biàn*	v	to change
27	民以食为天	民以食為天	*mín yǐ shí wéi tiān*		ordinary people consider food as important as heaven
28	句	句	*jù*	m	(measure word for sentences)
29	从来	從來	*cónglái*	adv	from past till present, always, at all times
30	老百姓	老百姓	*lǎobǎixìng*	n	ordinary people
31	尽可能	儘可能	*jǐn kěnéng*		as much as possible

表哥带张天明和丽莎去夫子庙尝南京的特色小吃。你知道哪些中国的特色小吃？

表哥帶張天明和麗莎去夫子廟嚐南京的特色小吃。你知道哪些中國的特色小吃？

At the Temple of Confucius, you see these tablets with personal wishes written on them. What did this student wish for? What would you write on your own tablet?

GET Real WITH CHINESE

No.	Simplified	Traditional	Pinyin	Part of Speech	Definition
32	厦	廈	*shà*	n	mansion, tall building
33	座	座	*zuò*	m	(measure word for buildings, mountains, bridges, cities and other large, solid things)
34	声音	聲音	*shēngyīn*	n	sound, voice
35	脚步	腳步	*jiǎobù*	n	footstep
36	拍	拍	*pāi*	v	to take a picture, to shoot a film
37	咕噜	咕嚕	*gūlū*	ono	(rumbling sound)
38	法国	法國	*Fǎguó*	pn	France
39	夫子庙	夫子廟	*Fūzǐmiào*	pn	Temple of Confucius

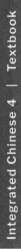

Grammar

The modal particle 啊

It's common, especially in spoken Chinese, to place a particle at the end of a sentence in order to convey a particular emotion. Among such particles, 啊 is the most frequently used, and it can express a wide range of emotions.

First, 啊 can be used in exclamatory sentences, as in this example from the Text of this lesson:

A 看起来，南京人真的是想尽可能保留老南京的特色、老南京的传统啊。

看起來，南京人真的是想儘可能保留老南京的特色、老南京的傳統啊。

It seems that Nanjingers really do want to preserve the character and traditions of old Nanjing as much as possible.

By adding 啊, Lisha heightens the effect of what she's saying. (B), (C), and (D) show the particle used in the same way.

B 你的字写得多好哇 (wa)！

你的字寫得多好哇 (wa)！

What great handwriting you have!

C 这里的青菜好新鲜哪 (na)！

這裡的青菜好新鮮哪 (na)！

The vegetables are really fresh here!

D 你听，鞭炮多响啊 (ŋa)！

你聽，鞭炮多響啊 (ŋa)！

Listen, the firecrackers are really loud!

As suggested by the parenthetical notations, the pronunciation of the particle is sometimes influenced by the preceding syllable. After "-ao," it can sound like (and be written as) 哇 (wa), as in (B). After "n," it can sound like (and be written as) 哪 (na), as in (C). After "-ng," it is pronounced "ŋa," as in (D). Note that after "-i," "-a," and "o," 呀 can be used in place of 啊 for ease of pronunciation, as in (E):

雨下得多大呀！

雨下得多大呀！

Wow, it's really pouring.

Second, 啊 can be placed at the end of a declarative sentence to emphasize the speaker's intention to explain or remind. (F), (G), and (H) present examples of this use of 啊 from the Text:

F

可是现在，你看到处都有外国游客啊！

可是現在，你看到處都有外國遊客啊！

But now, as you can see, there are foreign tourists everywhere!

G

那就是夫子庙啊。

那就是夫子廟啊。

That is the Temple of Confucius.

H

别忘了，"民以食为天"啊！

別忘了，"民以食為天"啊！

Don't forget, "Ordinary people consider food as important as heaven!"

Third, 啊 can have a softening effect. For example, it can be placed at the end of a yes-or-no question. Used in this way, 啊 usually expresses the speaker's skepticism or surprise and makes the speaker's tone slightly more gentle:

I

明天你给我们上课啊？

明天你給我們上課啊？

So you are going to teach our class tomorrow?

[The speaker is surprised.]

J　小马不去哈尔滨哪？

　　小馬不去哈爾濱哪？

So Little Ma isn't going to Harbin?

[The speaker had thought otherwise.]

This particle can also soften an affirmative question, as in (K), (L), and (M), or an alternative question, as in (N):

K　谁呀？

　　誰呀？

Who is it?

L　我们什么时候走啊？

　　我們什麼時候走啊？

When arc we leaving?

M　你怎么不说话呀？

　　你怎麼不說話呀？

How come you aren't saying anything?

N　我们是看电影还是听音乐呀？

　　我們是看電影還是聽音樂呀？

Are we going to watch a movie or listen to music?

啊 can tone down an imperative sentence:

O　小心点儿啊，别看错了！

　　小心點兒啊，別看錯了！

Be careful—look carefully so that you don't make any mistakes!

P　注意 (zhùyi) 啊，比赛马上开始了！

　　注意 (zhùyi) 啊，比賽馬上開始了！

Pay attention now, the competition is about to begin!

Q 我只是开个玩笑，别急呀！

我只是開個玩笑，別急呀！

I was just joking. Now please don't get upset!

Lastly, 啊 can sometimes convey urgency:

R 大家都等着听你的意见，你怎么不说话，说呀！

大家都等著聽你的意見，你怎麼不說話，說呀！

Everyone is waiting to hear your opinion. How come you're not talking?
Say something!

2 以 X 为/為 Y

"以 X 为/為 Y" means "to regard or treat X as Y." This construction is characteristic of classical Chinese. Note that 为/為 is a verb rather than a preposition here and is pronounced in the second tone.

A 民以食为天。

（老百姓把吃的东西看成是最重要的。）

民以食為天。

（老百姓把吃的東西看成是最重要的。）

Ordinary people consider food as important as heaven.

B 这位老师以校为家。

（这位老师把学校当作自己家一样。）

這位老師以校為家。

（這位老師把學校當作自己家一樣。）

This teacher considers the school his/her home.

我姐姐以帮助别人为自己最大的快乐。
（姐姐把帮助别人当作自己最大的快乐。）

我姐姐以幫助別人為自己最大的快樂。
（姐姐把幫助別人當作自己最大的快樂。）

My older sister thinks of helping others as her greatest joy.

3 | 一 + reduplicated measure word

The structure "一 + reduplicated measure word" is used to describe a large grouping of identical or similar, yet distinctly individual, objects. For example:

A 桌子上摆着一盘盘水果，一瓶瓶可乐。

桌子上擺著一盤盤水果，一瓶瓶可樂。

On the table there is plate after plate of fruit and bottle after bottle of cola.

B 我家门前有一座座高山，风景特别漂亮。

我家門前有一座座高山，風景特別漂亮。

In front of my house there are mountains upon mountains. The landscape is really pretty.

This construction differs from 很多 in both meaning and usage. If the speaker's focus is on simply and factually describing quantity, as in (C) and (D), then this kind of construction would not be appropriate.

C 书架上有很多书。

書架上有很多書。

On the bookshelf are many books.

D 教室里坐着很多学生。

教室裡坐著很多學生。

Many students are sitting in the classroom.

Words & Phrases

A | 要不是 (if it were not for; but for)

要不是 means "if it weren't for." It is used in spoken Chinese.

1 要不是丽莎叫天明跟她去看电影，天明根本不想进电影院。

要不是麗莎叫天明跟她去看電影，天明根本不想進電影院。

If Lisha hadn't asked Tianming to go to the movies with her, he'd never have stepped into the movie theater.

2 要不是看到报纸上的新闻，大家都不知道那栋大厦已经盖好了。

要不是看到報紙上的新聞，大家都不知道那棟大廈已經蓋好了。

If we hadn't seen that news story in the paper, no one would have known that that building was finished.

3 要不是有奖学金和政府贷款，他恐怕拿不到硕士学位。

要不是有獎學金和政府貸款，他恐怕拿不到碩士學位。

If it hadn't been for his scholarship and government loan, he probably wouldn't have been able to get his master's degree.

从来／從來 (from past till present, always, at all times)

从来／從來 is an adverb. It's often followed by a negator such as 不 or 没／沒.

1

我的外国朋友从来没过过端午节，也从来没吃过粽子。

我的外國朋友從來沒過過端午節，也從來沒吃過粽子。

My foreign friends have never celebrated the Dragon Boat Festival and never eaten *zongzi* before.

2

小王上课从来不迟到，老师们都很喜欢他。

小王上課從來不遲到，老師們都很喜歡他。

Little Wang is never late for class. The teachers all like him a lot.

3

林太太买衣服从来不在乎牌子。

林太太買衣服從來不在乎牌子。

Mrs. Lin never cares about brand names when she shops for clothes.

从来／從來 is sometimes used in an affirmative sense, for instance to contradict:

4   Person A

没想到你的房间这么干净。

沒想到你的房間這麼乾淨。

I didn't think that your room would be this clean!

Person B

我的房间从来就很干净。

我的房間從來就很乾淨。

My room is always very clean.

看起来/看起來 (it seems)

看起来/看起來, meaning "it seems" or "it appears," introduces a conclusion or opinion based on a previously stated fact or previously described situation:

1

你这么高兴，看起来一定有什么好事。

你這麼高興，看起來一定有什麼好事。

You seem so happy. There must be a really good reason.

2

听你刚才那么说，看起来你儿子暑假的活动你都已经安排好了。

聽你剛才那麼說，看起來你兒子暑假的活動你都已經安排好了。

From what you just said, it seems you have made all the arrangements for your son's summer activities.

3

我还得学五门课，看起来这个学期毕不了业了。

我還得學五門課，看起來這個學期畢不了業了。

I have to take five more classes. It looks like I won't be able to graduate this semester.

A WAY WITH WORDS

对面

張天明和柯林讨论选专业的对话很有意思。

今天晚上我们学校有篮球比赛，对手是纽约大学队。

Using the word/phrase in orange as a clue, try to figure out the meaning of the words/phrases in blue; consult a dictionary if necessary. Consider how the literal and extended senses are related in each case.

對面

張天明和柯林討論選專業的對話很有意思。

今天晚上我們學校有籃球比賽，對手是紐約大學隊。

尽可能/儘可能 (as much as possible, to do one's utmost)

1

别着急，我们会尽可能帮你找到钥匙。

別著急，我們會儘可能幫你找到鑰匙。

Don't stress. We'll do our best to help you find your keys.

2

有的人认为旅行的时候要尽可能少带东西，可是有的人喜欢带很多东西。

有的人認為旅行的時候要儘可能少帶東西，可是有的人喜歡帶很多東西。

Some people think that when you travel you should pack as lightly as possible. However, some people like to pack a bunch of stuff.

3

你明天尽可能早点来学校，别又迟到。要不然老师会生气。

你明天儘可能早點來學校，別又遲到。要不然老師會生氣。

Come to school tomorrow as early as you can. Don't be late again, or the teacher will be angry.

Language Practice

| INTERPERSONAL | **Astonished and astounded** | PRESENTATIONAL

First, in pairs, ask and answer questions about scenes that one might see in a busy urban area like New York City, e.g.:

 多

Q: 大城市里的人多吗？

大城市裡的人多嗎？

A: 大城市里的人非常多。

大城市裡的人非常多。

 多   1

 多   2

 高   3

Second, present a cohesive statement to your partner by connecting your responses and making them flow.

_____

_____

_____

_____

B | City getaway

In pairs, have a conversation about the cities and towns you've visited. Ask your partner where they've been, and which city or town they found most memorable. What was it like? Ask what they heard (or didn't hear) and what they saw (or didn't see) during their visit. Kick off the conversation by asking:

- 你去过哪些城市？
  你去過哪些城市？

- 你对哪一个城市的印象最好？
  你對哪一個城市的印象最好？

- 那个地方有什么特色小吃？
  那個地方有什麼特色小吃？

  ......

C | Getting all nostalgic

In pairs, talk about how your hometown has (or hasn't) changed in the past few years using these terms where appropriate:

- 我小时候…/我小時候…
- 到处都是/到處都是
- 要不是

- 保留
- 以前…，现在也…起…来了
  以前…，現在也…起…來了

Ask your partner to explain the reasons why he/she likes or dislikes those changes and jot them down.

1 _____

2 _____

3 _____

4 _____

Then, recap what your partner has told you and report to the class.

| **Expectations vs. reality** |

What would you expect of a popular historic tourist attraction in China? Don't forget to mention the sights, sounds, and food.

1 _____

2 _____

3 _____

4 _____

5 _____

In pairs, discuss whether or not you know of or have visited such a historic tourist sight. Describe where it is and when is the best time of year to visit.

Chinese Chat

A friend is messaging you on WeChat about her first few days in Beijing. How would you reply?

Marla Eisenberg

Marla:
北京很有特色，很热闹，到处都有好吃的，好玩儿的。

You:
…

Marla:
像我一样的"老外"很多，很好融入！你也来这儿旅游吧？

You:
…

This can't continue

In pairs, role-play a conversation between an older and younger sibling. Based on each of the scenarios below, the older sibling should use 担心这样下去/擔心這樣下去 to warn the younger sibling of a possible negative consequence that could arise if he/she keeps on doing things in the same way. The younger sibling should use 不会的/不會的 to respond that this negative consequence won't happen, and that any concerns are unfounded, e.g.:

Older Sibling	Your dorm is noisy. You won't be able to sleep, and you'll get sick.
Younger Sibling	I won't. I'm not afraid of noise. I fall asleep as soon as my head hits the pillow.
Older Sibling	你的宿舍很吵，你晚上睡不好觉。我担心这样下去，你会生病。 你的宿舍很吵，你晚上睡不好覺。我擔心這樣下去，你會生病。
Younger Sibling	不会的，我不怕吵，我一上床就睡着 (zháo) 了。 不會的，我不怕吵，我一上床就睡著 (zháo) 了。

1 Older Sibling You are a vegetarian, but most of the food at the cafeteria has meat in it. You will get too skinny.

    Younger Sibling I often cook for myself . . .

2 Older Sibling You haven't exercised in a long time. Your health is going to have big problems (出大问题/出大問題).

    Younger Sibling I used to not exercise . . . Now, I . . .

3 Older Sibling You never practice speaking Japanese. You will forget your Japanese/won't be able to speak it.

    Younger Sibling I found a Japanese friend . . .

4 Older Sibling You never call your friends. You will have fewer and fewer friends.

    Younger Sibling I often text them . . .

Better self

PRESENTATIONAL

Suppose you are leaving home for college and you want to alleviate your parents' concerns about your lifestyle on campus by pledging to do more or less of the following, e.g.:

我会尽可能少喝可乐。

我會儘可能少喝可樂。

1

2

3

4

5

6

Characterize it!

More
characters

❶ 店　❷ 庭

❸ 座　❹ 庙

| What do the characters mean? |
| What is the common radical? |
| What does the radical mean? |
| How does the radical relate to the overall meaning of the characters? |

1 店　2 庭

3 座　4 廟

You saved the day!

Based on the prompts, use 要不是 to thank a friend for averting an undesirable situation, e.g.:

> If you hadn't told me that computer science would have an exam today, I definitely wouldn't have studied last night. I would have done terribly on the test today.

要不是你告诉我今天电脑课有考试，昨天晚上我一定不会复习，今天一定考得很糟糕。

要不是你告訴我今天電腦課有考試，昨天晚上我一定不會復習，今天一定考得很糟糕。

1 The hospital was very difficult to find. If you hadn't gone with me, I definitely wouldn't have found it.

2 The place for the meeting was very far away. If you hadn't let me borrow your car, I definitely would have been late.

3 My boyfriend/girlfriend and I are still together. If you hadn't suggested that I sit down with him/her and talk, we definitely would have broken up.

4 If you hadn't told me about this scholarship, I definitely would have had to take out a loan from the bank.

A WAY WITH WORDS

保留

下个月我要去纽约，能不能麻烦你帮我保管电脑？

您今年七十五岁了，应该多休息，好好保养身体。

Using the word/phrase in orange as a clue, try to figure out the meaning of the words/phrases in blue; consult a dictionary if necessary. Consider how the literal and extended senses are related in each case.

保留

下個月我要去紐約，能不能麻煩你幫我保管電腦？

您今年七十五歲了，應該多休息，好好保養身體。

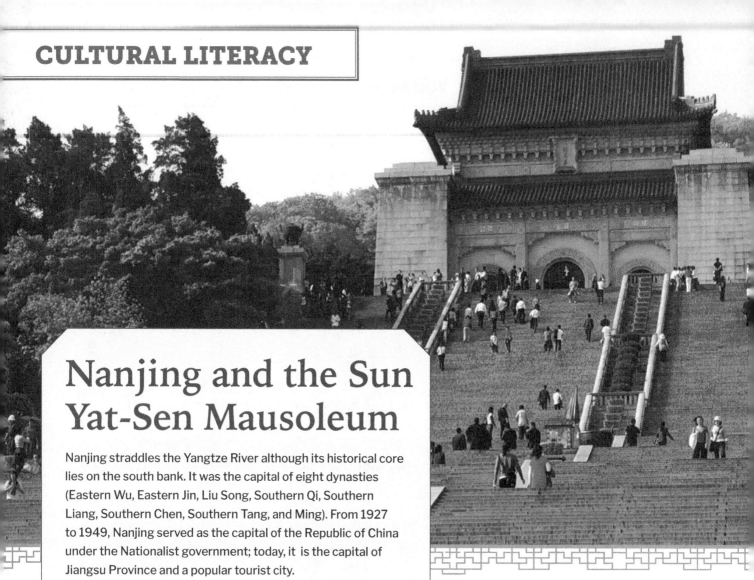

CULTURAL LITERACY

Nanjing and the Sun Yat-Sen Mausoleum

Nanjing straddles the Yangtze River although its historical core lies on the south bank. It was the capital of eight dynasties (Eastern Wu, Eastern Jin, Liu Song, Southern Qi, Southern Liang, Southern Chen, Southern Tang, and Ming). From 1927 to 1949, Nanjing served as the capital of the Republic of China under the Nationalist government; today, it is the capital of Jiangsu Province and a popular tourist city.

One of Nanjing's most famous landmarks is the Sun Yat-sen (孙中山/孫中山) (*Sūn Zhōngshān*, 1866–1925) Mausoleum. After Sun's death, the Nationalist government decided to build a tribute to "the Father of the Nation" (国父/國父) and held an open competition for the design of a grand mausoleum. The winner was Lu Yanzhi (吕彦直/呂彥直) (*Lǚ Yànzhí*, 1894–1929), a thirty-three-year-old architect who had spent part of his childhood in Paris and received his professional training at Cornell University. Drawing on Ming and Qing imperial tomb and Western Beaux Arts architecture, Lu conceived a strongly axial plan. Visitors are directed through a memorial archway, the mausoleum gate, and a stele pavilion, up three hundred and ninety-two stone steps, and across eight terraces.

A selection of Sun's ideals is inscribed in gold on each building along the processional route: 博爱/博愛 (*bó'ài*) (fraternity) on the memorial gateway and 天下为公/天下為公 (All under the heavens belongs to the public) on the mausoleum gate. The longest text at the mausoleum is Sun's "Platform for National Construction" (建国大纲/建國大綱) (*Jiànguó dàgāng*), which is reproduced in its entirety behind a marble statue of Sun in the ceremonial hall.

COMPARE & CONTRAST

In China as in other countries, the city center has been a site for thinking about social value. Keeping development away from the city center was seen as regressive. However, priorities are changing; some new developments in a number of Chinese cities are seeking to renovate, not demolish, older buildings, in the hope that their existing character might be preserved. Research the development of your city or a city close to you. What parts of the city are new, what parts of the city are old, and which parts do you prefer? Can you think of any initiatives in recent years that have been designed to correct what happened to the city in an earlier era?

Architectural Preservation and Liang Sicheng

Cities in China have undergone enormous change; in many places, traditional residential neighborhoods have been demolished to make way for high-rise apartment buildings. Courtyard houses known as 四合院 were once found in many Chinese cities, notably in Beijing.

The architect and architectural historian Liang Sicheng (梁思成 [Liáng Sīchéng], 1901–1972) argued that traditional courtyard houses, temples, and city walls should be preserved. In one of his most famous proposals, he suggested that the traditional city center of Beijing could be retained by moving some government departments outside of the city; this would reduce crowding and enable the preservation of much of old Beijing. Liang's proposal was rejected. However, some saw Liang's impact in the Chinese government's announcement in 2017 that some governmental functions would be moved outside of the city to the Xiong'an New Area in adjacent Hebei Province.

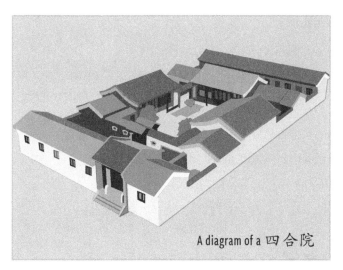

A diagram of a 四合院

Temples of Confucius

Temples dedicated to Confucius were once common in many Chinese towns. The most important ancient Chinese educator and philosopher 孔子 (Kǒngzǐ, 551–479 BCE) was colloquially known as 孔夫子 (Kǒngfūzǐ); hence his Latinized name Confucius in European languages. Confucian temples are called 孔庙/孔廟 (Kǒngmiào), 夫子庙/夫子廟 (Fūzǐmiào), or 文庙/文廟 (Wénmiào) (Temple of Literature). The most impressive temple of Confucius is found in the sage's birthplace, Qufu, Shandong. Its size, architectural style and color scheme were typically associated with imperial palaces. Behind a ceremonial gate are nine, instead of the usual two or three, courtyards with numerous steles commemorating imperial visits or grants of honorific titles on Confucius' descendants. The main structure, the Hall of Grand Synthesis (大成殿 Dàchéngdiàn), sits on top of a marble terrace and is accessed through an elaborately carved marble staircase. All the buildings feature vermilion walls and yellow glazed roof tiles.

Lesson Wrap-Up

Project

How much has your hometown changed in the last twenty or thirty years? Share its transformation with the class. Prepare a PowerPoint presentation. Begin with an introductory statement: 我来谈谈 (your hometown) 的变化 / 我來談談 (your hometown) 的變化. Where appropriate, your presentation should:

- describe your hometown's physical transformation (cityscape, traffic, construction, and so on)
- comment on how international it has become, e.g., are there many more types of restaurants or stores?
- explain the reasons for the transformation, e.g., immigration or economic change
- describe ways your community has stayed the same
- explain whether you are concerned that your community will lose its character
- predict the future of your community: what will it be like in ten, twenty years?

Keep It Flowing

Study the following description; pay particular attention to how the highlighted parts help the sentences flow smoothly from one to the next. Notice how:

- pronouns (他们 / 他們) replace proper nouns (天明和丽莎 / 天明和麗莎) in subsequent sentences
- certain words and phrases (听说 / 聽說, 没想到 / 沒想到, 比方说 / 比方說, 觉得 / 覺得) introduce hearsay, thoughts, examples, and feelings
- time words and conjunctions (以前, 现在 / 現在, 但是) suggest contrast

南京的变化很大

张天明和丽莎从上海坐高铁到了南京，天明的表哥来接他们。南京跟天明和丽莎听到的不一样。他们听说以前南京是一个很安静的城市，很少看到外国人。他们没想到现在到处都是新盖的高楼，大街上挤满了汽车，到处都有外国游客和外国商店。但是南京还是保留了很多有中国特色的东西，比如说夫子庙、南京小吃。天明觉得中国融入世界了，是一件好事。

南京的變化很大

　　張天明和麗莎從上海坐高鐵到了南京，天明的表哥來接他們。南京跟天明和麗莎聽到的不一樣。他們聽說以前南京是一個很安靜的城市，很少看到外國人。他們沒想到現在到處都是新蓋的高樓，大街上擠滿了汽車，到處都有外國遊客和外國商店。但是南京還是保留了很多有中國特色的東西，比如說夫子廟、南京小吃。天明覺得中國融入世界了，是一件好事。

How has your hometown (or another place of your choice) changed in the last few decades? Use as many of the cohesive devices highlighted in the example as possible to string together a response, based on the prompts:

- 那个地方几十年或几年前是什么样子？
  那個地方幾十年或幾年前是什麼樣子？

- 现在那个地方有哪些变化？
  現在那個地方有哪些變化？

- 那个地方哪些东西变化不大？
  那個地方哪些東西變化不大？

- 你喜欢这些变化吗？
  你喜歡這些變化嗎？

Can-Do Check List ✓

I can

Before proceeding to Lesson 13, make sure you can complete the following tasks in Chinese:

- ☐ Discuss how a place has or hasn't changed
- ☐ Specify how something differs from your previous expectations
- ☐ Voice your concern about the consequences of a persisting issue
- ☐ Draw comparisons between a place in its current form and what it used to be like

Zhāng Tiānmíng hé Lìshā shàng ge xuéqī mò shēnqǐng dào Zhōngguó xué Zhōngwén, yuánlái yǐwéi shíjiān huì lái bu jí, méi xiǎng dào xuéxiào hěn kuài jiù tóngyì le. Liǎng ge rén kěyǐ zài Zhōngguó xuéxí, shēnghuó sān, sì ge yuè, zhè ràng tāmen fēicháng gāoxìng.

Zhāng Tiānmíng hé Lìshā xiān dào Shànghǎi, ránhòu zuò gāotiě qù Nánjīng. Chē hěn kuài, yí ge duō xiǎoshí jiù dào le. Tiānmíng de biǎoge^a kāi chē lái jiē tāmen. Biǎogē jiàn dao tāmen hěn gāoxìng, shuō yuànyì dāng dǎoyóu, dài tāmen zài jiē shang zǒu zou, ràng tāmen hǎohāor kàn kan Nánjīng.

Bàba chángcháng shuō Nánjīng shì ge hěn ānjìng de chéngshì, méi xiǎng dào zhème rènao! Nǐ kàn, dàjiē shang dàochù dōu shì xīn gài de gāo lóu, dàochù dōu shì qìchē.

Zhè xiē nián Nánjīng de biànhuà shì hěn dà, wǒ yǐqián qí zìxíngchē shàng bān, xiànzài yě kāi qi chē lai le.

Zhè gēn wǒ yǐqián xiǎngxiàng de Zhōngguó wánquán bù yíyàng. Zài Shànghǎi de shíhou, yàobúshì dàochù dōu shì Zhōngwén, wǒ hái yǐwéi shì zài Měiguó ne.

Wǒ bàba shuō, tā xiǎo shíhou zài Nánjīng hěn shǎo kàn dào wàiguó rén, kěshì xiànzài, nǐ kàn, dàochù dōu yǒu wàiguó yóukè a¹!

Wǒmen bù yě shì liǎng ge "lǎowài" ma? Hā hā! Nǐ kàn mǎlù duìmiàn, Měiguó kuàicān diàn, Rìběn yínháng, Fǎguó fúzhuāng diàn . . .

Zhōngguó qítā dìfang yě zhèyàng, biànhuà zhēnde hěn dà.

Zhōngguó róngrù shìjiè le, zhè shì jiàn hǎo shì.

Kěshì wǒ dānxīn, zhèyàng xia qu^b, yǒu Zhōngguó tèsè de dōngxi huì bú huì yuè lái yuè shǎo ne?

Bú huì de. Nánjīng hái shì bǎoliú le hěn duō yǒu Zhōngguó tèsè de dōngxi. Bǐfāng shuō jiànzhù, Nánjīng zuì yǒu Zhōngguó tèsè de shì Fūzǐmiào, nàr hái yǒu chī de, hē de, wánr de . . .

Nà wǒmen xiànzài jiù qù Fūzǐmiào, cháng chang Nánjīng xiǎochī^c ba.

Hǎo a! Bùguǎn Zhōngguó zěnme biàn^d, Nánjīng zěnme biàn, dùzi è le yào chī méi biàn. Nǐmen tīngshuō guo "Mín yǐ shí wéi tiān"^{e 2} zhè jù huà ba?

Á? Shénme? Cónglái méi tīngshuō guo.

Zhè jù huà de yìsi, jiǎndān de shuō jiù shì, "chī" shì lǎobǎixìng shēnghuó zhōng zuì zhòngyào de shìr.

Āi, Tiānmíng, nǐ kàn, nà shì shénme dìfang? Rén nàme duō, pángbiān hǎoxiàng hái mài chī de, wánr de, wǔ yán liù sè, zhēn hǎokàn, zhēn rènao!

Nà jiù shì Fūzǐmiào a.

Kàn qi lai, Nánjīng rén zhēn de shì xiǎng jǐn kěnéng bǎoliú lǎo Nánjīng de tèsè, lǎo Nánjīng de chuántǒng a.

Nánjīng yìbiān shì yí dòng dòng gāo lóu dà shà, yìbiān shì yí zuò zuò³ chuántǒng jiànzhù, zhàn zài zhèr, wǒ hǎoxiàng tīng dào le yì zhǒng shēngyīn.

Shénme shēngyīn?

Lìshā de jiǎobù shēng. Lái Zhōngguó yǐqián bàba ràng wǒ zhǎo tā shàng de nà ge zhōngxué. Yíhuìr wǒ gěi tā fā Wēixìn, gàosu tā Nánjīng biànhuà tài dà, nà ge zhōngxué yǐjīng zhǎo bú dào le, zài bǎ jīntiān pāi de zhàopiàn fā gěi tā kàn kan.

Āi, wǒ yě tīng dào le yì zhǒng shēngyīn.

Shénme shēngyīn?

Dùzi gūlū gūlū jiào de shēngyīn. Zǒu le zhème duō lù, nǐmen hǎoxiàng bú lèi bú è, kěshì wǒ zhè ge dǎoyóu yòu kě yòu è. Bié wàng le, "Mín yǐ shí wéi tiān" a! Zǒu, chī fàn qù!

去云南旅游

去雲南旅遊

A TRIP TO YUNNAN

Learning Objectives

In this lesson, you will learn to:

- Describe what costs a package tour may cover
- Explain the differences between "soft" and "hard" sleeper cars
- Describe Yunnan's natural and cultural attractions
- Discuss high and low points of a trip

Relate and Get Ready

In your own culture/community:

- Do tourists prefer to travel by plane, car, bus, or train?
- How do people document their travels?
- Do travelers prefer to plan their own itinerary or join a tour group?
- What types of hotel accommodation are there? How do they differ?

课文

Text

Audio

Before You Study

Answer the following questions in Chinese to prepare for the reading.

1 你喜欢自然风景还是名胜古迹？

2 你喜欢坐火车还是开车旅行？

When You Study

Listen to the audio recording and skim the text; then answer the following questions in Chinese.

1 张天明觉得他们的导游怎么样？

2 张天明说中国火车有什么特别的地方？

3 张天明觉得自助游好还是参加旅行团好？为什么？

新学期开始前，张天明、丽莎和柯林、雪梅一起去云南旅游。他们约好星期天在昆明见面，然后在云南旅游一个星期。这次旅游，中国的火车、导游和云南美丽的风景，都给天明留下很深的印象。张天明每天发微信，跟朋友们分享自己的快乐。

张天明

去云南前，我们在网上报名参加了一个旅行团。团费包括[a]交通、旅馆、三餐和景点门票。

我们是坐火车去的云南。为了能跟别的旅客练习说中文，我们买了硬卧[b]票，因为硬卧车厢每个"房间"都没有门，容易找人聊天儿。我在上铺，上铺比下铺和中铺安静一点，晚上可以睡个好觉。

我也去软卧车厢看了看。那里每个小房间里有两个上铺，两个下铺，床比较软也比较大，房间的门可以关上。

1月22日

晚上，我们在餐车上吃了一顿饭。那里的饭，我觉得很贵，也不太好吃，还是买盒饭[c]或者方便面[d]好。

課文

新學期開始前，張天明、麗莎和柯林、雪梅一起去雲南旅遊。他們約好星期天在昆明見面，然後在雲南旅遊一個星期。這次旅遊，中國的火車、導遊和雲南美麗的風景，都給天明留下很深的印象。張天明每天發微信，跟朋友們分享自己的快樂。

張天明

去雲南前，我們在網上報名參加了一個旅行團。團費包括[a] 交通、旅館、三餐和景點門票。

我們是坐火車去的雲南。為了能跟別的旅客練習說中文，我們買了硬臥[b]票，因為硬臥車廂每個"房間"都沒有門，容易找人聊天兒。我在上鋪，上鋪比下鋪和中鋪安靜一點，晚上可以睡個好覺。

我也去軟臥車廂看了看。那裡每個小房間裡有兩個上鋪，兩個下鋪，床比較軟也比較大，房間的門可以關上。

晚上，我們在餐車上吃了一頓飯。那裡的飯，我覺得很貴，也不太好吃，還是買盒飯[c]或者方便麵[d]好。

1月22日

Before You Study

Answer the following questions in Chinese to prepare for the reading.

1 你喜歡自然風景還是名勝古蹟？

2 你喜歡坐火車還是開車旅行？

When You Study

Listen to the audio recording and skim the text; then answer the following questions in Chinese.

1 張天明覺得他們的導遊怎麼樣？

2 張天明說中國火車有什麼特別的地方？

3 張天明覺得自助遊好還是參加旅行團好？為什麼？

1月23日

我和丽莎在昆明下车后，等了两个多小时，雪梅和柯林他们的火车才到。我们一起走出火车站，看到导游正举着牌子找我们，牌子上写的是我们四个人的名字。我们的导游说话很幽默，不过有时^e他说的话我们三个人都听不懂，雪梅只好给我们当翻译。

导游介绍说云南是一个省，在中国的西南部，省会是昆明。云南自然风景很美^f，有山有水，这里住着很多少数民族。来云南旅游，可以看看不同民族的建筑、服装、饮食，了解各个民族的风俗习惯。

第一天我们游览了石林。这是一张石林的照片。石林有很多颜色很深的石头，远看就像树林一样。石头的样子千奇百怪[1]。我们在石林里一边走，一边听导游讲那些石头的故事，非常有意思。

1月24日

这是大理三塔，建筑很古老，很有名。大理城里有很多卖纪念品的商店，导游把我们带到那儿，希望大家多买东西。雪梅和丽莎很高兴，买了不少纪念品，而我跟柯林受不了，就抱怨说太浪费时间了。下次你们到中国旅游找旅行团，千万别找有"购物"的团。你们可以自助游^g，那样就自由多了。

我和麗莎在昆明下車後，等了兩個多小時，雪梅和柯林他們的火車才到。我們一起走出火車站，看到導遊正舉著牌子找我們，牌子上寫的是我們四個人的名字。我們的導遊說話很幽默，不過有時[e]他說的話我們三個人都聽不懂，雪梅只好給我們當翻譯。

導遊介紹說雲南是一個省，在中國的西南部，省會是昆明。雲南自然風景很美[f]，有山有水，這裡住著很多少數民族。來雲南旅遊，可以看看不同民族的建築、服裝、飲食，了解各個民族的風俗習慣。

第一天我們遊覽了石林。這是一張石林的照片。石林有很多顏色很深的石頭，遠看就像樹林一樣。石頭的樣子千奇百怪[1]。我們在石林裡一邊走，一邊聽導遊講那些石頭的故事，非常有意思。

這是大理三塔，建築很古老，很有名。大理城裡有很多賣紀念品的商店，導遊把我們帶到那兒，希望大家多買東西。雪梅和麗莎很高興，買了不少紀念品，而我跟柯林受不了，就抱怨說太浪費時間了。下次你們到中國旅遊找旅行團，千萬別找有"購物"的團。你們可以自助遊[g]，那樣就自由多了。

1月25日

第三天，到了有名的丽江古城[h]，我们非常喜欢这里。这个古城不大，从东边走到西边不过一两个小时。最特别的是有一条非常干净的小河[2]从城中间穿[i]过。小河两边有很多商店、茶馆、小饭馆。那天晚上，我们在一个很有云南特色的茶馆里喝茶，看着外边的小河，门旁的红灯笼，还有世界各国的游客，都不想回旅馆去睡觉了。

在丽江，我们住了两天家庭旅馆。房间虽然很小，但是很干净，也能上网。房东还给我们做了些家常菜，辣辣的，味道很不错。

云南各个地方的风景不一样，还有很多好玩的地方。我们明天要去游览大雪山。我过几天会把在那儿拍的照片放在博客上。

After You Study

Answer the following questions in Chinese.

1 石林为什么给人留下很深的印象？

2 丽江古城有什么特色？

3 简单地介绍一下云南的地理、风景、民族文化。

View & Explore

Video

For deeper language immersion and more cultural information, watch "Traveling to Yunnan," a short, supplemental video clip by Cheng & Tsui on this lesson's theme.

第三天，到了有名的麗江古城[h]，我們非常喜歡這裡。這個古城不大，從東邊走到西邊不過一兩個小時。最特別的是有一條非常乾淨的小河[2]從城中間穿[i]過。小河兩邊有很多商店、茶館、小飯館。那天晚上，我們在一個很有雲南特色的茶館裡喝茶，看著外邊的小河，門旁的紅燈籠，還有世界各國的遊客，都不想回旅館去睡覺了。

在麗江，我們住了兩天家庭旅館。房間雖然很小，但是很乾淨，也能上網。房東還給我們做了些家常菜，辣辣的，味道很不錯。

雲南各個地方的風景不一樣，還有很多好玩的地方。我們明天要去遊覽大雪山。我過幾天會把在那兒拍的照片放在博客上。

After You Study

Answer the following questions in Chinese.

1. 石林為什麼給人留下很深的印象？
2. 麗江古城有什麼特色？
3. 簡單地介紹一下雲南的地理、風景、民族文化。

Language Notes

a 包括
包括 is usually pronounced "bāokuò," but is sometimes pronounced "bāoguā" in Taiwan.

b 卧／臥
Here, 卧／臥 is short for 卧铺／臥鋪 (sleeping bunk).

c 盒饭／盒飯
The term 盒饭／盒飯 is used in Mainland China. In Taiwan, the term 便当／便當 (biàndāng), which is Japanese in origin, is used instead.

d 方便面／方便麵
方便面／方便麵 (lit. convenient noodles) are instant noodles. In Taiwan, the term 泡面／泡麵 (pàomiàn) (lit. soaked noodles) is preferred.

e 有时／有時
有时／有時 is short for and has a slightly more literary nuance than 有（的）时候／有（的）時候 (sometimes).

f 美 vs. 美丽／美麗
美 and 美丽／美麗 are synonymous. However, they are used differently. 美丽／美麗 is often placed before a noun as a modifier. 美, on the other hand, usually functions as a predicate after a noun. Furthermore, 美 is more colloquial than 美丽／美麗.

g 自助游／自助遊
自助游／自助遊 (lit. self-assisted travel) is travel that is undertaken not as part of a tour group. Here, 自 is short for 自己 (self), while 助 is short for 帮助／幫助 (help). The term 自由行, short for 自由旅行, is now also very common.

h 古城
In this phrase, 古 is short for 古老, and 城 is short for 城市.

i 穿
While 穿 can mean "to wear" or "to put on" in other contexts, here it means "to pass through."

Vocabulary

No.	Simplified	Traditional	Pinyin	Part of Speech	Definition
1	美丽	美麗	měilì	adj	beautiful
2	留（下）	留（下）	liú (xia)	v(c)	to leave behind, to stay behind
3	深	深	shēn	adj	deep, profound, dark (color)
4	分享	分享	fēnxiǎng	v	to share (joy, happiness, benefits, etc.) (lit. to divide and enjoy)
5	报名	報名	bào míng	vo	to sign up, to register
6	参加	參加	cānjiā	v	to participate, to take part, to attend
7	团	團	tuán	n	group, organization
8	包括	包括	bāokuò	v	to include, to consist of
9	交通	交通	jiāotōng	n	transportation, traffic (lit. to intersect and go through)
10	门票	門票	ménpiào	n	admission ticket, admission fee
11	旅客	旅客	lǚkè	n	passenger, voyager, traveler
12	硬	硬	yìng	adj	hard, stiff
13	卧铺	臥鋪	wòpù	n	sleeping bunk (on a train)
14	车厢	車廂	chēxiāng	n	train carriage
15	软	軟	ruǎn	adj	soft
16	关	關	guān	v	to close, to turn off
17	顿	頓	dùn	m	(measure word for meals)
18	盒饭	盒飯	héfàn	n	box lunch
19	面	麵	miàn	n	noodles
20	幽默	幽默	yōumò	adj	humorous
21	省会	省會	shěnghuì	n	provincial capital
22	美	美	měi	adj	beautiful, good
23	饮食	飲食	yǐnshí	n	diet, food and drink
24	风俗	風俗	fēngsú	n	custom
25	习惯	習慣	xíguàn	n/v	habit; to be accustomed to

No.	Simplified	Traditional	Pinyin	Part of Speech	Definition
26	游览	遊覽	*yóulǎn*	v/n	to go sightseeing, to tour; excursion
27	石头	石頭	*shítou*	n	stone, rock, pebble
28	树林	樹林	*shùlín*	n	woods, forest
29	讲	講	*jiǎng*	v	to speak, to tell
30	故事	故事	*gùshi*	n	story, tale
31	塔	塔	*tǎ*	n	tower, pagoda
32	古老	古老	*gǔlǎo*	adj	anclent, old
33	纪念品	紀念品	*jìniànpǐn*	n	souvenir, keepsake, memento
34	千万	千萬	*qiānwàn*	adv	by all means, absolutely must
35	河	河	*hé*	n	river
36	茶馆	茶館	*cháguǎn*	n	teahouse
37	灯笼	燈籠	*dēnglong*	n	lantern
38	房东	房東	*fángdōng*	n	landlord
39	昆明	昆明	*Kūnmíng*	pn	Kunming (capital of Yunnan Province)
40	石林	石林	*Shílín*	pn	The Stone Forest
41	大理	大理	*Dàlǐ*	pn	Dali
42	丽江	麗江	*Lìjiāng*	pn	Lijiang

How About You?

云南的风景给张天明留下了很深的印象。你呢？你对哪儿的自然风景印象很深？为什么？

雲南的風景給張天明留下了很深的印象。你呢？你對哪兒的自然風景印象最深？為什麼？

Grammar

1 ## Numbers in idioms

Many idioms in Chinese contain two numbers. These numbers are almost never literal in meaning. For instance, "千···百···" can mean "myriad" or "many," as in 千奇百怪 (strange in all sorts of ways) and 千娇百媚/千嬌百媚 (qiān jiāo bǎi mèi) (charming in myriad ways). 千 and 万/萬 emphasize a large quantity, as in 千变万化/千變萬化 (constantly changing), 千军万马/千軍萬馬 (qiān jūn wàn mǎ) (a large and powerful army), and 千家万户/千家萬戶 (qiān jiā wàn hù) (countless families and households).

In many idioms that contain numbers, the two numbers are consecutive. 一 and 二 frequently appear together, and imply that something is straightforward or clear-cut, as in 一干二净/一乾二淨 (quick and clean, complete) and 一清二楚 (crystal clear). 五 and 六 can sometimes mean many, as in 五颜六色/五顏六色 (colorful, variegated). 七 and 八 suggest messiness and chaos, as in 七上八下 (at an utter loss, feeling unsettled), 乱七八糟/亂七八糟 (messy), 七手八脚/七手八腳 (too many cooks spoiling the broth), and 七嘴八舌 (qī zuǐ bā shé) (everyone talking in confusion).

Some idioms involve non-consecutive numbers, such as 五光十色 (dazzlingly colored) and 五花八门/五花八門 (all manner of, every kind of). There are also idioms in which the numbers go from large to small, as in 三番两次/三番兩次 (repeatedly) and 三心二意 (half-hearted).

Chinese Chat

Ke Lin just posted a review on TripAdvisor 猫途鹰/貓途鷹 (Māotúyīng).
What tips does he offer other tourists?

⊙⊙⊙⊙○ 2018-01-25

柯林

KeLin_IC4

坐火车到云南以后，我和朋友们尝了尝地道的特色小吃，还游览了像树林一样的石林、古老的大理三塔、和美丽的丽江古城。我们的导游虽然很幽默，但是一直让我们买纪念品……下次来云南，我打算自助游。

柯林

坐火車到雲南以後，我和朋友們嚐了嚐地道的特色小吃，還遊覽了像樹林一樣的石林、古老的大理三塔、和美麗的麗江古城。我們的導遊雖然很幽默，但是一直讓我們買紀念品……下次來雲南，我打算自助遊。

Nouns with multiple attributives

A noun can take multiple attributives, but these attributives must follow a certain order. Typically, numeral-measure words must come first.

Two nouns with multiple attributives can be found in the Text of Lesson 11: 一套三室两厅两卫的公寓/一套三室兩廳兩衛的公寓 (an apartment with three bedrooms, a living room, a dining room, and two bathrooms) and 一张不大的红纸/一張不大的紅紙 (a not-too-large piece of red paper). Note that 一套 and 一张/一張 are numeral-measure words, whereas 三室两厅两卫/三室兩廳兩衛, 不大的, and 红/紅 are descriptive modifiers.

The Text of this lesson has 一条非常干净的小河/一條非常乾淨的小河 (a very clean stream), and 一个很有云南特色的茶馆/一個很有雲南特色的茶館 (a teahouse with distinct Yunnan characteristics). Similarly, 一条/一條 and 一个/一個 are numeral-measure words.

Numeral-measure words normally come before descriptive modifiers, as in 一件漂亮的毛衣 (a pretty sweater), 一位有名的教授 (a famous professor), 一个大红"福"字/一個大红"福"字 (a big red 福 character), 两个认识很久的朋友/兩個認識很久的朋友 (two friends who have known each other for a long time), and 五个性格不同的研究生/五個性格不同的研究生 (five graduate students with distinct personalities).

Sometimes, though, descriptive modifiers are placed before numeral-measure words for emphasis:

A 一室一厅的一套公寓就要一百万，太贵了。
一室一廳的一套公寓就要一百萬，太貴了。

> Even a one bedroom, one living-room apartment costs as much as a million. That's too expensive.

B 三岁大的一个孩子就能认识两千个汉字，太厉害了。
三歲大的一個孩子就能認識兩千個漢字，太厲害了。

> A three-year-old child can already recognize two thousand Chinese characters. That's incredible.

Words & Phrases

印象/印象 (impression)

印象/印象 often appears in the following constructions:

X 对 Y 的印象很好（or 不好 or 很深）
X 對 Y 的印象很好（or 不好 or 很深）

X has a very good (or bad, or very deep) impression of Y.

Y 给 X 留下很好（or 不好 or 很深）的印象
Y 給 X 留下很好（or 不好 or 很深）的印象

Y gives X a very good (or bad, or very deep) impression.

（没）有印象
（沒）有印象

to have (no) impression or recollection

1　Q: 你跟那个人第一次见面，对他的印象怎么样？
　　你跟那個人第一次見面，對他的印象怎麼樣？

This is the first time you've met that person. What's your impression of him?

A: 那个人很开朗，也很幽默，我对他的印象不错。
　　那個人很開朗，也很幽默，我對他的印象不錯。

That person is very outgoing and funny. My impression of him is pretty good.

2　Q: 中国的哪一个城市给你留下的印象最深？
　　中國的哪一個城市給你留下的印象最深？

Which city in China had the deepest impression on you?

A: 北京有很多古老建筑，给我留下的印象最深。
　　北京有很多古老建築，給我留下的印象最深。

Beijing has many ancient structures. It had the deepest impression on me.

3 Q: 听说你去过云南，你对那儿的印象好吗？

聽說你去過雲南，你對那兒的印象好嗎？

I hear you've been to Yunnan. Do you have a good impression of that place?

A: 云南的风景美，少数民族的饮食、服装、风俗习惯都很特别，给我的印象很好。

雲南的風景美，少數民族的飲食、服裝、風俗習慣都很特別，給我的印象很好。

Yunnan has beautiful scenery, and the food, clothing, customs, and habits of the ethnic minority groups are very unique. They gave me a very good impression.

4 这件事已经过去很多年了，我没有印象了。

這件事已經過去很多年了，我沒有印象了。

This happened many years ago. I have no recollection of it anymore.

B | 分享 (to share joy, happiness, benefit, or something pleasant or positive)

The object of 分享 is usually an abstract noun. The verb often occurs in the pattern "跟 (or 和) (someone) 分享."

1 知道自己考上研究生院，他非常高兴，马上发微信告诉朋友们，跟他们分享自己的快乐。

知道自己考上研究生院，他非常高興，馬上發微信告訴朋友們，跟他們分享自己的快樂。

After learning that he had gotten into graduate school, he was very happy. He sent his friends a WeChat message right away to share his happiness with them.

2 我当然愿意跟家人分享自己的幸福。

我當然願意跟家人分享自己的幸福。

Of course I want to share my good fortune with my family.

3

他有什么好事都跟女朋友分享。

他有什麼好事都跟女朋友分享。

He shares every positive thing in his life with his girlfriend.

C 只好 (have no choice but)

1

我今天很想看篮球赛，可是晚上到球场的时候，
票卖完了，我只好以后再看了。

我今天很想看籃球賽，可是晚上到球場的時候，
票賣完了，我只好以後再看了。

I really wanted to watch a basketball game today, but when I got to the stadium
tonight, the tickets were all sold out. I'll just have to wait till another time.

2

小张的父母不给他零用钱了，他只好去打工。

小張的父母不給他零用錢了，他只好去打工。

Little Zhang's parents stopped giving him an allowance, so he has to
work part-time.

3

朋友请他晚上去听演唱会，可是明天有考试，
他只好在家复习。

朋友請他晚上去聽演唱會，可是明天有考試，
他只好在家復習。

A friend invited him to go to a concert tonight, but there's a test tomorrow,
so he has to stay home and review.

D 千万/千萬 (by all means, absolutely must)

千万/千萬 is used in imperative sentences to advise or to urge.

1

明天考期末考，你千万别迟到了。

明天考期末考，你千萬別遲到了。

Tomorrow is the final exam. Make sure you aren't late.

2   这件事你千万别告诉妈妈，要不然她会着急的。

這件事你千萬別告訴媽媽，要不然她會著急的。

You absolutely can't tell Mom about this. She'd be very worried.

3   下午会下大雨，出门前千万记得关窗户。

下午會下大雨，出門前千萬記得關窗戶。

It's going to pour this afternoon. Make sure you close all the windows before heading out.

E | ## 不过/不過 (however, no more than)

As you may recall, 不过/不過 can serve as a conjunction indicating a turn in thought:

1   南京夏天很热，不过房间里有空调，就不那么难受了。

南京夏天很熱，不過房間裡有空調，就不那麼難受了。

Nanjing's summers are very hot, but [if] there's air conditioning in the room, it's not so unbearable. *[conjunction]*

In this lesson, 不过/不過 is used as an adverb meaning "only" or "no more than," and it can be modified by 只.

2   这个古城不大，从东边走到西边不过一两个小时。

這個古城不大，從東邊走到西邊不過一兩個小時。

This ancient town is not big. It takes less than a couple of hours to go from the east to the west side. *[adverb]*

3   我不过是跟你开个玩笑，你怎么哭了？

我不過是跟你開個玩笑，你怎麼哭了？

I was only joking with you. Why are you crying? *[adverb]*

Language Practice

| | **Had no choice** | PRESENTATIONAL |

Describe what you had to do using 只好 based on the following prompts. Avoid repeating the personal pronoun when the subject of the sentence remains the same, e.g.:

硬卧票都卖完了（软卧票）　　→　　所以我只好买软卧票。

硬臥票都賣完了（軟臥票）　　→　　所以我只好買軟臥票。

1　我没有钱了（我哥哥有钱）

　　我沒有錢了（我哥哥有錢）

2　我参加了一个有购物的旅游团（导游进商店）

　　我參加了一個有購物的旅遊團（導遊進商店）

3　去年我没有时间去云南（今年）

　　去年我沒有時間去雲南（今年）

4　我的朋友不会说中文（我跟他说英文）

　　我的朋友不會說中文（我跟他說英文）

5　火车上的盒饭和方便面都卖完了（去餐车吃饭）

　　火車上的盒飯和方便麵都賣完了（去餐車吃飯）

Characterize it!

More characters

❶ 馆　❷ 饺

❸ 饿　❹ 饼

What do the characters mean?

What is the common radical?

What does the radical mean?

How does the radical relate to the overall meaning of the characters?

❶ 館　❷ 餃

❸ 餓　❹ 餅

| | **Under no circumstances** | PRESENTATIONAL |

Based on each of the scenarios below, advise your friend against doing something by using
千万别/千萬別, e.g.:

火车上的东西又贵又不新鲜，千万别在火车上买东西吃。
火車上的東西又貴又不新鮮，千萬別在火車上買東西吃。

1 那个家庭旅馆又不干净，又不能上网，……
那個家庭旅館又不乾淨，又不能上網，……

2 云南南部八月非常热，……
雲南南部八月非常熱，……

3 对面茶馆卖的茶贵极了，……
對面茶館賣的茶貴極了，……

4 河边的那个景点这几天人太多，挤死了，……
河邊的那個景點這幾天人太多，擠死了，……

5 那个旅行社的旅行团每个纪念品商店都进，……
那個旅行社的旅行團每個紀念品商店都進，……

A WAY WITH WORDS

分享

老王最近太忙了，老钱
想帮他分担一些工作。

下午三点有两个重要的
会，我都想参加，可是
没办法分身。

Using the word/phrase
in orange as a clue, try to
figure out the meaning
of the words/phrases in
blue; consult a dictionary
if necessary. Consider
how the literal and
extended senses are
related in each case.

分享

老王最近太忙了，老錢
想幫他分擔一些工作。

下午三點有兩個重要的
會，我都想參加，可是
沒辦法分身。

Thrifty traveler

Imagine that you are planning a trip on a modest budget. In pairs, discuss the things you are and are not willing to spend money on.

愿意/願意

1 _____

2 _____

3 _____

不愿意/不願意

1 _____

2 _____

3 _____

Consider the possibility of traveling on your own instead of joining a tour group. Talk about the pros and the cons of a 自助游/自助遊 with your partner. After looking at both sides, explain to your partner whether you would like to join a tour group or travel by yourself.

好处/好處

1 _____

2 _____

3 _____

4 _____

坏处/壞處

1 _____

2 _____

3 _____

4 _____

In pairs, discuss the train as an option for a long-distance trip in China. Would you opt for the train? How do you feel about the price, speed, comfort level, food, hard vs. soft sleeper, opportunities to communicate with other travelers, etc.?

List some pros and the cons of traveling by train.

好处/好處

1 省钱/省錢

2 _____

3 _____

4 _____

坏处/壞處

1 _____

2 _____

3 _____

4 _____

Then, based on your pros and cons, discuss with your partner how the train compares with other means of transportation by using 比 and 没有/沒有, e.g.:

坐火车旅行比坐飞机旅行省钱。

坐火車旅行比坐飛機旅行省錢。

or

坐飞机旅行没有坐火车旅行省钱。

坐飛機旅行沒有坐火車旅行省錢。

Finally, poll the class and see whether the majority of the class prefers the train to other means of transportation.

It's June 3. You and your friends will travel from Jiujiang to Shenzhen tomorrow, but cannot decide on which type of tickets to buy. Zero in on the first line under the date. What are the five categories of fares?

GET
Real
WITH CHINESE

Sharing is caring

In pairs, share your travel experiences based on the prompts. The first person to speak should start by saying:

> 我和你分享一下我在 (place X) 的旅游经验。
>
> 我和你分享一下我在 (place X) 的旅遊經驗。

The second person to speak should choose a different place, and should start by saying:

> 我也和你分享一下我在 (place Y) 的旅游经验。
>
> 我也和你分享一下我在 (place Y) 的旅遊經驗。

In your description, be sure to incorporate the following:

- ○ positive impressions

  - ○ 我对 (place X or place Y) 印象最好的是······
    我對 (place X or place Y) 印象最好的是······

  - ○ (place X or place Y) 给我留下印象最好的是······
    (place X or place Y) 給我留下印象最好的是······

- ○ negative impressions

  - ○ 我对 (place X or place Y) 印象最不好的是······
    我對 (place X or place Y) 印象最不好的是······

  - ○ (place X or place Y) 给我留下印象最不好的是······
    (place X or place Y) 給我留下印象最不好的是······

- ○ things to see

  - ○ 在 (place X or place Y) 你一定要看······

- ○ things to eat

  - ○ 在 (place X or place Y) 你一定要吃······

○ things to avoid

○ 在 (place X or place Y) 你千万别……

在 (place X or place Y) 你千万别……

Nature lover `INTERPERSONAL`

What would a nature lover say about some of the most beautiful features in the natural landscape?

1 First, list some adjectives to describe each of the following:

○ 山： _____

○ 河： _____

○ 树/樹： _____

○ 石头/石頭： _____

○ 风景/風景： _____

2 Then, in pairs, ask your partner about the nature reserves or national parks (国家公园/ 國家公園) that he/she has visited:

○ 你游览过哪些国家公园？
你遊覽過哪些國家公園？

○ 你对那儿的印象怎么样？
你對那兒的印象怎麼樣？

○ 那儿的山（或者河、树、石头、风景）怎么样？
那兒的山（或者河、樹、石頭、風景）怎麼樣？

It's on my list

1 Apart from appreciating natural and cultural attractions, what else do you like to do as a tourist? From the list, select activities that you think you would enjoy.

参加旅行团	參加旅行團
拍照（片）	拍照（片）
尝小吃	嚐小吃
买纪念品	買紀念品
上网写博客	上網寫博客
听导游讲故事	聽導遊講故事
想了解少数民族的	想了解少數民族的
生活习惯	生活習慣

2 Combine the activities you have selected above with 一定, 常常, 有时候/有時候, or 从来不/從來不 to give your partner a sense of the kind of tourist you are. You can start by saying:

我旅行的时候…/我旅行的時候…

G

Exploring Yunnan

Complete the descriptions and/or statements based on the prompts.

1 Stone Forest

石林有很多＿＿＿＿＿＿＿＿＿＿＿＿＿＿＿＿＿＿＿，

颜色/顏色＿＿＿＿＿＿＿＿＿＿＿＿＿＿＿＿＿＿＿，

样子/樣子＿＿＿＿＿＿＿＿＿＿＿＿＿＿＿＿＿＿＿。

2 Dali

大理最有名的建筑是/大理最有名的建築是＿＿＿＿＿＿＿，

建筑很/建築很＿＿＿＿＿＿＿＿＿＿＿＿＿＿＿＿＿＿。

3 Lijiang

丽江古城有一条/麗江古城有一條＿＿＿＿＿＿＿＿＿＿，

两边有很多/兩邊有很多＿＿＿＿＿＿＿＿＿＿＿＿＿＿。

4 Minority architecture, different ethnic groups, different foods

去云南可以看到/去雲南可以看到＿＿＿＿＿＿＿＿＿＿，

可以吃到＿＿＿＿＿＿＿＿＿＿＿＿＿＿＿＿＿＿＿。

A WAY WITH WORDS

交通

小周和小张虽然是同学，可是平时交流不多。

他们俩交往了半年就决定结婚了。

Using the word/phrase in orange as a clue, try to figure out the meaning of the words/phrases in blue; consult a dictionary if necessary. Consider how the literal and extended senses are related in each case.

交通

小周和小張雖然是同學，可是平時交流不多。

他們倆交往了半年就決定結婚了。

The Stone Forest

石林, the Stone Forest, lies about fifty-three miles south of Kunming, the capital of Yunnan Province. Part of the karst topography of southern China, the Stone Forest is a UNESCO World Heritage Site. It is one of the most photographed scenic sights in Yunnan, and covers an area of about one hundred and sixty square miles. The name 石林 derives from the forest-like rock formations in the geological park, which lie at the core of the scenic area. Because of their unusual forms, many of these rocks have become associated with popular legends and have been given fanciful names.

In the oral tradition of the Sani people, who have historically lived in the area of the Stone Forest, there is an epic poem about a beautiful girl named Ashima. Though she is in love with a shepherd, Ahei, she catches the eye of the son of an influential landowner, Azhi, who tries to force Ashima to marry him. Azhi kidnaps Ashima; Ahei then confronts Azhi at home. Ahei and Azhi engage in a three-day singing duel to decide who will triumph. Ahei wins and goes to take Ashima away, but Azhi releases the floodgates keeping back a reservoir as they turn away, and Ashima, overcome by water, metamorphoses into one of the stone figures in the forest.

The Three Pagodas of Dali

Dali is the capital of Dali Bai Autonomous Prefecture in central Yunnan. The local Bai people are one of the province's main ethnic groups. The Three Pagodas of Dali, 大理三塔/大理三塔, are the only remnants of an extensive ninth-century Esoteric Buddhist temple complex built by the royal family of the ancient Nanzhao Kingdom. The three pagodas form an equilateral triangle. Unlike most pagodas in the Chinese hinterland, the Three Pagodas of Dali have an even number of floors. The central and tallest pagoda, at about two hundred and seven feet, has sixteen stories and bears a close resemblance to the famous Small Goose Pagoda in Xi'an. The two ten-story pagodas are about one hundred and twenty-six feet tall. Fronting a beautiful blue lake, these whitewashed pagodas are one of Yunnan's most memorable sights.

COMPARE & CONTRAST

Yunnan is widely known for its ethnic, geographic, biological, and even climatic diversity. This has to do not only with its wild terrain, stretching across river valleys and mountains, but also with its location on the borders of Laos, Myanmar, and Vietnam. Many of Yunnan's minority groups, for instance, may also be found across Chinese borders in surrounding countries. Kunming, the capital of Yunnan, will be the terminus for new high-speed rail links to Southeast Asia now being promoted by the Chinese government. Consider a border area in your country. Is it viewed as a gateway to another country or region? Is it characterized by ethnic, geographic, or biological diversity? Are there unique opportunities and challenges presented by its location?

Tiled rooftops in Lijiang

Lahu women in traditional dress

The Old City of Lijiang

Surrounded by snow-capped mountains and dotted with pristine lakes, Lijiang, 丽江/麗江, is located in northwestern Yunnan. The ancient city of Lijiang, 丽江古城/麗江古城, is one of the best preserved in China. It survived a major earthquake in 1996 and has since become extremely popular among tourists. The streets are paved with blue-gray flagstones, and small streams and rivulets ripple through the city. Most of the low-lying houses in Lijiang feature tiled roofs and carved wooden windows.

Yunnan is home to twenty-five officially recognized minority nationalities, who make up about a third of the province's population. About fifteen nationalities, including the Bai, Hani, Yi, Naxi, and Dai, call Yunnan their ancestral homeland. Many of these minority nationalities have their own distinct languages, cultures, and religious traditions. The Dai, for instance, practice Theravada Buddhism and speak a language related to Lao and Thai. The Yao and Miao are famous for their embroidery and their elaborate silver headdresses and jewelry. The largest and most widely dispersed minority are the Yi, who practice an animist religion.

Lesson Wrap-Up

Project

You work part-time as a tour guide on a hop-on, hop-off bus in your home state/province. Choose a city, a park, or a combination of natural and cultural sights and design a rewarding itinerary. In your presentation, be sure to:

· include at least four stops and research them

· introduce yourself (and perhaps the driver) and welcome the tourists on your bus

· give a summary of the stops and explain how long the tour will last

· come up with some introductory statements as the bus approaches and arrives at each stop, e.g., 我们马上（还有五分钟）就要到⋯⋯了/我們馬上（還有五分鐘）就要到⋯⋯了

· introduce each sight pointing out the most interesting features making sure to incorporate useful words and phrases from the Lesson Text

· invite the tourists to ask you questions

· think how you want to end the tour, e.g. bidding the tourists good-bye, asking them if they had a good time, inviting them to come visit again

Keep It Flowing

Study the following example; pay particular attention to how the highlighted parts help the sentences flow smoothly from one to the next. Notice how:

· time phrases (在中国的新学期开始前/在中國的新學期開始前) connect sentences

· following a timeline (第一天⋯, 第二天⋯, 第三天⋯, 过几天/過幾天⋯) organizes a narrative

· place words (那里/那裡) help bring cohesion to a narrative

· certain conjunctions (而且) introduce additional information

· certain expressions (特别是/特別是) single out examples

云南旅游

在中国的新学期开始前我跟丽莎、林雪梅还有柯林一起去云南旅游。

第一天我们游览了石林，那里石头的样子千奇百怪，而且很多石头还有故事。石林给我留下了很深的印象。

第二天我们去大理，那里有大理三塔，建筑很古老，很有名。

第三天我们到了有名的丽江古城，我们非常喜欢那里，特别是那条从城中间穿过的小河。我们在小河边上的茶馆坐着，都不想回去睡觉了。

云南各个地方的风景都不太一样，有很多好玩的地方。我拍了很多照片，过几天会把它们放在博客上。

雲南旅遊

在中國的新學期開始前我跟麗莎、林雪梅還有柯林一起去雲南旅遊。

第一天我們遊覽了石林，那裡石頭的樣子千奇百怪，而且很多石頭還有故事。石林給我留下了很深的印象。

第二天我們去大理，那裡有大理三塔，建築很古老，很有名。

第三天我們到了有名的麗江古城，我們非常喜歡那裡，特別是那條從城中間穿過的小河。我們在小河邊上的茶館坐著，都不想回去睡覺了。

雲南各個地方的風景都不太一樣，有很多好玩的地方。我拍了很多照片，過幾天會把它們放在博客上。

Have you gone on a trip recently? Use as many of the cohesive devices highlighted in the example on the previous page as possible to string together a response, based on the prompts:

◦ 先写时间。
　先寫時間。

◦ 去什么地方旅游?
　去什麼地方旅遊?

◦ 跟谁一起去的?
　跟誰一起去的?

◦ 简单写一下去的景点。
　簡單寫一下去的景點。

◦ 什么给你留下了很深的印象?
　什麼給你留下了很深的印象?

◦ 你在旅游休息的时候写博客或给朋友发微信了吗?
　你在旅遊休息的時候寫博客或給朋友發微信了嗎?

Can-Do Check List **I can**

Before proceeding to Lesson 14, make sure you can complete the following tasks in Chinese:

☐ Describe what costs a package tour may cover
☐ Explain the differences between "hard" and "soft" sleeper cars
☐ Describe Yunnan's natural and cultural attractions
☐ Discuss high and low points of a trip

Xīn xuéqī kāishǐ qián, Zhāng Tiānmíng, Lìshā hé Kē Lín, Xuěméi yìqǐ qù Yúnnán lǚyóu. Tāmen yuē hǎo xīngqītiān zài Kūnmíng jiàn miàn, ránhòu zài Yúnnán lǚyóu yí ge xīngqī. Zhè cì lǚyóu, Zhōngguó de huǒchē, dǎoyóu hé Yúnnán měilì de fēngjǐng, dōu gěi Tiānmíng liú xia hěn shēn de yìnxiàng. Zhāng Tiānmíng měitiān fā Wēixìn, gēn péngyou men fēnxiǎng zìjǐ de kuàilè.

Qù Yúnnán qián, wǒmen zài wǎng shang bàomíng cānjiā le yí ge lǚxíngtuán. Tuán fèi bāokuò[a] jiāotōng, lǚguǎn, sān cān hé jǐngdiǎn ménpiào.

Wǒmen shì zuò huǒchē qù de Yúnnán. Wèile néng gēn bié de lǚkè liànxí shuō Zhōngwén, wǒmen mǎi le yìngwò[b] piào, yīnwèi yìngwò chēxiāng měi ge "fángjiān" dōu méiyǒu mén, róngyì zhǎo rén liáo tiānr. Wǒ zài shàng pù, shàng pù bǐ xià pù hé zhōng pù ānjìng yì diǎn, wǎnshang kěyǐ shuì ge hǎo jiào.

Wǒ yě qù ruǎnwò chēxiāng kàn le kan. Nàli měi ge xiǎo fángjiān li yǒu liǎng ge shàng pù, liǎng ge xià pù, chuáng bǐjiào ruǎn yě bǐjiào dà, fángjiān de mén kěyǐ guān shang.

Wǎnshang, wǒmen zài cānchē shang chī le yí dùn fàn. Nàli de fàn, wǒ juéde hěn guì, yě bú tài hǎochī, háishi mǎi héfàn[c] huòzhě fāngbiàn miàn[d] hǎo.

Wǒ hé Lìshā zài Kūnmíng xià chē hòu, děng le liǎng ge duō xiǎoshí, Xuěméi hé Kē Lín tāmen de huǒchē cái dào. Wǒmen yìqǐ zǒu chu huǒchē zhàn, kàn dào dǎoyóu zhèng jǔ zhe páizi zhǎo wǒmen, páizi shang xiě de shì wǒmen sì ge rén de míngzi. Wǒmen de dǎoyóu shuō huà hěn yōumò, búguò yǒushí[e] tā shuō de huà wǒmen sān ge rén dōu tīng bu dǒng, Xuěméi zhǐhǎo gěi wǒmen dāng fānyì.

Dǎoyóu jièshào shuō Yúnnán shì yí ge shěng, zài Zhōngguó de xīnán bù, shěnghuì shì Kūnmíng. Yúnnán zìrán fēngjǐng hěn měi[f], yǒu shān yǒu shuǐ, zhèli zhù zhe hěn duō shǎoshù mínzú. Lái Yúnnán lǚyóu, kěyǐ kàn kan bù tóng mínzú de jiànzhù, fúzhuāng, yǐnshí, liǎojiě gè ge mínzú de fēngsú xíguàn.

Dì yī tiān wǒmen yóulǎn le Shílín. Zhè shì yì zhāng Shílín de zhàopiàn. Shílín yǒu hěn duō yánsè hěn shēn de shítou, yuǎn kàn jiù xiàng shùlín yíyàng. Shítou de yàngzi qiān qí bǎi guài[1]. Wǒmen zài Shílín li yìbiān zǒu, yìbiān tīng dǎoyóu jiǎng nà xiē shítou de gùshi, fēicháng yǒu yìsi.

Zhè shì Dàlǐ sān tǎ, jiànzhù hěn gǔlǎo, hěn yǒumíng. Dàlǐ chéng li yǒu hěn duō mài jìniànpǐn de shāngdiàn, dǎoyóu bǎ wǒmen dài dào nàr, xīwàng dàjiā duō mǎi dōngxi. Xuěméi hé Lìshā hěn gāoxìng, mǎi le bù shǎo jìniànpǐn, ér wǒ gēn Kē Lín shòu bu liǎo, jiù bàoyuàn shuō tài làngfèi shíjiān le. Xià cì nǐmen dào Zhōngguó lǚyóu zhǎo lǚxíngtuán, qiānwàn bié zhǎo yǒu "gòuwù" de tuán. Nǐmen kěyǐ zìzhùyóu[g], nàyàng jiù zìyóu duō le.

Dì sān tiān, dào le yǒumíng de Lìjiāng gǔchéng[h], wǒmen fēicháng xǐhuan zhèli. Zhè ge gǔchéng bú dà, cóng dōngbian zǒu dào xībian búguò yì liǎng ge xiǎoshí. Zuì tèbié de shì yǒu yì tiáo fēicháng gānjìng de xiǎo hé[2] cóng chéng zhōngjiān chuān[1] guo. Xiǎo hé liǎng biān yǒu hěn duō shāngdiàn, cháguǎn, xiǎo fànguǎn. Nà tiān wǎnshang, wǒmen zài yí ge hěn yǒu Yúnnán tèsè de cháguǎn li hē chá, kàn zhe wài bian de xiǎo hé, mén páng de hóng dēnglong, hái yǒu shìjiè gè guó de yóukè, dōu bù xiǎng huí lǚguǎn qù shuì jiào le.

Zài Lìjiāng, wǒmen zhù le liǎng tiān jiātíng lǚguǎn. Fángjiān suīrán hěn xiǎo, dànshì hěn gānjìng, yě néng shàng wǎng. Fángdōng hái gěi wǒmen zuò le xiē jiācháng cài, là là de, wèidao hěn búcuò.

Yúnnán gè ge dìfang de fēngjǐng bù yíyàng, hái yǒu hěn duō hǎowán de dìfang. Wǒmen míng tiān yào qù yóulǎn Dàxuě shān. Wǒ guò jǐ tiān huì bǎ zài nàr pāi de zhàopiàn fàng zài bókè shang.

生活与健康

生活與健康

LIFESTYLE AND HEALTH

Learning Objectives

In this lesson, you will learn to:

- Talk about various types of exercises
- Outline some healthy eating habits
- Compare exercise habits in China and the U.S.
- Point out the importance of a balanced diet
- Describe habits that could age people prematurely or harm their health

Relate and Get Ready

In your own culture/community:

- Do many people exercise in the morning?
- Do people tend to exercise at the gym or in parks?
- Are people conscientious about health and fitness?
- Are many people concerned about their weight?

课文

Text

Audio

Before You Study

Answer the following questions in Chinese to prepare for the reading.

1 你平常运动吗？打球、跑步还是游泳？

2 你一个星期运动几次？每次运动多长时间？

When You Study

Listen to the audio recording and skim the text; then answer the following questions in Chinese.

1 丽莎看到中国老人怎么锻炼身体？

2 丽莎为什么喜欢做瑜伽？

3 李文为什么非熬夜不可？

丽莎到北京后没有住留学生公寓，为了更多地了解中国人的生活，她住进了一个中国家庭。房东夫妻二人已¹退休，女儿李文在博物馆工作，与²父母住在一起。李文很想去美国留学，所以请丽莎做她的英文家教，这样丽莎就不必付房租了。因为丽莎每天都跟李文的父母说中文，所以她的中文进步得很快。

丽莎每天早上都出去散步，在她住的这个小区，在街边，在公园，都能看见很多人，特别是老人，在锻炼身体。他们有的跳广场舞，有的打太极拳。这些早晨锻炼ª的人们，成为北京特别的"风景"。

这一天早上丽莎正要出门，李文从房间走出来。

丽莎，今天是星期六，怎么这么早就起床了？

我本来想跟叔叔、阿姨去学太极拳，没想到他们那么早就出去了。

我以为你只喜欢做瑜伽ᵇ，怎么对太极拳也有兴趣？

太极拳和瑜伽一样，不但对身体有好处，而且动作很美。

課文

麗莎到北京後沒有住留學生公寓，為了更多地了解中國人的生活，她住進了一個中國家庭。房東夫妻二人已¹退休，女兒李文在博物館工作，與²父母住在一起。李文很想去美國留學，所以請麗莎做她的英文家教，這樣麗莎就不必付房租了。因為麗莎每天都跟李文的父母說中文，所以她的中文進步得很快。

麗莎每天早上都出去散步，在她住的這個小區，在街邊，在公園，都能看見很多人，特別是老人，在鍛煉身體。他們有的跳廣場舞，有的打太極拳。這些早晨鍛煉ᵃ的人們，成為北京特別的"風景"。

這一天早上麗莎正要出門，李文從房間走出來。

麗莎，今天是星期六，怎麼這麼早就起床了？

我本來想跟叔叔、阿姨去學太極拳，沒想到他們那麼早就出去了。

我以為你只喜歡做瑜伽ᵇ，怎麼對太極拳也有興趣？

太極拳和瑜伽一樣，不但對身體有好處，而且動作很美。

Before You Study

Answer the following questions in Chinese to prepare for the reading.

1 你平常運動嗎？打球、跑步還是游泳？

2 你一個星期運動幾次？每次運動多長時間？

When You Study

Listen to the audio recording and skim the text; then answer the following questions in Chinese.

1 麗莎看到中國老人怎麼鍛煉身體？

2 麗莎為什麼喜歡做瑜伽？

3 李文為什麼非熬夜不可？

丽莎，你看大树下边，我爸、我妈正在跟那些退休老人打太极拳呢！你去找他们吧。

好，一会儿就去。他们打得真棒。我每天早晨出去散步，看见到处都是运动的人。中国人真重视锻炼身体啊！

对，现在大家都越来越注意身体健康了。哎，丽莎，美国人一般怎么锻炼身体？

一般是跑步、游泳、打球等等，有些人也去健身房。我平常做瑜伽，有的时候也跑步。

难怪你的身体这么健康。

我觉得如果希望身体健康，除了多运动以外，还应该注意饮食。

你一点儿都不胖，还需要注意饮食吗？

注意饮食不等于减肥。我认为只要身体健康就³好，胖瘦不重要。

我工作忙，没时间好好儿吃饭，常常随便乱吃。你是怎么注意饮食的呢？

多喝水，多吃青菜、水果。另外，即使非常忙，也⁴一定要吃早饭，而且早饭要有营养；午饭要吃饱，因为下午还要学习和工作；晚饭就要少吃一点，不然会越来越胖，因为离上床睡觉的时间太近了。

我们中国人有一句话：早餐要吃好，午餐要吃饱，晚餐^c要吃少，跟你说的差不多一样。

麗莎，你看大樹下邊，我爸、我媽正在跟那些退休老人打太極拳呢！你去找他們吧。

好，一會兒就去。他們打得真棒。我每天早晨出去散步，看見到處都是運動的人。中國人真重視鍛煉身體啊！

對，現在大家都越來越注意身體健康了。哎，麗莎，美國人一般怎麼鍛煉身體？

一般是跑步、游泳、打球等等，有些人也去健身房。我平常做瑜伽，有的時候也跑步。

難怪你的身體這麼健康。

我覺得如果希望身體健康，除了多運動以外，還應該注意飲食。

你一點兒都不胖，還需要注意飲食嗎？

注意飲食不等於減肥。我認為只要身體健康就[3]好，胖瘦不重要。

我工作忙，沒時間好好兒吃飯，常常隨便亂吃。你是怎麼注意飲食的呢？

多喝水，多吃青菜、水果。另外，即使非常忙，也[4]一定要吃早飯，而且早飯要有營養；午飯要吃飽，因為下午還要學習和工作；晚飯就要少吃一點，不然會越來越胖，因為離上床睡覺的時間太近了。

我們中國人有一句話：早餐要吃好，午餐要吃飽，晚餐[c]要吃少，跟你說的差不多一樣。

真的？ 大家都这么说，可能是有科学道理的。

我觉得想要身体好，在其他方面也必须[d]注意。

你的意思是要有良好的生活习惯，对不对？

对。不吸烟[e]，不喝酒，早睡早起，最好不要熬夜。别的都没问题，就是不熬夜我做不到。我晚上常常得开夜车[f]准备考研究生。

那你必须尽可能找时间补充睡眠。

你说得对，我是得注意了，要不然我的两只眼睛都快变成熊猫[g]眼了。

Language Notes

a 晨练/晨練

在早晨进行练习或锻炼/在早晨進行練習或鍛煉 can be shortened to 晨练/晨練.

b 瑜伽

瑜伽 can also be written as 瑜珈. The pronunciation is the same.

c 早餐，午餐，晚餐

早餐, 午餐, and 晚餐 are interchangeable with 早饭/早飯, 午饭/午飯, and 晚饭/晚飯, respectively. 餐 sounds more formal than 饭/飯.

d 必须/必須

The negative form of 必须/必須 is 不必 or 不用.

e 煙 vs. 菸

The simplified character 烟 corresponds to two traditional variants, 煙 and 菸. Although 煙 and 菸 are sometimes used interchangeably, 菸 is recommended when referring to the tobacco plant and tobacco-related products and activities, as in 菸草 (yāncǎo) (tobacco), 香菸 (xiāngyān) (cigarette), 吸菸 (to smoke), and 禁菸 (jìn yān) (to ban smoking). By contrast, 煙 is associated primarily with smoke and smoke-like vapor or mist, as in 炊煙 (chuīyān) (cooking smoke) and 煙霧 (yānwù) (clouds and mist). Note that 煙 and 菸 have different radicals: 火 (huǒ) (fire) and 艹 (cǎo) (grass), respectively. 煙草, 香煙, 吸煙, and 禁煙 are acceptable; ✖ 炊菸 and ✖ 菸霧 are not.

f 开夜车/開夜車

开夜车/開夜車 (lit. to drive the night car) means "to stay up late (to work or study)."

g 熊猫/熊貓

The term 熊猫/熊貓 (lit. bear cat) is used in Mainland China. However, in Taiwan, the term 猫熊/貓熊 (lit. cat bear) is preferred.

真的？大家都這麼說，可能是有科學道理的。

我覺得想要身體好，在其他方面也必須^d注意。

你的意思是要有良好的生活習慣，對不對？

對。不吸菸^e，不喝酒，早睡早起，最好不要熬夜。別的都沒問題，就是不熬夜我做不到。我晚上常常得開夜車^f準備考研究生。

那你必須儘可能找時間補充睡眠。

你說得對，我是得注意了，要不然我的兩隻眼睛都快變成熊貓^g眼了。

After You Study

Answer the following questions in Chinese.

1 在北京，如果早上到公園走走，會看到什麼？

2 良好的生活習慣包括哪些？

3 怎麼樣才能身體健康？

View & Explore

For deeper language immersion and more cultural information, watch "Wellness," a short, supplemental video clip by Cheng & Tsui on this lesson's theme.

Video

Vocabulary

No.	Simplified	Traditional	Pinyin	Part of Speech	Definition
1	与	與	yǔ	conj/prep	and; with [See Grammar 2.]
2	夫妻	夫妻	fūqī	n	husband and wife, couple
3	退休	退休	tuìxiū	v	to retire
4	博物馆	博物館	bówùguǎn	n	museum
5	不必	不必	búbì	adv	need not, do not need to
6	散步	散步	sàn bù	vo	to take a walk, to go for a walk
7	锻炼	鍛煉	duànliàn	v	to exercise, to work out, to undergo physical training
8	广场	廣場	guǎngchǎng	n	public square
9	太极拳	太極拳	tàijíquán	n	tai chi (a form of traditional Chinese shadowboxing)
10	早晨	早晨	zǎochen	n	morning, early morning
11	成为	成為	chéngwéi	v	to become, to turn into
12	出门	出門	chū mén	vo	to go out, to leave home
13	瑜伽	瑜伽	yújiā	n	yoga
14	动作	動作	dòngzuò	n	movement, action
15	树	樹	shù	n	tree
16	重视	重視	zhòngshì	v	to attach importance to
17	注意	注意	zhùyì	v/n	to pay attention to; attention
18	等	等	děng	p	and so forth, etc.
19	健身房	健身房	jiànshēnfáng	n	fitness center, gym
20	等于	等於	děngyú	v	to equal, to be equivalent to, to amount to
21	减肥	減肥	jiǎn féi	vo	to lose weight (lit. to reduce fat)
22	只要	只要	zhǐyào	conj	as long as, provided

No.	Simplified	Traditional	Pinyin	Part of Speech	Definition
23	随便	隨便	*suíbiàn*	adj/vo	casual, careless; to do as one pleases
24	即使	即使	*jíshǐ*	conj	even if
25	营养	營養	*yíngyǎng*	n	nutrition, nourishment
26	饱	飽	*bǎo*	adj	full, satiated (after a meal)
27	科学	科學	*kēxué*	n/adj	science; scientific
28	方面	方面	*fāngmiàn*	n	aspect, respect
29	必须	必須	*bìxū*	adv	must, have to, be obliged to
30	吸烟	吸菸	*xī yān*	vo	to smoke a cigarette
31	熬夜	熬夜	*áo yè*	vo	to stay up late or all night
32	补充	補充	*bǔchōng*	v	to supplement, to replenish
33	睡眠	睡眠	*shuìmián*	n	sleep
34	只	隻	*zhī*	m	(measure word for one of certain paired things and some animals)
35	熊猫	熊貓	*xióngmāo*	n	panda
36	李文	李文	*Lǐ Wén*	pn	(a personal name)

丽莎平常做瑜伽、跑步来锻炼身体。你平常怎么锻炼身体？

麗莎平常做瑜伽、跑步來鍛鍊身體。你平常怎麼鍛鍊身體？

How About You?

Grammar

1 Monosyllabic forms of disyllabic words

Two-syllable modal verbs, adverbs, conjunctions, and so on often appear in monosyllabic form in formal Chinese. Some examples are:

已经/已經   →   已 (already)   比较/比較 → 较/較 (relatively, rather)

应该/應該   →   应/應 (should)   多半   → 多 (most, mostly)

可以   →   可 (can, may)   虽然/雖然 → 虽/雖 (although)

因为/因為   →   因 (because)   但是   → 但 (but, however)

2 The conjunction and preposition 与/與

与/與 is a conjunction as well as a preposition. It appears in formal Chinese. 与/與 is a conjunction in 生活与健康/生活與健康 and is synonymous with 和 and 跟, e.g.:

A   教师与学生 / 教師與學生
teachers and students

B   沙漠与河流 / 沙漠與河流
deserts and rivers

Like 和 and 跟, 与/與 can serve as a preposition, e.g.:

C   李文与父母住在一起。
李文與父母住在一起。
Li Wen lives with her parents.

D   丽莎与天明一起去云南旅行。
麗莎與天明一起去雲南旅行。
Lisha travels to Yunnan with Tianming.

E　我购物的标准与你们不同。

我購物的標準與你們不同。

My shopping criteria are different from yours.

---

3 ┌──┐
　 │　　　　　　　　只要…就…　　　　　　　　│
　 └──┘

In the construction "只要…就…," 只要 introduces a necessary condition for the result expressed by the word or phrase following 就.

A　小林租房子，只要环境好就行，其他的他都不在乎。

小林租房子，只要環境好就行，其他的他都不在乎。

In looking for an apartment, Little Lin is okay with renting anything as long as the environment is good. He doesn't care about anything else.

B　只要你好好儿用功学习，你的中文就一定会进步。

只要你好好兒用功學習，你的中文就一定會進步。

As long as you study diligently, your Chinese will definitely improve.

C　很多父母认为，只要孩子平安、健康，就是自己最大的幸福。

很多父母認為，只要孩子平安、健康，就是自己最大的幸福。

Many parents consider their greatest happiness to be the safety and health of their children.

Characterize it!

What do the characters mean?

What is the common radical?

What does the radical mean?

How does the radical relate to the overall meaning of the characters?

More characters

即使…也…

In the structure "即使…也…," 即使… usually presents an extreme scenario, and 也… indicates the result or conclusion that will be reached even if the previously mentioned hypothetical occurs.

A
即使熬夜不睡觉，我也要把这篇文章写完。

即使熬夜不睡覺，我也要把這篇文章寫完。

Even if I [have to] stay up all night, I will finish writing this article.

B
我啊，即使不吃东西只喝水，也会胖。

我啊，即使不吃東西只喝水，也會胖。

For me, even if I didn't eat anything and just drank water, I'd still put on weight.

C
他的事业非常成功，但是太忙。即使是感恩节，也在办公室工作。

他的事業非常成功，但是太忙。即使是感恩節，也在辦公室工作。

He's been very successful in his career, but he is too busy. He has to work in the office even on Thanksgiving.

A WAY WITH WORDS

退休

我两个星期没有练习说中文了，老师说我的中文退步了。

小李家只有她和爸爸两个人。最近她爸爸病得很厉害，她想退学回家去照顾爸爸。

Using the word/phrase in orange as a clue, try to figure out the meaning of the words/phrases in blue; consult a dictionary if necessary. Consider how the literal and extended senses are related in each case.

退休

我兩個星期沒有練習說中文了，老師說我的中文退步了。

小李家只有她和爸爸兩個人。最近她爸爸病得很厲害，她想退學回家去照顧爸爸。

Words & Phrases

A 有的…，有的…

1 中午，旅行团的人都累了，他们有的躺在椅子上睡觉，有的靠在椅子上休息，都不说话了。

中午，旅行團的人都累了，他們有的躺在椅子上睡覺，有的靠在椅子上休息，都不說話了。

At midday, everyone in the tour group was tired. Some lay down on the chairs to nap, and some leaned back against the chairs to take a rest. Everybody stopped talking.

2 我到公园的时候，看见有的人在散步，有的人打太极拳，有的人跳广场舞。

我到公園的時候，看見有的人在散步，有的人打太極拳，有的人跳廣場舞。

When I got to the park, I saw some people taking walks, some practicing tai chi, and others dancing in open spaces.

3 我进学校的时候，看见孩子们有的在打球，有的在玩游戏，有的坐在地上休息。

我進學校的時候，看見孩子們有的在打球，有的在玩游戲，有的坐在地上休息。

When I arrived at the school, I saw that some children were playing ball, some were playing games, and some were sitting on the ground taking a break.

105

B 重视/重視 (to attach importance to, to think highly of)

重视/重視 is generally followed by an object, as in (1) and (2).

1 公司很重视我舅舅，又给他加工资了。

公司很重視我舅舅，又給他加工資了。

The company thinks very highly of my uncle and gave him another raise. *[predicate]*

2 我们大学很重视科学研究，我们的教授在研究方面都很有名。

我們大學很重視科學研究，我們的教授在研究方面都很有名。

Our university places a great deal of importance on scientific research. Our professors are all very famous for their research. *[predicate]*

重视/重視 is also sometimes used as an attributive, as in (3).

3 我爸爸现在最重视的是我的学习。

我爸爸現在最重視的是我的學習。

What my dad cares the most about now is my studies. *[attributive]*

C 等于/等於 (to equal, to be equivalent to, to amount to)

等于/等於 can mean that two numbers or two things are equal to each other.

1 已经一个星期了，你男朋友打电话你一直不接，不等于告诉他你要跟他分手吗？

已經一個星期了，你男朋友打電話你一直不接，不等於告訴他你要跟他分手嗎？

You haven't taken your boyfriend's phone calls for a week now. Doesn't that amount to you telling him you want to break up with him?

2　孩子要什么就给什么不<u>等于</u>爱孩子，可能会让孩子变坏。

孩子要什麼就給什麼不<u>等於</u>愛孩子，可能會讓孩子變壞。

Giving a child whatever he/she wants isn't the same as loving the child. You might spoil the child instead.

3　二加二<u>等于</u>四。

二加二<u>等於</u>四。

Two plus two equals four.

4　十五减九<u>等于</u>六。

十五減九<u>等於</u>六。

Fifteen minus nine equals six.

Chinese Chat

A friend is chatting with you on Google Hangouts. What advice would you give on how to maintain a healthy lifestyle?

Alex:
我昨天开夜车，夜里三点才睡觉，两只眼睛都快变成熊猫眼了。🐼

You:
…

Alex:
好，我以后不熬夜了！我还没吃早饭呢，陪我去补充点营养吧！

You:
…

我昨天開夜車，夜裡三點才睡覺，兩隻眼睛都快變成熊貓眼了。🐼

Alex · Mon, 11:45 PM

…

好，我以後不熬夜了！我還沒吃早飯呢，陪我去補充點營養吧！

Alex · Mon, 11:50 PM

…

Send a message

随便/隨便 (casual, careless, as one pleases)

随便/隨便 literally means "to follow one's convenience." In this lesson, 随便/隨便 connotes "to do whatever one wants," regardless of whether the action or behavior is appropriate. It can be a predicate, as in (1) and (2).

1 Q: 明天的欢迎晚会我穿什么衣服好？

　　　明天的歡迎晚會我穿什麼衣服好？

　　　What should I wear to tomorrow's welcome party?

　　A: 随便。你想穿什么就穿什么。

　　　隨便。你想穿什麼就穿什麼。

　　　Wear whatever. Wear what you want to. *[predicate]*

2 现在是上课时间，你一会儿出去，一会儿进来，
太随便了。

现在是上課時間，你一會兒出去，一會兒進來，
太隨便了。

It's class time now. You're going in and out of the classroom, and you're doing whatever you want. *[predicate]*

It can also be an adverbial, as in (3) and (4).

3 上课不能随便说话，有问题要举手。

上課不能隨便說話，有問題要舉手。

You can't speak whenever you feel like it. If you have a question, raise your hand.
[adverbial]

4 Q: 你为什么问他交没交女朋友？

　　　你為什麼問他交沒交女朋友？

　　　Why did you ask if he had a girlfriend?

　　A: 没什么，只是随便问问。

　　　沒什麼，只是隨便問問。

　　　No reason. I was just asking. *[adverbial]*

Language Practice

A | **Number cruncher** | INTERPERSONAL

In pairs, complete these math problems in Chinese, e.g.:

135 + 40 = ?

Q: 一百三十五加四十等于多少？

一百三十五加四十等於多少？

A: 一百三十五加四十等于一百七十五。

一百三十五加四十等於一百七十五。

1 76 + 36 = ?

2 308 + 699 = ?

3 1122 − 34 = ?

4 253 − 148 = ?

B | **As you wish** | INTERPERSONAL

You are known for your easygoing, agreeable nature. Respond to the queries accordingly using 随便/隨便, e.g.:

Q: 你叫我给你写几个汉字？写什么好？

你叫我給你寫幾個漢字？寫什麼好？

A: 随便写。/ 隨便寫。

1 Q: 我把地图还给你。放哪儿？

我把地圖還給你。放哪兒？

A: _____

2 Q: 你这儿这么多杂志，我能不能拿一本？

你這兒這麼多雜誌，我能不能拿一本？

A: _____

3 Q: 我忘了带手机，能用一下你的手机吗？

我忘了帶手機，能用一下你的手機嗎？

A: _____

Take turns to form questions and answers with 随便/隨便, e.g.:

What would you like for dinner?

Q: 今天晚餐想吃点儿什么？

今天晚餐想吃點兒什麼？

A: 随便，你做什么就吃什么。

隨便，你做什麼就吃什麼。

1 Which outfit should I wear for tonight's party?

2 Which color should we choose for the walls in the living room?

3 Where should we go for spring break?

4 Which tour group should we sign up for?

A WAY WITH WORDS

减肥

你车开得太快了，太危险，赶快减速！

这些孩子每天都要学这学那，太累了，父母应该给孩子减压了。

Using the word/phrase in orange as a clue, try to figure out the meaning of the words/phrases in blue; consult a dictionary if necessary. Consider how the literal and extended senses are related in each case.

減肥

你車開得太快了，太危險，趕快減速！

這些孩子每天都要學這學那，太累了，父母應該給孩子減壓了。

You've been warned

Warn a friend of the likely negative consequence if he/she fails to do something, e.g.:

复习/復習

你得复习，要不然考试会考得不好。

你得復習，要不然考試會考得不好。

1　锻炼/鍛煉

2　注意饮食/注意飲食

3　早睡早起/早睡早起

Chinese and American workout routines

Answer the question based on the prompts.

中国人和美国人常常怎么锻炼身体？

中國人和美國人常常怎麼鍛煉身體？

中国人/中國人

 1　 2　

美国人/美國人

 1　　2　

In pairs, have a conversation about how you try to keep in shape. If you don't work out at all, explain why. Ask and answer these questions.

○ 你平常锻炼身体吗？／你平常鍛煉身體嗎？

○ 你平常怎么锻炼身体？／你平常怎麼鍛煉身體？

○ 你多长时间锻炼一次？／你多長時間鍛煉一次？

○ 你每次锻炼多长时间？／你每次鍛煉多長時間？

○ 你觉得锻炼身体有什么好处？／你覺得鍛煉身體有什麼好處？

Connect your answers to form a coherent paragraph and tell your class about your exercise routine.

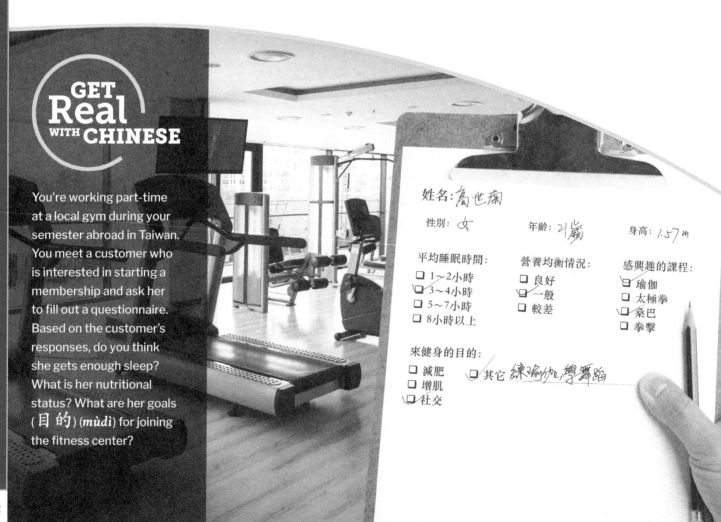

GET Real WITH CHINESE

You're working part-time at a local gym during your semester abroad in Taiwan. You meet a customer who is interested in starting a membership and ask her to fill out a questionnaire. Based on the customer's responses, do you think she gets enough sleep? What is her nutritional status? What are her goals (目的) (mùdì) for joining the fitness center?

姓名：高世菊

性別：女　　　　年齡：21歲　　　　身高：1.57 m

平均睡眠時間：　　　營養均衡情況：　　　感興趣的課程：
☐ 1～2小時　　　☐ 良好　　　　　☑ 瑜伽
☑ 3～4小時　　　☑ 一般　　　　　☐ 太極拳
☐ 5～7小時　　　☐ 較差　　　　　☑ 桑巴
☐ 8小時以上　　　　　　　　　　　☐ 拳擊

來健身的目的：
☐ 減肥　　　☑ 其它　練瑜伽，學舞蹈
☐ 增肌
☑ 社交

F Health nut

PRESENTATIONAL

What would a doctor, dietitian, or personal trainer advise you to do to stay healthy and fit? Write their advice on the following chart.

多	少	别/別
____________	____________	____________
____________	____________	____________
____________	____________	____________
____________	____________	____________
____________	____________	____________
____________	____________	____________

In addition to the above, what other advice can you think of?

G Eat right, from morning to night

PRESENTATIONAL

What do Chinese people say about the proper portions for the three meals of the day?

早饭要/早飯要 ____________________。

午饭要/午飯要 ____________________。

晚饭要/晚飯要 ____________________。

Cultivating Vitality

"Cultivating vitality" (养生/養生) (yǎng shēng) is an influential concept with an ancient philosophical lineage. It is a holistic view of health and longevity emphasizing the connection between mind and body. 养/養 means nurturing, preserving, and supplementing one's life force, while 生 is associated with life, existence, and growth. 养生/養生 blends traditional Chinese medicine, nutrition, qigong, and the teachings of Daoism, Buddhism, and Confucianism. A diet that balances yin and yang, regular breathing exercises and massaging of acupuncture points, meditation, tonics, and so on, are all deemed essential to living a long and healthy life. In many Chinese cities, there are establishments called "vitality clubhouses" (养生馆/養生館, 养生会馆/養生會館, or 养生会所/養生會所) that provide acupuncture, massage, cupping, aromatherapy, and an assortment of other services to enhance or restore one's vitality.

Within the system of Chinese medicine, it is believed that most health problems can be cured or prevented through dietary adjustments. Certain foods such as watercress and mung beans are thought to have a yin (阴/陰), or cooling effect, while others such as onions and certain meats have a yang (阳/陽), or a heating effect. The overconsumption of spicy, oily, or other "hot" foods is thought to cause an excessive accumulation of heat within the body, a condition termed 上火. This can manifest as feverishness, irritated skin, or just general discomfort. Illnesses caused by "hot" foods can be treated with "cold" foods, and vice versa.

Therapeutic Practices

A foot - bath powder containing ginger and seaweed

In China, aside from diet and exercise, massage is popular for maintaining good health. Traditional massage techniques come in many forms, and are believed to promote circulation throughout the body. Establishments offering 足浴 (zúyù) (foot massage, lit. "foot bath") services abound. Each session lasts about an hour and involves soaking the feet in a hot bath of medicinal herbs and vigorous pinching of various pressure points of the feet and calves. Therapeutic body massage based on the traditional theory of acupuncture points called 推拿 (tuīná) is a part of Chinese medicine. Its name comes from the two major actions of the system, pushing and grasping.

Smoking

China is the world's largest tobacco producer and consumer. Forty-four percent of the world's tobacco is sold in China, where smokers, mostly men, exceed three hundred million. According to the World Health Organization (WHO), tobacco use causes approximately one million deaths in China each year. Health experts and the WHO have urged the Chinese government for years to discourage smoking. Beijing, Shenzhen, and Shanghai became the first three major Chinese cities to outlaw smoking in all enclosed public spaces such as restaurants, airports, and train stations. Other cities have also passed legislation to ban public smoking.

COMPARE & CONTRAST

1 Are there similarities between the 养生/養生 philosophy and health practices in your country? Is the medical community generally supportive or skeptical of these practices? How do such practices compare to your health regimen?

2 In China, many people prefer hot rather than icy beverages, even in the middle of summer; hot beverages are believed to be better for health. People of all ages carry flasks of hot tea, and customers are often asked whether they want sodas with ice or at room temperature. In your community, do people prefer hot or cold beverages?

Lesson Wrap-Up

Project

In pairs, role-play a diet and nutrition consultation session at a community health and nutrition center where some clients are recent immigrants from China. One partner takes the role of a physical fitness major who is interning at the center, while the other takes the role of a client. In your session, make sure that you and your partner complete the following tasks:

STUDENT INTERN

- get to know the client by finding out where he/she is from and when he/she immigrated as well as his/her occupation and age
- tell him/her that you will take his/her height, weight, and blood pressure: 我给您量身高 (or 体重 or 血压 [xuèyā])/我給您量身高 (or 體重 or 血壓 [xuèyā])
- find out if the client has any health problems
- inquire about the client's diet and lifestyle, and determine whether he/she pays attention to diet; in addition, ask whether he/she exercises (e.g., practices tai chi or yoga), and if so, how often
- suggest ways for the client to modify his/her diet and lifestyle

CLIENT

- express concern about your weight and blood pressure
- tell the intern that you have been eating too much meat and not a lot of vegetables because meat is inexpensive and Chinese vegetables are hard to find in America, and that you work through the night and do not get enough sleep
- ask for suggestions on how to pay more attention to diet and exercise
- explain to the intern how you will change the way you eat and exercise

Study the following example; pay particular attention to how the highlighted parts help the sentences flow smoothly from one to the next. Notice how:

- pronouns (他们/他們) replace nouns (中国人/中國人) in subsequent sentences
- time words and phrases (早上, 晚饭后/晚飯後) connect sentences
- certain phrases (有的⋯，有的⋯) introduce examples
- certain conjunctions (除了⋯以外，也⋯) signify addition
- certain conjunctions (所以) introduce conclusions

中国老人很注意身体健康

中国人退休比较早，有的60岁，有的55岁。他们退休以后花很多时间锻炼身体，早上，在公园或街边跳广场舞、打太极拳，晚饭后，常常去散步。除了锻炼以外，他们也非常重视饮食健康和良好的生活习惯。所以中国老人活得越来越久了。

中國老人很注意身體健康

中國人退休比較早，有的60歲，有的55歲。他們退休以後花很多時間鍛煉身體，早上，在公園或街邊跳廣場舞、打太極拳，晚飯後，常常去散步。除了鍛煉以外，他們也非常重視飲食健康和良好的生活習慣。所以中國老人活得越來越久了。

How do people in your country exercise? Use as many of the cohesive devices highlighted in the example on the previous page as possible to string together a response, based on the prompts:

○ 你们国家的人注意锻炼身体吗？

　你們國家的人注意鍛煉身體嗎？

○ 他们一般喜欢哪些运动？

　他們一般喜歡哪些運動？

○ 老年人为了身体健康，除了运动以外，还应该注意
　什么？

　老年人為了身體健康，除了運動以外，還應該注意
　什麼？

○ 你注意自己的身体健康吗？

　你注意自己的身體健康嗎？

○ 为了身体健康，你怎样做？

　為了身體健康，你怎樣做？

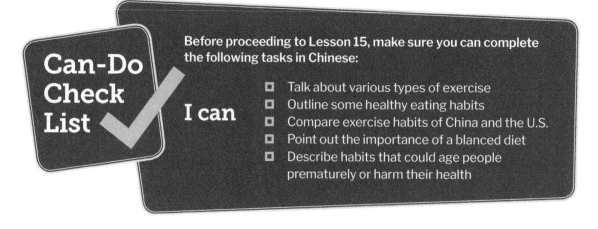

Can-Do Check List ✔ **I can**

Before proceeding to Lesson 15, make sure you can complete the following tasks in Chinese:

☐ Talk about various types of exercise
☐ Outline some healthy eating habits
☐ Compare exercise habits of China and the U.S.
☐ Point out the importance of a blanced diet
☐ Describe habits that could age people prematurely or harm their health

Lìshā dào Běijīng hòu méiyǒu zhù liúxuéshēng gōngyù, wèile gèng duō de liǎojiě Zhōngguó rén de shēnghuó, tā zhù jìn le yí ge Zhōngguó jiātíng. Fángdōng fūqī èr rén yǐ[1] tuì xiū, nǚ'ér Lǐ Wén zài bówùguǎn gōngzuò, yǔ[2] fùmǔ zhù zài yìqǐ. Lǐ Wén hěn xiǎng qù Měiguó liú xué, suǒyǐ qǐng Lìshā zuò tā de Yīngwén jiājiào, zhèyàng Lìshā jiù búbì fù fángzū le. Yīnwèi Lìshā měi tiān dōu gēn Lǐ Wén de fùmǔ shuō Zhōngwén, suǒyǐ tā de Zhōngwén jìnbù de hěn kuài.

Lìshā měi tiān zǎoshang dōu chū qu sàn bù, zài tā zhù de zhè ge xiǎoqū, zài jiē biān, zài gōngyuán, dōu néng kàn jiàn hěn duō rén, tèbié shì lǎorén, zài duànliàn shēntǐ. Tāmen yǒude tiào guǎngchǎng wǔ, yǒude dǎ tàijíquán. Zhè xiē zǎochen duànliàn[a] de rénmen, chéngwéi Běijīng tèbié de "fēngjǐng".

Zhè yì tiān zǎoshang Lìshā zhèng yào chū mén, Lǐ Wén cóng fángjiān zǒu chu lai.

Lìshā, jīntiān shì xīngqīliù, zěnme zhème zǎo jiù qǐ chuáng le?

Wǒ běnlái xiǎng gēn shūshu, āyí qù xué tàijíquán, méi xiǎng dào tāmen nàme zǎo jiù chū qu le.

Wǒ yǐwéi nǐ zhǐ xǐhuan zuò yújiā[b], zěnme duì tàijíquán yě yǒu xìngqù?

Tàijíquán hé yújiā yíyàng, búdàn duì shēntǐ yǒu hǎochu, érqiě dòngzuò hěn měi.

Lìshā, nǐ kàn dà shù xià bian, wǒ bà, wǒ mā zhèngzài gēn nà xiē tuì xiū lǎorén dǎ tàijíquán ne! Nǐ qù zhǎo tāmen ba.

Hǎo, yí huìr jiù qù. Tāmen dǎ de zhēn bàng. Wǒ měi tiān zǎochen chū qu sàn bù, kàn jiàn dàochù dōu shì yùndòng de rén. Zhōngguó rén zhēn zhòngshì duànliàn shēntǐ a!

Duì, xiànzài dàjiā dōu yuè lái yuè zhùyì shēntǐ jiànkāng le. Āi, Lìshā, Měiguó rén yìbān zěnme duànliàn shēntǐ?

Yìbān shì pǎo bù, yóu yǒng, dǎ qiú děng děng, yǒu xiē rén yě qù jiànshēnfáng. Wǒ píngcháng zuò yújiā, yǒude shíhou yě pǎo bù.

Nánguài nǐ de shēntǐ zhème jiànkāng.

Wǒ juéde rúguǒ xīwàng shēntǐ jiànkāng, chúle duō yùndòng yǐwài, hái yīnggāi zhùyì yǐnshí.

Nǐ yì diǎnr dōu bú pàng, hái xūyào zhùyì yǐnshí ma?

Zhùyì yǐnshí bù děngyú jiǎn féi. Wǒ rènwéi zhǐyào shēntǐ jiànkāng jiù³ hǎo, pàng shòu bú zhòngyào.

 Wǒ gōngzuò máng, méi shíjiān hǎo hāor chī fàn, chángcháng suíbiàn luàn chī. Nǐ shì zěnme zhùyì yǐnshi de ne?

 Duō hē shuǐ, duō chī qīngcài, shuǐguǒ. Lìngwài, jíshǐ fēicháng máng, yě⁴ yídìng yào chī zǎofàn, érqiě zǎofàn yào yǒu yíngyǎng; wǔfàn yào chī bǎo, yīnwèi xiàwǔ hái yào xuéxí hé gōngzuò; wǎnfàn jiù yào shǎo chī yì diǎn, bùrán huì yuè lái yuè pàng, yīnwèi lí shàng chuáng shuì jiào de shíjiān tài jìn le.

 Wǒmen Zhōngguó rén yǒu yí jù huà: Zǎocān yào chī hǎo, wǔcān yào chī bǎo, wǎncān yào chī shǎoᶜ, gēn nǐ shuō de chàbuduō yíyàng.

 Zhēn de? Dàjiā dōu zhème shuō, kěnéng shì yǒu kēxué dàoli de.

 Wǒ juéde xiǎng yào shēntǐ hǎo, zài qítā fāngmiàn yě bìxūᵈ zhùyì.

 Nǐ de yìsi shì yào yǒu liánghǎo de shēnghuó xíguàn, duì bu duì?

 Duì. Bù xī yānᵉ, bù hē jiǔ, zǎo shuì zǎo qǐ, zuìhǎo bú yào áo yè. Bié de dōu méi wèntí, jiù shì bù áo yè wǒ zuò bú dào. Wǒ wǎnshang chángcháng děi kāi yèchēᶠ zhǔnbèi kǎo yánjiūshēng.

 Nà nǐ bìxū jǐn kěnéng zhǎo shíjiān bǔchōng shuìmián.

 Nǐ shuō de duì, wǒ shì děi zhùyì le, yàobùrán wǒ de liǎng zhī yǎnjing dōu kuài biàn chéng xióngmāoᵍ yǎn le.

男女平等

GENDER EQUALITY

Learning Objectives	Relate and Get Ready

In this lesson, you will learn to:

- Talk about equal treatment in relationships
- Discuss gender equality in the workplace
- Summarize the changes in Chinese women's social status since 1950
- Describe how couples share household chores

In your own culture/community:

- Do married couples split chores at home?
- What roles are men and women expected to live up to?
- Are men and women equally compensated for their work?

课文

Text

Audio

在历史上，中国是一个重男轻女的社会，妇女的家庭地位和社会地位都比男人低得多。一九五〇年以后，情况逐渐[a]发生了变化。特别是在城市里，女孩子和男孩子一样有受教育和参加工作的机会，妇女的社会地位也有了很大的提高。

改革开放以来，在一些企业和事业单位[b]，又出现了男女不平等的现象。比方说，找工作的时候，妇女常常比男人更难；一些工厂和公司还没有做到男女同工同酬。当然，也有一些女性，无论在工作上还是收入上，都超过一般男人。不过她们在女性中只是少数。

但是在很多中国家庭中，丈夫和妻子都是互相照顾，所以，家庭可能是现在中国社会男女最平等的地方。拿林雪梅的舅舅来说吧，他是个大球迷，只有在看电视里的足球赛的时候才什么家务都不做。可是比赛一完，他就忙着帮舅妈做饭、洗碗，又成了一位"模范丈夫"。

課文

在歷史上，中國是一個重男輕女的社會，婦女的家庭地位和社會地位都比男人低得多。一九五〇年以後，情況逐漸[a]發生了變化。特別是在城市裡，女孩子和男孩子一樣有受教育和參加工作的機會，婦女的社會地位也有了很大的提高。

改革開放以來，在一些企業和事業單位[b]，又出現了男女不平等的現象。比方說，找工作的時候，婦女常常比男人更難；一些工廠和公司還沒有做到男女同工同酬。當然，也有一些女性，無論在工作上還是收入上，都超過一般男人。不過她們在女性中只是少數。

但是在很多中國家庭中，丈夫和妻子都是互相照顧，所以，家庭可能是現在中國社會男女最平等的地方。拿林雪梅的舅舅來說吧，他是個大球迷，只有在看電視裡的足球賽的時候才什麼家務都不做。可是比賽一完，他就忙著幫舅媽做飯、洗碗，又成了一位"模範丈夫"。

Before You Study

Answer the following questions in Chinese to prepare for the reading.

1 在你們國家裡，夫妻之間，一般誰在外工作掙錢，誰在家照顧孩子？

2 在你們的社會裡，男女做同樣的工作掙的錢一樣多嗎？

When You Study

Listen to the audio recording and skim the text; then answer the following questions in Chinese.

1 從哪些方面能看出中國婦女的社會地位有了提高？

2 在工作上，男女不平等的現象有哪些？

3 什麼決定女子職業運動員的收入？

舅舅，今天怎么您洗碗呀？

哈哈，因为我洗碗比你舅妈洗得干净啊。

我来洗吧！我洗碗也是洗得很干净的[1]。

别、别、别，你们从云南旅游回来，就忙着找工作、面试，还没休息过来[2]呢。再说，你舅舅呀，昨天晚上看球看到夜里一点，今天还不得好好表现表现？

舅舅，昨天晚上是什么比赛啊？

男子足球赛，北京队对上海队。

那有什么好看的？我最讨厌那些男足队员了，平常骄傲得不得了，可是比赛的时候老输球。所以，我只看中国女足，她们比男足棒多了。

不错，女足是比男足成绩好，可是我听说女足队员挣的钱只有男足的十分之一[c]，真不公平。

别忘了，他们的收入是由市场来决定的。美国职业女篮队员的薪水跟职业男篮比，也少多了。

哎，别老说中国男足输球了。我刚看到网上的消息说，中国男足昨天赢了世界冠军队。

舅舅，今天怎麼您洗碗呀？

哈哈，因為我洗碗比你舅媽洗得乾淨啊。

我來洗吧！我洗碗也是洗得很乾淨的[1]。

別、別、別，你們從雲南旅遊回來，就忙著找工作、面試，還沒休息過來[2]呢。再說，你舅舅呀，昨天晚上看球看到夜裡一點，今天還不得好好表現表現？

舅舅，昨天晚上是什麼比賽啊？

男子足球賽，北京隊對上海隊。

那有什麼好看的？我最討厭那些男足隊員了，平常驕傲得不得了，可是比賽的時候老輸球。所以，我只看中國女足，她們比男足棒多了。

不錯，女足是比男足成績好，可是我聽說女足隊員掙的錢只有男足的十分之一[c]，真不公平。

別忘了，他們的收入是由市場來決定的。美國職業女籃隊員的薪水跟職業男籃比，也少多了。

哎，別老說中國男足輸球了。我剛看到網上的消息說，中國男足昨天贏了世界冠軍隊。

After You Study

Answer the following questions in Chinese.

1 重男轻女的社会是一个什么样的社会?

2 为什么有人认为家庭是中国社会男女最平等的地方?

3 这一百年以来，中国妇女的社会地位有些什么变化?

 我不相信，是网上乱说的吧?

好像是真的。网上说，这次中国男足踢得不错，比分一直是0比0。最后一分钟，中国男足才踢进一球，以1比0赢了比赛。

没想到，真的没想到，太棒了！那这个世界冠军队是德国队还是西班牙队?

中国乒乓球女队。

啊?

那一定是什么人在开男足的玩笑！

View & Explore

Video

For deeper language immersion and more cultural information, watch "Men and Women of the Mosuo," a short, supplemental video clip by Cheng & Tsui on this lesson's theme.

我不相信，是網上亂說的吧？

好像是真的。網上說，這次中國男足踢得不錯，比分一直是0比0。最後一分鐘，中國男足才踢進一球，以1比0贏了比賽。

沒想到，真的沒想到，太棒了！那這個世界冠軍隊是德國隊還是西班牙隊？

中國乒乓球女隊。

啊？

那一定是什麼人在開男足的玩笑！

Language Notes

a 逐漸/逐漸

逐漸/逐漸 and 漸漸/漸漸 both mean "gradually," but 漸漸/漸漸 is more colloquial.

b 企業單位/企業單位 vs. 事業單位/事業單位

單位/單位 means "work unit," but in contemporary usage, it is close to "company." 企業單位/企業單位 are enterprises that are engaged in profit-generating activities such as manufacturing, construction, and trade. Factories, mines, and railroads are typical 企業單位/企業單位. 事業單位/事業單位, on the other hand, are units that are financed through government funding, such as schools and hospitals.

c 十分之一

十分之一 (lit. one of ten parts) means "one-tenth."

Vocabulary

No.	Simplified	Traditional	Pinyin	Part of Speech	Definition
1	平等	平等	*píngděng*	adj/n	equal; equality (lit. level and equal)
2	重男轻女	重男輕女	*zhòng nán qīng nǚ*		to regard males as superior to females, to privilege men over women
3	妇女	婦女	*fùnǚ*	n	women
4	地位	地位	*dìwèi*	n	position, status
5	情况	情況	*qíngkuàng*	n	situation, condition, circumstances
6	逐渐	逐漸	*zhújiàn*	adv	gradually, little by little
7	机会	機會	*jīhuì*	n	opportunity
8	改革开放	改革開放	*gǎigé kāifàng*	v/n	to reform and open up; Reform and Opening-Up
9	以来	以來	*yǐlái*	t	since
10	企业	企業	*qǐyè*	n	enterprise, business, company, firm
11	单位	單位	*dānwèi*	n	unit
12	出现	出現	*chūxiàn*	v	to appear, to arise, to emerge
13	现象	現象	*xiànxiàng*	n	phenomenon, appearance
14	工厂	工廠	*gōngchǎng*	n	factory
15	同工同酬	同工同酬	*tóng gōng tóng chóu*		equal pay for equal work
16	女性	女性	*nǚxìng*	n	female gender, woman
17	超过	超過	*chāoguò*	v	to surpass, to exceed
18	丈夫	丈夫	*zhàngfu*	n	husband
19	妻子	妻子	*qīzi*	n	wife
20	互相	互相	*hùxiāng*	adv	mutually, each other, reciprocally
21	家务	家務	*jiāwù*	n	household chores, household duties

庆祝"三八"国际妇女节
实现男女平等,推动社会进步

While shopping in Chengdu on spring break, you come across this banner outside of a subway station. What event does the banner celebrate, and when does this event occur every year?

GET Real WITH CHINESE

No.	Simplified	Traditional	Pinyin	Part of Speech	Definition
22	模范	模範	*mófàn*	adj/n	exemplary; model, fine example
23	表现	表現	*biǎoxiàn*	v/n	to display, to manifest; performance; manifestation
24	男子	男子	*nánzǐ*	n	man, male
25	队	隊	*duì*	n	team, a row or line of people, (measure word for teams and lines)
26	讨厌	討厭	*tǎoyàn*	v/adj	to dislike, to loathe; disgusting, disagreeable
27	队员	隊員	*duìyuán*	n	team member
28	骄傲	驕傲	*jiāo'ào*	adj/n	proud, arrogant, full of oneself; pride
29	输	輸	*shū*	v	to lose, to be defeated
30	成绩	成績	*chéngjì*	n	performance, achievement, result, score, grade
31	公平	公平	*gōngpíng*	adj	fair, just, impartial, equitable
32	由	由	*yóu*	prep	by

No.	Simplified	Traditional	Pinyin	Part of Speech	Definition
33	市场	市場	shìchǎng	n	market
34	职业	職業	zhíyè	n	occupation, profession, vocation
35	薪水	薪水	xīnshuǐ	n	salary, pay, wages
36	消息	消息	xiāoxi	n	news, message, information
37	赢	贏	yíng	v	to win
38	冠军	冠軍	guànjūn	n	champion, first place in a competition
39	相信	相信	xiāngxìn	v	to believe, to trust
40	比分	比分	bǐfēn	n	score
41	乒乓球	乒乓球	pīngpāngqiú	n	ping pong, table tennis
42	德国	德國	Déguó	pn	Germany
43	西班牙	西班牙	Xībānyá	pn	Spain

林雪梅帮舅舅、舅妈洗碗。你平常在家做什么家务？

林雪梅幫舅舅、舅媽洗碗。你平常在家做什麼家務？

How About You?

Grammar

Sentences with 是…的 (II)

In L14, IC2 and L1, IC3, we learned that the "是…的" construction should be used when discussing the particulars (e.g., the time, place, or manner) of an action that has already taken place.

The Text of this lesson introduces another use of the "是…的" construction: namely, it can be used to persuade someone.

A Xuemei

我洗碗也是洗得很干净的。

我洗碗也是洗得很乾淨的。

I also do a good job at washing dishes.

Here, by bracketing her statement with 是…的, Xuemei tries to convince her aunt that she can do a good job, too. In the same vein, (B), (C), (D), and (E) illustrate how 是…的 is used to reassure or sway someone.

B

别担心，医生说你父亲的身体健康情况是很不错的。

別擔心，醫生說你父親的身體健康情況是很不錯的。

Don't worry. The doctor says that your father's health is quite good.

More neutral:

别担心，医生说你父亲的身体健康情况不错。

別擔心，醫生說你父親的身體健康情況不錯。

C

我相信住在校内是很安全的。

我相信住在校內是很安全的。

I believe it is very safe to live on campus.

More neutral:

我相信住在校内很安全。

我相信住在校內很安全。

D

只知道减肥，不注意饮食与睡眠，也不锻炼，对你是没有好处的。

只知道減肥，不注意飲食與睡眠，也不鍛煉，對你是沒有好處的。

Focusing only on losing weight while ignoring diet and sleep and not exercising won't do you any good.

[Here, 有好处/有好處 functions as an adjective.]

More neutral:

只知道减肥，不注意饮食与睡眠，也不锻炼，对你没有好处。

只知道減肥，不注意飲食與睡眠，也不鍛煉，對你沒有好處。

E

我们是很重视学生的健康的。

我們是很重視學生的健康的。

We do take students' health very seriously.

More neutral:

我们很重视学生的健康。

我們很重視學生的健康。

(A), (B), (C), and (D) all show the "是···的" construction used with adjectives or adjectival phrases. These often take 很 when serving as predicates.

However, verbs can also be used with the "是···的" construction. They have to follow a modal verb, as in (F) and (G), have a potential complement as in (H), or be mental verbs that can be modified by 很, as in (E). Generally, verbs alone cannot be inserted into the construction, as shown in the incorrect examples alongside (F), (G), and (H).

F　他是会丢三拉四的。[✗ 他是丢三拉四的。]

他是會丟三拉四的。[✗ 他是丟三拉四的。]

He does get scatterbrained.

G　小张这个人是不会忘这忘那的。
[✗ 小张这个人是不忘这忘那的。]

小張這個人是不會忘這忘那的。
[✗ 小張這個人是不忘這忘那的。]

LIttle Zhang isn't someone who is careless and forgetful.

H　你的电脑是找得到的。[✗ 你的电脑是找到的。]

你的電腦是找得到的。[✗ 你的電腦是找到的。]

Your computer will be found.

2

过来/過來 as a complement

As a complement, 过来/過來 can express a resultative meaning: a return to a normal active state.

A　你昨天太累了，现在休息过来了吗？

你昨天太累了，現在休息過來了嗎？

You were so tired yesterday. Have you rested up [and recovered]?

B　他病得很厉害，医生费了好大力气才把他救 *(jiù)* 过来。

他病得很厲害，醫生費了好大力氣才把他救 *(jiù)* 過來。

He was seriously ill. The doctor barely managed to save him [from the brink of death].

c

他不清楚这件事他错在哪里，老师给他讲了很长时间，他才明白过来。

他不清楚這件事他錯在哪裡，老師給他講了很長時間，他才明白過來。

It was unclear to him where he made the mistake on this. The teacher gave him a very long explanation; only then did it become clear to him.

The opposite of 过来/過來 is 过去/過去. Some examples of 过去/過去 as a complement include 死过去了/死過去了 (passed away), 睡过去了/睡過去了 (fell asleep), and 晕过去了/暈過去了 (*yūn guo qu le*) (lost consciousness).

Chinese Chat

You are looking up the score of a soccer game and see this post and a follower's comment on Weibo. What comment would you leave?

我爱足球
4-1 10:00 PM 来自华为

好消息！在下半场第44分钟，中国男足踢进一球，以1比0赢得了与世界冠军——中国乒乓球女队的比赛！

@莎莎：博主是在开玩笑？

⤴ 转发 | 💬1评论 | 👍赞

我愛足球：
好消息！在下半場第44分鐘，中國男足踢進一球，以1比0贏得了與世界冠軍——中國乒乓球女隊的比賽！

@莎莎：
博主是在開玩笑？

Words & Phrases

A | 逐渐/逐漸 (gradually, little by little)

逐渐/逐漸 is an adverb.

1 春天了，天气逐渐暖和了。

春天了，天氣逐漸暖和了。

It's spring, and the weather has gradually begun to warm up.

2 我开始有点儿讨厌我的同屋，后来对他逐渐了解了，也逐渐喜欢他了。

我開始有點兒討厭我的同屋，後來對他逐漸了解了，也逐漸喜歡他了。

I didn't like my roommate all that much at first, but later I gradually got to know him and came to like him more and more.

3 柯林到北京一两个月了，逐渐适应这个城市的生活了。

柯林到北京一兩個月了，逐漸適應這個城市的生活了。

Ke Lin has been in Beijing for a couple of months now. He is slowly getting used to life in the city.

提高 (to improve, to raise; improvement)

提高 can be a verb, as in (1) and (2).

1
要是你这个学期好好学习，成绩一定会提高。

要是你這個學期好好學習，成績一定會提高。

If you study hard this semester, your grades will definitely improve. *[verb]*

2
这个城市的房租又提高了。

這個城市的房租又提高了。

Housing rents in this city have risen again. *[verb]*

提高 can also be a noun, as in (3).

3
今年小林的汉语水平有很大的提高。

今年小林的漢語水平有很大的提高。

Little Lin's Chinese has improved a great deal this year. *[noun]*

…以来/…以來 (since)

…以来/…以來 means "from … till now."

1
年初以来，已经下了好几次雪了。

年初以來，已經下了好幾次雪了。

Since the beginning of the year, it has already snowed several times.

2
丽莎住在李文家以来，已经逐渐习惯中国人的生活了。

麗莎住在李文家以來，已經逐漸習慣中國人的生活了。

Ever since Lisha started living at Li Wen's place, she's gradually been getting used to the lifestyles of Chinese people.

3

改革开放以来，中国的经济发生了很大的变化。

改革開放以來，中國的經濟發生了很大的變化。

Since the beginning of the Reform and Opening-Up, China's economy has gone through huge changes.

拿…来说 / 拿…來說 (take . . . for example)

The structure "拿…来说 / 拿…來說" is used to cite examples, and in spoken Chinese is often followed by 吧:

1

我们小区退休的老人都很喜欢运动，拿我爷爷来说吧，天天锻炼，一天不锻炼，就觉得不舒服。

我們小區退休的老人都很喜歡運動，拿我爺爺來說吧，天天鍛煉，一天不鍛煉，就覺得不舒服。

All the retirees in our residential subdivision love to exercise. My grandfather, for example, exercises every day. If he doesn't exercise for even one day, he doesn't feel well.

2

一九九〇年以来，中国的城市变化很大，拿北京来说吧，老北京的样子差不多都找不到了。

一九九〇年以來，中國的城市變化很大，拿北京來說吧，老北京的樣子差不多都找不到了。

Since 1990, Chinese cities have undergone tremendous change. Take Beijing for example; there is hardly anything left of the old Beijing anymore.

只有…才… (only if)

The structure "只有…才…" indicates that only under a certain condition can a particular result be reached.

1

只有你去请这位教授，他才会来。

只有你去請這位教授，他才會來。

This professor will come only if you invite him.

2

我只有不去上课的时候，才能来你家帮助你练习写汉字。

我只有不去上課的時候，才能來你家幫助你練習寫漢字。

Only when I'm not in class can I come to your house to help you practice writing Chinese characters.

3

只有过春节的时候，从农村到城市打工的人才能回家和孩子团圆。

只有過春節的時候，從農村到城市打工的人才能回家和孩子團圓。

Only during Chinese New Year can people from rural areas who work in the cities go home to reunite with their children.

F | 表现/表現 (to show, to display, to manifest; performance, manifestation)

表现/表現 can be a verb:

1

只有每天练球，比赛时才能好好儿表现。

只有每天練球，比賽時才能好好兒表現。

Only with daily practice can we perform well in competitions. *[verb]*

Characterize it!

More characters

What do the characters mean?

What is the common radical?

What does the radical mean?

How does the radical relate to the overall meaning of the characters?

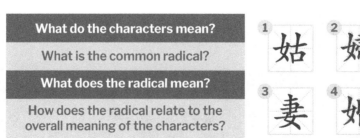

It is often followed by 出 or 出来/出來 as a complement, as in (2) and (3):

2 看见我的游戏机，弟弟表现出极大的兴趣。

看見我的遊戲機，弟弟表現出極大的興趣。

Upon seeing my video game console, my younger brother showed a great deal of interest. *[verb]*

3 等一会儿看见律师，你即使很紧张，也不要表现出来。

等一會兒看見律師，你即使很緊張，也不要表現出來。

When you meet the lawyer in a moment, even if you feel nervous, don't show it. *[verb]*

表现/表現 can also be a noun, as in (4):

4 他见到你有什么表现？生气还是高兴？

他見到你有什麼表現？生氣還是高興？

How did he seem when he saw you? Was he angry or happy? *[noun]*

(When he saw you, what body language did he show? Was he angry or happy?)

A WAY WITH WORDS

平等

这条高速公路很平整，在上面开车真的很舒服。

小张今天跟女朋友分手了，心里很难受，很长时间平静不下来。

Using the word/phrase in orange as a clue, try to figure out the meaning of the words/phrases in blue; consult a dictionary if necessary. Consider how the literal and extended senses are related in each case.

平等

這條高速公路很平整，在上面開車真的很舒服。

小張今天跟女朋友分手了，心裡很難受，很長時間平靜不下來。

由 (by)

由 is a preposition that introduces the person or entity performing an action.

1

他的学习时间由你安排，我不担心。

他的學習時間由你安排，我不擔心。

His study hours are set by you. [That's why] I don't have to worry.

2

学什么专业由我自己选择，我父母不管。

學什麼專業由我自己選擇，我父母不管。

It's up to me to choose my major. My parents don't interfere.

3

小林的学费完全由父母负担。

小林的學費完全由父母負擔。

Little Lin's tuition is entirely taken care of by her parents.

A WAY WITH WORDS

公平

学校餐馆服务员的工资太低了，我们应该帮他们说几句公道话。

历史是公正的，如果我们现在不好好保护这里的传统建筑，将来人们会抱怨我们的。

Using the word/phrase in orange as a clue, try to figure out the meaning of the words/phrases in blue; consult a dictionary if necessary. Consider how the literal and extended senses are related in each case.

公平

學校餐館服務員的工資太低了，我們應該幫他們說幾句公道話。

歷史是公正的，如果我們現在不好好保護這裡的傳統建築，將來人們會抱怨我們的。

Language Practice

A INTERPERSONAL **Delegating responsibility** PRESENTATIONAL

In pairs, plan a party for your class. First, with your partner, designate which classmates should be in charge of different tasks, e.g.:

找音乐/找音樂

Q: 音乐由谁来找？
音樂由誰來找？

A: 音乐由 Jeff 和 Katie 来找。
音樂由 Jeff 和 Katie 來找。

Tasks:

- 请客人/請客人
- 买饮料/買飲料
- 准备游戏/準備遊戲
- 搬桌子、椅子
- 晚会后打扫/晚會後打掃

Then send out the assignment list to your class in a WeChat group.

B **Equality begins at home** INTERPERSONAL

In pairs, discuss relationships and housework. Based on the prompts, ask your partner how both partners in a couple can share or split household responsibilities.

买菜/買菜   洗衣服

做饭/做飯   打扫屋子/打掃屋子

洗碗   教育孩子

141

My ideal partner

In addition to a willingness to share household chores, what other qualities would you want in a future spouse? Would you want your spouse to be cheerful, attentive, able to earn a good income, funny, or not forgetful? Would you want them to have a similar educational background and similar interests?

First, list ideal qualities you would want in a future spouse:

1 _____

2 _____

3 _____

4 _____

5 _____

Then, describe your ideal partner based on your list. You may start by saying:

我希望我的丈夫（或者妻子）除了能帮我做家务以外，还必须…

我希望我的丈夫（或者妻子）除了能幫我做家務以外，還必須…

My ideal workplace

Would your dream job be in a company, a factory, or another setting? List the features that your ideal workplace would have. You may want to mention that it should be a place where people trust and care for each other, where nobody dislikes you, where people are paid well, where men and women get equal pay for equal work, etc.

1 _____

2 _____

3 _____

4 _____

5 _____

6 _____

Then, make a presentation on your ideal workplace to the class.

E | # Women's empowerment | PRESENTATIONAL

Briefly summarize the important changes that took place in terms of women's social status since 1950.

After 1950	After the Reform and Opening-Up
_____	_____
_____	_____
_____	_____

Ask yourself if there have been similar changes in women's social status in your own society. What were the historical turning points, and what has been achieved since then? Try to focus on women's situations in the family and the workplace. You may use English for proper nouns.

1 _____

2 _____

3 _____

4 _____

5 _____

Women in the Workforce

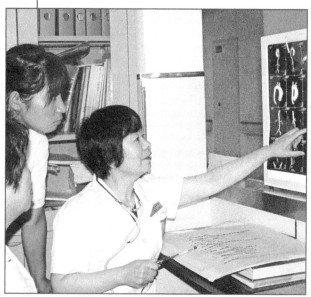

The role of women in Chinese society underwent dramatic change from the 1950s to the late 1970s, when China had a planned economy, 计划经济/計劃經濟. Under this system, national economic plans were formulated by the central government and implemented by all enterprises. The government actively sought to establish gender equality in China, setting up policies for equal opportunities and equal pay. Reflecting this situation, Mao Zedong coined the phrase 妇女能顶半边天/婦女能頂半邊天 (*Fùnǚ néng dǐng bàn biān tiān*), meaning "Women can hold up half the sky." While women saw an improvement in workforce participation rates, they often held jobs different from those of men.

Through economic reform in recent decades, China has gradually evolved into a market economy, 市场经济/市場經濟, referred to by the Chinese government as a "socialist market economy." The Chinese Reform and Opening-Up, known as 改革开放/改革開放, started in 1978. Since then, tens of millions of people have been lifted out of poverty, and opportunities for women continue to improve. But even today, the desire to have boys over girls remains very strong in some rural areas, which has resulted in a gender imbalance in the country's population.

Gender Terms

In step with changes in the role of women in Chinese society, gendered terms in Chinese have also seen a shift. During the Republican era, 先生 and 太太 were the default informal terms for "husband" and "wife," but were dismissed as "feudal" and "bourgeois" after 1949 in Mainland China, replaced by the gender-neutral term 爱人/愛人. In recent years, terms for partners have diverged among Chinese speakers of different regions, ages, and socioeconomic groups. In Mainland China, 爱人/愛人 remains common among educated, middle-aged people, but has a different nuance in Taiwan, where it means "lover." 先生 and 太太 have been revived but remain uncommon, particularly among the working class. 老公 and 老婆 have become trendy among some young people. In formal contexts, such as on official forms, 丈夫 and 妻子 are used (a couple is 夫妻); while people may sometimes refer to their spouse with these terms, they are rarely used when talking with friends and acquaintances.

Several sets of terms for men and women are used in different contexts. 男人 and 女人 can refer to unfamiliar or non-specific people, as in 一个男人/一個男人 (a man) and 一个女人/一個女人 (a woman). However, it is disrespectful and impolite to use these to refer to specific people, especially acquaintances. Instead of asking 那个男人是你的男朋友吗？/那個男人是你的男朋友嗎？ ("Is that man your boyfriend?"), it sounds better to say: 那个男的是你的男朋友吗？/那個男的是你的男朋友嗎？ 男的 and 女的 are more neutral. When 男人 and 女人 are used as collective nouns, there is no question of being impolite: 男人的问题和女人不同/男人的問題和女人不同 ("Men and women have different issues").

The terms 男子 and 女子 are often used to refer to gender-specific categories or institutions, as in 男子100米 (men's hundred-meter dash), 女子跳高 (women's high jump), 女子时装/女子時裝 (women's fashion), and 女子学院/女子學院 (women's college). 男性 and 女性 are usually used as collective nouns and are more polite than 男人 and 女人. 男生 and 女生 literally refer to male and female students. However, in Taiwan these terms often refer to men and women in general. This usage has also caught on among some young people in Mainland China. Finally, the word 妇女/婦女 often has social and political connotations, e.g., 妇女节/婦女節 (Women's Day) and 妇女运动/婦女運動 (women's movement). There isn't a corresponding term for men.

Women's Script

Traditional Chinese culture placed heavy emphasis on gender roles in society and favored men over women. The old saying 男主外，女主内/男主外，女主內 (*Nán zhǔ wài, nǚ zhǔ nèi*) ("The man takes care of [the family's] external affairs; the woman takes care of [the family's] internal affairs") largely encapsulates these roles. Because women were deemed unworthy of a formal education, most never learned to read or write.

But hundreds of years ago in a southern county of Hunan Province, women developed a script of their own, a willowy phonetic writing system distinct from rectangular, logographic Chinese characters. The writing system, known as 女书/女書 (*Nǚshū*) or "women's script," was adapted from hundreds of different Chinese characters. 女书/女書 is an extraordinary example of female expression. Local women used the script to exchange poems and share private feelings about family and marriage. While the last original writers of 女书/女書 have passed away, the tradition has been kept alive through a local museum, an influential documentary, and young women who have taken up the script.

COMPARE & CONTRAST

1 Married people sometimes informally call their spouses 老公 (*lǎogōng*) (lit. old man) or 老婆 (*lǎopó*) (lit. old woman). Some young people have adopted these terms to refer to longtime boyfriends or girlfriends; however, traditionalists object to this usage as crude. Are there similar terms used in your culture or community that diverge from their intended use or are preferred by some and not others?

2 Research the accomplishments of Chinese women like Tu Youyou (屠呦呦), Li Yinhe (李银河/李銀河), Hu Shuli (胡舒立), Lang Ping (郎平), and Zhang Xin (张欣/張欣). How many prominent female leaders in different spheres can you name? Is there still a glass ceiling for women in business and politics? How does your country compare with the rest of the world in terms of gender equality?

Lesson Wrap-Up

Prepare a talk on the status of women in your country that you will give to a visiting Chinese women's delegation. Begin with an overview of women's status before citing statistics and describing women's progress or lack thereof. How much has women's status changed in the last twenty, thirty years? Be sure to:

· research the percentage of female professionals in medicine, education, law, etc.

· find out the percentage of female undergraduate and graduate students

· investigate the percentage of female business leaders

· indicate whether there is income equality between men and women

· explain what the statistics suggest

· forecast the future of women's status in your country

Keep It Flowing

Study the following example; pay particular attention to how the highlighted parts help the sentences flow smoothly from one to the next. Notice how:

· time and place expressions (在一九五〇年以前,那时候/那時候,一九五〇年以后/一九五〇年以後,改革开放以后/改革開放以後,在家里/在家裡) serve as cohesive devices

· certain phrases (特别是/特別是) single out examples

· some conjunctions (而且) introduce additional information

· other conjunctions (但是) signify a turn of thought

中国的男女平等问题

在一九五〇年以前，中国男女很不平等。那时候很多女人不能上学，也不工作，只能在家里带孩子、做饭等等，地位很低。一九五〇年以后，中国妇女的地位大大提高了，特别是城市里，女孩和男孩一样有受教育的机会，女人跟男人一样出来工作。改革开放以后，女人找工作有时比男人难，而且有些地方不同工同酬。但是有些女硕士或女博士，可以找到很好的工作，而且工资很高。

中國的男女平等問題

在一九五〇年以前，中國男女很不平等。那時候很多女人不能上學，也不工作，只能在家裡帶孩子、做飯等等，地位很低。一九五〇年以後，中國婦女的地位大大提高了，特別是城市裡，女孩和男孩一樣有受教育的機會，女人跟男人一樣出來工作。改革開放以後，女人找工作有時比男人難，而且有些地方不同工同酬。但是有些女碩士或女博士，可以找到很好的工作，而且工資很高。

Is there gender equality in your country? Use as many of the cohesive devices highlighted in the example as possible to string together a response, based on the prompts:

- 你们国家几十年前，在工作方面男女平等不平等？
  你們國家幾十年前，在工作方面男女平等不平等？

- 你们国家几十年前，在家庭中男女平等吗？
  你們國家幾十年前，在家庭中男女平等嗎？

- 现在你们国家男女平等吗？在哪些方面平等？
  現在你們國家男女平等嗎？在哪些方面平等？

- 你们国家现在还有男女不平等的情况吗？在哪些方面？
  你們國家現在還有男女不平等的情況嗎？在哪些方面？

- 谈谈你对男女平等的看法。
  談談你對男女平等的看法。

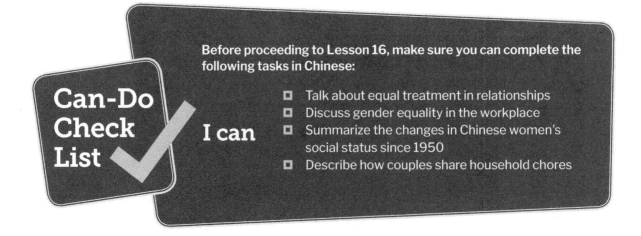

Can-Do Check List ✔

I can

Before proceeding to Lesson 16, make sure you can complete the following tasks in Chinese:

- ☐ Talk about equal treatment in relationships
- ☐ Discuss gender equality in the workplace
- ☐ Summarize the changes in Chinese women's social status since 1950
- ☐ Describe how couples share household chores

Zài lìshǐ shang, Zhōngguó shì yí ge zhòng nán qīng nǚ de shèhuì, fùnǚ de jiātíng dìwèi hé shèhuì dìwèi dōu bǐ nánrén dī de duō. Yī jiǔ wǔ líng nián yǐhòu, qíngkuàng zhújiàn[a] fāshēng le biànhuà. Tèbié shì zài chéngshì li, nǚ háizi hé nán háizi yíyàng yǒu shòu jiàoyù hé cānjiā gōngzuò de jīhuì, fùnǚ de shèhuì dìwèi yě yǒu le hěn dà de tígāo.

Gǎigé kāifàng yǐlái, zài yì xiē qǐyè hé shìyè dānwèi[b], yòu chūxiàn le nánnǚ bù píngděng de xiànxiàng. Bǐfāng shuō, zhǎo gōngzuò de shíhou, fùnǚ chángcháng bǐ nánrén gèng nán; yìxiē gōngchǎng hé gōngsī hái méiyǒu zuò dào nánnǚ tóng gōng tóng chóu. Dāngrán, yě yǒu yì xiē nǚxìng, wúlùn zài gōngzuò shang háishi shōurù shang, dōu chāoguò yìbān nánrén. Búguò tāmen zài nǚxìng zhōng zhǐ shì shǎoshù.

Dànshì zài hěn duō Zhōngguó jiātíng zhōng, zhàngfu hé qīzǐ dōu shì hùxiāng zhàogù, suǒyǐ, jiātíng kěnéng shì xiànzài Zhōngguó shèhuì nánnǚ zuì píngděng de dìfang. Ná Lín Xuěméi de jiùjiu lái shuō ba, tā shì ge dà qiúmí, zhǐ yǒu zài kàn diànshì li de zúqiú sài de shíhou cái shénme jiāwù dōu bú zuò. Kěshì bǐsài yì wán, tā jiù máng zhe bāng jiùmā zuò fàn, xǐ wǎn, yòu chéng le yí wèi "mófàn zhàngfu".

Jiùjiu, jīntiān zěnme nín xǐ wǎn ya?

Hā ha, yīnwèi wǒ xǐ wǎn bǐ nǐ jiùmā xǐ de gānjìng a.

Wǒ lái xǐ ba! Wǒ xǐ wǎn yě shì xǐ de hěn gānjìng de[1].

Bié, bié, bié, nǐmen cóng Yúnnán lǚyóu huí lai, jiù máng zhe zhǎo gōngzuò, miànshì, hái méi xiūxi guo lai[2] ne. Zàishuō, nǐ jiùjiu ya, zuótiān wǎnshang kàn qiú kàn dào yèli yī diǎn, jīntiān hái bù děi hǎo hāo biǎoxian biǎoxian?

Jiùjiu, zuótiān wǎnshang shì shénme bǐsài a?

Nánzǐ zúqiú sài, Běijīng duì duì Shànghǎi duì.

Nà yǒu shénme hǎokàn de? Wǒ zuì tǎoyàn nà xiē nán zú duìyuán le, píngcháng jiāo'ào de bùdéliǎo, kěshì bǐsài de shíhou lǎo shū qiú. Suǒyǐ, wǒ zhǐ kàn Zhōngguó nǚ zú, tāmen bǐ nán zú bàng duō le.

Búcuò, nǚ zú shì bǐ nán zú chéngjì hǎo, kěshì wǒ tīngshuō nǚ zú duìyuán zhèng de qián zhǐ yǒu nán zú de shí fēn zhī yī[c], zhēn bù gōngpíng.

Bié wàng le, tāmen de shōurù shì yóu shìchǎng lái juédìng de. Měiguó zhíyè nǚ lán duìyuán de xīnshuǐ gēn zhíyè nán lán bǐ, yě shǎo duō le.

Āi, bié lǎo shuō Zhōngguó nán zú shū qiú le. Wǒ gāng kàn dào wǎng shang de xiāoxi shuō, Zhōngguó nán zú zuótiān yíng le shìjiè guànjūn duì.

Wǒ bù xiāngxìn, shì wǎng shang luàn shuō de ba?

Hǎoxiàng shì zhēn de. Wǎng shang shuō, zhè cì Zhōngguó nán zú tī de búcuò, bǐfēn yìzhí shì líng bǐ líng. Zuìhòu yì fēnzhōng, Zhōngguó nán zú cái tī jìn yì qiú, yǐ yī bǐ líng yíng le bǐsài.

Méi xiǎng dào, zhēn de méi xiǎng dào, tài bàng le! Nà zhè ge shìjiè guànjūn duì shì Déguó duì háishi Xībānyá duì?

Zhōngguó pīngpāngqiú nǚ duì.

Á?

Nà yídìng shì shénme rén zài kāi nán zú de wánxiào!

<u>A</u>

Chinese character crossword puzzles

Many of the new words and phrases from Lessons 11–15 share the same characters. In these puzzles, the common character is positioned in the center of the cluster of bubbles. The triangular points indicate which way you should read the words. Work with a partner and see how many association bubbles you can complete, adding more bubbles if you can think of additional words/phrases, e.g.:

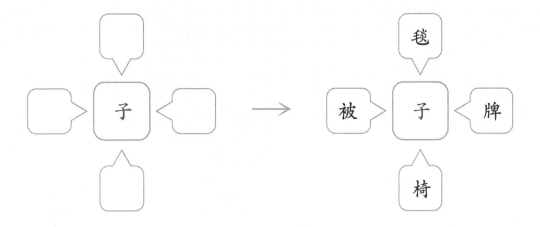

1

2

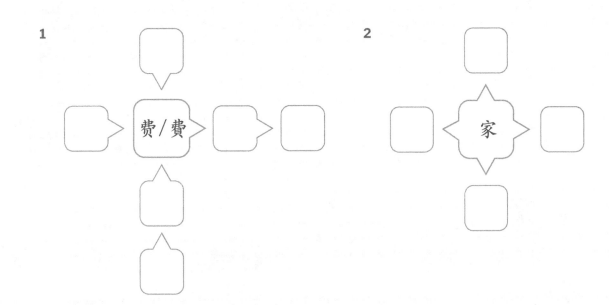

3

4

5

6

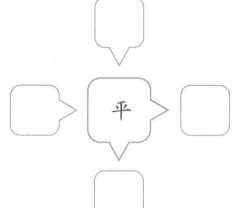

7   Create your own

Matching words

1 Draw lines to connect each verb with its proper object.

锻炼/鍛煉	睡眠/睡眠
取得	快乐/快樂
出现/出現	比赛/比賽
保留	身体/身體
分享	变化/變化
补充/補充	特色
参加/參加	成绩/成績
发生/發生	现象/現象

2 Draw lines to connect each noun with its proper adjective that can best describe it.

事业/事業	美
地位	深
工作	高
风景/風景	成功
印象/印象	顺利/順利

Put your thoughts into words

1 Brainstorm with a partner and ask each other what words or phrases you can use when you want to:

- describe festivities during Chinese New Year

foods	activities	atmosphere
_____	_____	_____
_____	_____	_____
_____	_____	_____
_____	_____	_____

- plan a trip or join a tour group

people	expenses
_____	_____
_____	_____
_____	_____
_____	_____

attractions	activities
_____	_____
_____	_____
_____	_____
_____	_____

- talk about changes in a city

past	present
_____	_____
_____	_____
_____	_____
_____	_____

- offer advice and share ways to stay healthy and fit

eating habits	other ways
_____	_____
_____	_____
_____	_____
_____	_____

- describe a model couple that are nice to each other or a model company that is fair to its employees

couple	company
_____	_____
_____	_____
_____	_____

Study these words/phrases with a few classmates. Using the list that follows, group the words/phrases according to their meanings and usages. Feel free to add other words/phrases if you can.

尽可能/儘可能

只要…就…

要不是

不管

要不然

即使…也…

看起来/看起來

等（等）

包括

没有…那么/沒有…那麼

是…的

- When you wish to state the certainty of an outcome regardless: _____

- When you wish to state what might have happened if something else hadn't: _____

- When you wish to mean doing one's best: _____

- When you wish to warn or deter people: _____

- When you wish to predict the outcome if the condition is met: _____

- When you wish to infer based on what has occurred: _____

- When you wish to cite examples: _____

- When you wish to compare: _____

- When you wish to assure someone or affirm something: _____

Present your thoughts

With a partner, give a brief presentation on Chinese festivals, travel in China, the modernization of Chinese cities, morning exercises in a Chinese city, or gender issues in Chinese society.

First, discuss with your partner:

· which topic you will select, and why
· what aspects of the topic you want to focus on
· what words or phrases from the first part of (C) should be used in your presentation
· what information should be presented first, next, and last
· what transitions may be needed between parts of the presentation
· what linking devices should be used to connect your sentences
· what words or phrases from the second part of (C) can be useful in presenting your point of view

It's a good idea to jot down sentences that you wish to say, then number them in the order you think they should be presented. Consider how you can make your list into a coherent discourse. Once you've finished, present your work to the class.

Speak methodically

Reorganize the following sentences to compose a well-connected paragraph praising Mr. Wang's devotion to his wife. Pay attention to time expressions, location expressions, and pronouns.

不管妻子要他做什么，他都会尽可能做到。

不管妻子要他做什麼，他都會儘可能做到。

从公园回来，他就买菜、整理房间、做家务。

從公園回來，他就買菜、整理房間、做家務。

王先生自己的看法呢？

王先生自己的看法呢？

王先生对太太很好。
王先生對太太很好。

他说他太太对他也很好。
他說他太太對他也很好。

要不是自己看到，很多人不相信王先生对太太那么好。
要不是自己看到，很多人不相信王先生對太太那麼好。

他认为夫妻就应该互相照顾。
他認為夫妻就應該互相照顧。

一天三顿都是他做饭，他洗碗，但他从来都不抱怨。
一天三頓都是他做飯，他洗碗，但他從來都不抱怨。

每天早晨陪太太去公园散步。
每天早晨陪太太去公園散步。

大家都觉得他爱太太，尊重太太，是个模范丈夫。
大家都覺得他愛太太，尊重太太，是個模範丈夫。

妻子的健康、快乐就是他最大的幸福。
妻子的健康、快樂就是他最大的幸福。

第十六课

第十六課

环境保护与节约能源

環境保護與節約能源

ENVIRONMENTAL PROTECTION AND ENERGY CONSERVATION

Learning Objectives

In this lesson, you will learn to:

- Describe how to get close to and relax in nature
- Talk about indicators of a clean environment
- Discuss green and renewable energy
- Explain what government can do to reduce pollution
- Identify what individuals can do to protect the environment

Relate and Get Ready

In your own culture/community:

- Are people concerned about pollution and environmental degradation?
- Are there barriers to the wider use of green energy, and if so, what are they?
- How have people changed their habits to consume less energy?

课文

Text

Audio

Before You Study

Answer the following questions in Chinese to prepare for the reading.

1 你平常怎么去学校上课？走路、开车还是坐公共汽车？

2 要是学习或者工作压力大，你怎么让自己轻松一下？

When You Study

Listen to the audio recording and scan the text; then answer the following questions in Chinese.

1 天明和朋友们为什么去爬山？

2 天明和朋友们为什么觉得城外比城里好？

3 多用风能、太阳能发电有什么好处？

　　张天明他们四个人来北京已经两三个月了，天气也逐渐暖和了。他们每天上课的上课[1]，找工作的找工作，半个月没见面了。今天是星期六，大家都想轻松轻松[2]，天明建议去爬山，丽莎和雪梅不反对，柯林也觉得这个建议不错，他说正好他的德国朋友马克也想去。

　　可是怎么去呢？坐出租车吧，太贵，而且也没意思；坐公交[a]车吧[3]，人太多，太挤。柯林想出了一个主意，骑自行车！大家马上就同意了，觉得骑自行车又能锻炼身体，又省钱，而且有益于[4]环境保护。

　　他们早上很早就出发了。骑了很长的一段路以后，有点热，也有点累，就下了车，一边推着车，一边聊了起来。

这儿的空气比城里好，雾霾也没有那么严重。

到处都是绿色，看着真舒服！

課文

張天明他們四個人來北京已經兩三個月了，天氣也逐漸暖和了。他們每天上課的上課[1]，找工作的找工作，半個月沒見面了。今天是星期六，大家都想輕鬆輕鬆[2]，天明建議去爬山，麗莎和雪梅不反對，柯林也覺得這個建議不錯，他說正好他的德國朋友馬克也想去。

可是怎麼去呢？坐出租車吧，太貴，而且也沒意思；坐公交[a]車吧[3]，人太多，太擠。柯林想出了一個主意，騎自行車！大家馬上就同意了，覺得騎自行車又能鍛煉身體，又省錢，而且有益於[4]環境保護。

他們早上很早就出發了。騎了很長的一段路以後，有點熱，也有點累，就下了車，一邊推著車，一邊聊了起來。

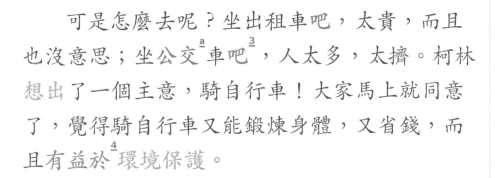
這兒的空氣比城裡好，霧霾也沒有那麼嚴重。

到處都是綠色，看著真舒服！

Before You Study

Answer the following questions in Chinese to prepare for the reading.

1 你平常怎麼去學校上課？走路、開車還是坐公共汽車？

2 要是學習或者工作壓力大，你怎麼讓自己輕鬆一下？

When You Study

Listen to the audio recording and scan the text; then answer the following questions in Chinese.

1 天明和朋友們為什麼去爬山？

2 天明和朋友們為什麼覺得城外比城裡好？

3 多用風能、太陽能發電有什麼好處？

哎呀，渴死了，……你们看，一瓶水都喝完了！这儿有垃圾回收筒吗？空瓶子不能随便乱扔。

对，我们应该注意环保[b]，垃圾回收筒……，你看，在树下边。

我好久没买瓶装水了。我们班有的同学建议，为了保护绿色的地球，自己带水喝，不买瓶装水。

这个建议不错。哎，你们看，那边房子上有些亮亮的东西，是什么？

是太阳能[c]板吧？我在美国也看见过。

用太阳能发电，太好了！

要是自行车也能用太阳能发电，那多酷啊！

现在世界上很多国家都有能源危机，如果世界各国都用太阳能和风能，那能节约多少石油和煤啊！而且多……

环保！哈哈……

我听说中国政府规定办公室和公共场所[d]，冬天暖气的温度不能高于[5]摄氏[e]20度，夏天空调的温度不能低于26度。

 哎呀，渴死了，……你們看，一瓶水都喝完了！這兒有垃圾回收筒嗎？空瓶子不能隨便亂扔。

對，我們應該注意環保[b]，垃圾回收筒……，你看，在樹下邊。

我好久沒買瓶裝水了。我們班有的同學建議，為了保護綠色的地球，自己帶水喝，不買瓶裝水。

這個建議不錯。哎，你們看，那邊房子上有些亮亮的東西，是什麼？

是太陽能[c]板吧？我在美國也看見過。

用太陽能發電，太好了！

要是自行車也能用太陽能發電，那多酷啊！

現在世界上很多國家都有能源危機，如果世界各國都用太陽能和風能，那能節約多少石油和煤啊！而且多……

環保！哈哈……

我聽說中國政府規定辦公室和公共場所[d]，冬天暖氣的溫度不能高於[5]攝氏[e]20度，夏天空調的溫度不能低於26度。

这个规定我举双手赞成。你们还记得吗，我们美国学校的教室，冬天穿衬衫还出汗，夏天穿毛衣还冷得不得了。

可不是吗，太浪费了。

我听说现在不少人去餐厅吃饭自己带餐具，不用一次性^f的。

我觉得这个做法很好，要不然每年要砍多少树啊？

除了上餐馆自己带筷子，买东西也得自己带包了。

对，现在中国超市不给塑料袋，要自己买，所以很多人都自己带包，这样一年不知道能减少多少白色污^g染！

还有汽车，不但要用很多能源，而且还对空气造成严重污染。

大家都应该像我们这样，少开车、多骑车、多走路，又环保节能^h、又有益于健康。

对，地球是我们的家，我们应该好好保护它！

這個規定我舉雙手贊成。你們還記得嗎，我們美國學校的教室，冬天穿襯衫還出汗，夏天穿毛衣還冷得不得了。

可不是嗎，太浪費了。

我聽說現在不少人去餐廳吃飯自己帶餐具，不用一次性[f]的。

我覺得這個做法很好，要不然每年要砍多少樹啊？

除了上餐館自己帶筷子，買東西也得自己帶包了。

對，現在中國超市不給塑料袋，要自己買，所以很多人都自己帶包，這樣一年不知道能減少多少白色汙[g]染！

還有汽車，不但要用很多能源，而且還對空氣造成嚴重汙染。

大家都應該像我們這樣，少開車、多騎車、多走路，又環保節能[h]、又有益於健康。

對，地球是我們的家，我們應該好好保護它！

 我们应该从小地方做起，比如随手关灯，节约用水。

好！同意！

哎，你们看，都到了山下了。我们开始爬山吧，看谁先到山上！加油！

Language Notes

a 公交

公交 is abbreviated from 公共交通.

b 环保/環保

环保/環保 is abbreviated from 环境保护/環境保護.

c 太阳能/太陽能

能 here is short for 能量, meaning "energy" or "power." 能量 is often abbreviated and attached to another word indicating the source of energy, e.g., 太阳能/太陽能 (solar power), 电能/電能 (electric power), 风能/風能 (wind power), and 水能 (hydraulic power).

d 场所/場所 vs. 地方

场所/場所 refers to indoor or outdoor places for specific activities or purposes and generally requires a modifier, e.g. 办公场所/辦公場所, 休息场所/休息場所, etc. By contrast, 地方 can be used on its own and can also refer to a part or aspect of someone or something, e.g. 我们有很多地方不一样/我們有很多地方不一樣 (We differ in many respects).

e 摄氏/攝氏

摄氏/攝氏 is the term for Celsius. Fahrenheit is 华氏/華氏 (Huáshì). The word 氏, meaning "surname,"

is often attached to the family name of a famous person or expert, here the abbreviated family names of the astronomer Anders Celsius (1701–1744) and the physicist Daniel Gabriel Fahrenheit (1686–1736), respectively. As a Chinese family name, 华/華 is usually pronounced in the falling tone (Huà).

f 一次性

Here, 一次性 refers to things that are discarded after being used only once—that is, "disposable" objects.

g 污 vs. 汙

污 is the standard simplified form and is also frequently seen in Taiwan. Although 汙 is the official traditional form, Taiwanese newspapers use 污 instead of 汙 by a wide margin.

h 节能/節能

节能/節能 is abbreviated from 节约能源/節約能源.

i 比如 vs. 比方说/比方說

These are synonymous. 比如 is more literary than 比方说/比方說.

j 都…了

都…了, like 已经…了/已經…了, means "already."

我們應該從小地方做起，比如隨手關燈，節約用水。

好！同意！

哎，你們看，都到了山下了。我們開始爬山吧，看誰先到山上！加油！

After You Study

Answer the following questions in Chinese.

1 怎麼樣才能減少垃圾，減少白色汙染？

2 政府應該怎麼做來節約能源，保護環境？

3 老百姓應該從哪些小地方做起來節約能源，保護環境？

View & Explore

For deeper language immersion and more cultural information, watch "Protecting the Environment," a short, supplemental video clip by Cheng & Tsui on this lesson's theme.

Video

Vocabulary

Audio

Flashcards

No.	Simplified	Traditional	Pinyin	Part of Speech	Definition
1	保护	保護	bǎohù	v	to protect, to safeguard
2	节约	節約	jiéyuē	v	to economize, to save, to conserve
3	能源	能源	néngyuán	n	energy, energy source
4	爬山	爬山	pá shān	vo	to hike in the mountains, to climb a mountain
5	有益	有益	yǒuyì	adj	beneficial, useful [See Grammar 4.]
6	于	於	yú	prep	towards, in, on, at, (indicating comparison) [See Grammar 4 and Grammar 5.]
7	段	段	duàn	m	(measure word for section, segment, or part)
8	推	推	tuī	v	to push, to shove
9	空气	空氣	kōngqì	n	air, atmosphere
10	雾霾	霧霾	wùmái	n	smog
11	回收	回收	huíshōu	v	to recycle
12	筒	筒	tǒng	n	thick tube-shaped container
13	扔	扔	rēng	v	to throw, to toss, to throw away
14	瓶装水	瓶裝水	píngzhuāng shuǐ	n	bottled water
15	地球	地球	dìqiú	n	the earth, the globe
16	亮	亮	liàng	adj	bright, light
17	太阳	太陽	tàiyáng	n	sun
18	太阳能	太陽能	tàiyángnéng	n	solar energy, solar power
19	板	板	bǎn	n	board, plank, panel
20	发电	發電	fā diàn	vo	to generate electricity
21	国家	國家	guójiā	n	country, nation

No.	Simplified	Traditional	Pinyin	Part of Speech	Definition
22	危机	危機	*wēijī*	n	crisis
23	风	風	*fēng*	n	wind
24	石油	石油	*shíyóu*	n	petroleum, oil
25	煤	煤	*méi*	n	coal
26	规定	規定	*guīdìng*	v/n	to regulate, to specify; rules and regulations, provisions
27	公共场所	公共場所	*gōnggòng chǎngsuǒ*	n	public place or space
28	暖气	暖氣	*nuǎnqì*	n	heating (lit. warm air)
29	温度	溫度	*wēndù*	n	temperature
30	度	度	*dù*	m	(measure word for degrees of temperature, heat, hardness, humidity, etc.)
31	赞成	贊成	*zànchéng*	v	to approve, to support
32	出汗	出汗	*chū hàn*	vo	to sweat
33	餐具	餐具	*cānjù*	n	eating utensil, tableware
34	一次性	一次性	*yícìxìng*	adj	one-time

柯林他们觉得骑自行车又节能又环保，你在生活中怎么节能环保？

柯林他們覺得騎自行車又節能又環保，你在生活中怎麼節能環保？

GET Real WITH CHINESE

轻 轻 的 您 来 了,
也 请 您 轻 轻 的 将 垃 圾 带 走,
保 护 湖 泊 人 人 有 责。

武昌区水务局宣

No.	Simplified	Traditional	Pinyin	Part of Speech	Definition
35	砍	砍	*kǎn*	v	to cut, to chop
36	超市	超市	*chāoshì*	n	supermarket (short for 超级市场/超級市場)
37	塑料袋	塑料袋	*sùliào dài*	n	plastic bag
38	减少	減少	*jiǎnshǎo*	v	to reduce, to decrease, to lessen
39	污染	汙染	*wūrǎn*	v/n	to pollute, to contaminate; pollution, contamination
40	造成	造成	*zào chéng*	vc	to cause, to give rise to
41	比如	比如	*bǐrú*	v	for example
42	随手	隨手	*suíshǒu*	adv	without extra effort or motion, conveniently
43	加油	加油	*jiā yóu*	vo	to make an extra effort, to work harder, to refuel
44	马克	馬克	*Mǎkè*	pn	Mark
45	摄氏	攝氏	*Shèshì*	pn	Celsius, centigrade

Grammar

<u>1</u> | **Verb 1 的 verb 1, verb 2 的 verb 2**

Take a closer look at this sentence from the Text of this lesson:

A 他们每天上课的上课，找工作的找工作，半个月
没见面了。

他們每天上課的上課，找工作的找工作，半個月
沒見面了。

Every day, some of them are taking classes and some of them are looking for jobs.
They haven't seen each other for half a month.

Here, the 上课的/上课的 in 上课的上课/上课的上课 acts like a noun. Similarly,
the 找工作的 in 找工作的找工作 also acts like a noun. This structure is used to
imply that everyone is occupied doing his/her own thing; no one is idle.

B 下班了，人们回家的回家，约朋友吃饭的约朋友
吃饭，办公室很快就没有人了。

下班了，人們回家的回家，約朋友吃飯的約朋友
吃飯，辦公室很快就沒有人了。

After work, some went home, and some made plans to eat out with friends. The office
emptied out quickly.

C 运动场上学生们踢球的踢球，跑步的跑步，都在
锻炼身体。

運動場上學生們踢球的踢球，跑步的跑步，都在
鍛鍊身體。

On the athletic field, some students are playing soccer and some are jogging. They're
all working out.

171

D 硬卧车厢里，旅客聊天儿的聊天儿，唱歌的唱歌，热闹极了。

硬臥車廂裡，旅客聊天兒的聊天兒，唱歌的唱歌，熱鬧極了。

In the hard-sleeper car, some passengers are chatting and some are singing. It's extremely lively.

2 | Adjective reduplication (II)

As we learned in IC2, adjectives can be reduplicated in the form XXYY: so, the reduplicated form of the adjective 轻松/輕鬆 is 轻轻松松/輕輕鬆鬆. [See Grammar 6, L12, IC2.] This kind of reduplication has a heightening effect:

A 这次考试不难，她轻轻松松地就考了100分。

這次考試不難，她輕輕鬆鬆地就考了100分。

This time, the exam wasn't difficult. She coasted along and easily scored one hundred.

[轻轻松松/輕輕鬆鬆 = 很轻松/很輕鬆]

This lesson introduces another kind of adjective reduplication. Namely, adjectives like 轻松/輕鬆 can be reduplicated, like verbs, in XYXY form. XYXY reduplication is used to indicate that someone wants to do something to realize the state indicated by the adjective.

B 今天是星期六，大家都想轻松轻松。

今天是星期六，大家都想輕鬆輕鬆。

Today is Saturday. Everyone wants to relax a little.

[Here, 轻松轻松/輕鬆輕鬆 indicates that everyone wants to do something in order to realize the state of being 轻松/輕鬆.]

轻松轻松/輕鬆輕鬆 in the above example means "to have some fun" or "do whatever to make one feel more relaxed."

C

洗个澡，舒服舒服。

洗個澡，舒服舒服。

Take a bath/shower to unwind.

(Here, 舒服舒服 indicates a desire to do something (i.e., take a bath/shower) in order to feel comfortable.)

D

爷爷今年过八十岁生日，我们应该好好儿地热闹热闹。

爺爺今年過八十歲生日，我們應該好好兒地熱鬧熱鬧。

This year is Grandpa's eightieth birthday. We should have a big celebration and have a great time.

(热闹热闹/熱鬧熱鬧 indicates going out of one's way to make the celebration a lively, festive occasion.)

A reduplicated adjective in this form is sometimes preceded by the verb 让/讓 or 叫:

E

你把这个好消息告诉他，让他高兴高兴。

你把這個好消息告訴他，讓他高興高興。

Tell him the good news to cheer him up.

(让他高兴高兴/讓他高興高興 indicates that the person wants to make someone else happy.)

3 | Suggesting multiple alternatives with ⋯吧，⋯吧

This construction is usually found in spoken Chinese. It is used to indicate that the speaker is in a dilemma and unable to make a decision among the alternatives.

A

可是怎么去呢？坐出租车吧，太贵，而且也没意思；坐公交车吧，人太多，太挤。

可是怎麼去呢？坐出租車吧，太貴，而且也沒意思；坐公交車吧，人太多，太擠。

But how should they get there? Taking a cab would be too expensive, and boring, too. Public transportation has too many people, and is too crowded.

B

我的车旧了，最近老有问题。买新的吧，没有钱，
不买新的吧，旧车又不可靠，真难办。

我的車舊了，最近老有問題。買新的吧，沒有錢，
不買新的吧，舊車又不可靠，真難辦。

My car is old, and lately it's had many problems. I could buy a new one, but I don't
have the money. I could keep the old one, but it's not reliable. I don't know what to do.

C

Q: 你说住在城里好，还是住在城外好？

你說住在城裡好，還是住在城外好？

Do you think it's better to live in or outside the city?

A: 很难说。住在城里吧，上、下班，购物都很方便，
可是空气不太好；住在城外吧，环境好，空气新
鲜，但做什么都不太方便。

很難說。住在城裡吧，上、下班，購物都很方便，
可是空氣不太好；住在城外吧，環境好，空氣新
鮮，但做什麼都不太方便。

It's hard to say. If you live in the city, commuting and shopping are convenient, but
the air quality is not so good. If you live outside the city, the environment is good
and the air is fresh, but it's quite inconvenient to do anything.

D

他女朋友的妹妹明天过生日，有个生日晚会。他想，
去吧，没有钱买礼物；不去吧，又怕女朋友生气。
怎么办呢？

他女朋友的妹妹明天過生日，有個生日晚會。他想，
去吧，沒有錢買禮物；不去吧，又怕女朋友生氣。
怎麼辦呢？

Tomorrow is his girlfriend's younger sister's birthday. There will be a birthday party in
the evening. He thinks if he goes, he won't have the money to buy a present; but if he
doesn't go, he's afraid that his girlfriend will be angry. What should he do?

4 ｜ （有益）于/（有益）於

The preposition 于/於 is generally used in formal Chinese, often after a verb. 于/於 has many meanings. In 有益于/有益於, 于/於 means 对/對 (to). 有益于/有益於 has the same meaning as 对…有好处/對…有好處 (It's good or beneficial to …).

A　大家觉得骑自行车又能锻炼身体，又省钱，而且有益于环境保护。

大家覺得騎自行車又能鍛煉身體，又省錢，而且有益於環境保護。

Everybody feels that biking is good exercise and saves money. Furthermore, it helps to protect the environment.

B　多听录音，有益于中文学习。

多聽錄音，有益於中文學習。

Listening to recordings more is beneficial for learning Chinese.

C　多听别人意见，有益于与人相处。

多聽別人意見，有益於與人相處。

Listening to others more is helpful for getting along with people.

D　体育运动有益于身体健康。

體育運動有益於身體健康。

Sports are good for your health.

Adjective + 于/於

Used after an adjective, 于/於 has the same meaning as 比. 高于 X/高於 X is synonymous with 比 X 高. Similarly, 低于 X/低於 X has the same meaning as 比 X 低.

A

今天的温度低于昨天。

今天的溫度低於昨天。

Today's temperature is lower than yesterday's.

or in other words:

今天的温度比昨天低。

今天的溫度比昨天低。

B

四大于三。

四大於三。

Four is greater than three.

or in other words:

四比三大。

四比三大。

C

那个国家水贵于油。

那個國家水貴於油。

In that country, water is more expensive than oil.

or in other words:

那个国家的水比油贵。

那個國家的水比油貴。

Words & Phrases

A | 想出（来）/想出（來） (to come up with)
vs. 想起（来）/想起（來） (to recall)

想出来/想出來 means "to come up with (a new way, method, name, etc.)." 想起来/想起來 means "to recall (something that has been forgotten)."

1 Q: 你的孩子快出生了，叫什么名字，你想出来了吗？

你的孩子快出生了，叫什麼名字，你想出來了嗎？

Your child will be born soon. Have you come up with a name yet?

A: 我们给孩子想出来一个很好听的名字。

我們給孩子想出來一個很好聽的名字。

Yes, we've come up with a very nice-sounding name for the child.

2 这件事虽然很麻烦，但是他想来想去，还是想出来一个解决的办法。

這件事雖然很麻煩，但是他想來想去，還是想出來一個解決的辦法。

Although this problem is very complicated, he dwelled on it for a long time and came up with a way to solve it.

3 这个人我十年前见过，他叫什么名字我想不起来了。

這個人我十年前見過，他叫什麼名字我想不起來了。

I met this person ten years ago. I can't remember his name.

4 Q: 你知道小区健身房在哪儿吗？

你知道小區健身房在哪兒嗎？

Do you know where the community gym is?

A: 我去过，可是忘了……我想起来了，就在老人活动中心旁边。

我去過，可是忘了……我想起來了，就在老人活動中心旁邊。

I've been there, but I've forgotten . . . I remember now. It's next to the senior center.

B ┃ ## Four-character phrases

When a two-syllable abstract verb and a two-syllable abstract noun are combined to form a four-character phrase in formal speech and writing, the noun usually comes before the verb (e.g. 环境保护/環境保護. This is especially true when the phrase functions as the subject, object, or attributive in a sentence.

1 能源管理是大问题。

能源管理是大問題。

Energy management is a big problem. *[能源管理 as a subject]*

2 ……有益于环境保护

……有益於環境保護

. . . beneficial for environmental protection *[环境保护/環境保護 as an object]*

3 注意垃圾回收工作

注意垃圾回收工作

to pay attention to the work on garbage recycling *[垃圾回收 as an attributive]*

可不是吗/可不是嗎 (Isn't that so? How true!)

可不是吗/可不是嗎 is used to second someone's opinion. It is used in spoken Chinese. 吗/嗎 is optional.

1 Person A　雪梅的舅舅和舅妈结婚以来，生活一直很幸福。
　　　　　　　雪梅的舅舅和舅媽結婚以來，生活一直很幸福。

　　　　　　　Xuemei's uncle and aunt have always had a happy marriage.

　　Person B　可不是吗，他们从来没吵过架。
　　　　　　　可不是嗎，他們從來沒吵過架。

　　　　　　　That's so true. They've never argued with each other.

2 Person A　最近能源危机越来越严重。
　　　　　　　最近能源危機越來越嚴重。

　　　　　　　The energy crisis has been getting even worse recently.

　　Person B　可不是吗？我们每个人都应该尽可能节约能源。从小地方做起，比如随手关灯、节约用水、少开车等等。
　　　　　　　可不是嗎？我們每個人都應該儘可能節約能源。從小地方做起，比如隨手關燈、節約用水、少開車等等。

　　　　　　　How true! We should all do our best to save energy, starting with small things like turning off the lights on the way out, conserving water, driving less, and so on.

3 Person A　这两天热得不得了。
　　　　　　　這兩天熱得不得了。

　　　　　　　It's been unbearably hot the last couple of days.

　　Person B　可不是，非开空调不可。
　　　　　　　可不是，非開空調不可。

　　　　　　　So true. You can't do without turning on the air conditioner.

造成 (to cause, to give rise to)

造成 is a verb. The object of 造成 is usually a two-syllable noun denoting an undesirable or unfavorable result.

1

汽车要用很多能源，而且还对空气造成严重污染。

汽車要用很多能源，而且還對空氣造成嚴重汙染。

Automobiles consume a lot of energy and cause severe pollution to the atmosphere.

2

他的政治学教授这个学期上课常常迟到，造成很坏的影响。

他的政治學教授這個學期上課常常遲到，造成很壞的影響。

His political science professor has frequently been late to class this semester, which has had a very negative impact.

3

坏影响已经造成了，你只能好好儿表现，让大家慢慢忘了吧。

壞影響已經造成了，你只能好好兒表現，讓大家慢慢忘了吧。

The damage has already been done. All you can do is be on your best behavior and let everyone slowly forget about it.

Characterize it!

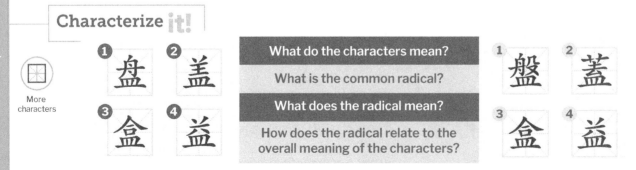

More characters

❶ 盘　❷ 盖
❸ 盒　❹ 益

What do the characters mean?
What is the common radical?
What does the radical mean?
How does the radical relate to the overall meaning of the characters?

❶ 盤　❷ 蓋
❸ 盒　❹ 益

从⋯做起/從⋯做起 (to start with)

从⋯做起/從⋯做起 means "to start with." 起/起 means "to begin."

1

节约大家应该从小地方做起。

節約大家應該從小地方做起。

Conservation begins with our doing small things.

2

保护环境应该从节约能源做起。

保護環境應該從節約能源做起。

Protecting the environment should start with energy conservation.

3

男女平等应该从日常生活、从每个家庭做起。

男女平等應該從日常生活、從每個家庭做起。

Equality between men and women should begin with the everyday life of every family.

A WAY WITH WORDS

回收

我的童年生活非常快乐，让人回味。

三十年前的上海和今天的上海很不一样。让我们回顾一下上海这三十年的变化。

Using the word/phrase in orange as a clue, try to figure out the meaning of the words/phrases in blue; consult a dictionary if necessary. Consider how the literal and extended senses are related in each case.

回收

我的童年生活非常快樂，讓人回味。

三十年前的上海和今天的上海很不一樣。讓我們回顧一下上海這三十年的變化。

Language Practice

A   **A busy scene**   PRESENTATIONAL

In pairs, imagine what these locations look like when busy, e.g.:

医院里，看病的看病，拿药的拿药。

醫院裡，看病的看病，拿藥的拿藥。

1   2   3   4

B   **Tough to say**   PRESENTATIONAL

Little Lin sees pros and cons in everything and never gives straightforward advice. In pairs, take turns role-playing Little Lin and Little Lin's advice-seeking friend. The advice-seeking friend should ask a question based on the prompt; in response, Little Lin should present two equally viable options by using ⋯吧，⋯吧, e.g.:

旅行　参加旅行团/參加旅行團　自助游/自助遊

Q: 你觉得出去旅行，参加旅行团好还是自助游好？

你覺得出去旅行，參加旅行團好還是自助遊好？

A: 参加旅行团吧，由导游安排管理，不必担心，但没有那么自由；自助游吧，很自由，但什么都由自己安排，有点儿麻烦。哪个好，很难说，要看自己的情况。

參加旅行團吧，由導遊安排管理，不必擔心，但沒有那麼自由；自助遊吧，很自由，但什麼都由自己安排，有點兒麻煩。哪個好，很難說，要看自己的情況。

1	大一新生 住校內	住校內	住校外
2	大学毕业以后 大學畢業以後	工作	念研究生
3	查资料 查資料	上网查 上網查	去图书馆查 去圖書館查
4	过春节 過春節	待在家里 待在家裡	出去旅游 出去旅遊

C

Back to nature

INTERPERSONAL

In pairs, ask each other what you do to get close to nature and relax on weekends. Answer the question based on the prompts below.

你周末怎么接近大自然放松放松?

你週末怎麼接近大自然放鬆放鬆？

1

2

3

4

You're writing a children's book about the quest to find an amazingly beautiful but imaginary place. For an interesting challenge, you've decided to write the book in Chinese. First, connect each of these features with the adjective that fits best.

1 山　　　　　　　　　　　　美

2 树/樹　　　　　　　　　　新鲜/新鮮

3 河水　　　　　　　　　　　少

4 风景/風景　　　　　　　　安静/安靜

5 地　　　　　　　　　　　　高

6 人和车/人和車　　　　　　干净/乾淨

7 空气/空氣　　　　　　　　大

8 环境/環境　　　　　　　　绿/綠

Then, describe what you hope that imaginary place looks like:

我希望这个地方⋯⋯

我希望這個地方⋯⋯

A WAY WITH WORDS

随手

他的建议我们还没有讨论，你怎么就随口同意了呢？

你要是有问题，可以随时给我发微信。

Using the word/phrase in orange as a clue, try to figure out the meaning of the words/phrases in blue; consult a dictionary if necessary. Consider how the literal and extended senses are related in each case.

隨手

他的建議我們還沒有討論，你怎麼就隨口同意了呢？

你要是有問題，可以隨時給我發微信。

| INTERPERSONAL | **Go green!** | PRESENTATIONAL |

1 First, ask three classmates what energy sources their country/state/province uses to generate electricity, and list their answers in the table. Make sure that each energy source is listed in the appropriate column.

同学 同學	传统能源 傳統能源	绿色能源 綠色能源
_____	_____	_____
_____	_____	_____
_____	_____	_____

2 Then, report to your class the traditional or green energy sources that your classmates indicated are used in their home countries/states/provinces, e.g.:

Mike 的国家（或者州、省）用_____来发电。

Mike 的國家（或者州、省）用_____來發電。

_____

_____

_____

3 What else can government do to reduce pollution?

政府还可以做什么来减少污染？

政府還可以做什麼來減少汙染？

4 Finally, as a class, discuss the advantages and disadvantages of each energy source.

Do your part

First, ask your partner what kinds of pollution could result from these activities:

开汽车/開汽車

用很多洗衣粉

用塑料袋

Q: 开汽车会造成什么污染？
开汽車會造成什麼汙染？

A: 开汽车会造成空气污染。
開汽車會造成空氣汙染。

Then, ask what he/she could do to reduce air pollution, water pollution, and plastic waste, e.g.:

Q: 你怎么减少空气污染？
你怎麼減少空氣汙染?

Finally, based on the prompts, explain what you do or don't do to help the environment, e.g.:

我用节能冰箱。
我用節能冰箱。

1 ✓

2 ✓

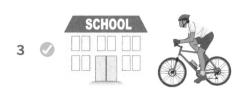

3 ✓

4 ✗

5 ✗

Plastic Bag

Become a conservation advocate

In pairs, prepare a brief oral presentation to promote conservation in daily life. Encourage people to start with the small things and feel free to add other ways to help conserve resources.

节约能源，从小地方做起/節約能源，從小地方做起：

1 _____

2 _____

3 _____

4 _____

5 _____

6 _____

Chinese Chat

A friend is chatting with you on HipChat about an upcoming hiking trip. What suggestions would you give to make the trip more environmentally friendly?

Aisha Rollins:
周末去爬山，我带些吃的和瓶装水，你带些一次性餐具吧。

You:
...

Aisha Rollins:
好，听你的！对了，我们坐公交车还是骑车到山下？

You:
...

9:48 PM   85%

● Aisha Rollins

Aisha Rollins 9:41 PM
週末去爬山，我帶些吃的和瓶裝水，你帶些一次性餐具吧。

You 9:42 PM
...

Aisha Rollins 9:44 PM
好，聽你的！對了，我們坐公交車還是騎車到山下？

You 9:45 PM
...

Send

Green Initiatives

With rising public consciousness, China has adopted a slate of policies to mitigate the ecological impact of development. In particular, reducing China's reliance on fossil fuels has become a major concern. Although coal remains the largest source of energy in China as well as a major source of air pollution, China is investing heavily in green energy, particularly solar and wind power. China is already a major exporter of solar panels and is a world leader in renewable energy production, with the largest installed capacity of hydroelectric, wind, and solar power facilities. This can be seen from the vast wind farms in Inner Mongolia, Xinjiang, and Gansu to the compact solar-powered water heaters on the roofs of many residential buildings. To tighten regulatory loopholes, China passed legislation in 2016 to implement a comprehensive environmental tax beginning in 2018. To combat global warming, the government started the world's largest carbon trading market in 2017, using a scheme known as cap-and-trade to encourage companies to cut emissions.

Not all policies have been at the macro level. In June 2008, the Chinese government banned the production, sale, and use of "super-thin" (less than 0.025 millimeter) plastic shopping bags. Supermarkets and shopping centers can no longer give away free plastic bags. Instead, shoppers have to purchase them or bring their own shopping bags. This effort has significantly cut down on plastic pollution, also known as "white pollution," or 白色污染/白色汙染.

Endangered Species

As a biodiverse but rapidly developing country, China is home to many endangered and vulnerable species, such as the giant panda (大熊猫/大熊貓). Fortunately, conservation efforts such as those at the Wolong National Nature Reserve (卧龙自然保护区/臥龍自然保護區) have led to an increase in the population of pandas in the wild. Pandas living in captivity attract hundreds of thousands of visitors to conservation centers each year. The relative success story of the giant panda has raised hopes for the protection of other endangered and vulnerable animals in China as well.

Sustainability in Ancient Thought

In Chinese discourses on sustainability, one often hears the warning against "draining the pond to catch the fish" (竭泽而渔/竭澤而漁) (jié zé ér yú). This expression comes from an ancient text called *The Spring and Autumn Annals of Lü [Buwei]* (吕氏春秋/呂氏春秋) (Lǚshì Chūnqiū). In 636 BCE, the capital of the state of Song was besieged by the powerful army of the state of Chu. King Cheng of Song sought help from King Wen of Jin, who in turn asked his uncle, Huyan, for advice. Huyan thought that aiding Song would increase Jin's prestige, and suggested using deception to defeat the superior Chu army. King Wen's minister, Yongji, however, found Huyan's counsel shortsighted and cautioned, "If one drains the pond, one will certainly catch all the fish. However, there will be no more fish to catch next year. If one burns down the forest, one will certainly catch all the prey. However, there will be no more beasts to catch next year. One may get away with chicanery and deception temporarily. However, one cannot repeat it. Therefore, it's not a viable long-term strategy." The phrase 竭泽而渔/竭澤而漁 has become a familiar metaphor for the unsustainable exploitation of natural resources.

COMPARE & CONTRAST

How green is your country? Can you pinpoint the start of environmentalism as a grassroots movement? What citizen initiatives and public policies have resulted in much cleaner air and water? In China as in other countries, some have argued that an emphasis on environmental protection hampers development. Can you find evidence for this view in your country, and how would you argue for or against it?

Lesson Wrap-Up

Project

Find out about environmental initiatives in Chinese-speaking communities by researching recycling programs in Taipei and Shanghai. Consult international media coverage (*New York Times*, *Washington Post*, etc.) and relevant municipal websites and report to the class on the following questions:

- Does Taipei or Shanghai receive high marks on recycling? Why?

- What role did women play in Taiwan's "recycling revolution?"

- Looking at government websites, investigate whether recycling takes on a schedule. Are there specific days on which flat (平面类/平面類) (*píngmiàn lèi*) and bulky (立体类/立體類) (*lìtǐ lèi*) items are recycled? List three examples of each. Use a dictionary if necessary.

- What efforts is Shanghai making to recycle the city's garbage? How successful are they?

- How does Shanghai's "green account" system work? What kinds of products can you redeem with your "green points" on the city government's website?

Keep It Flowing

Study the following example; pay particular attention to how the highlighted parts help the sentences flow smoothly from one to the next. Notice how:

- pronouns (他们/他們) replace nouns in subsequent sentences (张天明/張天明, 丽莎/麗莎, 柯林和林雪梅)
- time expressions (上个周末/上個週末) serve as connective devices
- certain prepositions (为了/為了) introduce purposes (环保/環保)
- certain adverbs (也, 还/還, 而是) suggest similarity, addition, or contrast

张天明他们很注意环保

张天明、丽莎、柯林和林雪梅都很注意环保。他们上个周末去爬山，为了环保，没有坐出租车，也没坐公共汽车，而是骑自行车。他们不乱扔空瓶子，而是把它们扔进树下的垃圾回收筒里。他们也同意不买瓶装水的建议，还希望全世界都能多用太阳能和风能发电。

張天明他們很注意環保

　　張天明、麗莎、柯林和林雪梅都很注意環保。他們上個週末去爬山，為了環保，沒有坐出租車，也沒坐公共汽車，而是騎自行車。他們不亂扔空瓶子，而是把它們扔進樹下的垃圾回收筒裡。他們也同意不買瓶裝水的建議，還希望全世界都能多用太陽能和風能發電。

What do you do to protect the environment? Use as many of the cohesive devices highlighted in the example on the previous page/above as possible to string together a response, based on the prompts.

○ 你以前注意环保吗？现在呢？

你以前注意環保嗎？現在呢？

○ 为了环保，你注意做这些事情吗：吃饭自己带餐具、不买瓶装水、不随便扔垃圾？

為了環保，你注意做這些事情嗎：吃飯自己帶餐具、不買瓶裝水、不隨便扔垃圾？

○ 你对用太阳能和风能发电有什么看法？

你對用太陽能和風能發電有什麼看法？

Can-Do Check List ✓

I can

Before proceeding to Lesson 17, make sure you can complete the following tasks in Chinese:

☐ Describe how to get close to and relax in nature
☐ Talk about indicators of a clean environment
☐ Discuss green and renewable energy
☐ Explain what government can do to reduce pollution
☐ Identify what individuals can do to protect the environment

Zhāng Tiānmíng tāmen sì ge rén lái Běijīng yǐjīng liǎng sān ge yuè le, tiānqì yě zhújiàn nuǎnhuo le. Tāmen měi tiān shàng kè de shàng kè[1], zhǎo gōngzuò de zhǎo gōngzuò, bàn ge yuè méi jiàn miàn le. Jīntiān shì xīngqīliù, dàjiā dōu xiǎng qīngsong qīngsong[2], Tiānmíng jiànyì qù pá shān, Lìshā hé Xuěméi bù fǎnduì, Kē Lín yě juéde zhè ge jiànyì búcuò, tā shuō zhènghǎo tā de Déguó péngyou Mǎkè yě xiǎng qù.

Kěshì zěnme qù ne? Zuò chūzūchē ba, tài guì, érqiě yě méi yìsi; zuò gōngjiāo[a] chē ba[3], rén tài duō, tài jǐ. Kē Lín xiǎng chu le yí ge zhǔyi, qí zìxíngchē! Dàjiā mǎshàng jiù tóngyì le, juéde qí zìxíngchē yòu néng duànliàn shēntǐ, yòu shěng qián, érqiě yǒuyì yú[4] huánjìng bǎohù.

Tāmen zǎoshang hěn zǎo jiù chūfā le. Qí le hěn cháng de yí duàn lù yǐhòu, yǒu diǎn rè, yě yǒu diǎn lèi, jiù xià le chē, yìbiān tuī zhe chē, yìbiān liáo le qǐ lai.

Zhèr de kōngqì bǐ chéng li hǎo, wùmái yě méiyǒu nàme yánzhòng.

Dàochù dōu shì lǜsè, kàn zhe zhēn shūfu!

Āiyā, kě sǐ le, . . . Nǐmen kàn, yì píng shuǐ dōu hē wán le! Zhèr yǒu lājī huíshōu tǒng ma? Kōng píngzi bù néng suíbiàn luàn rēng.

Duì, wǒmen yīnggāi zhùyì huánbǎo[b]. Lājī huíshōu tǒng . . . , nǐ kàn, zài shù xiàbian.

Wǒ hǎo jiǔ méi mǎi píngzhuāng shuǐ le. Wǒmen bān yǒude tóngxué jiànyì, wèile bǎohù lǜsè de dìqiú, zìjǐ dài shuǐ hē, bù mǎi píngzhuāng shuǐ.

Zhè ge jiànyì búcuò. Āi, nǐmen kàn, nà bian fángzi shang yǒu xiē liàng liàng de dōngxi, shì shénme?

Shì tàiyángnéng[c] bǎn ba? Wǒ zài Měiguó yě kàn jian guo.

Yòng tàiyángnéng fā diàn, tài hǎo le!

Yàoshi zìxíngchē yě néng yòng tàiyángnéng fādiàn, nà duō kù a!

Xiànzài shìjiè shang hěn duō guójiā dōu yǒu néngyuán wēijī, rúguǒ shìjiè gè guó dōu yòng tàiyángnéng hé fēngnéng, nà néng jiéyuē duōshao shíyóu hé méi a! Érqiě duō . . .

Huánbǎo! Hā hā . . .

Wǒ tīngshuō Zhōngguó zhōngfǔ guīdìng bàngōngshì hé gōnggòng chǎngsuǒ[d], dōngtiān nuǎnqì de wēndù bù néng gāo yú[5] Shèshì[e] èrshí dù, xiàtiān kōngtiáo de wēndù bù néng dī yú èrshíliù dù.

Zhè ge guīdìng wǒ jǔ shuāng shǒu zànchéng. Nǐmen hái jìde ma, wǒmen Měiguó xuéxiào de jiàoshì, dōngtiān chuān chènshān hái chū hàn, xiàtiān chuān máoyī hái lěng de bù déliǎo.

Kě bu shì ma, tài làngfèi le.

Wǒ tīngshuō xiànzài bù shǎo rén qù cāntīng chī fàn zìjǐ dài cānjù, bú yòng yícìxìng[f] de.

Wǒ juéde zhè ge zuòfǎ hěn hǎo. Yàobùrán měi nián yào kǎn duōshao shù a?

Chúle shàng cānguǎn zìjǐ dài kuàizi, mǎi dōngxi yě děi zìjǐ dài bāo le.

Duì, xiànzài Zhōngguó chāoshì bù gěi sùliào dài, yào zìjǐ mǎi, suǒyǐ hěn duō rén dōu zìjǐ dài bāo, zhèyàng yì nián bù zhīdào néng jiǎnshǎo duōshao báisè wū[g]rǎn!

Hái yǒu qìchē, búdàn yào yòng hěn duō néngyuán, érqiě hái duì kōngqì zàochéng yánzhòng wūrǎn.

Dàjiā dōu yīnggāi xiàng wǒmen zhèyang, shǎo kāi chē, duō qí chē, duō zǒu lù, yòu huánbǎo jiénéng[h], yòu yǒuyì yú jiànkāng.

Duì, dìqiú shì wǒmen de jiā, wǒmen yīnggāi hǎo hāo bǎohù tā!

Wǒmen yīnggāi cóng xiǎo dìfang zuò qǐ, bǐrú[i] suíshǒu guān dēng, jiéyuē yòng shuǐ.

Hǎo! Tóngyì!

Āi, nǐmen kàn, dōu dào le shān xia le[j]. Wǒmen kāishǐ pá shān ba, kàn shéi xiān dào shān shang! Jiā yóu!

理财通

我的交易单

黄金
基金
股票
期货

Daily Unique Sales by Country

stomization

Daily Product Sales by Country

理财与投资

理財與投資

WEALTH MANAGEMENT AND INVESTING

Learning Objectives

Relate and Get Ready

In this lesson, you will learn to:

- Discuss whether you're a saver or a spender
- Identify ways to invest money
- List ways to purchase a big-ticket item
- Describe your spending habits
- Recount in basic terms the ups and downs of the stock market

In your own culture/community:

- How do people perceive saving money?
- Do many people invest in the stock market or real estate?
- Is it more common to get a mortgage or to pay cash when purchasing a house?

课文

Text

Audio

Before You Study

Answer the following questions in Chinese to prepare for the reading.

1 你每个月生活花的是打工挣的钱、学校给的奖学金，还是父母给的零用钱？

2 如果存钱，你去银行存还是在网上存？

3 你计划工作几年以后买房？

When You Study

Listen to the audio recording and scan the text; then answer the following questions in Chinese.

1 很多家庭觉得把钱存在银行里有什么好处、坏处？

2 最近几年，中国人觉得哪些投资不错？

3 姑妈为什么突然想投资股市？

中国老百姓一般都比较节俭，所以不少家庭有存款。改革开放以后，他们中间不少人开始考虑投资理财的问题。最近一些年，中国的房价[a]涨得很快，买房子成为一些人投资的选择。也有人看见别人"炒股[b]"，也炒起股来。还有一些人更愿意把[1]钱花在子女教育上，他们觉得让子女受到最好的教育，将来事业成功、生活幸福，才是最好的投资。

张天明平常不大考虑投资理财的事，今天他表哥跟他在网上聊了半天这个问题，才引起他的思考。他吃完晚饭，就跟丽莎聊了起来。

最近姑妈跟表哥有点儿矛盾，表哥好像有点儿郁闷。

为什么？

姑妈退休前省吃俭用存了一笔钱，要留给孙子孙女上大学用。

表哥还没结婚呢！这钱可能还得存二十年啊。

可不是，表哥也这样说。后来姑妈想出了一个花钱的主意。

什么主意？

表哥不是计划明年结婚吗？姑妈要给表哥的未婚妻买一辆新车，算是结婚礼物。

課文

中國老百姓一般都比較節儉，所以不少家庭有存款。改革開放以後，他們中間不少人開始考慮投資理財的問題。最近一些年，中國的房價[a]漲得很快，買房子成為一些人投資的選擇。也有人看見別人"炒股[b]"，也炒起股來。還有一些人更願意把[1]錢花在子女教育上，他們覺得讓子女受到最好的教育，將來事業成功、生活幸福，才是最好的投資。

張天明平常不大考慮投資理財的事，今天他表哥跟他在網上聊了半天這個問題，才引起他的思考。他吃完晚飯，就跟麗莎聊了起來。

最近姑媽跟表哥有點兒矛盾，表哥好像有點兒鬱悶。

為什麼？

姑媽退休前省吃儉用存了一筆錢，要留給孫子孫女上大學用。

表哥還沒結婚呢！這錢可能還得存二十年啊。

可不是，表哥也這樣說。後來姑媽想出了一個花錢的主意。

什麼主意？

表哥不是計劃明年結婚嗎？姑媽要給表哥的未婚妻買一輛新車，算是結婚禮物。

Before You Study

Answer the following questions in Chinese to prepare for the reading.

1 你每個月生活花的是打工掙的錢、學校給的獎學金，還是父母給的零用錢？

2 如果存錢，你去銀行存還是在網上存？

3 你計劃工作幾年以後買房？

When You Study

Listen to the audio recording and scan the text; then answer the following questions in Chinese.

1 很多家庭覺得把錢存在銀行裡有什麼好處、壞處？

2 最近幾年，中國人覺得哪些投資不錯？

3 姑媽為什麼突然想投資股市？

姑妈真好。

可是表哥他们不同意买车。他们俩上班的地方很近，合用一辆车就行了。他们劝姑妈买房子，说姑妈辛苦了几十年，应该住一套大一些的房子，舒舒服服地享受退休生活。

他们说得太对了！再说，买房子也是一种不错的投资啊。

可是姑妈说她的钱不够买一套房子。我表哥说他可以为姑妈贷款，还给姑妈讲了一个两位老太太[c]买房子的故事。

这个故事我以前也听说过。说的是，有一个老太太存了三十年钱，利息很少，钱增加得很慢，到了老年才买到一套房子，住了进去。另外一个老太太，三十年前就贷款买房子住进去了。比一比，哪个老太太更会生活？

对，表哥就用这个故事说服[d]了姑妈，姑妈最后同意买房子了。

好啊，问题算是解决了。

事情还没完。两个星期前，他们觉得有一套三室一厅两卫的房子不错，原来后天就要去签购房合同了，没想到姑妈的想法突然变了。

怎么了？

姑妈退休以后常跟在一起做义工的朋友们打打[2]麻将，聊聊天儿。前几天姑妈听说有几个姑媽真好。

可是表哥他們不同意買車。他們倆上班的地方很近，合用一輛車就行了。他們勸姑媽買房子，說姑媽辛苦了幾十年，應該住一套大一些的房子，舒舒服服地享受退休生活。

他們說得太對了！再說，買房子也是一種不錯的投資啊。

可是姑媽說她的錢不夠買一套房子。我表哥說他可以為姑媽貸款，還給姑媽講了一個兩位老太太[c]買房子的故事。

這個故事我以前也聽說過。說的是，有一個老太太存了三十年錢，利息很少，錢增加得很慢，到了老年才買到一套房子，住了進去。另外一個老太太，三十年前就貸款買房子住進去了。比一比，哪個老太太更會生活？

對，表哥就用這個故事說服[d]了姑媽，姑媽最後同意買房子了。

好啊，問題算是解決了。

事情還沒完。兩個星期前，他們覺得有一套三室一廳兩衛的房子不錯，原來後天就要去簽購房合同了，沒想到姑媽的想法突然變了。

怎麼了？

姑媽退休以後常跟在一起做義工的朋友們打打[2]麻將，聊聊天兒。前幾天姑媽聽說有幾個

人这两年只要炒股就赚钱[e],所以变主意了,不想买房子了。

她想投资股市[f]?

可不是吗?

可是姑妈不知道炒股有风险吗?跟李文父母一起打太极拳的一位老先生,把房子抵押给银行,然后把钱都买了股票,没想到股市一直跌,不到三个月,赔了一半。

买房子是不是就没有风险呢?

房价太高的时候买房子,当然有风险。

看起来投资真不是一件简单的事,不知道姑妈最后会怎么决定。

View & Explore

Video

For deeper language immersion and more cultural information, watch "Spending Habits," a short, supplemental video clip by Cheng & Tsui on this lesson's theme.

人這兩年只要炒股就賺錢[e]，所以變主意了，不想買房子了。

她想投資股市[f]？

可不是嗎？

可是姑媽不知道炒股有風險嗎？跟李文父母一起打太極拳的一位老先生，把房子抵押給銀行，然後把錢都買了股票，沒想到股市一直跌，不到三個月，賠了一半。

買房子是不是就沒有風險呢？

房價太高的時候買房子，當然有風險。

看起來投資真不是一件簡單的事，不知道姑媽最後會怎麼決定。

After You Study

Answer the following questions in Chinese.

1 中國退休老人怎麼享受退休生活？

2 哪種投資對你最合適？為什麼？

3 有人覺得有錢就該消費，錢花了才是自己的。你的看法呢？

Language Notes

a 房价/房價

房价/房價, meaning "house price," is short for 房子的价格 (jiàgé) / 房子的價格 (jiàgé).

b 炒股

炒股 is a slang expression. 炒 means "to stir fry" or "to sauté," as in 炒菜/炒菜 (to stir-fry a dish) and 炒饭/炒飯 (fried rice). 股 is short for 股票 (stock, share). 炒 is sometimes used in colloquial speech, as in 炒冷饭/炒冷飯 (to rehash an old topic) and 炒鱿鱼/炒鱿魚 (yóuyú, squid) (to fire someone).

c 老太太

In China, traditional respect for the elderly remains important. The word 老 carries no stigma. 老师/老師 is widely used to refer not just to one's teacher but to anyone accomplished in some discipline or field. An elderly female relative in one's immediate family may be referred to as 老太太. The equivalent term for an elderly male relative is 老爷子/老爺子. However, these terms are rarely used as forms of direct address.

d 说服/說服

说服/說服 is pronounced "shuìfú" in Taiwan. When 说/說 means "to say," "to speak," or "to explain," it is pronounced "shuō". When it means "to verbally influence" or "to sway," it is traditionally pronounced "shuì", e.g., 游说/遊說 (yóushuì) (to lobby), 说客/說客 (shuìkè) (lobbyist). 服 means "to convince."

e 赚钱/賺錢

赚钱/賺錢 means to make a profit through a business venture, whereas 挣钱/掙錢 means to earn wages through labor or providing a service.

f 股市

股市, meaning "stock market," is short for 股票市场/股票市場.

Vocabulary

Audio

Flashcards

No.	Simplified	Traditional	Pinyin	Part of Speech	Definition
1	节俭	節儉	jiéjiǎn	adj	thrifty, frugal
2	存款	存款	cúnkuǎn	n/vo	bank savings; to deposit money at a bank
3	投资	投資	tóu zī	vo/n	to invest capital; investment (financial) (lit. to throw or cast capital)
4	理财	理財	lǐcái	vo	to manage wealth
5	涨	漲	zhǎng	v	to rise, to surge, to go up (of water, prices, etc.)
6	炒股	炒股	chǎo gǔ	vo	to flip stocks
7	引起	引起	yǐnqǐ	v	to give rise to, to lead to
8	思考	思考	sīkǎo	v/n	to think deeply, to ponder over; contemplation, cogitation
9	姑妈	姑媽	gūmā	n	aunt (father's sister)
10	矛盾	矛盾	máodùn	n/adj	contradiction, conflict; contradictory, conflicting
11	郁闷	鬱悶	yùmèn	adj	gloomy, depressed
12	省吃俭用	省吃儉用	shěng chī jiǎn yòng		to be frugal (with food and other living expenses)
13	笔	筆	bǐ	m	(measure word for sums of money)
14	孙子	孫子	sūnzi	n	grandson (son's son)
15	孙女	孫女	sūnnü	n	granddaughter (son's daughter)
16	未婚妻	未婚妻	wèihūnqī	n	fiancée
17	算	算	suàn	v	to count as, to be considered as
18	合	合	hé	v	to combine, to join
19	劝	勸	quàn	v	to persuade, to advise, to urge
20	辛苦	辛苦	xīnkǔ	adj/v	hard, strenuous; to work hard

No.	Simplified	Traditional	Pinyin	Part of Speech	Definition
21	享受	享受	*xiǎngshòu*	v/n	to enjoy; enjoyment, pleasure
22	老太太	老太太	*lǎotàitai*	n	elderly lady
23	利息	利息	*lìxī*	n	interest (on invested funds)
24	增加	增加	*zēngjiā*	v	to increase, to add
25	老年	老年	*lǎonián*	n	old age
26	说服	說服	*shuōfú*	v	to persuade, to convince
27	签	簽	*qiān*	v	to sign, to autograph
28	合同	合同	*hétong*	n	agreement, contract
29	想法	想法	*xiǎngfǎ*	n	idea, opinion
30	突然	突然	*tūrán*	adv/adj	suddenly, unexpectedly; sudden, unexpected
31	义工	義工	*yìgōng*	n	volunteer work (lit. righteous work), volunteer
32	麻将	麻將	*májiàng*	n	mahjong
33	赚钱	賺錢	*zhuànqián*	vo	to make a profit
34	股市	股市	*gǔshì*	n	stock market

How About You?

天明的姑妈考虑投资，要么买房，要么炒股。你认为哪种投资风险低些？

天明的姑媽考慮投資，要麼買房，要麼炒股。你認為哪種投資風險低些？

You are studying at a Chinese university over the summer. In the hallway after class, you notice this poster advertising an upcoming presentation. What is the message of the poster? Do you agree with it? Find out what 理 means besides 'to manage.'

你不理财
财不理你

无财可理？岂有此理！
觉得打工挣的钱不多，所以不必理财？正是因为你不理财，所以才变成月光族。

钱信一教授
经济系教学楼201室
星期三下午4:30

GET Real WITH CHINESE

No.	Simplified	Traditional	Pinyin	Part of Speech	Definition
35	风险	風險	*fēngxiǎn*	n	risk, danger, hazard
36	抵押	抵押	*dǐyā*	v	to mortgage
37	股票	股票	*gǔpiào*	n	stock, share (lit. stock certificate)
38	跌	跌	*diē*	v	to fall
39	赔	賠	*péi*	v	to lose (money, etc.), to suffer a loss in a deal

Grammar

---

1   Review of the 把 construction (I)

As you will recall from IC2, it is best to use the 把 construction to describe what someone has done to something, if that something is known to the listener. [See Grammar 4, Lesson 15, and Grammar 2, Lesson 20, IC2.]

A   把你在云南买的纪念品给我们看看。

         把你在雲南買的紀念品給我們看看。

         Would you show us the souvenirs that you bought in Yunnan?

B   Q: 你新买的被子呢？怎么不用？

         你新買的被子呢？怎麼不用？

         What happened to the comforters you just bought? Why aren't you using them?

     A: 我把它们送给我表哥了，算是给他和他未婚妻的结婚礼物。

         我把它們送給我表哥了，算是給他和他未婚妻的結婚禮物。

         I gave them to my cousin and his fiancée as a wedding gift.

C   房间里空气太不好了，把窗户打开吧。

         房間裡空氣太不好了，把窗戶打開吧。

         The air in the room is really bad. Why don't you open the windows?

The 把 construction takes the following form:

> **Subject + 把 + noun + verb + another element (complement, reduplicated verb, etc.)**

把 is a preposition. In a typical 把 sentence, the noun after 把 is not only the object of 把, but also the object of the verb. In (A), 纪念品/紀念品 is the object of both 把 and 看. In (B), 它们/它們 is the object of both 把 and 送. In (C), 窗户/窗戶 is the object of both 把 and 开/開.

203

Note the following when using the 把 structure.

First, the object of 把 must be known or at least recognizable to the listener. If you suddenly say to someone:

D Person A 你把杂志给我。

你把雜誌給我。

Give me the magazine.

That person may get confused if the magazine was not mentioned or defined previously, and ask:

Person B: 什么杂志？

什麼雜誌？

What magazine?

Second, the verb in a 把 sentence is usually followed by a complement indicating a result or some other element. This is because such sentences usually describe how an object is impacted as a result of someone's action. (E), (F), and (G) are examples of 把 sentences with complements after the verb:

E 大雨把花打下来了。

大雨把花打下來了。

The heavy rain knocked down the flowers.

F 请把这封信拿给老师。

請把這封信拿給老師。

Please give this letter to the teacher.

[Your giving will cause the letter to be in the teacher's possession.]

G 昨天的剩菜把我的肚子吃坏了。

昨天的剩菜把我的肚子吃壞了。

The leftovers from yesterday upset my stomach.

It is also common for other elements to follow the verb in 把 sentences. 了 following a verb, for instance, can sometimes mean "to disappear," as in (H) and (I):

H

小明，把桌子上的药吃了。

小明，把桌子上的藥吃了。

Xiaoming, take the medicine on the table.

I

妈妈担心我会把信用卡丢了。

媽媽擔心我會把信用卡丢了。

My mother worries I'll lose my credit card.

[Here, 了 conveys a result, namely, loss.]

In addition, the verb in a 把 sentence can also appear in reduplicated form, as in (J) and (K):

J

请你把刚买回来的月饼给我尝尝。

請你把剛買回來的月餅給我嚐嚐。

Please let me try the moon cakes that you've just bought.

K

他把那个合同看了看，又放下了。

他把那個合同看了看，又放下了。

He took a look at the contract and put it down.

To sum up, when using the 把 construction, be sure to include a complement or some other element after the verb. See L20 for more on the 把 construction.

A WAY WITH WORDS

投资

在美国十八岁就能投票。

他昨天晚上很晚才到，找不到旅馆了，只好去朋友家投宿。

Using the word/phrase in orange as a clue, try to figure out the meaning of the words/phrases in blue; consult a dictionary if necessary. Consider how the literal and extended senses are related in each case.

投資

在美國十八歲就能投票。

他昨天晚上很晚才到，找不到旅館了，只好去朋友家投宿。

Verb reduplication (II)

In Grammar 6, Lesson 13, IC2, we studied how a reduplicated verb can make the tone of a sentence milder, as in (A) and (B):

A

请你谈谈应该怎样理财。

請你談談應該怎樣理財。

Can you please talk a bit on how to manage wealth?

B

你看看这本书，写的是环境保护方面的事情，写得非常好。

你看看這本書，寫的是環境保護方面的事情，寫得非常好。

Take a look at this book. It's about environmental protection, and it's very well written.

Both (A) and (B) feature imperative sentences with actions (谈谈/談談, 看看) that are yet to happen.

The Text in this lesson introduces a different kind of reduplicated verb, shown in (C):

C

姑妈退休以后常跟在一起做义工的朋友们打打麻将，聊聊天儿。

姑媽退休以後常跟在一起做義工的朋友們打打麻將，聊聊天兒。

Since she retired, [Tianming's] aunt often plays mahjong and chats with her volunteer friends.

Here, the reduplicated verbs aren't time-specific, as they are in (A) and (B)—rather, they indicate actions that occur frequently. Reduplicated verbs of this kind usually appear in pairs or threes, and often suggest a sense of leisure and casualness.

D

Q: 你周末都做些什么？

你週末都做些什麼？

What do you do on weekends?

A: 要么上网聊聊天儿，要么打打球，一般不学习。

要麼上網聊聊天兒，要麼打打球，一般不學習。

I either chat online [with friends] or play ball for a bit. I don't usually study.

E

老人们每天早晨跳跳舞、打打拳、散散步，挺高兴。

老人們每天早晨跳跳舞、打打拳、散散步、挺高興。

Every morning the elderly people have a pleasant time dancing, practicing tai chi, or walking. They're quite happy.

Chinese Chat

A friend is texting you on Facebook Messenger about her investment plan. How would you reply?

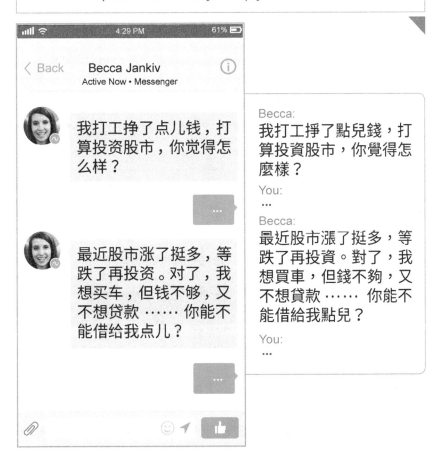

4:29 PM   61%

‹ Back   Becca Jankiv   ⓘ
Active Now • Messenger

我打工挣了点儿钱，打算投资股市，你觉得怎么样？

...

最近股市涨了挺多，等跌了再投资。对了，我想买车，但钱不够，又不想贷款 …… 你能不能借给我点儿？

...

Becca:
我打工掙了點兒錢，打算投資股市，你覺得怎麼樣？

You:
…

Becca:
最近股市漲了挺多，等跌了再投資。對了，我想買車，但錢不夠，又不想貸款 …… 你能不能借給我點兒？

You:
…

Words & Phrases

A

引起/引起 (to give rise to, to lead to)

The verb 引起/引起 usually takes as objects two-syllable abstract nouns, such as 注意, 思考, 重视/重視, 反对/反對, 讨论/討論, 兴趣/興趣, or 危机/危機.

1

这两个孩子的教育问题还没有引起他们父母的注意。

這兩個孩子的教育問題還沒有引起他們父母的注意。

The issue of these two children's education has not attracted their parents' attention.

2

环保问题已经引起各个国家的重视。

環保問題已經引起各個國家的重視。

The issue of environmental protection has drawn much attention in different countries.

3

小王的建议引起同学们的反对。

小王的建議引起同學們的反對。

Little Wang's proposal met with objections from other students.

B

算（是）(to count as, to be considered as)

The basic meaning of 算 is "to count." In this lesson 算 means "to count as," or "can be taken as." 是 is optional.

1

姑妈要给表哥的未婚妻买一辆新车，算是结婚礼物。

姑媽要給表哥的未婚妻買一輛新車，算是結婚禮物。

[Tianming's] aunt wanted to buy a new car for [Tianming's] cousin's fiancée as a wedding gift.

2

这钱算我借给你的，你什么时候还给我都行。

這錢算我借給你的，你什麼時候還給我都行。

Take this money as a loan from me. You can return it whenever.

3 这个孩子算是他的儿子吧。

这個孩子算是他的兒子吧。

This child could be considered his son.

While 算是 sometimes has about the same meaning as 是—in (1) the car is a wedding gift, and in (2), the money is a loan—算是 does not always have the same meaning as 是.

In (3), "this child" is definitely not his biological son, but is "considered" his son.

C

合 (to combine, to join)

合 is used to describe sharing or doing something together.

1 他们俩上班的地方很近，合用一辆车就行了。

他們倆上班的地方很近，合用一輛車就行了。

Their workplaces are close to one another. They can share a car.

2 丽莎打算跟雪梅合租一套公寓。

麗莎打算跟雪梅合租一套公寓。

Lisha plans to rent an apartment with Xuemei.

3 我跟李教授合写了一本书。

我跟李教授合寫了一本書。

I coauthored a book with Professor Li.

More examples: 合唱一个歌/合唱一個歌 (to sing a song together), 合开一家饭馆/合開一家飯館 (to open a restaurant with a partner).

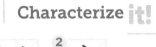

Characterize it!

What do the characters mean?

What is the common radical?

What does the radical mean?

How does the radical relate to the overall meaning of the characters?

More characters

突然 (sudden, unexpected)

突然 is an adjective. It can be used as an adverbial, as in (1) and (2); a predicate, as in (3); or as a complement following 得, as in (4).

1

没想到姑妈的想法突然变了。

沒想到姑媽的想法突然變了。

Who would have imagined Aunt would suddenly change her mind. *[adverbial]*

2

刚才天气很好，可是突然下起雨来。

剛才天氣很好，可是突然下起雨來。

The weather was fine just now, but all of a sudden it started to rain. *[adverbial]*

3

这件事很突然，我一点儿准备也没有。

這件事很突然，我一點兒準備也沒有。

This thing was too sudden. I wasn't prepared for it at all. *[predicate]*

4

他病得太突然了，大家根本没想到。

他病得太突然了，大家根本沒想到。

He got sick so suddenly. No one expected it at all. *[complement]*

A WAY WITH WORDS

义工

义工

不用谢我，你是我的
同学，我有帮助你的
义务。

他是个讲义气的人，为
了帮好朋友的孩子交学
费，把自己的车卖了。

Using the word/phrase in orange as a clue, try to figure out the meaning of the words/phrases in blue; consult a dictionary if necessary. Consider how the literal and extended senses are related in each case.

義工

不用謝我，你是我的
同學，我有幫助你的
義務。

他是個講義氣的人，為
了幫好朋友的孩子交學
費，把自己的車賣了。

Language Practice

Happy-go-lucky

PRESENTATIONAL

Li Zhe has earned enough credits for graduation and is currently waiting for word about an internship opportunity, so he's been taking it easy and relaxing these past few weeks. Based on the images, describe Li Zhe's daily activities by using reduplicated verbs, e.g.:

1

2

每天早晨李哲要么打打篮球，要么打打太极拳。

每天早晨李哲要麼打打籃球，要麼打打太極拳。

1　Morning:

2　Afternoon:

3　After dinner:

I insist

Imagine that an old friend of yours is experiencing financial difficulties. You want to help him/her out with some money, but he/she refuses to take it. Try to talk your old friend into accepting the money by using 算 or 算是, e.g.:

a loan from me

这点儿钱算是我借给你的。

這點兒錢算是我借給你的。

1 birthday gift

2 Chinese New Year gift

3 my investment in you

Ups and downs

Using 只要, practice describing how people's moods are affected by the fluctuation of different factors, e.g.:

Some people's moods are determined by the weather.

只要天气好，出太阳，就很高兴。只要天气不好，下雨，就很郁闷。

只要天氣好，出太陽，就很高興。只要天氣不好，下雨，就很鬱悶。

1 Some people's moods are set by the rising and falling of the stock market.

_____

2 Some people's moods are set by the appreciation and depreciation of the value of their house.

_____

Save up, give up, or something else? [INTERPERSONAL]

First, ask a partner what big-ticket item he/she would like to purchase. Is it a TV, a laptop, a car, a video game console (游戏机/遊戲機), or a house?

Second, ask him/her how he or she plans to pay for it. Is he/she going to save up for it, use bank savings, get a loan, ask his/her parents to lend him/her money, ask his/her parents for money as a gift, get a part-time job to pay for it, or give up?

你打算怎么买？还是不打算买了？

你打算怎麼買？還是不打算買了？

_____

_____

_____

_____

_____

_____

Finally, see if you can offer your partner any advice:

我觉得你应该_____。

我覺得你應該_____。

E [INTERPERSONAL]

Money matters [PRESENTATIONAL]

First, in pairs, brainstorm some ways to invest money.

_____

_____

_____

_____

Next, discuss with your partner the profitability and risk factors of the methods you brainstormed. Rank them, listing the most profitable and least risky method first.

Finally, present your conclusion to the class:

我们认为 ＿＿＿＿＿＿＿＿ 是最好的投资，不但安全，风险低，而且又赚钱。

我們認為 ＿＿＿＿＿＿＿＿ 是最好的投資，不但安全，風險低，而且又賺錢。

In your presentation, be sure to comment on the other items on your list in terms of their relative profitability and risk.

F INTERPERSONAL | **Spenders and savers** | PRESENTATIONAL

1 Sort these words/phrases based on whether they characterize spenders or savers.

整天叫外卖／整天叫外賣
常常乱买东西／常常亂買東西
把钱存在银行里／把錢存在銀行裡
省吃俭用／省吃儉用
借钱炒股／借錢炒股
投资买房／投資買房
享受生活／享受生活
贷款买车／貸款買車

Spender	Saver
＿＿＿＿＿＿	＿＿＿＿＿＿
＿＿＿＿＿＿	＿＿＿＿＿＿
＿＿＿＿＿＿	＿＿＿＿＿＿
＿＿＿＿＿＿	＿＿＿＿＿＿
＿＿＿＿＿＿	＿＿＿＿＿＿

2 In pairs, compare your lists. Discuss how your lists are the same or different.

3 Finally, ask your partner whether he/she considers himself or herself a spender or a saver, and why.

Be a financial consultant

In pairs, role-play a financial consultant and a person seeking advice. The financial consultant should take a look at the advice-seeker's monthly income and spending, and try to offer advice.

1   List your partner's sources of income: wages, allowance, scholarships, etc.

收入 _____

_____

_____

_____

_____

List your partner's expenditures: rent, groceries, utilities, car loan, cell phone, Internet, books, restaurant take-out, etc.

支出 (*zhīchū*) _____

_____

_____

_____

_____

2   Finally, take a look at the two lists and advise your partner on where he/she can cut expenses in order to put more money in the bank or stock market:

。   你可以少（不）_____，把省下来的钱存到银行里。

你可以少（不）_____，把省下來的錢存到銀行裡。

。   你可以少（不）_____，把省下来的钱投资股市。

你可以少（不）_____，把省下來的錢投資股市。

3   Switch roles and repeat Steps 1 and 2.

The Housing Market

China's housing market is another facet of its economy that has been drastically changed by reform. Before the early 1990s, housing was allocated to city residents by the government. Rent was minimal, and most people purchased their rentals at very inexpensive prices when the government began to commercialize housing. This kind of subsidized housing was called "welfare housing." Currently, housing stock in China includes "low-rent housing" (廉租房) (*lián zū fáng*), "economical, practical housing" (经济适用房 / 經濟適用房) sold below market rates to low-income people, and "commercial housing" (商品房). In large cities such as Beijing and Shanghai, the price of real estate has skyrocketed. Regardless of housing type, however, all land is owned by the state, and land-use rights technically have a term of seventy years. While the Chinese government has considered implementing a residential housing tax to scale back real estate prices, it has yet to do so.

Stock Exchanges

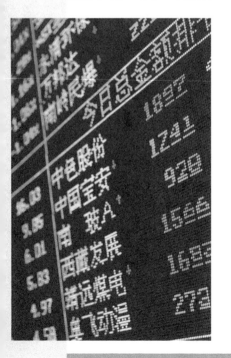

There are two stock exchanges in Mainland China: the Shanghai Stock Exchange and the Shenzhen Stock Exchange, each with its own stock index. The origins of the Shanghai Stock Exchange can be found in the city's history of foreign concessions, in which the Shanghai Sharebrokers' Association was founded in the late 1800s. The Shanghai Stock Exchange was registered in the early 1900s and operated for several decades.

After closing during wartime and periods of revolution, the Shanghai Stock Exchange reopened in 1990. The Shenzhen Stock Exchange opened in the same year. Unlike the stock exchanges in Hong Kong and Taiwan, the stock exchanges in Mainland China are not completely open to foreign investors. Nevertheless, all stock exchanges in the Greater China region rank within the top twenty in the entire world.

Saving

Due in part to periods of widespread poverty in the past and lack of a generous, comprehensive social safety net, the majority of Chinese people are known to save most of what they earn. The Chinese national savings rate is close to fifty percent, which is the highest among the world's major economies. The average family puts away approximately a third of its income in savings.

However, with the rise of its middle class, China has seen a shift from saving to spending, catalyzed by the convenience of online shopping, fast delivery, and mobile payment methods. Consumerism is at an all-time high as luxury retailers pop up across the country. Even in retail stores abroad, it is not uncommon to see signage catering to Chinese-speaking shoppers.

Income Inequality

While there has been astonishing growth since the reform of the planned economy began in the 1980s, there is a high level of income inequality in China. According to Forbes, the number of billionaires in China was second only to the United States in 2016 (251 vs. 540). China surpasses the rest of the world in number of female billionaires.

At the same time, an estimated 1% of the population owns one-third of the country's wealth. Many of China's richest people surpass the GDP of small nations in personal wealth and are therefore literal examples of the Chinese expression 富可敌国/富可敵國 (fù kě dí guó) (having wealth rivaling that of a country). There is also a wide urban–rural and coastal–inland disparity in income distribution, with few signs of the situation changing significantly anytime soon.

COMPARE & CONTRAST

Perhaps one of the most common greetings on Chinese New Year now is 恭喜发财/恭喜發財. Traditionally, Chinese literati, or 文人, would have found the saying unspeakably vulgar. Orthodox communism also frowns upon the naked pursuit of wealth. During the early years of reform, China's "paramount leader" Deng Xiaoping was famously reported to have said, "Poverty is not socialism. To get rich is glorious," thus repudiating the earlier official ideology of asceticism and planned economy. However, he also stressed the importance of sharing the prosperity. What is the attitude towards wealth in your country? Are questions about people's finances considered impolite or crass?

Lesson Wrap-Up

Project

Research the savings and homeownership rates in China and your country. In pairs, discuss whether your and your partner's findings are in broad agreement. Be sure to:

- compare the average percentage of income households in the two countries put away
- look up the interest rate (利率) (lìlǜ) in China and your country
- try to explain why the average savings rate among Chinese families is so high
- find out how much real estate prices increased or decreased in China and your country last year
- compare the percentage of young people, or "millennials" (九〇后、〇〇后/九〇後、〇〇後) (jiǔ líng hòu, líng líng hòu), who own their homes in China and your country
- describe how young people finance home purchases in China
- explain some of the reasons for the difference in homeownership rates among young people between the two countries

Keep It Flowing

First, study the following example; pay particular attention to how the highlighted parts help the sentences flow smoothly from one to the next. Notice how:

- certain conjunctions (但是, 可是) suggest turns in thought
- certain conjunctions (因为/因為) introduce cause
- pronouns (她) replace nouns (姑妈/姑媽) in subsequent sentences
- certain conjunctions (不但⋯还/還) signify addition
- time expressions (后来/後來) serve as connective devices and suggest change
- certain adverbs (也) signify addition
- certain verbs (看起来/看起來) introduce perceptions or tentative conclusions

张天明他们认为应该怎样理财

张天明的姑妈存了一笔钱，但是应该怎样理财呢？

天明的表哥认为姑妈应该买房子，因为这不但能让她舒舒服服地享受生活，还是一种不错的投资。姑妈被说服了，可是后来她的想法又变了，因为她看到有些人炒股赚了不少钱，也想炒股。丽莎认为炒股有风险，张天明认为买房子也不是没有风险，看起来没有什么又赚钱又没有风险的理财办法。

張天明他們認為應該怎樣理財

張天明的姑媽存了一筆錢，但是應該怎樣理財呢？

天明的表哥認為姑媽應該買房子，因為這不但能讓她舒舒服服地享受生活，還是一種不錯的投資。姑媽被說服了，可是後來她的想法又變了，因為她看到有些人炒股賺了不少錢，也想炒股。麗莎認為炒股有風險，張天明認為買房子也不是沒有風險，看起來沒有什麼又賺錢又沒有風險的理財辦法。

What are your thoughts on wealth management? Use as many of the cohesive devices highlighted in the example on the previous page/above as possible to string together your response, based on the prompts.

。我现在是学生，没有钱，好像不用理财。
我現在是學生，沒有錢，好像不用理財。

。我对理财有兴趣。
我對理財有興趣。

。在美国，最好投资股市，选好的公司，长期投资，一定会赚钱。
在美國，最好投資股市，選好的公司，長期投資，一定會賺錢。

○ 买房子也是投资，在房子不贵的时候买，在房子很贵的时候卖。

買房子也是投資，在房子不貴的時候買，在房子很貴的時候賣。

○ 还有很多投资的办法，我现在不懂，不能随便乱说。

還有很多投資的辦法，我現在不懂，不能隨便亂說。

Before proceeding to Lesson 18, make sure you can complete the following tasks in Chinese:

☐ Discuss whether I'm a saver or a spender
☐ Identify ways to invest
☐ List ways to purchase a big-ticket item
☐ Describe my spending habits
☐ Recount in basic terms the ups and downs of the stock market

Zhōngguó lǎobǎixìng yìbān dōu bǐjiào jiéjiǎn, suǒyǐ bù shǎo jiātíng yǒu cúnkuǎn. Gǎigé kāifàng yǐhòu, tāmen zhōngjiān bù shǎo rén kāishǐ kǎolǜ tóuzī lǐcái de wèntí. Zuìjìn yì xiē nián, Zhōngguó de *fáng jià*[a] zhǎng de hěn kuài, mǎi fángzi chéngwéi yì xiē rén tóuzī de xuǎnzé. Yě yǒu rén kàn jiàn biérén "*chǎo gǔ*"[b], yě chǎo qi gǔ lai. Hái yǒu yì xiē rén gèng yuànyì *bǎ*[1] qián huā zài zǐnǚ jiàoyù shang, tāmen juéde ràng zǐnǚ shòu dào zuì hǎo de jiàoyù, jiānglái shìyè chénggōng, shēnghuó xìngfú, cái shì zuì hǎo de tóuzī.

Zhāng Tiānmíng píngcháng bú dà kǎolǜ tóuzī lǐcái de shì, jīntiān tā biǎogē gēn tā zài wǎng shang liáo le bàntiān zhè ge wèntí, cái *yǐnqǐ* tā de sīkǎo. Tā chī wán wǎnfàn, jiù gēn Lìshā liáo le qi lai.

 Zuìjìn gūmā gēn biǎogē yǒu diǎnr máodùn, biǎogē hǎoxiàng yǒu diǎnr yùmèn.

 Wèishénme?

 Gūmā tuìxiū qián shěng chī jiǎn yòng cún le yì bǐ qián, yào liú gěi sūnzi sūnnǚ shàng dàxué yòng.

 Biǎogē hái méi jié hūn ne! Zhè qián kěnéng hái děi cún èrshí nián a.

 Kě bu shì, biǎogē yě zhèyàng shuō. Hòulái gūmā xiǎng chu le yí ge huā qián de zhúyi.

 Shénme zhúyi?

 Biǎogē bú shì jìhuà míngnián jié hūn ma? Gūmā yào gěi biǎogē de wèihūnqī mǎi yí liàng xīn chē, *suàn shì* jié hūn lǐwù.

 Gūmā zhēn hǎo.

 Kěshì biǎogē tāmen bù tóngyì mǎi chē. Tāmen liǎ shàng bān de dìfāng hěn jìn, *hé* yòng yí liàng chē jiù xíng le. Tāmen quàn gūmā mǎi fángzi, shuō gūmā xīnkǔ le jǐ shí nián, yīnggāi zhù yí tào dà yì xiē de fángzi, shū shu fú fú de xiǎngshòu tuìxiū shēnghuó.

 Tāmen shuō de tài duì le! Zàishuō, mǎi fángzi yě shì yì zhǒng búcuò de tóuzī a.

 Kěshì gūmā shuō tā de qián bú gòu mǎi yí tào fángzi. Wǒ biǎogē shuō tā kěyǐ wèi gūmā dài kuǎn, hái gěi gūmā jiǎng le yí ge liǎng wèi *lǎotàitai*[c] mǎi fángzi de gùshi.

Zhè ge gùshi wǒ yǐqián yě tīngshuō guo. Shuō de shì, yǒu yí ge lǎotàitai cún le sānshí nián qián, lìxī hěn shǎo, qián zēngjiā de hěn màn, dào le lǎonián cái mǎi dao yí tào fángzi, zhù le jin qu. Lìngwài yí ge lǎotàitai, sān shí nián qián jiù dài kuǎn mǎi fángzi zhù jin qu le. Bǐ yì bǐ, nǎ ge lǎotàitai gèng huì shēnghuó?

Duì, biǎogē jiù yòng zhè ge gùshi shuōfú[d] le gūmā, gūmā zuìhòu tóngyì mǎi fángzi le.

Hǎo a, wèntí suàn shì jiějué le.

Shìqing hái méi wán. Liǎng ge xīngqī qián, tāmen juéde yǒu yí tào sān shì yì tīng liǎng wèi de fángzi búcuò, yuánlái hòutiān jiù yào qù qiān gòu fáng hétong le, méi xiǎng dào gūmā de xiǎngfǎ tūrán biàn le.

Zěnme le?

Gūmā tuìxiū yǐhòu cháng gēn zài yìqǐ zuò yìgōng de péngyou men dǎ dǎ[2] májiàng, liáo liao tiānr. Qián jǐ tiān gūmā tīngshuō yǒu jǐ ge rén zhè liǎng nián zhǐyào chǎo gǔ jiù zhuàn qián[e], suǒyǐ biàn zhúyì le, bù xiǎng mǎi fángzi le.

Tā xiǎng tóuzī gǔshì[f]?

Kě bu shì ma?

Kěshì gūmā bù zhīdào chǎo gǔ yǒu fēngxiǎn ma? Gēn Lǐ Wén fùmǔ yìqǐ dǎ tàijíquán de yí wèi lǎoxiānsheng, bǎ fángzi dǐyā gěi yínháng, ránhòu bǎ qián dōu mǎi le gǔpiào, méi xiǎng dào gǔshì yìzhí diē, bú dào sān ge yuè, péi le yí bàn.

Mǎi fángzi shì bú shì jiù méiyǒu fēngxiǎn ne?

Fáng jià tài gāo de shíhou mǎi fángzi, dāngrán yǒu fēngxiǎn.

Kàn qi lai tóuzī zhēn bú shì yí jiàn jiǎndān de shì, bù zhīdào gūmā zuìhòu huì zěnme juédìng.

中国历史

中國歷史

CHINA'S HISTORY

Learning Objectives

In this lesson, you will learn to:

- Narrate the general timeline of Chinese history
- Describe the historical significance of major Chinese dynasties
- Talk about important Chinese material and cultural artifacts
- Discuss the contributions of key Chinese historical figures

Relate and Get Ready

In your own culture/community:

- In what ways is history remembered?
- What historical events are perceived as foundational?
- Do people lay claim to any world-famous inventions?

课文

Text

Audio

Before You Study

Answer the following questions in Chinese to prepare for the reading.

1 你们国家的历史有多长？

2 你参观过哪些博物馆？哪个给你留下的印象最深？

3 你对哪个国家的历史有兴趣？为什么？

When You Study

Listen to the audio recording and scan the text; then respond to the following prompts in Chinese.

1 请说说秦始皇的贡献是什么。

2 请说说汉朝为什么重要。

3 请说说中国的四大发明是什么。

4 请说说为什么清朝是中国最后的一个朝代。

丽莎这个学期除了中文课以外还选了一门中国历史课。中国是世界文明古国之一[1]，有文字记载的历史就有四千多年。为了对中国历史有更多的了解，她请李文带她去中国国家博物馆参观。张天明和柯林对中国历史也有兴趣，听说丽莎要参观博物馆，也要跟着一起去。李文很高兴地答应了。

中国国家博物馆很大，中国历史只是其中[2]的一部分。李文建议今天只看几个朝代，以后再慢慢参观。丽莎他们觉得这个建议很好。

你们都是学生，我就先给你们介绍中国历史上最重要的一位教育家。你们知道是谁吗？

是孔子吧？

对。孔子是中国历史上最伟大的教育家和思想家，到现在对中国教育还有很大的影响。

我的一件 T 恤衫上有孔子的一句话："有朋自远方来，不亦乐乎[a]。"

现在我们来到了秦朝的展厅。秦始皇是中国的第一个皇帝。

我的历史老师说秦始皇对统一中国有很大的贡献。

課文

麗莎這個學期除了中文課以外還選了一門中國歷史課。中國是世界文明古國之一[1]，有文字記載的歷史就有四千多年。為了對中國歷史有更多的了解，她請李文帶她去中國國家博物館參觀。張天明和柯林對中國歷史也有興趣，聽說麗莎要參觀博物館，也要跟著一起去。李文很高興地答應了。

中國國家博物館很大，中國歷史只是其中[2]的一部分。李文建議今天只看幾個朝代，以後再慢慢參觀。麗莎他們覺得這個建議很好。

你們都是學生，我就先給你們介紹中國歷史上最重要的一位教育家。你們知道是誰嗎？

是孔子吧？

對。孔子是中國歷史上最偉大的教育家和思想家，到現在對中國教育還有很大的影響。

我的一件 T 恤衫上有孔子的一句話："有朋自遠方來，不亦樂乎[a]。"

現在我們來到了秦朝的展廳。秦始皇是中國的第一個皇帝。

我的歷史老師說秦始皇對統一中國有很大的貢獻。

Before You Study

Answer the following questions in Chinese to prepare for the reading.

1 你們國家的歷史有多長？

2 你參觀過哪些博物館？哪個給你留下的印象最深？

3 你對哪個國家的歷史有興趣？為什麼？

When You Study

Listen to the audio recording and scan the text; then respond to the following prompts in Chinese.

1 請說說秦始皇的貢獻是什麼。

2 請說說漢朝為什麼重要。

3 請說說中國的四大發明是什麼。

4 請說說為什麼清朝是中國最後的一個朝代。

对，他还统一了文字。

还让老百姓修长城。

秦始皇做的事都对吗？

他杀了几百个读书人，烧了很多古书，是吗？

他还让很多很多人给他修宫殿、修坟墓。

你们说得都很对。你们看，这就是秦始皇的兵马俑，他死了以后还让这么多"兵马"保护他。

......

秦朝时间不长，下一个重要的朝代是汉朝。汉朝在政治、经济各个方面都有很大的发展。汉族^b这个名字就是从汉朝来的。

"丝绸之路^c"也跟汉朝有关系吧？

对，跟西方进行^d贸易是从汉朝开始的。

你们看，我们来到唐朝了。我爸爸常跟我说中国唐诗最有名。

没错，唐朝出现了很多大诗人。你学过谁的诗？

我学过李白的诗。

Top to bottom:
Terracotta warriors
and a section of the Silk Road

對，他還統一了文字。

還讓老百姓修長城。

秦始皇做的事都對嗎？

他殺了幾百個讀書人，燒了很多古書，是嗎？

他還讓很多很多人給他修宮殿、修墳墓。

你們說得都很對。你們看，這就是秦始皇的兵馬俑，他死了以後還讓這麼多"兵馬"保護他。

……

秦朝時間不長，下一個重要的朝代是漢朝。漢朝在政治、經濟各個方面都有很大的發展。漢族[b]這個名字就是從漢朝來的。

"絲綢之路[c]"也跟漢朝有關係吧？

對，跟西方進行[d]貿易是從漢朝開始的。

你們看，我們來到唐朝了。我爸爸常跟我說中國唐詩最有名。

沒錯，唐朝出現了很多大詩人。你學過誰的詩？

我學過李白的詩。

Top to bottom:
Terracotta horses and a
caravan in Dunhuang, a city
along the Silk Road

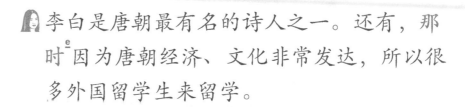

李白是唐朝最有名的诗人之一。还有，那时[e]因为唐朝经济、文化非常发达，所以很多外国留学生来留学。

跟我们一样。

你们知道吗，在历史上，中国科学技术曾经是很先进的。

你是说四大发明吗？

我知道，是造纸、火药、指南针、活字印刷。

对，造纸、火药发明得较早。活字印刷是宋朝发明的，指南针也在宋朝发展到了很高的水平。

……

我们现在来到中国最后一个朝代：清朝。

为什么是最后一个？

因为一九一一年孙中山领导革命[f]，一九一二年建立了中华民国，就再也没有皇帝了。

我们真不简单，一两个小时就走过了几千年。

我好像听到一个声音。

Top to bottom:
A Tang pottery figure of a
Sogdian merchant on camelback
and a reconstruction of an
ancient compass

李白是唐朝最有名的詩人之一。還有，那時因為唐朝經濟、文化非常發達，所以很多外國留學生來留學。

跟我們一樣。

你們知道嗎，在歷史上，中國科學技術曾經是很先進的。

你是說四大發明嗎？

我知道，是造紙、火藥、指南針、活字印刷。

對，造紙、火藥發明得較早。活字印刷是宋朝發明的，指南針也在宋朝發展到了很高的水平。

……

我們現在來到中國最後一個朝代：清朝。

為什麼是最後一個？

因為一九一一年孫中山領導革命，一九一二年建立了中華民國，就再也沒有皇帝了。

我們真不簡單，一兩個小時就走過了幾千年。

我好像聽到一個聲音。

Top to bottom:
A postage stamp featuring
Tang poetry and Chinese
movable type

1 为什么中国人认为秦始皇是中国历史上最重要的皇帝之一？

2 请说说为什么中国人认为孔子很重要。

3 跟唐朝一样，现在有很多外国人去中国留学，为什么？

4 中国的四大发明是什么？

5 为什么清朝以后再也没有皇帝了？

什么声音？

历史的脚步声。

我也听到了一个声音。

你要说肚子叫的……

对了。

你们在说什么呀？

Language Notes

a 有朋自远方来，不亦乐乎 / 有朋自遠方來，不亦樂乎

This saying is from *The Analects* of Confucius. It is often quoted to mean, "Isn't it a great joy to have friends from far away?" According to the Tang commentator 孔颖达 / 孔頴達 (*Kǒng Yǐngdá*, 574–648), 朋 here means "classmate" or "study companion" (同门 / 同門). The Song philosopher 朱熹 (*Zhū Xī*, 1130–1200) glosses 朋 as "kindred spirit" or "like-minded person" (lit. same type [of person]), 同类 / 同類. [自 = 从 / 從; 不亦⋯乎 = 不是⋯吗 / 不是⋯嗎; 乐 / 樂 = 快乐 / 快樂].

b 汉族 / 漢族

汉族 / 漢族 is short for 汉民族 / 漢民族, the Han ethnic group.

c 丝绸之路 / 絲綢之路

丝绸之路 / 絲綢之路 is the Chinese translation of "Silk Road," a term coined by the German traveler and geographer Ferdinand von Richtholfen (1833–1905).

d 进行 / 進行

进行 / 進行 must be followed by a two-syllable verb denoting an extended activity of some importance, e.g., 研究, 讨论 / 討論, 教育, 贸易 / 貿易, etc. It can't be used with verbs denoting brief, ordinary activities. For instance, we wouldn't say ❌ 进行洗澡 / 進行洗澡. 进行 / 進行 can be omitted without affecting the meaning. 进行贸易 / 進行貿易 is more formal than 贸易 / 貿易.

e 那时 / 那時

那时 / 那時 is short for 那个时候 / 那個時候 (at that time).

f 革命

"Revolution" here refers to 辛亥革命 (*Xīnhài Gémìng*), the Xinhai Revolution, also known as the Revolution of 1911.

什麼聲音？

歷史的腳步聲。

我也聽到了一個聲音。

你要說肚子叫的⋯⋯

對了。

你們在說什麼呀？

After You Study

Answer the following questions in Chinese.

1 為什麼中國人認為秦始皇是中國歷史上最重要的皇帝之一？

2 請說說為什麼中國人認為孔子很重要。

3 跟唐朝一樣，現在有很多外國人去中國留學，為什麼？

4 中國的四大發明是什麼？

5 為什麼清朝以後再也沒有皇帝了？

View & Explore

For deeper language immersion and more cultural information, watch "The History of a Village," a short, supplemental video clip by Cheng & Tsui on this lesson's theme.

Video

Vocabulary

Audio

Flashcards

No.	Simplified	Traditional	Pinyin	Part of Speech	Definition
1	文明	文明	wénmíng	n/adj	civilization, civilized
2	之	之	zhī	p	(literary equivalent of 的)
3	文字	文字	wénzì	n	characters, written form of a language
4	记载	記載	jìzǎi	v/n	to put down in writing, to record; record, account
5	参观	參觀	cānguān	v	to visit, to look around
6	其中	其中	qízhōng		among which/whom, in which/whom, of which/whom [See Grammar 2.]
7	部分	部分	bùfen	n	portion, part
8	朝代	朝代	cháodài	n	dynasty
9	伟大	偉大	wěidà	adj	great, outstanding, magnificent
10	思想	思想	sīxiǎng	n	thinking, ideology, thoughts
11	展厅	展廳	zhǎntīng	n	exhibition hall, gallery
12	皇帝	皇帝	huángdì	n	emperor
13	统一	統一	tǒngyī	v/adj	to unify, to unite; unified, centralized
14	贡献	貢獻	gòngxiàn	v/n	to contribute, to devote; contribution
15	修	修	xiū	v	to build, to repair
16	杀	殺	shā	v	to kill
17	烧	燒	shāo	v	to burn, to set fire to, to cook
18	宫殿	宮殿	gōngdiàn	n	palace
19	坟墓	墳墓	fénmù	n	grave, tomb
20	兵马俑	兵馬俑	bīngmǎyǒng	n	terracotta warriors and horses
21	发展	發展	fāzhǎn	v/n	to develop; development
22	丝绸	絲綢	sīchóu	n	silk, silk fabric
23	关系	關係	guānxì	n	relation, relationship, connection

No.	Simplified	Traditional	Pinyin	Part of Speech	Definition
24	进行	進行	jìnxíng	v	to carry on, to carry out, to conduct
25	贸易	貿易	màoyì	n/v	trade; to trade
26	诗	詩	shī	n	poetry, poem
27	诗人	詩人	shīrén	n	poet
28	发达	發達	fādá	adj	developed, flourishing
29	技术	技術	jìshù	n	technology, technique
30	曾经	曾經	céngjīng	adv	once; at some time in the past
31	先进	先進	xiānjìn	adj	advanced
32	发明	發明	fāmíng	n/v	invention; to invent
33	造纸	造紙	zào zhǐ	vo	to make paper
34	火药	火藥	huǒyào	n	gunpowder (lit. fire chemical)
35	指南针	指南針	zhǐnánzhēn	n	compass
36	活字印刷	活字印刷	huózì yìnshuā	n	moveable-type printing; letterpress printing
37	领导	領導	lǐngdǎo	v/n	to lead; leadership, leader (lit. to lead and guide)

How About You?

孔子、李白和孙中山都是中国历史上的名人。现在请你介绍一、两位历史人物，谈谈他们对世界有什么贡献，为什么重要。

孔子、李白和孫中山都是中國歷史上的名人。現在請你介紹一、兩位歷史人物，談談他們對世界有什麼貢獻，為什麼重要。

233

Your history teacher has asked you to help label some pictures to be used in your Chinese history class. What is this building, and what does the red banner commemorate? Figure out what 辛亥 and 周年 mean in order to determine when this photo was taken.

GET Real WITH CHINESE

No.	Simplified	Traditional	Pinyin	Part of Speech	Definition
38	革命	革命	*gémìng*	n	revolution
39	建立	建立	*jiànlì*	v	to build, to establish
40	孔子	孔子	*Kǒngzǐ*	pn	Confucius
41	秦朝	秦朝	*Qíncháo*	pn	Qin dynasty
42	秦始皇	秦始皇	*Qínshǐhuáng*	pn	First Emperor of the Qin dynasty
43	汉朝	漢朝	*Hàncháo*	pn	Han dynasty
44	西方	西方	*Xīfāng*	pn	the West
45	唐朝	唐朝	*Tángcháo*	pn	Tang dynasty
46	李白	李白	*Lǐ Bái*	pn	Li Bai
47	宋朝	宋朝	*Sòngcháo*	pn	Song dynasty
48	清朝	清朝	*Qīngcháo*	pn	Qing dynasty
49	孙中山	孫中山	*Sūn Zhōngshān*	pn	Sun Yat-sen
50	中华民国	中華民國	*Zhōnghuá Mínguó*	pn	Republic of China

Grammar

之一

之 is a structural particle inherited from classical Chinese. Among its many usages, it can be used in a way similar to 的. 之一 means "one of."

A 中国是世界文明古国之一。

中國是世界文明古國之一。

China is one of the world's ancient civilizations.

B 造纸是中国的四大发明之一。

造紙是中國的四大發明之一。

Papermaking is one of the four great inventions of China.

C 石林是云南最有名的旅游景点之一。

石林是雲南最有名的旅遊景點之一。

The Stone Forest is one of the most famous tourist sights in Yunnan.

之一 must be preceded by a phrase denoting scope, such as 世界文明古国/世界文明古國 (world's ancient civilizations) in (A), 四大发明/四大發明 (four great inventions) in (B), and 旅游景点/旅遊景點 (tourist sights) in (C).

A **W**AY
WITH **W**ORDS

火药

火藥

Using the word/phrase in orange as a clue, try to figure out the meaning of the words/phrases in blue; consult a dictionary if necessary. Consider how the literal and extended senses are related in each case.

日本有很多火山，有的成了有名的旅游景点。

他今天考试没考好，所以火气很大，为了一点小事就跟同屋吵起来了。

日本有很多火山，有的成了有名的旅遊景點。

他今天考試沒考好，所以火氣很大，為了一點小事就跟同屋吵起來了。

2 其中

其 is a pronoun with the same meaning as 那 or 那些. 其中 means "among them" or "within it."

A
中国国家博物馆很大，中国历史只是其中的一部分。

中國國家博物館很大，中國歷史只是其中的一部分。

The National Museum of China is very large, and the exhibit of Chinese history is only one part of it.

B
我去过中国很多省旅游，其中我对云南和四川的印象最深。

我去過中國很多省旅遊，其中我對雲南和四川的印象最深。

Of all the Chinese provinces I've traveled to, Yunnan and Sichuan had the biggest impression on me.

C
上个学期我选了三门课，其中金融课最难。

上個學期我選了三門課，其中金融課最難。

Last semester I took three courses. Among them, Finance was the hardest.

When using 其中, there must be an antecedent to 其 to make it clear to what 其 refers. In (A), it is 中国国家博物馆/中國國家博物館 (the National Museum of China); in (B), it is 很多省 (many provinces); and in (C), it is 三门课/三門課 (three courses).

Characterize it!

More characters

What do the characters mean?	
What is the common radical?	
What does the radical mean?	
How does the radical relate to the overall meaning of the characters?	

Words & Phrases

参观/參觀 (to visit, to look around) vs. 游览/遊覽
(to go sightseeing, to tour; excursion)

游/遊 means "to roam about"; 览/覽 means "to view." 游览/遊覽 is "to go on a sightseeing excursion," and usually implies a destination like a scenic or historic attraction. 参观/參觀 is often used to describe a visit for educational purposes, e.g., 参观学校/參觀學校 (to visit a school), 参观博物馆/參觀博物館 (to visit a museum), and 参观工厂/參觀工廠 (to visit a factory).

1　昨天我们去参观一个建筑公司，他们给我们介绍了他们正在盖的大厦。

昨天我們去參觀一個建築公司，他們給我們介紹了他們正在蓋的大廈。

Yesterday we visited a construction company. They briefed us on the high-rise they were building.

2　我想参观附近那个科学研究单位，不知道让不让参观。

我想參觀附近那個科學研究單位，不知道讓不讓參觀。

I'd like to visit that scientific research institute nearby. I don't know if they allow visits.

3　我去中国一定要游览长城。

我去中國一定要遊覽長城。

If I go to China, I'll definitely tour the Great Wall.

4　寒假我去中国西北高原游览，拍了很多照片。

寒假我去中國西北高原遊覽，拍了很多照片。

During winter break I toured China's northwest plateau region and took many photographs.

在…方面 (in terms of, in the area of)

1　在学习方面，他帮助我，在生活方面，我帮助他。

在學習方面，他幫助我，在生活方面，我幫助他。

He helps me with my studies. I help him with matters of daily life.

2　在找工作方面，他的经验很多，你可以听听他的意见。

在找工作方面，他的經驗很多，你可以聽聽他的意見。

When it comes to looking for a job, he is very experienced. You can listen to his opinions.

3　她在各个方面的表现都很好。

她在各個方面的表現都很好。

Her performance in many different areas is outstanding.

Chinese Chat

Your friend is texting you on iMessage to make plans to visit a museum tomorrow. How would you reply?

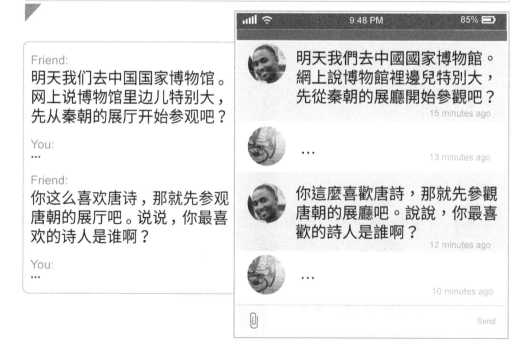

Friend:
明天我们去中国国家博物馆。网上说博物馆里边儿特别大，先从秦朝的展厅开始参观吧？

You:
...

Friend:
你这么喜欢唐诗，那就先参观唐朝的展厅吧。说说，你最喜欢的诗人是谁啊？

You:
...

X 跟 Y 有关（系）/ X 跟 Y 有關（係）
(related to, having to do with)

跟…有关（系）/跟…有關（係） can act as a predicate or as an attributive:

1 节约能源跟每一个人都有关系，你不能不重视。

節約能源跟每一個人都有關係，你不能不重視。

Energy conservation concerns everyone. You cannot dismiss it. *[predicate]*

2 最近跟环保有关（系）的新闻特别多。

最近跟環保有關（係）的新聞特別多。

There has been much news related to environmental protection recently. *[attributive]*

When the construction is used as an attributive, 系/係 is often omitted, especially in written Chinese. However, when 没有关系/沒有關係 occurs at the end of a sentence as a predicate, 系/係 cannot be omitted.

3 比赛的事跟我没有关系，我走了。

比賽的事跟我沒有關係，我走了。

The game doesn't concern me, so I'm going to head out. *[predicate]*

4 对不起，跟投资理财有关系的事情，我完全不懂。

對不起，跟投資理財有關係的事情，我完全不懂。

Sorry, I know nothing about investment or financial management. *[attributive]*

再也没…了/再也沒…了，再也不…了
(no more, not anymore)

再也没…了/再也沒…了，再也不…了 carries a strong feeling of negation.

1 建立了中华民国，就再也没有皇帝了。

建立了中華民國，就再也沒有皇帝了。

After the founding of the Republic of China, there were no more emperors.

2　他老是跟我抱怨这，抱怨那，我再也不想见他了。

他老是跟我抱怨這，抱怨那，我再也不想見他了。

He's always complaining to me about this or that. I don't want to see him ever again.

3　这个城市非常重视环保，现在买东西都得自己带包，商店再也不给免费的塑料袋了。

這個城市非常重視環保，現在買東西都得自己帶包，商店再也不給免費的塑料袋了。

People place a lot of importance on environmental protection in this city. Now you have to bring your own shopping bags, and the stores no longer provide free plastic shopping bags.

A WAY WITH WORDS

领导　　　　　　　　　　　　　　　　領導

昨天要不是老王在前面开车引导我们，我们差一点就找不到回家的路了。

Using the word/phrase in orange as a clue, try to figure out the meaning of the words/phrases in blue; consult a dictionary if necessary. Consider how the literal and extended senses are related in each case.

昨天要不是老王在前面開車引導我們，我們差一點就找不到回家的路了。

小周中文考试考得不好，很难过，说下学期不想学下去了。老师花了很多时间劝导她。

小周中文考試考得不好，很難過，說下學期不想學下去了。老師花了很多時間勸導她。

Language Practice

One among many

Let's talk about China in a global context. Form sentences with 之一, e.g.:

China   old civilizations

中国是世界文明古国之一。

中國是世界文明古國之一。

1 Beijing   biggest cities

2 Yangtze River   longest rivers

3 papermaking   most important inventions

4 the Great Wall   most famous historic attractions

Take your pick

In pairs, discuss your favorite tourist spot, the most famous political leader, the most important historical figure, and the most famous poet, e.g.:

cities   most impressive

Q: 你去过那么多城市，其中哪个城市给你的印象最深？

   你去過那麼多城市，其中哪個城市給你的印象最深？

A: 我去过很多城市，其中纽约给我的印象最深。

   我去過很多城市，其中紐約給我的印象最深。

1 tourist sights   favorite

2 political leaders (人物)   most famous

3 historical figures (人物)   most influential

4 poets   most important

Getting the facts straight

1 Work with a partner to match each dynasty with the historical phenomenon that that dynasty is often associated with.

丝绸之路／絲綢之路   秦朝

活字印刷   唐朝

文字统一／文字統一   清朝

外国人去中国留学／外國人去中國留學   宋朝

历史上最后一个皇帝／歷史上最後一個皇帝   汉朝／漢朝

2 Next, take turns with your partner to quiz each other about each phenomenon, e.g.:

丝绸之路／絲綢之路

Q: 丝绸之路跟哪个朝代有关系？

丝綢之路跟哪個朝代有關係？

A: 丝绸之路跟汉朝有关系。

絲綢之路跟漢朝有關係。

○ _____

○ _____

○ _____

○ _____

Never again

People often claim that they won't repeat their mistakes. In pairs, take turns with a partner and use the prompts to practice vowing never to do things again, e.g.:

> joining a tour

柯林决定再也不参加旅行团了。

柯林決定再也不參加旅行團了。

1   dining in a dining car

2   staying up late

3   watching men's soccer

4   drinking bottled water

5   using disposable chopsticks

INTERPERSONAL

Chinese History 101

In pairs, use the prompts and the table that follows to prepare an outline for someone who is just starting to learn some basic historical facts about China.

1   中国的历史有多长?

中國的歷史有多長？

2   中国历史上有那么多朝代，其中哪些朝代比较重要，
比较有影响?

中國歷史上有那麼多朝代，其中哪些朝代比較重要，
比較有影響？

3 写出那些朝代名，说说它们为什么重要。

寫出那些朝代名，說說它們為什麼重要。

朝代名	历史重要性/歷史重要性
_____	_____
_____	_____
_____	_____
_____	_____

4 Number these dynasties chronologically. Refer to the dynastic chart in the Cultural Literacy section if necessary.

清朝　　汉朝　　宋朝　　唐朝　　元朝　　秦朝　　明朝
　　　　漢朝

_____　_____　_____　_____　_____　_____　_____

F | **Chinese history buff** | PRESENTATIONAL |

In pairs, complete the sentences to describe these material and cultural artifacts from Chinese history.

1 _____让老百姓_____。

　　　 _____讓老百姓_____。

2 _____死后还让千千万万的_____保护他。

　　　 _____死後還讓千千萬萬的_____保護他。

3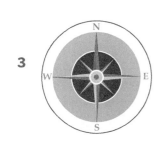

_____是在_____发明的。

_____是在_____發明的。

4

_____也是中国的四大发明_____。

_____也是中國的四大發明_____。

5

_____发明得比活字印刷_____。

_____發明得比活字印刷_____。

6

中国的_____很_____。

中國的_____很_____。

_____之路和_____朝有关系。

_____之路和_____朝有關係。

7

唐朝的_____很_____。

唐朝的_____很_____。

唐朝最有名的诗人是_____。

唐朝最有名的詩人是_____。

8　茶叶／茶葉 *(cháyè)* (lit. tea leaves)

和_____一样，_____在中国和_____的贸易中
很_____。

和_____一樣，_____在中國和_____的貿易中
很_____。

<u>G</u>　| INTERPERSONAL | **Know your own country** | PRESENTATIONAL |

1　In pairs, brainstorm some of your country's great historical figures. The names do not have to be in Chinese.

- 教育家: _____
- 画家／畫家: _____
- 哲学家／哲學家: _____

2　Report the results of your brainstorming to the class by saying:

我们认为（person's name）是我国历史上最伟大的
_____之一。

我們認為（person's name）是我國歷史上最偉大的
_____之一。

3　Next, work with your partner to name some of your country's inventions and their inventors. The inventors' names do not have to be in Chinese.

发明／發明	发明人／發明人
○ _____	_____
○ _____	_____
○ _____	_____

...

4 Report the results of your brainstorming to the class by saying:

我们国家发明了_____，是（name of inventor）发明的。

我們國家發明了_____，是（name of inventor）發明的。

---

1 In pairs, discuss what should be included when writing a biography of a famous historical figure. Record what you come up with:

○ _____

○ _____

○ _____

○ _____

○ _____

2 Prepare to write a brief sketch of Confucius or Sun Yat-sen. Use the list you made in (1) to gather information, and the checklist below to organize your findings. (Note that "BCE" is 公元前 and "to pass away" is 去世).

○ 他是哪一年出生的？
他是哪一年出生的？

○ 他是在哪个省出生的？
他是在哪個省出生的？

○ 他是哪一年去世的？

○ 他是中国历史上伟大的_____家。
他是中國歷史上偉大的_____家。

○ 他对中国历史和社会有什么贡献或者影响？
他對中國歷史和社會有什麼貢獻或者影響？

3 Based on your list in (1) and answers in (2), compose a short bio of Confucius or Sun Yat-sen.

THE IMPERIAL ERA

A series of dynasties arose and fell over the course of China's history. Often, the collapse of a dynasty was followed by a period of disunity before a leader arose who could reunify the country. The first and perhaps the most important unifier was Qin Shihuangdi, often called the "First Emperor." He enacted sweeping legal reforms, created a uniform system of weights and measures, and standardized the Chinese written script. Although the Qin dynasty would be overthrown shortly after the First Emperor's death, many of the institutions he created were adopted by subsequent dynasties. In Xi'an, tourists can see the awe-inspiring terracotta army commissioned by the First Emperor.

COMPARE & CONTRAST

Like the First Emperor, the framers of the U.S. Constitution hoped to create a strong, unified country. In Article 1, Section 8 of the Constitution, they gave the government the power to set standard weights and measures and to create a shared, national currency. Why are these important powers for a national government to have?

A Brief Chronology of
CHINESE DYNASTIES

Major dynasties are in purple.

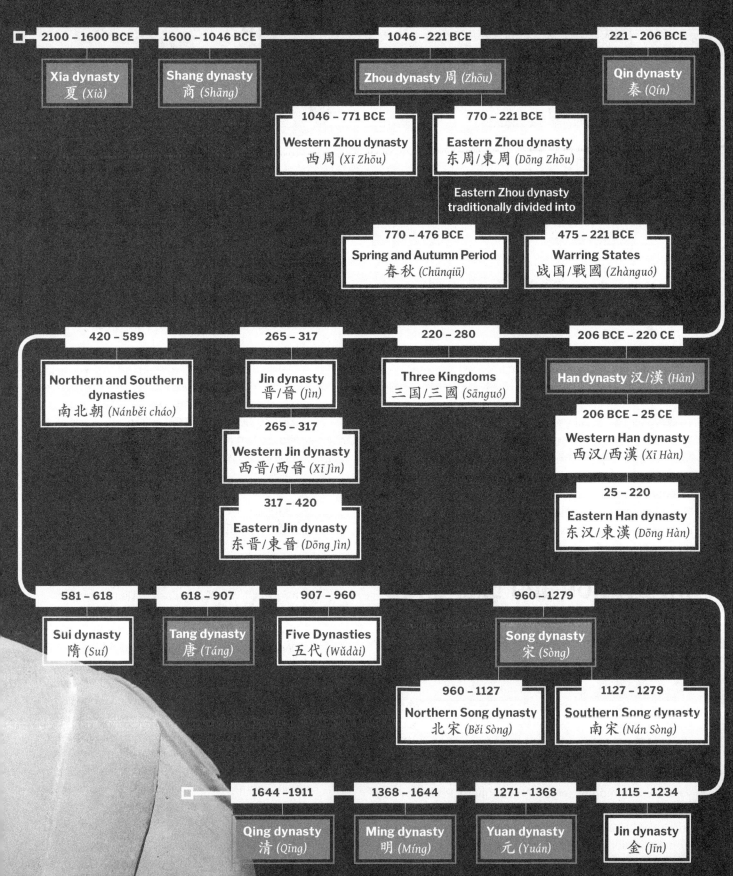

2100 – 1600 BCE

Xia dynasty
夏 *(Xià)*

1600 – 1046 BCE

Shang dynasty
商 *(Shāng)*

1046 – 221 BCE

Zhou dynasty 周 *(Zhōu)*

221 – 206 BCE

Qin dynasty
秦 *(Qín)*

1046 – 771 BCE

Western Zhou dynasty
西周 *(Xī Zhōu)*

770 – 221 BCE

Eastern Zhou dynasty
东周/東周 *(Dōng Zhōu)*

Eastern Zhou dynasty traditionally divided into

770 – 476 BCE

Spring and Autumn Period
春秋 *(Chūnqiū)*

475 – 221 BCE

Warring States
战国/戰國 *(Zhànguó)*

420 – 589

Northern and Southern dynasties
南北朝 *(Nánběi cháo)*

265 – 317

Jin dynasty
晋/晉 *(Jìn)*

220 – 280

Three Kingdoms
三国/三國 *(Sānguó)*

206 BCE – 220 CE

Han dynasty 汉/漢 *(Hàn)*

265 – 317

Western Jin dynasty
西晋/西晉 *(Xī Jìn)*

317 – 420

Eastern Jin dynasty
东晋/東晉 *(Dōng Jìn)*

206 BCE – 25 CE

Western Han dynasty
西汉/西漢 *(Xī Hàn)*

25 – 220

Eastern Han dynasty
东汉/東漢 *(Dōng Hàn)*

581 – 618

Sui dynasty
隋 *(Suí)*

618 – 907

Tang dynasty
唐 *(Táng)*

907 – 960

Five Dynasties
五代 *(Wǔdài)*

960 – 1279

Song dynasty
宋 *(Sòng)*

960 – 1127

Northern Song dynasty
北宋 *(Běi Sòng)*

1127 – 1279

Southern Song dynasty
南宋 *(Nán Sòng)*

1644 – 1911

Qing dynasty
清 *(Qīng)*

1368 – 1644

Ming dynasty
明 *(Míng)*

1271 – 1368

Yuan dynasty
元 *(Yuán)*

1115 – 1234

Jin dynasty
金 *(Jīn)*

SUN YAT-SEN
Father of Modern China

Sun Yat-sen (1866-1925) was born in Xiangshan (香山), Guangdong (广东/廣東) Province. His original name was Sun Wen, 孙文/孫文. Yat-sen (逸仙) (Yìxiān in Mandarin) is the Cantonese pronunciation of his courtesy name. Sun trained as a doctor, but his opposition to the ruling Qing dynasty drew him into politics. In 1895, he took part in a failed uprising and went into exile in Japan for 16 years. During this time, he adopted the alias 中山樵 (Zhōngshānqiáo) and, as a result, he is most widely known as 孙中山/孫中山 (Sūn Zhōngshān) in China. Even while abroad, Sun worked tirelessly to organize Chinese revolutionaries. After the Revolution of 1911, which overthrew the Qing dynasty, he was elected the first interim president of the Republic of China, and he continues to be revered as the father of modern China.

Innovation and Exchange

China is the source of innumerable innovations, including kites, noodles, and soybean cultivation. Among these, paper, printing, gunpowder, and the compass are known as China's Four Great Inventions, 四大发明/四大發明. However, it was demand for two other inventions, silk and ceramics, which drove much of the trade between Imperial China and lands to the west. The Chinese successfully guarded the secret of sericulture for centuries, effectively establishing a monopoly over the product. Merchants risked life and limb to bring this valuable commodity across the continent. Perhaps even more important than the exchange of goods was the spread of ideas. Buddhism, for instance, entered China from India along Silk Road trade routes.

Zhang Qian, Ban Chao, and the Silk Road

The ancient trade route extending from China to the eastern rim of the Mediterranean was named after silk. In 138 BCE, Emperor Wu of the Han Dynasty sent Zhang Qian, 张骞/張騫 (Zhāng Qiān, 164–113 BCE) and an entourage of about a hundred people westward on a diplomatic mission. He reported what he had seen in Central Asian countries and suggested that the Han Empire establish a friendly relationship with them. In 119 BCE, Emperor Wu sent Zhang Qian on a second mission to Central Asia. Zhang Qian and his delegation visited many Central Asian countries. Subsequently, contact between the Han Empire and Central Asia became increasingly frequent. In 73 CE, the Eastern Han envoy Ban Chao, 班超 (Bān Chāo, 32–102 CE) went to Central Asia. Ban Chao sent a diplomat to the Persian Gulf, then part of the Roman Empire. In 166, an envoy visited Luoyang, capital of the Eastern Han. Chinese historians view this visit as the first direct contact between Europe and China. Although archaeological finds in Central and West Asia suggest that the Silk Road may have started long before Zhang Qian's diplomatic missions, he is still remembered today along with Ban Chao as pioneers of East-West exchanges. Later on, maritime trade routes were also developed.

Lesson Wrap-Up

Like silk and tea, porcelain or fine china (瓷器) *(cíqì)* was of great cultural importance and a major Chinese export item for centuries. Research Chinese porcelain and prepare an oral report with slides. Be sure to:

- define porcelain, its principal material (主要原料) *(zhǔyào yuánliào)*, color, and firing temperature (烧制温度/燒製溫度) *(shāozhì wēndù)*

- explain why blue-and-white porcelain is called 青花瓷/青花瓷, and when it began to be mass produced (大量生产/大量生產) *(dàliàng shēngchǎn)*

- mention why cobalt, the blue glaze material, was called 回回青

- include why Jingdezhen (景德镇/景德鎮) *(Jǐngdézhèn)* is called "the Capital of Porcelain" (瓷都) due to its location and proximity to the main porcelain material, *kaolin* (高岭土/高嶺土) *(gāolǐngtǔ)*

- describe the popularity of Chinese blue-and-white porcelain in the Middle East (中东/中東) and the West, when porcelain began to be exported (出口), and when the West began to produce real porcelain

- compare the popularity of Chinese silk, tea, and porcelain in your country; 中国丝绸、茶和瓷器，哪个最受欢迎/中國絲綢、茶和瓷器，哪個最受歡迎？

First, study the following example; pay particular attention to how the highlighted parts help the sentences flow smoothly from one to the next. Notice how:

- key words and phrases (中国/中國, 中国历史上/中國歷史上) state the theme or topic at the beginning of a sentence

- time phrases (比较早的/比較早的, 后来/後來) serve as connective devices

- pronouns (他) replace proper nouns (秦始皇) in subsequent sentences

- following a historical timeline (秦朝, 汉朝/漢朝, 唐朝, 宋朝, 明朝, 清朝, 一九四九年) helps organize a narrative

说说中国重要的朝代

中国有文字记载的历史最少有三千三百多年。中国历史上有很多朝代，我们只说说几个重要的朝代。比较早的是秦朝，秦始皇统一了那时的六国，他的重要贡献是统一了文字。汉朝有了丝绸之路，开始和西方进行贸易。唐朝出现了很多大诗人，李白是最有名的之一。宋朝有四大发明。明朝以后是清朝。清朝是最后一个朝代，后来孙中山领导革命，建立了中华民国。一九四九年，中华人民共和国建立了。

說說中國重要的朝代

中國有文字記載的歷史最少有三千三百多年。中國歷史上有很多朝代，我們只說說幾個重要的朝代。比較早的是秦朝，秦始皇統一了那時的六國，他的重要貢獻是統一了文字。漢朝有了絲綢之路，開始和西方進行貿易。唐朝出現了很多大詩人，李白是最有名的之一。宋朝有四大發明。明朝以後是清朝。清朝是最後一個朝代，後來孫中山領導革命，建立了中華民國。一九四九年，中華人民共和國建立了。

What are your thoughts on your country's history? Use as many of the cohesive devices highlighted in the example on the previous page as possible to string together a response, based on the prompts. Other phrases to consider include 可是, 不但, 还是/還是, 因为/因為, and 也.

- 你们国家的历史有多少年了？
  你們國家的歷史有多少年了？

- 你们国家的历史可以分成多少时期 *(shíqī)* (period)？
  你們國家的歷史可以分成多少時期 *(shíqī)* (period)？

- 每一个时期有什么重要的事情？比如哪个时期经济最好、哪个时期文化最发达、哪个时期跟别的国家开始进行贸易，等等。
  每一個時期有什麼重要的事情？比如哪个時期經濟最好、哪個時期文化最發達、哪個時期跟別的國家開始進行貿易，等等。

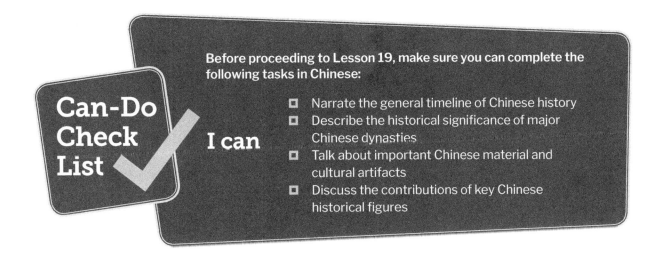

Before proceeding to Lesson 19, make sure you can complete the following tasks in Chinese:

☐ Narrate the general timeline of Chinese history
☐ Describe the historical significance of major Chinese dynasties
☐ Talk about important Chinese material and cultural artifacts
☐ Discuss the contributions of key Chinese historical figures

Can-Do Check List ✔ **I can**

Lìshā zhè ge xuéqī chúle Zhōngwén kè yǐwài hái xuǎn le yì mén Zhōngguó lìshǐ kè. Zhōngguó shì shìjiè wénmíng gǔguó zhī yī[1], yǒu wénzì jìzǎi de lìshǐ jiù yǒu sì qiān duō nián. Wèile duì Zhōngguó lìshǐ yǒu gèng duō de liǎojiě, tā qǐng Lǐ Wén dài tā qù Zhōngguó Guójiā Bówùguǎn cānguān. Zhāng Tiānmíng hé Kē Lín duì Zhōngguó lìshǐ yě yǒu xìngqù, tīngshuō Lìshā yào cānguān bówùguǎn, yě yào gēn zhe yìqǐ qù. Lǐ Wén hěn gāoxìng de dāying le.

Zhōngguó Guójiā Bówùguǎn hěn dà, Zhōngguó lìshǐ zhǐ shì qízhōng[2] de yí bùfen. Lǐ Wén jiànyì jīntiān zhǐ kàn jǐ ge cháodài, yǐhòu zài màn mān cānguān. Lìshā tāmen juéde zhè ge jiànyì hěn hǎo.

 Nǐmen dōu shì xuésheng, wǒ jiù xiān gěi nǐmen jièshào Zhōngguó lìshǐ shang zuì zhòngyào de yí wèi jiàoyùjiā. Nǐmen zhīdao shì shéi ma?

 Shì Kǒngzǐ ba?

 Duì. Kǒngzǐ shì Zhōngguó lìshǐ shang zuì wěidà de jiàoyùjiā hé sīxiǎngjiā, dào xiànzài duì Zhōngguó jiàoyù hái yǒu hěn dà de yǐngxiǎng.

 Wǒ de yí jiàn tīxùshān shang yǒu Kǒngzǐ de yí jù huà: "Yǒu péng zì yuǎnfāng lái, bú yì lè hū[a]."

 Xiànzài wǒmen lái dào le Qíncháo de zhǎntīng. Qínshǐhuáng shì Zhōngguó de dì yī ge huángdì.

 Wǒ de lìshǐ lǎoshī shuō Qínshǐhuáng duì tǒngyī Zhōngguó yǒu hěn dà de gòngxiàn.

 Duì, tā hái tǒngyī le wénzì.

 Hái ràng lǎobǎixìng xiū Chángchéng.

 Qínshǐhuáng zuò de shì dōu duì ma?

 Tā shā le jǐ bǎi ge dúshū rén, shāo le hěn duō gǔ shū, shì ma?

 Tā hái ràng hěn duō hěn duō rén gěi tā xiū gōngdiàn, xiū fénmù.

 Nǐmen shuō de dōu hěn duì. Nǐmen kàn, zhè jiù shì Qínshǐhuáng de bīngmǎyǒng, tā sǐ le yǐhòu hái ràng zhème duō "bīng mǎ" bǎohù tā.

. . .

 Qíncháo shíjiān bù cháng, xià yí ge zhòngyào de cháodài shì Hàncháo. Hàncháo zài zhèngzhì, jīngjì gè ge fāngmiàn[b] dōu yǒu hěn dà de fāzhǎn. Hànzú[b] zhè ge míngzi jiù shì cóng Hàncháo lái de.

 "Sīchóu zhī lù[c]" yě gēn Hàncháo yǒu guānxi ba?

 Duì, gēn Xīfāng jìnxíng[d] màoyì shì cóng Hàncháo kāishǐ de.

 Nǐmen kàn, wǒmen lái dào Tángcháo le Wǒ bàba cháng gēn wǒ shuō Zhōngguó Táng shī zuì yǒumíng.

 Méicuò, Tángcháo chūxiàn le hěn duō dà shīrén. Nǐ xué guo shéi de shī?

 Wǒ xué guo Lǐ Bái de shī.

 Lǐ Bái shì Tángcháo zuì yǒumíng de shīrén zhī yī. Háiyǒu, nà shí[e] yīnwèi Tángcháo jīngjì, wénhuà fēicháng fādá, suǒyǐ hěn duō wàiguó liúxuéshēng lái liúxué.

 Gēn wǒmen yíyàng.

 Nǐmen zhīdào ma, zài lìshǐ shang, Zhōngguó kēxué jìshù céngjīng shì hěn xiānjìn de.

 Nǐ shì shuō sì dà fāmíng ma?

 Wǒ zhīdào, shì zào zhǐ, huǒyào, zhǐnánzhēn, huózì yìnshuā.

 Duì, zào zhǐ, huǒyào fāmíng de jiào zǎo. Huózì yìnshuā shì Sòngcháo fāmíng de, zhǐnánzhēn yě zài Sòngcháo fāzhǎn dào le hěn gāo de shuǐpíng.

. . .

 Wǒmen xiànzài lái dào Zhōngguó zuìhòu yí ge cháodài—Qīngcháo.

 Wèishénme shì zuìhòu yí ge?

 Yīnwèi yī jiǔ yī yī nián Sūn Zhōngshān lǐngdǎo gémìng[f], yī jiǔ yī èr nián jiànlì le Zhōnghuá Mínguó, zài yě méi yǒu huángdì le.

 Wǒmen zhēn bù jiǎndān, yì liǎng ge xiǎoshí jiù zǒu guo le jǐ qiān nián.

 Wǒ hǎoxiàng tīng dào yí ge shēngyīn.

 Shénme shēngyīn?

 Lìshǐ de jiǎobù shēng.

 Wǒ yě tīng dào le yí ge shēngyīn.

 Nǐ yào shuō dùzi jiǎo de . . .

 Duì le.

 Nǐmen zài shuō shénme ya?

面试

面試

JOB INTERVIEW

Learning Objectives

In this lesson, you will learn to:

- Explain why China has been able to attract talent and corporations from overseas
- Describe overseas returnees and their nickname
- Recount a nerve-racking interview
- Handle typical job interview questions

Relate and Get Ready

In your own culture/community:

- Are there many returnees from overseas with foreign college degrees?
- How extensive is the interviewing process for entry-level positions?
- What are some typical questions you'd expect to be asked during a job interview?

课文

21世纪初以来，中国的经济有了很大的发展，不少跨国公司进入中国。这些大公司吸引了世界各地不少的人材[a]，包括一些在国外学习毕业的中国留学生。他们从海外归来，被叫做"海归"。有的人还开玩笑地把他们叫做"海龟[b]"。林雪梅现在就是其中的一只新"海龟"。

雪梅回到中国以后不久，就开始上网查资料、找工作。她去过几家公司实习，但是都不太满意。昨天有一家她非常喜欢的大公司叫她今天上午去面试销售经理的工作。面试以后，刚回到家里就接到丽莎的电话。

哎，"海龟"小姐，今天的面试怎么样？

哈，开始有些紧张，出了好多汗，套装的上衣都快湿了。

你已经不是第一次面试了，干吗那么紧张？

给我面试的是他们公司的总经理，挺严肃的，第一句话就是："你是不是在美国找不到工作才回中国来的？"

这个总经理可真的挺吓人的！难怪你紧张。

Before You Study

Answer the following questions in Chinese to prepare for the reading.

1 你觉得面试前应该怎么准备？

2 你觉得面试的时候怎么能让自己不紧张？

3 你觉得面试的时候应该注意些什么？

When You Study

Listen to the audio recording and scan the text; then answer the following questions in Chinese.

1 雪梅到底为什么回中国工作？

2 雪梅觉得自己的缺点是什么？

3 总经理对雪梅的面试表现满意不满意？为什么？

課文

Audio

21世紀初以來，中國的經濟有了很大的發展，不少跨國公司進入中國。這些大公司吸引了世界各地不少的人材[a]，包括一些在國外學習畢業的中國留學生。他們從海外歸來，被叫做"海歸"。有的人還開玩笑地把他們叫做"海龜[b]"。林雪梅現在就是其中的一隻新"海龜"。

雪梅回到中國以後不久，就開始上網查資料、找工作。她去過幾家公司實習，但是都不太滿意。昨天有一家她非常喜歡的大公司叫她今天上午去面試銷售經理的工作。面試以後，剛回到家裡就接到麗莎的電話。

哎，"海龜"小姐，今天的面試怎麼樣？

哈，開始有些緊張，出了好多汗，套裝的上衣都快濕了。

你已經不是第一次面試了，幹嗎那麼緊張？

給我面試的是他們公司的總經理，挺嚴肅的，第一句話就是："你是不是在美國找不到工作才回中國來的？"

這個總經理可真的挺嚇人的！難怪你緊張。

Before You Study

Answer the following questions in Chinese to prepare for the reading.

1 你覺得面試前應該怎麼準備？

2 你覺得面試的時候怎麼能讓自己不緊張？

3 你覺得面試的時候應該注意些什麼？

When You Study

Listen to the audio recording and scan the text; then answer the following questions in Chinese.

1 雪梅到底為什麼回中國工作？

2 雪梅覺得自己的缺點是什麼？

3 總經理對雪梅的面試表現滿意不滿意？為什麼？

257

我越紧张就越[1]解释不清楚。后来我突然想出了一个主意，什么也不说了，从包里拿出两张纸，放到他前面。他一看，脸上马上阴转多云[c]了。

什么纸？我也去买两张准备着。

是加州的两家公司五月寄给我的录用通知。总经理看了接着问："既然[2]你在美国公司找到了工作，为什么还要回中国工作呢？"

这个问题不难回答，你的男朋友在中国留学嘛！

我要是这样说，他很可能会以为我在中国找工作，只是短期打算。好在这个时候我已经不紧张了。我就从中国经济发展，谈到他们公司的产品，再谈产品的销售，然后解释为什么希望去他们公司工作。总经理听着听着[3]，脸上多云转晴[d]了。

面试完了吧？

还没呢！这时候总经理突然笑着问："你觉得你自己最大的缺点是什么？"

哈，我觉得，你最大的缺点就是爱吃零食[e]。

那他不是要把我看成小女孩了？

那你是怎么回答的？

我越緊張就越[1]解釋不清楚。後來我突然想出了一個主意,什麼也不說了,從包裡拿出兩張紙,放到他前面。他一看,臉上馬上陰轉多雲[c]了。

什麼紙?我也去買兩張準備著。

是加州的兩家公司五月寄給我的錄用通知。總經理看了接著問:"既然[2]你在美國公司找到了工作,為什麼還要回中國工作呢?"

這個問題不難回答,你的男朋友在中國留學嘛!

我要是這樣說,他很可能會以為我在中國找工作,只是短期打算。好在這個時候我已經不緊張了。我就從中國經濟發展,談到他們公司的產品,再談產品的銷售,然後解釋為什麼希望去他們公司工作。總經理聽著聽著[3],臉上多雲轉晴[d]了。

面試完了吧?

還沒呢!這時候總經理突然笑著問:"你覺得你自己最大的缺點是什麼?"

哈,我覺得,你最大的缺點就是愛吃零食[e]。

那他不是要把我看成小女孩了?

那你是怎麼回答的?

我说，一个好的销售管理人材，应该能科学地安排自己的时间，善于工作的人往往也是善于休息的，我在这方面还很不够。实习的时候，我工作一有压力就熬夜加班。所以，不太会休息可能是我最大的缺点。

雪梅，你到底是在说自己的缺点还是优点啊？

我又说，只要我们能把缺点变成优点，缺点就没那么可怕了。说到这儿，总经理站起来，一边跟我握手，一边笑着说，他相信我的能力，让我等他们的好消息。

太棒了！恭喜你，林经理！

View & Explore

Video

For deeper language immersion and more cultural information, watch "Job Interview," a short, supplemental video clip by Cheng & Tsui on this lesson's theme.

我說，一個好的銷售管理人材，應該能科學地安排自己的時間，善於工作的人往往也是善於休息的，我在這方面還很不夠。實習的時候，我工作一有壓力就熬夜加班。所以，不太會休息可能是我最大的缺點。

雪梅，你到底是在說自己的缺點還是優點啊？

我又說，只要我們能把缺點變成優點，缺點就沒那麼可怕了。說到這兒，總經理站起來，一邊跟我握手，一邊笑著說，他相信我的能力，讓我等他們的好消息。

太棒了！恭喜你，林經理！

After You Study

Answer the following questions in Chinese.

1 什麼樣的人被叫做"海龜"？為什麼？

2 怎麼樣才算是優秀的銷售管理人材？

3 什麼樣的面試才算是成功的面試？

Language Notes

a 人材 vs. 人才

人材 can also be written as 人才. For all intents and purposes, they are interchangeable. 材 means "timber" or "material." As a noun, 才 means "talent" or "ability."

b 海龟/海龜

海龟/海龜, meaning "sea turtle," is a facetious pun. It is pronounced the same as 海归/海歸 ("a returnee from overseas," typically someone highly educated or qualified). The opposite of 海龟/海龜 is 土鳖/土鳖 (tǔbiē), or "rustic soft-shelled turtle," often used self-deprecatingly by people who have never studied abroad.

c 阴转多云/陰轉多雲

阴转多云/陰轉多雲 means "from overcast to partly cloudy." It is a phrase borrowed from weather forecasts that is often jokingly used to describe a slight improvement in a person's mood as reflected by a change in his/her facial expression.

d 多云转晴/多雲轉晴

多云转晴/多雲轉晴, another weather phrase, means "from partly cloudy to sunny." It is sometimes used to describe the brightening of a person's facial expression.

e 零食 vs. 小吃

零食 refers to things like candies, crackers, melon seeds, chips, and so on. 小吃, on the other hand, are informal, light meals. 零食 are store-bought whereas 小吃 are made at home, in specialized restaurants, or at roadside food stands. Furthermore, unlike 小吃, 零食 is not generally associated with any particular region. For these reasons, 零食 and 小吃 cannot be used interchangeably.

Vocabulary

No.	Simplified	Traditional	Pinyin	Part of Speech	Definition
1	世纪	世紀	shìjì	n	century
2	跨国	跨國	kuàguó	adj	transnational, multinational
3	进入	進入	jìnrù	v	to enter, to get into
4	吸引	吸引	xīyǐn	v	to attract, to draw, to fascinate
5	人材	人材	réncái	v	person of ability and talent
6	国外	國外	guówài	n	abroad
7	海外	海外	hǎiwài	n	overseas
8	归来	歸來	guīlái	v	to return, to come back
9	叫做	叫做	jiào zuò	vc	to be called, to be known as
10	海龟	海龜	hǎiguī	n	sea turtle
11	满意	滿意	mǎnyì	v	to be satisfied, to be pleased
12	销售	銷售	xiāoshòu	v	to sell, to market
13	经理	經理	jīnglǐ	n	manager
14	套装	套裝	tàozhuāng	n	suit, a set of matching outer garments
15	上衣	上衣	shàngyī	n	upper outer garment, jacket
16	湿	濕	shī	adj	wet
17	干吗	幹嗎	gànmá	qpr	why, why on earth, whatever for
18	总	總	zǒng	adj	general, chief
19	严肃	嚴肅	yánsù	adj	stern, serious
20	吓人	嚇人	xiàrén	adj	scary, frightening
21	解释	解釋	jiěshì	v	to explain
22	阴	陰	yīn	adj	overcast, hidden from the sun

No.	Simplified	Traditional	Pinyin	Part of Speech	Definition
23	转	轉	*zhuǎn*	v	to turn, to shift, to change
24	云	雲	*yún*	n	cloud
25	寄	寄	*jì*	v	to mail, to send
26	录用	錄用	*lùyòng*	v	to take someone on staff, to employ
27	通知	通知	*tōngzhī*	n/v	notice; to notify, to inform
28	既然	既然	*jìrán*	conj	since, as, now that [See Grammar 2.]
29	接着	接著	*jiēzhe*	v	to follow, to continue
30	回答	回答	*huídá*	v	to reply, to answer
31	短期	短期	*duǎnqī*	n	short term
32	好在	好在	*hǎozài*	adv	fortunately, luckily
33	产品	產品	*chǎnpǐn*	n	product, merchandise
34	晴	晴	*qíng*	adj	sunny

林雪梅希望到跨国公司做销售经理。你将来想做什么工作？为什么？

林雪梅希望到跨國公司做銷售經理。你將來想做什麼工作？為什麼？

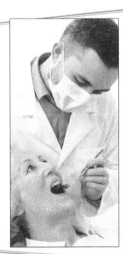

No.	Simplified	Traditional	Pinyin	Part of Speech	Definition
35	缺点	缺點	*quēdiǎn*	n	shortcoming, defect, weakness
36	零食	零食	*língshí*	n	snack
37	善于	善於	*shànyú*		to be good at, to be adept in
38	往往	往往	*wǎngwǎng*	adv	more often than not
39	加班	加班	*jiā bān*	vo	to work overtime, to work extra shifts
40	优点	優點	*yōudiǎn*	n	merit, strong point, advantage
41	可怕	可怕	*kěpà*	adj	awful, terrible, fearful
42	握手	握手	*wò shǒu*	vo	to shake hands, to clasp hands
43	能力	能力	*nénglì*	n	ability, capacity, competence

GET Real WITH CHINESE

Having just graduated from college, you've decided to start looking for jobs in Taiwan. You come across this ad on an online job posting site. What position is being advertised? What kind of company posted the ad, and are you qualified for the position? Based on the information on job responsibilities and benefits, would you be interested in applying?

Grammar

The structure 越 X 越 Y

"越 X 越 Y" means that Y changes in accordance with X, or "the more X, the more Y."

A

我越紧张就越解释不清楚。

我越緊張就越解釋不清楚。

The more nervous I got, the more incoherent my explanation became.

B

你别说了，你越说我越不懂。

你別說了，你越說我越不懂。

Stop, please. The more you explain, the less I understand.

C

他很着急，车越开越快。

他很著急，車越開越快。

He was in a big rush. He began to drive [his car] faster and faster.

D

明天你尽可能早点来，越早越好。

明天你儘可能早點來，越早越好。

Tomorrow, come as early as you can. The earlier, the better.

The conjunction 既然

既然 is used in the first clause of a compound sentence. It restates a known scenario, reason, or premise. The main clause presents the logical conclusion derived from the condition outlined in the first clause.

A

既然你在美国公司找到了工作，为什么还要回中国工作呢？

既然你在美國公司找到了工作，為什麼還要回中國工作呢？

Since you've already found a job with an American company, why do you still want to come back to work in China?

[The speaker knows that the other person found a job at an American company.]

B Person A

老师，今天下午我应该去你的办公室谈我这个学期的表现，可是我病了。

老師，今天下午我應該去你的辦公室談我這個學期的表現，可是我病了。

Teacher, I was supposed to go to your office to discuss my performance this semester, but I got sick.

Person B

既然你病了，就换个时间吧。

既然你病了，就換個時間吧。

Since you're sick, let's find another time.

C Person A

昨天我们看的那套公寓，听说已经卖了。

昨天我們看的那套公寓，聽說已經賣了。

I heard that the apartment we saw yesterday has already been sold.

Person B

既然那套卖了，那么我们再看看别的房子吧。

既然那套賣了，那麼我們再看看別的房子吧。

Since that apartment has been sold, let's look at some other ones.

Note that although 既然 also indicates a reason, it must already be known or stated. It is not interchangeable with 因为/因為.

Verb 着 verb 着···/Verb 著 verb 著···

The pattern "Verb 着 verb 着···/Verb 著 verb 著···" must be followed by a verbal phrase. It signifies that while the action denoted in the phrase "Verb 着 verb 着···/Verb 著 verb 著···" is going on, a second action happens as an unintended result or by surprise. The adverb 就 often appears in the second verbal phrase, as in (B) and (C), but it can be omitted, as in (A) and (D).

A 总经理听着听着，脸上多云转晴了。

總經理聽著聽著，臉上多雲轉晴了。

As the general manager listened to me, his gloomy face gradually brightened up.

B 妈妈走了以后，那个孩子哭着哭着就睡着了。

媽媽走了以後，那個孩子哭著哭著就睡著了。

After his mother left, the child cried and cried and fell asleep.

C 我第一次来这个城市，开车出去，开着开着就不知道东南西北了。

我第一次來這個城市，開車出去，開著開著就不知道東南西北了。

The first time I came to this city, I drove around and around and lost my sense of direction before I knew it.

D 弟弟躺在床上想下午刚看的电影，想着想着笑了起来。

弟弟躺在床上想下午剛看的電影，想著想著笑了起來。

Lying in bed and thinking about the movie he had just seen this afternoon, my younger brother burst out laughing.

Words & Phrases

叫做 (to be called, to be known as)

叫做 is a "verb + complement" construction. It occurs mainly in formal speech.

1

他们从海外归来，被叫做"海归"。

他們從海外歸來，被叫做"海歸"。

They are returnees from abroad. They are called "repatriates."

2

我们把一年级的学生叫做"新生"。

我們把一年級的學生叫做"新生"。

We call first-year students "freshmen."

3

"花生"在中国南方有的地方叫做"土豆"。

"花生"在中國南方有的地方叫做"土豆"。

In some parts of southern China, "peanuts" (花生/花生) are called 土豆.

Characterize it!

More characters

❶ 春	**❷** 晨
❸ 暖	**❹** 晴

What do the characters mean?

What is the common radical?

What does the radical mean?

How does the radical relate to the overall meaning of the characters?

1 春	**2** 晨
3 暖	**4** 晴

好在 (fortunately, luckily)

好在 is used to point out something in someone's favor in an otherwise unfavorable situation.

1
好在这个时候我已经不紧张了。

好在這個時候我已經不緊張了。

Luckily, by that time I was no longer nervous.

2 Person A
哎呀，我的录用通知拉在房间了。

哎呀，我的錄用通知拉在房間了。

Shoot, I left my job offer letter in the room.

Person B
快回去拿吧，好在我们走得不远。

快回去拿吧，好在我們走得不遠。

Go back and get it. Fortunately, we haven't gone very far.

3
今天老师突然说要考汉字，好在我这几天练习写汉字了，要不然一定考得很糟糕。

今天老師突然說要考漢字，好在我這幾天練習寫漢字了，要不然一定考得很糟糕。

Today the teacher suddenly announced that there would be a test on Chinese characters. Luckily, I had been practicing writing characters over the last few days. Otherwise I definitely would have flunked the test.

善于/善於 (to be good at, to be adept in)

善于/善於 means "to excel in something." It occurs in formal Chinese.

1
善于工作的人往往也是善于休息的人。

善於工作的人往往也是善於休息的人。

People who know how to work often also know how to rest.

2

这个人在大家面前很善于表现自己的优点。

這個人在大家面前很善於表現自己的優點。

This person is good at showing off his strong points to everyone.

3

很多人不善于理财投资，这可能会影响他们退休后的
生活。

很多人不善於理財投資，這可能會影響他們退休後的
生活。

Many people are not good at financial planning and investing. This might affect
their lives after retirement.

D 往往 (more often than not) vs. 常常 (often)

往往 is an adverb indicating that a certain action is likely to occur under certain circumstances.

1

周末我往往跟家人在一起，很少去公司加班。

週末我往往跟家人在一起，很少去公司加班。

On weekends, more often than not I am with my family. I rarely put in extra time
at work.

2

在跨国贸易公司工作的人，往往必须跟不同国家的
人打交道。

在跨國貿易公司工作的人，往往必須跟不同國家的
人打交道。

People who work at multinational companies often have to interact with people
from different countries.

3

这个健身房中午往往一个客人也没有，我想不是太
贵，就是管理得不好。

這個健身房中午往往一個客人也沒有，我想不是太
貴，就是管理得不好。

This gym is often completely empty at midday. I think it's either because it is too
expensive or because it is badly managed.

往往 is used in reference to predictable circumstances based on past experience. By contrast, 常常 refers to actions that do not follow any set pattern. 常常 can refer to future events. 往往 cannot.

4

请你以后常常来我们工厂参观。

請你以後常常來我們工廠參觀。

Please come visit our factory often.

[✕ 请你以后往往来我们工厂参观。]

[✕ 請你以後往往來我們工廠參觀。]

When the sentence is about a habitual action or behavior that is not bound to a specific time, only 常常 can be used.

5

爷爷奶奶很重视锻炼身体，常常去公园打太极拳。

爺爺奶奶很重視鍛煉身體，常常去公園打太極拳。

Grandpa and Grandma take exercising seriously. They often go to the park to do tai chi.

A WAY WITH WORDS

严肃

嚴肅

Using the word/phrase in orange as a clue, try to figure out the meaning of the words/phrases in blue; consult a dictionary if necessary. Consider how the literal and extended senses are related in each case.

我小时候每次做错了事爸爸都严厉地骂我，所以我很怕他。

老师对我们的要求很严格，每个汉字都要我们写二十遍。

我小時候每次做錯了事爸爸都嚴厲地罵我，所以我很怕他。

老師對我們的要求很嚴格，每個漢字都要我們寫二十遍。

Language Practice

A | **Well, why don't you?** | INTERPERSONAL

Suppose someone asks you a question that you aren't in a position to answer. In pairs, practice suggesting that the other person try another source for the information. Complete the answers using 干吗不/幹嗎不, e.g.:

Person A 我们星期几有考试？

我們星期幾有考試？

Person B 老师知道，今天下午→你干吗不今天下午问老师？

老師知道，今天下午→你幹嗎不今天下午問老師？

1 **Person A** 我肚子疼，不知道应该吃什么药。

我肚子疼，不知道應該吃什麼藥。

Person B 医生知道，现在→

醫生知道，現在→

2 **Person A** 你觉得那家跨国公司会不会录用我？

你覺得那家跨國公司會不會錄用我？

Person B 面试你的人知道，等几天→

面試你的人知道，等幾天→

3 **Person A** 那家服装店的衣服什么时候打折？

那家服裝店的衣服什麼時候打折？

Person B 上网查，马上→

上網查，馬上→

4　Person A　糖醋鱼怎么做？

糖醋魚怎麼做？

　　Person B　哥哥会做，明天→

哥哥會做，明天→

5　Person A　现在炒股，会赚钱还是赔钱？

现在炒股，會賺錢還是賠錢？

　　Person B　钱教授常常炒股，下个星期→

錢教授常常炒股，下個星期→

More, more, more

PRESENTATIONAL

Use the pattern "越 X 越 Y" to express the idea of "the more X, the more Y," e.g.:

李文忙　　　　　　　　　　　李文睡不好觉

李文忙　　　　　　　　　　　李文睡不好覺

李文越忙越睡不好觉。

李文越忙越睡不好覺。

1　丽莎学太极拳　　　　　　　丽莎喜欢太极拳
　　麗莎學太極拳　　　　　　　麗莎喜歡太極拳

2　总经理听雪梅说话　　　　　总经理觉得雪梅是个人材
　　總經理聽雪梅說話　　　　　總經理覺得雪梅是個人材

3　柯林开车开得快　　　　　　雪梅紧张
　　柯林開車開得快　　　　　　雪梅緊張

4 王爷爷不锻炼身体　　　　　　王爷爷容易生病

　　　王爺爺不鍛煉身體　　　　　　王爺爺容易生病

5 你不理财　　　　　　　　　　你没有钱

　　　你不理財　　　　　　　　　　你沒有錢

C 　　　　　**If that's the case . . .**　　　　INTERPERSONAL

In pairs, take turns role-playing two friends. One friend is always busy, messy, late, and forgetful. The other friend is flexible and quick to respond appropriately. Use 既然, e.g.:

  Occasion: playing mahjong

  Excuse: working an extra shift

  Suggestion: find another person

Person A　　对不起，我今天晚上得加班，不能跟你打麻将了。

　　　　　　　對不起，我今天晚上得加班，不能跟你打麻將了。

Person B　　既然你得加班，我就找别人吧。

　　　　　　　既然你得加班，我就找別人吧。

1 Occasion: hosting a birthday party

  Excuse: room being a mess

  Suggestion: come to your house

2 Occasion: traveling to Harbin to see the ice lanterns

  Excuse: must take classes during winter break

  Suggestion: go next year

3 Occasion: going hiking in the mountains

  Excuse: feet hurt

  Suggestion: take him/her to see the doctor

4 Occasion: going to see a ball game

  Excuse: forgot the tickets at home

  Suggestion: go to his/her place to get tickets together

Pure luck

Imagine a potentially disadvantageous or even disastrous situation. What would be the best thing that could happen? Based on the prompts, use 好在 to state how lucky you are/were, e.g.:

Teacher gave a pop quiz today.　　　　　　　　　　　I reviewed last night.

老师今天突然给我们考试，好在我昨天晚上复习了。

老師今天突然給我們考試，好在我昨天晚上復習了。

1　The stock market dropped one hundred points today.　　I no longer flip stocks.

2　The air conditioner broke last night.　　It's only twenty-seven degrees Celsius today.

3　The cost of electricity is skyrocketing.　　My house is powered by solar power.

4　The energy crisis seems to be more and more serious.　　More and more countries use solar and wind power.

5　There were too many dynasties and emperors in Chinese history.　　I'm not a Chinese history major.

Human resources

A business leader needs to know what expertise is necessary to succeed at a particular job. Imagine that you're forming a new company. Who would you hire? Practice describing the kinds of employees you need for various departments, e.g.:

marketing department

我们必须录用善于销售的人材。

我們必須錄用善於銷售的人材。

1　management

2　research department

3　energy conservation department

4　financial planning department

Bundle of nerves

For first-time job seekers, interviewing can be a nerve-racking experience. In pairs, take turns describing how nervous a first-time interviewee could be, e.g.:

being informed about the interview in a phone call   was startled

接到面试电话通知时，我紧张得吓了一跳。

接到面試電話通知時，我緊張得嚇了一跳。

1	leaving for the interview	left my car keys in my house
2	meeting the company's manager	forgot to shake her hand
3	answering the first question	couldn't speak
4	answering the second question	couldn't explain clearly
5	sitting in the manager's office	was sweating a lot
6	before the interview ended	forgot to ask when I would hear back
7	saying goodbye to the manager	forgot to shake her hand

A WAY WITH WORDS

可怕

小林每天都找中国同学
练习说中文，这种学习
态度是很可贵的。

我认识她好几年了，知
道她做事非常可靠。

Using the word/phrase in orange as a clue, try to figure out the meaning of the words/phrases in blue; consult a dictionary if necessary. Consider how the literal and extended senses are related in each case.

可怕

小林每天都找中國同學
練習說中文，這種學習
態度是很可貴的。

我認識她好幾年了，知
道她做事非常可靠。

Now that you've followed the adventures of Zhang Tianming and his friends for more than six months, do you know them well?

1   In pairs, discuss and list the strengths and weaknesses of Zhang Tianming and his friends. Start off by saying:

张天明有什么优点、缺点？

張天明有什麼優點、缺點？

	优点/優點	缺点/缺點
	_____	_____
	_____	_____
	_____	_____
	_____	_____
	_____	_____

2   Then use your list to present your thoughts to the class. Start by saying:

我们认为 (character's name) 的优点是……缺点是……

我們認為 (character's name) 的優點是……缺點是……

3   Finally, present to the class on which strengths and weaknesses you do and don't share with the characters:

我跟 (character's name)（不）一样，我的优点是……
缺点是……

我跟 (character's name)（不）一樣，我的優點是……
缺點是……

I'm so happy for you

Alongside 太好了, 太棒了, and 我真为你高兴/我真為你高興, 恭喜 is another good word to express happiness that someone has received good news or accomplished something. In pairs, take turns expressing happiness for your partner, e.g.:

passed the college entrance exam

太棒了，恭喜你考上大学。

太棒了，恭喜你考上大學。

1 passed the graduate school entrance exam

2 bought a new house

3 won the competition

4 won first prize

5 aced the interview and got the job

Opportunities and obstacles

What advantages and disadvantages might there be for people and companies deciding whether to move to or start operations in China?

1 Connect each noun with a predicate to form possible reasons why people might or might not want to work, live, or do business in China.

中国吸引人的地方：

中國吸引人的地方：

衣食住行	很美
经济发展/經濟發展	越来越先进/越來越先進
机会/機會	很快
有特色的小吃	越来越方便/越來越方便
科学技术/科學技術	非常多
旅游景点/旅遊景點	又多又好吃

Add your own: _____ _____

中国不吸引人的地方：

中國不吸引人的地方：

人口	太吵
空气污染/空氣汙染	太多
交通	太大
环境/環境	很严重/很嚴重
投资风险/投資風險	太乱/太亂

Add your own: _____   _____

2 In pairs, discuss the desirable and undesirable aspects you've identified, and your own thoughts. Would you want to work, live, and do business in China?

3 A transnational company is investigating opening a branch office in China. With your partner, discuss what your advice to this company would be.

Chinese Chat

Lin Xuemei just posted this on Qzone after her job interview. What would you say to her?

‹动态   好友动态   ⊕

雪梅
今天08:32 PM

下午的面试真吓人，从来没碰见过这么严肃的总经理！在中国当"海龟"不容易啊……

👍 💬 ↗

👍 2人觉得很赞

柯林: 中国经济需要你这样的跨国人材，你一定能找到满意的工作的！

You: ...

雪梅
下午的面試真嚇人，從來沒碰見過這麼嚴肅的總經理！在中國當"海龜"不容易啊……

柯林: 中國經濟需要你這樣的跨國人材，你一定能找到滿意的工作的！

You: ...

MULTI-NATIONAL Companies

Many of the world's largest and best-known multinational companies have set up shop in China in recent decades, hoping to take advantage of the purchasing power of the country's burgeoning middle class. Starbucks and most of the fast-food franchises have become familiar sights to Chinese urbanites. Retailers such as Walmart and Ikea have also found success in China. This is a significant change from the beginning of the century, when China was known mainly as "the world's factory," while its tantalizing market potential remained elusive. Today, China continues to be a manufacturing powerhouse. Many Fortune 500 companies such as GM, Ford, Volkswagen, Motorola, Nokia, Siemens, Exxon Mobil, Sony, and Toyota have joint ventures or wholly owned subsidiaries in China. Other companies, especially social networking services like Facebook, have struggled to find ways to enter the Chinese market.

COMPARE & CONTRAST

1 What types of questions are expected during job interviews in your country? What questions are considered inappropriate or off limits? Do universities in your country help graduating seniors prepare for job interviews?

2 Job seekers desperate to find a job often send their resumes out in large quantities, a practice called 海投 (lit. ocean toss). Would you take a similar approach to applying for jobs, or would you be more selective in your process?

3 What are some unspoken do's and don't's at workplaces in your country? Research Chinese business etiquette online and see how it compares to what you're accustomed to.

Repatriated Students

According to Chinese government sources, from 1978 to 2015, more than 230,000 of the Chinese students who studied abroad returned to settle in China. With the help of money allocated by the government, many returnees from overseas have opened businesses in China and become successful entrepreneurs. The majority of China's universlty presidents, doctoral advisors, and high-ranking scientists have studied abroad. Many of China's earlier leaders, including Sun Yat-sen, Zhou Enlai, and Deng Xiaoping, can also be considered 海归/海歸.

Interviews

If a candidate's resume catches the attention of an employer, he/she may be invited to participate in an initial interview (一面), a second interview (二面), and a final interview (终面/終面). Some interviews are conducted in groups (群面), and some include a written test (笔试/筆試).

Lesson Wrap-Up

Project

You are interested in a marketing job that has opened up at the branch office of a Chinese company in your country. In pairs, conduct a mock interview. First, study this resume template to get an idea of what information Chinese employers look for. Next, rehearse appropriate questions and responses together—how to begin, carry out, and conclude the interview. Finally, take turns role-playing the interviewer and the applicant.

个 人 简 历

填表日期：

姓名			性别		年龄		[贴照片]
地址	邮政编码			电子邮件			
	电话			传真			
毕业学校及专业							
应聘职务							
教育							
奖励							
语言							
工作经历							
推荐							
技能							
获得证书							

個人簡歷

填表日期：

姓名		性別		年齡		[貼照片]

地址						[貼照片]
	郵政編碼		電子郵件			
	電話		傳真			

畢業學校及專業	

應聘職務	

教育		

獎勵	

語言	

工作經歷	

推薦	

技能	

獲得證書	

ESSENTIAL WORDS

Chinese	Pinyin	English
性别/性別	xìngbié	gender
年龄/年齡	niánlíng	age
地址	dìzhǐ	address
应聘职务/應聘職務	yìngpìn zhíwù	position applied for
教育背景	jiàoyù bèijǐng	educational background

Chinese	Pinyin	English
奖励/獎勵	*jiǎnglì*	awards
语言/語言	*yǔyán*	languages
工作经历/工作經歷	*gōngzuò jīnglì*	work experience
推荐/推薦	*tuījiàn*	recommendations
技能	*jìnéng*	skills
获得证书/獲得證書	*huòdé zhèngshū*	certificates received

Keep It Flowing

First, study the following example; pay particular attention to how the highlighted parts help the sentences flow smoothly from one to the next. Notice how:

- an introductory statement (我是从中国 X 大学毕业的/我是從中國 X 大學畢業的) launches a narrative
- following a timeline (三年前, 今年) organizes a narrative
- certain prepositions (因为/因為) introduce reason
- certain adverbs (也) signify addition
- certain conjunctions (如果) introduce a hypothetical scenario
- certain prepositions (为/為) introduce purpose (公司的发展/公司的發展)

林雪梅这样介绍自己

我是从中国X大学毕业的。三年前到美国X大学学习工商管理，今年想在中国找一个适合自己的工作。

你们公司（贵公司）在世界上很有名，我来这里工作一定能学到很多东西，也相信我来这里工作，会对贵公司有贡献。因为我非常了解贵公司的情况，也对公司以后怎样发展有一些想法。如果你们录用了我，我一定和公司的其他人一起，为公司的发展好好地工作。

林雪梅這樣介紹自己

我是從中國X大學畢業的。三年前到美國X大學學習工商管理，今年想在中國找一個適合自己的工作。

你們公司（貴公司）在世界上很有名，我來這裡工作一定能學到很多東西，也相信我來這裡工作，會對貴公司有貢獻。因為我非常了解貴公司的情況，也對公司以後怎樣發展有一些想法。如果你們錄用了我，我一定和公司的其他人一起，為公司的發展好好地工作。

How would you introduce yourself to a potential employer? Use as many of the cohesive devices highlighted in the example on the previous page/above as possible to string together your response, based on the prompts. Other connective words and phrases to consider include 不但⋯而且 and 在⋯方面.

- 你是在哪个大学学习，或是从哪个大学（或者研究生院）毕业的？

  你是在哪個大學學習，或是從哪個大學（或者研究生院）畢業的？

- 你在学校是哪个系、哪个专业的学生？

  你在學校是哪個系、哪個專業的學生？

- 为什么要到这个公司或学校来实习或工作？

  為什麼要到這個公司或學校來實習或工作？

- 你觉得为什么这个公司或学校应该录用你？

  你覺得為什麼這個公司或學校應該錄用你？

- 如果这个公司或学校录用你，你会怎样工作？

  如果這個公司或學校錄用你，你會怎樣工作？

Can-Do Check List ✔

Before proceeding to Lesson 20, make sure you can complete the following tasks in Chinese:

- ☐ Explain why China has been able to attract talent and corporations from overseas
- ☐ Describe overseas returnees and their nickname
- ☐ Recount a nerve-racking interview
- ☐ Handle typical job interview questions

Èrshí yī shìjì chū yǐlái, Zhōngguó de jīngjì yǒu le hěn dà de fāzhǎn, bù shǎo kuàguó gōngsī jìn rù Zhōngguó. Zhè xiē dà gōngsī xīyǐn le shìjiè gè dì bù shǎo de réncái[a], bāokuò yì xie zài guówài xuéxí bìyè de Zhōngguó liúxuéshēng. Tāmen cóng hǎiwài guīlái, bèi jiào zuò "hǎiguī". Yǒude rén hái kāi wánxiào de bǎ tāmen jiào zuò "hǎiguī[b]". Lín Xuěméi jiù shì qízhōng de yì zhī xīn "hǎiguī".

Xuěméi huí dào Zhōngguó yǐhòu bù jiǔ, jiù kāishǐ shàng wǎng chá zīliào, zhǎo gōngzuò. Tā qù guo jǐ jiā gōngsī shíxí, dànshì dōu bú tài mǎnyì. Zuótiān yǒu yì jiā tā fēicháng xǐhuan de dà gōngsī jiào tā jīntiān shàngwǔ qù miànshì xiāoshòu jīnglǐ de gōngzuò. Miànshì yǐhòu, gāng huí dào jiā li jiù jiē dào Lìshā de diànhuà.

 Āi, "hǎiguī" xiǎojie, jīntiān de miànshì zěnmeyàng?

 Hā, kāishǐ yǒu xiē jǐnzhāng, chū le hǎo duō hàn, tàozhuāng de shàngyī dōu kuài shī le.

 Nǐ yǐjīng bú shì dì yī cì miànshì le, gànmá nàme jǐnzhāng?

 Gěi wǒ miànshì de shì tāmen gōngsī de zǒng jīnglǐ, tǐng yánsù de, dì yī jù huà jiù shì: "Nǐ shì bú shì zài Měiguó zhǎo bú dào gōngzuò cái huí Zhōngguó lái de?"

 Zhè ge zǒng jīnglǐ kě zhēn de tǐng xiàrén de! Nánguài nǐ jǐnzhāng.

 Wǒ yuè jǐnzhāng jiù yuè[1] jiěshì bù qīngchu. Hòulái wǒ tūrán xiǎng chū le yí ge zhúyi, shénme yě bù shuō le, cóng bāo li ná chu liǎng zhāng zhǐ, fàng dào tā qiánmian. Tā yí kàn, liǎn shang mǎshàng yīn zhuǎn duō yún[c] le.

 Shénme zhǐ? Wǒ yě qù mǎi liǎng zhāng zhǔnbèi zhe.

 Shì Jiāzhōu de liǎng jiā gōngsī wǔyuè jì gěi wǒ de lùyòng tōngzhī. Zǒng jīnglǐ kàn le jiēzhe wèn: "Jìrán[2] nǐ zài Měiguó gōngsī zhǎo dào le gōngzuò, wèishénme hái yào huí Zhōngguó gōngzuò ne?"

 Zhè ge wèntí bù nán huídá, nǐ de nán péngyou zài Zhōngguó liú xué ma!

 Wǒ yàoshi zhèyàng shuō, tā hěn kěnéng huì yǐwéi wǒ zài Zhōngguó zhǎo gōngzuò, zhǐ shì duǎnqī dǎsuàn. Hǎozài zhè ge shíhou wǒ yǐjīng bù jǐnzhāng le. Wǒ jiù cóng Zhōngguó jīngjì fāzhǎn, tán dào tāmen gōngsī de chǎnpǐn, zài tán chǎnpǐn de xiāoshòu, ránhòu jiěshì wèishénme xīwàng qù tāmen gōngsī gōngzuò. Zǒng jīnglǐ tīng zhe tīng zhe[3], liǎn shang duō yún zhuǎn qíng[d] le.

 Miànshì wán le ba?

 Hái méi ne! Zhè shíhou zǒng jīnglǐ tūrán xiào zhe wèn: "Nǐ juéde nǐ zìjǐ zuì dà de quēdiǎn shì shénme?"

 Hā, wǒ juéde, nǐ zuì dà de quēdiǎn jiù shì ài chī língshí[e].

 Nà tā bú shì yào bǎ wǒ kàn chéng xiǎo nǚhái le?

 Nà nǐ shì zěnme huídá de?

 Wǒ shuō, yí ge hǎo de xiāoshòu guǎnlǐ réncái, yīnggāi néng kēxué de ānpái zìjǐ de shíjiān, shànyú gōngzuò de rén wǎngwǎng yě shì shànyú xiūxi de, wǒ zài zhè fāngmiàn hái hěn bú gòu. Shíxí de shíhou, wǒ gōngzuò yì yǒu yālì jiù áo yè jiā bān. Suǒyǐ, bú tài huì xiūxi kěnéng shì wǒ zuì dà de quēdiǎn.

 Xuěméi, nǐ dàodǐ shì zài shuō zìjǐ de quēdiǎn háishi yōudiǎn a?

 Wǒ yòu shuō, zhǐyào wǒmen néng bǎ quēdiǎn biàn chéng yōudiǎn, quēdiǎn jiù méi nàme kěpà le. Shuō dào zhèr, zǒng jīnglǐ zhàn qi lai, yìbiān gēn wǒ wò shǒu, yìbiān xiào zhe shuō, tā xiāngxìn wǒ de nénglì, ràng wǒ děng tāmen de hǎo xiāoxi.

 Tài bàng le! Gōngxǐ nǐ, Lín jīnglǐ!

世界变小了

世界變小了

THE WORLD IS GETTING SMALLER

Learning Objectives

In this lesson, you will learn to:

- Explain the purpose of a gathering
- Request and offer help
- Discuss adjusting to life in a new country
- Describe how the world is getting smaller

Relate and Get Ready

In your own culture/community:

- How do people welcome visitors from far away?
- How do people send off friends before a long trip?
- Is it considered appropriate to ask about someone's profession when meeting for the first time?

课文

Text

Audio

Before You Study

Answer the following questions in Chinese to prepare for the reading.

1 要是开晚会，你会准备一些什么吃的、喝的、玩儿的？

2 你们学校一般怎么欢迎从国外来的客人？

3 你们学校的国际留学生多不多？学校怎么帮助他们适应新的学习环境？

When You Study

Listen to the audio recording and scan the text; then answer the following questions in Chinese.

1 大家为什么到雪梅住的地方聚会？

2 请说说马克有什么工作经验，对自己在中国的生活满意不满意。

3 李文为什么说世界变小了？

雪梅面试后，那家公司通知她下周开始上班。雪梅和柯林都很高兴，他们决定请朋友们到雪梅住的地方来聚会，庆祝一下。

张天明的好朋友李哲也来到中国了，他接受了天明的建议，到一家跨国公司来实习。结果，庆祝晚会也成了给李哲接风[a]的晚会。

张天明和丽莎很快就要回美国了，所以这次聚会也是给他们饯行[b]的晚会。

来的客人除了天明、丽莎、李哲外，还有李文和马克。

柯林去超市买了很多饮料、零食和水果[1]。雪梅准备了一个火锅，还从附近的一家餐馆叫了外卖[c]。

今天我们大家聚在一起，是为了给李哲接风，给天明和丽莎饯行，也庆祝雪梅找到工作。

对，大家不要客气，好好吃，好好玩儿。

雪梅，恭喜你找到了好工作。什么时候上班？

下个星期一，星期五就要到欧洲出差，推销太阳能板和节能电池。

課文

Audio

雪梅面試後，那家公司通知她下週開始上班。雪梅和柯林都很高興，他們決定請朋友們到雪梅住的地方來聚會，慶祝一下。

張天明的好朋友李哲也來到中國了，他接受了天明的建議，到一家跨國公司來實習。結果，慶祝晚會也成了給李哲接風[a]的晚會。

張天明和麗莎很快就要回美國了。所以這次聚會也是給他們餞行[b]的晚會。

來的客人除了天明、麗莎、李哲外，還有李文和馬克。

柯林去超市買了很多飲料、零食和水果[1]。雪梅準備了一個火鍋，還從附近的一個餐館叫了外賣[c]。

今天我們大家聚在一起，是為了給李哲接風，給天明和麗莎餞行，也慶祝雪梅找到工作。

對，大家不要客氣，好好吃，好好玩兒。

雪梅，恭喜你找到了好工作。什麼時候上班？

下個星期一，星期五就要到歐洲出差，推銷太陽能板和節能電池。

Before You Study

Answer the following questions in Chinese to prepare for the reading.

1 要是開晚會，你會準備一些什麼吃的、喝的、玩兒的？

2 你們學校一般怎麼歡迎從國外來的客人？

3 你們學校的國際留學生多不多？學校怎麼幫助他們適應新的學習環境？

When You Study

Listen to the audio recording and scan the text; then answer the following questions in Chinese.

1 大家為什麼到雪梅住的地方聚會？

2 請說說馬克有什麼工作經驗，對自己在中國的生活滿意不滿意。

3 李文為什麼說世界變小了？

太阳能板和节能电池？太好了！最近跟环保和节能有关系的绿色产品市场上都卖得很火[d]。

哎，马克，李文，你们过来，我来介绍一下，这是我们美国大学的校友，李哲，刚从美国来。

欢迎来北京。

大家好！请多关照[e]。

李哲，你来北京哪家公司实习？

我已经告诉天明了，就是你要去的那个公司。他没把这个消息告诉你[2]？那天面试你的是我哥哥的好朋友。

真的？那我们不就是同事了吗？太好了，以后我们可以互相帮助，互相照顾。

所以我说请多关照嘛。

还不知道谁关照谁呢。

马克，你来中国多长时间了？

六年了。

马克，你在中国都做什么工作？

我是个"自由"职业者[f]，当过英文家教，演过电视剧，还拍过广告，有时候也搞点儿翻译。

我说怎么有点儿面熟呢，我看过你演的电视剧。你演得很不错。

太陽能板和節能電池？太好了！最近跟環保和節能有關係的綠色產品市場上都賣得很火[d]。

哎，馬克，李文，你們過來，我來介紹一下，這是我們美國大學的校友，李哲，剛從美國來。

歡迎來北京。

大家好！請多關照[e]。

李哲，你來北京哪家公司實習？

我已經告訴天明了，就是你要去的那個公司。他沒把這個消息告訴你[2]？那天面試你的是我哥哥的好朋友。

真的？那我們不就是同事了嗎？太好了，以後我們可以互相幫助，互相照顧。

所以我說請多關照嘛。

還不知道誰關照誰呢。

馬克，你來中國多長時間了？

六年了。

馬克，你在中國都做什麼工作？

我是個"自由"職業者[f]，當過英文家教，演過電視劇，還拍過廣告，有時候也搞點兒翻譯。

我說怎麼有點兒面熟呢，我看過你演的電視劇。你演得很不錯。

不过是三流演员而已。

看起来你的工作机会很多，很忙啊。

不一定，有的时候很忙，有的时候没事做。说白了，实际上是工作有点儿不稳定。不过没关系，生活没问题。在这儿，我生活得很快乐，交了很多中国朋友。

难怪你的中文这么好。

李哲，你哥哥的朋友真不简单啊，这么年轻就当上总经理了。

他不但懂销售，也是个很好的管理人才。听说在他的领导下，公司越办越好。

现在在中国的外国人越来越多，你们习惯中国的生活吗？

你说呢？我在你们家，每天跟你父母打太极拳，吃他们做的又好吃、又健康的饭菜，都不想回去了。

我更没问题了。

你还写博客吗？

当然。在这里，我每天都会看到、听到新鲜的事，永远也写不完。

我就不用说了，要不然怎么会住这么久呢？我觉得自己已经融入这个社会了。

我原来还怕自己适应不了这儿的生活。听了你们的话，我放心多了。

不過是三流演員而已。

看起來你的工作機會很多，很忙啊。

不一定，有的時候很忙，有的時候沒事做。說白了[g]，實際上是工作有點兒不穩定。不過沒關係，生活沒問題。在這兒，我生活得很快樂，交了很多中國朋友。

難怪你的中文這麼好。

李哲，你哥哥的朋友真不簡單啊，這麼年輕就當上總經理了。

他不但懂銷售，也是個很好的管理人材。聽說在他的領導下，公司越辦越好。

現在在中國的外國人越來越多，你們習慣中國的生活嗎？

你說呢？我在你們家，每天跟你父母打太極拳，吃他們做的又好吃、又健康的飯菜，都不想回去了。

我更沒問題了。

你還寫博客嗎？

當然。在這裡，我每天都會看到、聽到新鮮的事，永遠也寫不完。

我就不用說了，要不然怎麼會住這麼久呢？我覺得自己已經融入這個社會了。

我原來還怕自己適應不了這兒的生活。聽了你們的話，我放心多了。

现在外国人来中国发展，中国人到国外学习、工作，大家的联系多了，关系近了，世界变小了。

李文说得真好。朋友们，来，大家举起杯来，为我们的友谊干杯！

为你们在中国事业成功干杯！

祝天明和丽莎一路平安！

祝大家身体健康！

干杯！

Language Notes

a 接风/接風

接风/接風 refers to welcoming and entertaining a friend who has just returned from a long, "windy" trip. It is often used together with 洗尘/洗塵 (xǐchén) (lit., to wash off the dust [with wine]), e.g., 给（为）李哲接风洗尘/給（為）李哲接風洗塵 (to throw a banquet for Li Zhe and wash off the dust from his long trip).

b 饯行/餞行

饯行/餞行 literally means to send off a friend on a long trip with food preserved in sugar or honey. Candied fruit is called 蜜饯/蜜餞 (mìjiàn); 蜜 is honey. Like 接风洗尘/接風洗塵, 饯行/餞行 is a literary expression. Either of the prepositions 给/給 or 为/為 can also be used, e.g., 给（为）天明和丽莎饯行/給（為）天明和麗莎餞行.

c 叫外卖/叫外賣

叫外卖/叫外賣 (lit. to shout takeout) means "to order takeout." We can also say 叫车/叫車 (to hail a cab) and 叫菜/叫菜 (to order a dish).

d 火

火 can describe a brisk, flourishing business or a product that is "selling like hotcakes."

e 请多关照/請多關照

请多关照/請多關照 is a formulaic expression that approximately means "Please be liberal with your help and consideration." People often say this when introducing themselves to new colleagues for the first time. The expression is meant to convey modesty.

f 自由职业者/自由職業者

自由职业者/自由職業者 refers to members of the "liberal professions," 自由职业/自由職業 —occupations that emphasize special professional qualifications and individual responsibility, e.g., medicine and law. The term was introduced from the West. Here, Mark is making a joke: he puts the stress on 自由, and means that he is a freelancer.

g 说白了/說白了

说白了/說白了 means "to speak frankly." 白 here means "plain" or "unadorned."

 現在外國人來中國發展，中國人到國外學習、工作，大家的聯繫多了，關係近了，世界變小了。

李文說得真好。朋友們，來，大家舉起杯來，為我們的友誼乾杯！

為你們在中國事業成功乾杯！

祝天明和麗莎一路平安！

祝大家身體健康！

 乾杯！

After You Study

Answer the following questions in Chinese.

1 給人接風聚會時，說些什麼話合適？

2 給人餞行聚會時，說些什麼話合適？

3 進新公司，見到新同事，說些什麼話合適？

View & Explore

For deeper language immersion and more cultural information, watch "Foreigners in China," a short, supplemental video clip by Cheng & Tsui on this lesson's theme.

Video

Vocabulary

No.	Simplified	Traditional	Pinyin	Part of Speech	Definition
1	周	週	*zhōu*	n	week
2	聚会	聚會	*jùhuì*	v/n	to get together, to congregate; party, get-together, social gathering
3	庆祝	慶祝	*qìngzhù*	v	to celebrate
4	接受	接受	*jiēshòu*	v	to accept, to take on, to undertake
5	接风	接風	*jiēfēng*	v	to host a welcome meal for a visitor from afar
6	饯行	餞行	*jiànxíng*	v	to host a farewell meal
7	客人	客人	*kèren*	n	guest, visitor
8	火锅	火鍋	*huǒguō*	n	hotpot
9	聚	聚	*jù*	v	to gather, to get together, to congregate
10	出差	出差	*chū chāi*	vo	to be away on business or on a business trip
11	推销	推銷	*tuīxiāo*	v	to market, to promote the sale (of goods/merchandise)
12	电池	電池	*diànchí*	n	battery
13	火	火	*huǒ*	adj/n	thriving, flourishing; fire, flame
14	校友	校友	*xiàoyǒu*	n	schoolmate, alumnus, alumna
15	关照	關照	*guānzhào*	v	to take care of, to look after
16	同事	同事	*tóngshì*	n	colleague, coworker
17	者	者	*zhě*		(suffix meaning person)

No.	Simplified	Traditional	Pinyin	Part of Speech	Definition
18	电视剧	電視劇	*diànshìjù*	n	TV drama, TV series
19	搞	搞	*gǎo*	v	to do, to carry on, to be engaged in
20	面熟	面熟	*miànshú*	adj	familiar-looking
21	流	流	*liú*	n	class, level, rank, category
22	演员	演員	*yǎnyuán*	n	actor, performer
23	而已	而已	*éryǐ*	p	and no more
24	稳定	穩定	*wěndìng*	adj/v	stable, steady; to stabilize, to be steady
25	年轻	年輕	*niánqīng*	adj	young

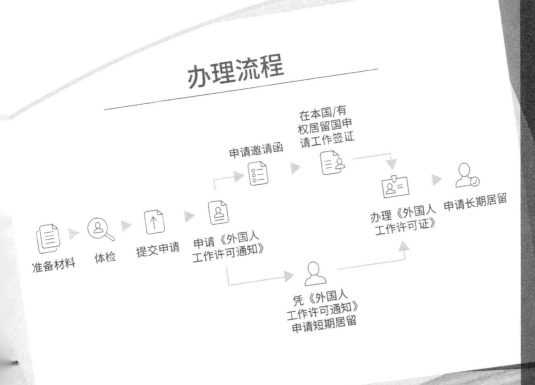

GET Real WITH CHINESE

You've received an employment offer from a Chinese company. To prepare for your move, you're studying this flow chart of the step-by-step process to apply for a long-term residency permit in China. What does the second step entail? What documentation do you need from your future employer? Where should you go in order to apply for a work visa?

No.	Simplified	Traditional	Pinyin	Part of Speech	Definition
26	永远	永遠	*yǒngyuǎn*	adv	always, forever
27	放心	放心	*fàng xīn*	vo	to feel relieved, to be at ease
28	联系	聯繫	*liánxì*	v/n	to contact, to get in touch; connection, relation (lit. to combine and tie)
29	友谊	友誼	*yǒuyì*	n	friendship
30	欧洲	歐洲	*Ōuzhōu*	pn	Europe

马克当过家教、做过翻译、拍过广告，是个自由职业者。你认为做什么工作的人也算是自由职业者？

馬克當過家教、做過翻譯、拍過廣告，是個自由職業者。你認為做什麼工作的人也算是自由職業者？

How About You?

Grammar

---

1 | **Summary of word order in Chinese**

Basic sentence structure

As you will recall from "Important Grammatical Features" in Basics and Grammar 1, Lesson 4, IC1, the basic Chinese sentence structure can be outlined as follows:

Subject/agent—(adverbial)—verb—(complement)—(object/
recipient of the action)

A

我们	下个星期	学	完	《中文听说读写》。
我們	下個星期	學	完	《中文聽說讀寫》。
Subject	Adverbial	Verb	Complement	Object

We will finish studying *Integrated Chinese* next week.

B

学生慢慢地走进了教室。

學生慢慢地走進了教室。

Students walked into the classroom slowly.

C

很多大学毕业生找不到满意的工作。

很多大學畢業生找不到滿意的工作。

Many college graduates can't find jobs they like.

Attributives in Chinese appear before what they modify:

D

小李是广东人，不太爱吃又酸又辣的菜。

小李是廣東人，不太愛吃又酸又辣的菜。

Little Li is Cantonese. He doesn't really like to eat food that is sour and spicy.

E

昨天给我打电话的人刚才来看我。

昨天給我打電話的人剛才來看我。

The person who called me yesterday just came to visit me.

Word order variation

Chinese word order can vary in special types of sentences.

Topic-comment sentences

As you will recall from Grammar 1, Lesson 10, IC1 and Grammar 1, Lesson 3, IC3, when something has already been mentioned or is understood, it becomes known information. Known information may appear at the beginning of a sentence as a topic:

F

面试你的那个人	我	认识。
面試你的那個人	我	認識。
Recipient of the Action	Agent	Verb
Topic		Comment

The person who interviewed you—I know [him/her].

G

（我们公司已经决定录用你了，）

录用通知	你	收到了吗?

（我們公司已經決定錄用你了，）

錄用通知	你	收到了嗎？
Recipient of the Action	Agent	Verb + Complement
Topic		Comment

Our company has decided to hire you. The offer letter—have you received it?

Sentences with 把

A 把 sentence also deviates from the regular sentence order.

H

请 你 把	那个炒菜锅	给	我。
請 你 把	那個炒菜鍋	給	我。
Subject	Direct Object	Verb	Indirect Object
Agent			

Please give that wok to me.

I

Q: 我的自行车呢?

我的自行車呢？

Where's my bike?

A: 你妹妹把它骑走了。

你妹妹把它騎走了。

Your younger sister took it.

Sentences with 被

In a 被 sentence, the object/recipient of the action is placed at the beginning of the sentence.

J

店里的新手机　都　被　人　买走了。

店裡的新手機　都　被　人　買走了。

Recipient of the Action　　　　　　　Agent　Verb + Complement

All the new cell phones in the store were sold out.

Other principles that affect word order

Chinese word order can also be affected by other cognitive and organizational principles.

General before specific

K

中国上海市静安区南京西路288号

中國上海市靜安區南京西路288號

China—Shanghai—Jing'an District—West Nanjing Road—No. 288
(the exact opposite of the organization of addresses in English)

L

2020年5月27号上午9点30分

2020年5月27號上午9點30分

Year 2020—May 27th —a.m.—9:30

Arranging events or situations according to their time of occurrence

Events or situations described in a Chinese sentence are usually in chronological order, i.e., whatever happens first is stated first. For example:

M

我常常在图书馆学习。

我常常在圖書館學習。

[Whereas in English, one would say "I often study in the library," the events here are stated in the order of their occurrence: being in the library, and then studying.]

表哥明天会开车到机场来接我们。

表哥明天會開車到機場來接我們。

[Whereas in English, one would say "My cousin will come to the airport to pick us up by car tomorrow," the events here are stated in the order of their occurrence: driving, arriving at the airport, then picking us up.]

O

我在房间用电脑写文章。

我在房間用電腦寫文章。

[Whereas in English, one would say, "I was writing an article on my computer in my room," the events here are stated in the order of their occurrence: being in the room, turning on the computer, and then writing the article.]

2 | Review of the 把 construction (II)

The 把 construction should be used if the object in a sentence is specific or known to both the speaker and the listener, the agent of the action has also been explicitly mentioned, and the following circumstances are in place:

There is an indirect object in the sentence:

A

你	把	这张照片	送给	我	吧。
你	把	這張照片	送給	我	吧。
Subject Agent		Direct Object (known information)		Indirect Object	

Will you please give this photo to me?

[❌ 你送这张照片给我吧。]

[❌ 你送這張照片給我吧。]

There is a phrase indicating the location of the object after the action has been executed:

B

他把筷子和方便面放在了桌子上。

他把筷子和方便麵放在了桌子上。

He put the chopsticks and instant noodles on the table.

[❌ 他放了筷子和方便面在桌子上。]

[❌ 他放了筷子和方便麵在桌子上。]

The verb is followed by the complement 成:

C

考试的时候，我不小心把"天"字写成了"夫"字。

考試的時候，我不小心把"天"字寫成了"夫"字。

I was careless and wrote 天 incorrectly as 夫 on the exam.

[My writing resultcd in a wrong character.]

D

他把宿舍房间变成了一个垃圾场。

他把宿舍房間變成了一個垃圾場。

He turned the dorm room into a trash dump.

[✘ 他变宿舍房间成了一个垃圾场。]

[✘ 他變宿舍房間成了一個垃圾場。]

Sentences with the 把 construction need a subject—that is to say, an agent that is responsible for the action, as in (A), (B), (C), and (D). Under certain circumstances, the subject can be omitted if it is clearly understood:

E

（你）把门关上。

（你）把門關上。

Close the door.

If the agent responsible for the action is unknown, unspecified, or not the focus, the 把 construction need not be used, as shown in (F) and (G):

F

钥匙　　丢了。

鑰匙　　丟了。

Topic　　comment

The key was lost.

[This is a topic-comment sentence. The focus is on what happened to the key rather than who lost it.]

G

这个红包给你，那个红包给小王。

這個紅包給你，那個紅包給小王。

This red envelope is for you. That red envelope is for Little Wang.

In 把 sentences, negative adverbs must be placed before 把:

H
哎呀，糟糕，我没把你要的地图带来。

哎呀，糟糕，我沒把你要的地圖帶來。

Shoot, I forgot to bring the map that you wanted.

[✗ ……我把你要的地图没带来。]

[✗ ……我把你要的地圖沒帶來。]

I
你老是丢三拉四的，要是不把护照放在我这里，过两天你肯定找不到。

你老是丟三拉四的，要是不把護照放在我這裡，過兩天你肯定找不到。

You are so scatterbrained. If you don't leave your passport with me, you won't be able to find it in a couple of days.

[✗ ……要是把护照不放在我这里……]

[✗ ……要是把護照不放在我這裡……]

Note that potential complements cannot be used in 把 sentences:

[✗ 我把购房合同找不到了。]

[✗ 我把購房合同找不到了。]

[✗ 舅舅说舅妈把碗洗不干净。]

[✗ 舅舅說舅媽把碗洗不乾淨。]

The 把 construction is one of the most complex structures in Chinese grammar. The application of the 把 construction also has to do with the larger linguistic context and other factors. As you practice recognizing and using the 把 construction, you'll soon catch on to its nuances.

Words & Phrases

A 接受 (to accept, to take on, to undertake)

接受 can be followed by an abstract noun such as 建议/建議 (suggestion), 意见/意見 (opinion), 领导/領導 (leadership), 好意 (goodwill), or 批评/批評 (*pīpíng*) (criticism).

1 张天明的好朋友李哲也来到中国了，他接受了天明的建议，到一家跨国公司来实习。

張天明的好朋友李哲也來到中國了，他接受了天明的建議，到一家跨國公司來實習。

Zhang Tianming's good friend Li Zhe also arrived in China. He had accepted Tianming's suggestion to intern at a multinational company.

2 国际销售部经理不愿意接受总经理的领导。

國際銷售部經理不願意接受總經理的領導。

The manager of the international sales department is unwilling to accept the general manager's leadership.

It can also be followed by a concrete noun or pronoun such as 礼物/禮物 (gift), as in (3).

3 我不能接受你这么贵的礼物。

我不能接受你這麼貴的禮物。

I can't accept such an expensive gift from you.

我说/我說 (I was wondering why)

我说/我說 is a colloquialism that is typically used at the beginning of a sentence as a comment on a newly discovered situation:

1

我说汽车钥匙怎么不见了，原来妹妹拿走了。

我說汽車鑰匙怎麼不見了，原來妹妹拿走了。

I was wondering why the car key was nowhere to be found. It turned out my younger sister took it.

2

你是小张的哥哥？我说你们俩怎么长得这么像呢。

你是小張的哥哥？我說你們倆怎麼長得這麼像呢。

You're Little Zhang's older brother? I was wondering why you two look so alike.

3

你说今天92度？我说怎么这么热。

你說今天92度？我說怎麼這麼熱。

Did you say the temperature today was ninety-two degrees? I was wondering why it was so hot.

而已 (and no more)

而已 is used at the end of a descriptive statement to downplay or minimize the significance of something. Another phrase that can be used in place of 而已 is 罢了/罷了 (bà le).

1

我不过是三流演员而已。

我不過是三流演員而已。

I'm just a third-rate actor.

2

我只是开玩笑而已，你别生气。

我只是開玩笑而已，你別生氣。

I was just teasing. You don't need to get angry.

3

这件套装质量不错，才500块**而已**，买了吧。

這件套裝質量不錯，才500塊**而已**，買了吧。

The suit is very good quality, and it's only five hundred yuan. Why don't you buy it?

4

这不过是一次小考**而已**，又不是期末考，你不用太担心。

這不過是一次小考**而已**，又不是期末考，你不用太擔心。

This is just a small quiz. It's not the final exam. There's no need to worry.

在…下 (under)

在…下 expresses a condition and appears before the verb or subject of a sentence.

1

在他的领导下，公司越办越好，我哥哥还买了他们公司很多股票呢。

在他的領導下，公司越辦越好，我哥哥還買了他們公司很多股票呢。

Under his leadership the company is becoming better and better managed. My older brother has even bought a lot of the company's stock.

2

在大家的说服下，他同意不炒股了。

在大家的說服下，他同意不炒股了。

Persuaded by everybody, he agreed not to flip stocks.

3

虽然小明化学学得不太好，可是在老师的帮助下，成绩提高得很快。

雖然小明化學學得不太好，可是在老師的幫助下，成績提高得很快。

Although Xiaoming isn't doing so well in his chemistry class, with the teacher's help, his grade is quickly improving.

你说呢？/你說呢？ (What do you say?; What do you think?)

你说呢?/你說呢？ can be used to elicit an opinion, for example:

1
我这笔钱应该存在银行里，还是拿去炒股？老王，
你说呢？

我這筆錢應該存在銀行裡，還是拿去炒股？老王，
你說呢？

Should I deposit this money in the bank or use it to speculate on stocks? What do you say, Old Wang?

It can also be used rhetorically in response to a question, when the speaker thinks the answer is obvious or self-evident:

2   Li Wen
现在在中国的外国人越来越多，你们习惯中国的
生活吗？

現在在中國的外國人越來越多，你們習慣中國的
生活嗎？

Nowadays there are more and more foreign nationals in China. Are you used to life in China?

Lisha
你说呢？（我当然习惯。）
你說呢？（我當然習慣。）

What do you think? (Of course, I am.)

3   Wife
今天是什么日子，你怎么做了这么多菜？
今天是什麼日子，你怎麼做了這麼多菜？

What day is it today? How come you made so much food?

Husband
你说呢？
你說呢？

What do you think?

Wife
啊，我想起来了，今天是我的生日！谢谢你！
啊，我想起來了，今天是我的生日！謝謝你！

Oh, I remember now. Today's my birthday. Thank you!

Language Practice

A

Party planning

PRESENTATIONAL

Imagine that you're orchestrating a huge wedding reception in Shanghai, and you need to tell your helpers what they need to do and where things should go. To make sure they understand you, jot down some instructions that you might need to say in Chinese.

1 Open the windows, please.

2 Place the cake and the flowers on the table.

3 Move those chairs out of the room.

4 Move the piano into the room.

5 Don't paste the 囍 character upside down.

6 Tidy up the kitchen.

7 Turn off the lights before you go home.

8 Don't forget to give me back the key to the room.

Other useful sentences: _____

_____

A WAY WITH WORDS

联系

一百位科学家联名给政
府写信，希望增加对环
境保护的投资。

两家跨国公司联手，两
年半就建成了这栋五十
层的高楼。

Using the word/phrase in orange as a clue, try to figure out the meaning of the words/phrases in blue; consult a dictionary if necessary. Consider how the literal and extended senses are related in each case.

聯繫

一百位科學家聯名給政
府寫信，希望增加對環
境保護的投資。

兩家跨國公司聯手，兩
年半就建成了這棟五十
層的高樓。

309

Be a good host

What would you say to your party guests? In pairs, take turns practicing what to say to your guests at a party, based on the following prompts.

1 Explain that the party is to:

    a welcome Little Chen back from a long trip

    b send off Little Tian on a long trip

    c celebrate Little Bai having found a good job

我们聚在一起是为了……

我們聚在一起是為了……

2 Ask the guests not to stand on ceremony, enjoy the food and have a good time:

请大家……

請大家……

3 Offer to help and take care of each other to a new acquaintance:

我们互相……，互相……

我們互相……，互相……

Characterize it!

More
characters

What do the characters mean?
What is the common radical?
What does the radical mean?
How does the radical relate to the overall meaning of the characters?

How to say the right thing

When welcoming new friends or saying goodbye to old friends, what formal expressions would you say to mark the occasion?

接风/接風　　　　　　　　　　　　　饯行/餞行

1 _____　　　　_____

2 _____　　　　_____

3 _____　　　　_____

4 _____　　　　_____

5 _____　　　　_____

D

I'm new here

When meeting new colleagues or friends for the first time, in addition to stating your name and saying how happy you are to meet them, you might need to ask for assistance as you get acquainted with your surroundings. Based on the prompts, practice asking for help and guidance, e.g.:

school

我刚到学校来工作，对很多情况都不太了解，请多关照。

我剛到學校來工作，對很多情況都不太了解，請多關照。

1 company

2 factory

3 this city

4 this country

There's so much you could do in China

As Li Wen says, more and more people from all over the world are working and studying in China. First, list some of their activities:

学习中文/學習中文, _____

_____

_____

当家教/當家教, _____

Then, circle the activities that you might do when you go to China.

Finally, based on what you have circled, report your own thoughts to the class. Use either "不是⋯就是⋯," "要么⋯要么⋯/要麼⋯要麼⋯," or "不但⋯而且⋯" in your presentation, and start with:

我将来去中国⋯⋯

我將來去中國⋯⋯

A WAY WITH WORDS

稳定

林太太八十多岁了，可是走起路来还是很稳健。

他这个人很稳重，跟别人打交道时从来不随便乱说话。

Using the word/phrase in orange as a clue, try to figure out the meaning of the words/phrases in blue; consult a dictionary if necessary. Consider how the literal and extended senses are related in each case.

穩定

林太太八十多歲了，可是走起路來還是很穩健。

他這個人很穩重，跟別人打交道時從來不隨便亂說話。

Do in Rome as the Romans do

Take turns with a partner describing how well the characters in IC4 have adjusted to life in China, e.g.:

 practices tai chi and eats with Li Wen's parents

 acts, does interpreting and translation work

天明呢？他习惯不习惯中国的生活？

天明呢？他習慣不習慣中國的生活？

李哲担心不担心他能不能适应中国的生活？

李哲擔心不擔心他能不能適應中國的生活？

Conclusion:

他们都＿＿＿＿＿＿＿＿＿＿＿＿＿＿＿＿＿＿＿＿＿＿＿＿＿＿＿＿＿＿。

他們都＿＿＿＿＿＿＿＿＿＿＿＿＿＿＿＿＿＿＿＿＿＿＿＿＿＿＿＿＿＿。

How could one adjust to a new country such as China? Think of some tips based on the prompts:

1   Seek help from people who are more experienced than you

＿＿＿＿＿＿＿＿＿＿＿＿＿＿＿＿＿＿＿＿＿＿＿＿＿＿＿＿＿

2   Try to meld into Chinese society as much as possible by

eating Chinese food

＿＿＿＿＿＿＿＿＿＿＿＿＿＿＿＿＿＿＿＿＿＿＿＿＿＿＿＿＿

making Chinese friends

＿＿＿＿＿＿＿＿＿＿＿＿＿＿＿＿＿＿＿＿＿＿＿＿＿＿＿＿＿

More tips:

＿＿＿＿＿＿＿＿＿＿＿＿＿＿＿＿＿＿＿＿＿＿＿＿＿＿＿＿＿

＿＿＿＿＿＿＿＿＿＿＿＿＿＿＿＿＿＿＿＿＿＿＿＿＿＿＿＿＿

Small world

Based on the prompts, take turns with a partner describing examples of increasing exchanges and interactions using 越来越/越來越.

1 Chinese people going abroad to study, Westerners going to China to study and/or teach

越来越多的中国人（或西方人）＿＿＿＿＿＿＿＿＿＿＿＿。

越來越多的中國人（或西方人）＿＿＿＿＿＿＿＿＿＿＿＿。

2 Chinese people doing yoga, Westerners doing tai chi

越来越多的中国人（或西方人）＿＿＿＿＿＿＿＿＿＿＿＿。

越來越多的中國人（或西方人）＿＿＿＿＿＿＿＿＿＿＿＿。

Based on the prompts, fill in the blanks with 越来越/越來越 and an appropriate adjective:

3 people using computers and cell phones to email and call one another

中国和世界的联系＿＿＿＿＿＿＿＿＿＿＿＿。

中國和世界的聯繫＿＿＿＿＿＿＿＿＿＿＿＿。

4 Chinese tourists going abroad, foreign tourists visiting China

中国和世界的关系＿＿＿＿＿＿＿＿＿＿＿＿。

中國和世界的關係＿＿＿＿＿＿＿＿＿＿＿＿。

Fill in the blanks with 越来越/越來越 and an appropriate adjective:

各国之间的来往 (comings and goings)_____了。

各國之間的來往 (comings and goings)_____了。

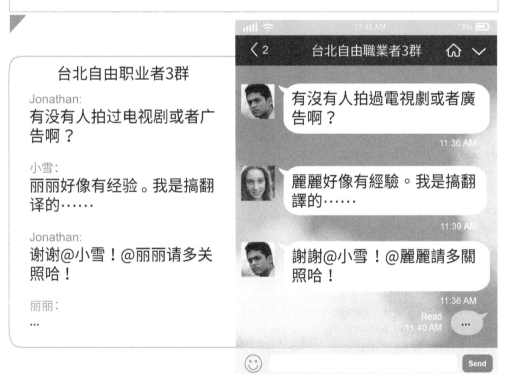

Chinese Chat

Jonathan just joined a LINE group of freelancers based in Taipei. What would Lili say to Jonathan after he reached out to her?

Foreign Students and Teachers

In recent years, there has been a marked increase in the number of foreign students studying in China. In 2016 alone, more than four hundred thousand students from over two hundred countries attended schools in China. About half of them are enrolled in degree programs, while the rest are short-term exchange students focused on Chinese language, history, and culture. Among foreign students, more than half come from Asian nations, and South Korea sends more students to China than any other country. Beijing, home to a large number of colleges and universities, has the largest population of foreign students, followed closely by Shanghai.

Teaching has also become a popular career choice for foreigners in China. It is estimated that there are more than one hundred thousand native English-speaking teachers in China. While most of them teach at private schools, some programs, such as Teach for China, aim to send teachers to understaffed rural schools.

COMPARE & CONTRAST

1 Many people go to China for educational or business opportunities. What factors have drawn people to your country, both now and in the past? Are the immigration trends in China similar to or different from the trends in your country?

2 Is there a significant Chinese population in your country? If so, where have Chinese immigrants chosen to settle? How have these immigrants contributed to their communities?

Welcomes and Goodbyes

Food plays an important role in Chinese culture. Guests are often welcomed with an elaborate meal. Before a friend or relative leaves on a long journey, he or she is invited to a farewell dinner party. In ancient China when travel was often arduous, people would accompany departing relatives and friends for miles passing through multiple rest pavilions before finally bidding their loved ones farewell; hence the expression 十里长亭相送/十里長亭相送 (*shílǐ chángtíng xiāngsòng*) (passing through pavilions spaced ten *li* apart to send someone off).

Yiwu: China's Laboratory of Multiculturalism

Yiwu (义乌/義烏) (*Yìwū*), three hundred kilometers south of Shanghai in Zhejiang Province, is the location of the world's largest wholesale market for small commodities. More than seventy percent of all the Christmas decorations in the world, for instance, are sourced from Yiwu. Nearly eighty thousand stalls covering more than two square miles sell a mind-boggling array of goods from lighters, toys, and luggage tags to kitchenware, candles, and socks—anything one can think of and more. The local government has actively sought to make the city's thirteen thousand resident foreign businessmen and businesswomen feel welcome. Signs are in Chinese, English, and Arabic at the train station. Yiwu's large, active mosque is important to the city's many Muslim residents from the Middle East and North Africa. The local government has held celebrations for both Muslim and Hindu festivals. In addition, Yiwu's officials organize an annual meeting at which foreign residents have a chance to discuss issues in the community.

Doing business in Guangzhou

Long-term Expats

Some long-term foreign residents open businesses in China or work at foreign-owned companies. Still others find employment as foreign language teachers, tutors, translators, or models and actors. A few have become household names after hosting gigs on TV. However, China's expat population is not evenly distributed throughout the country. Diplomats tend to be based in Beijing, while foreigners in commercial enterprises are spread throughout the major cities along the coast. In addition, different groups of foreigners may cluster according to their region of origin. Guangzhou, for example, is known for having a large sub-Saharan African community. While the size of the city's African population fluctuates, Guangzhou is home to one of the largest African populations in Asia. African merchants are attracted by Guangzhou's close proximity to the Pearl River Delta, a giant manufacturing center where everything from home appliances to clothes is produced. Most of these businesspeople visit Guangzhou only briefly to purchase merchandise to sell in Africa, but a small number settle in China more permanently.

View of the Yiwu International Trade City

Lesson Wrap-Up

Project

Choose a foreign celebrity in China or a person of Chinese descent in your country and prepare an oral report with slides. Be sure to:

- begin with a brief biography of your subject: when, where was the person born and grew up, his or her education and family background, etc.

- describe his or her career or claim to fame: what does he/she do, what are his/her accomplishments?

- describe how well integrated or adjusted he/she is or feels

- describe how he/she is received in China or in your country

- explain what your subject illustrates in terms of world exchanges

Keep It Flowing

First, study the following example; pay particular attention to how the highlighted parts help the sentences flow smoothly from one to the next. Notice how:

- time expressions (中国改革开放以后/中國改革開放以後, 现在/現在) can launch a narrative and connect sentences

- pronouns (他们/他們) replace nouns (外国人/外國人) in preceding sentences

- certain words (有的, 其中, 最多的) single out examples

- certain expressions (也就是) introduce clarifications or paraphrases (中国的国际留学生/中國的國際留學生)

外国人在中国

中国改革开放以后，吸引了很多外国人。他们有的是去教外语，特别是教英语。有的当演员，其中有几个人已经很有名了。有的在跨国公司工作，是优秀的管理人材。最多的是到中国留学，也就是中国的国际留学生。现在跟中国人结婚的外国人也不少，他们在中国建立了家庭，慢慢地融入中国社会了。

外國人在中國

中國改革開放以後，吸引了很多外國人。他們有的是去教外語，特別是教英語。有的當演員，其中有幾個人已經很有名了。有的在跨國公司工作，是優秀的管理人材。最多的是到中國留學，也就是中國的國際留學生。現在跟中國人結婚的外國人也不少，他們在中國建立了家庭，慢慢地融入中國社會了。

In your country, were many people born abroad? Use as many of the cohesive devices highlighted in the example on the previous page/above as possible to string together your response to the prompts.

- 你们国家的外国人多不多？

  你們國家的外國人多不多？

- 外国人在你们国家做什么？上大学、念硕士博士、做翻译、当演员，还是在跨国公司工作？

  外國人在你們國家做什麼？上大學、念碩士博士、做翻譯、當演員，還是在跨國公司工作？

- 你觉得很多外国人去你们国家，对你们国家有什么贡献？

  你覺得很多外國人去你們國家，對你們國家有什麼貢獻？

Can-Do Check List ✔

I can

Before finishing the *Integrated Chinese* series, make sure you can complete the following tasks in Chinese:

- ☐ Explain the purpose of a gathering
- ☐ Request and offer help
- ☐ Discuss adjusting to life in a new country
- ☐ Describe how the world is getting smaller

Xuěméi miànshì hòu, nà jiā gōngsī tōngzhī tā xià zhōu kāishǐ shàng bān. Xuěméi hé Kē Lín dōu hěn gāoxìng, tāmen juédìng qǐng péngyou men dào Xuěméi zhù de dìfang lái jùhuì, qìngzhù yí xià.

Zhāng Tiānmíng de hǎo péngyou Lǐ Zhé yě lái dào Zhōngguó le, tā jiēshòu le Tiānmíng de jiànyì, dào yì jiā kuàguó gōngsī lái shíxí. Jiéguǒ, qìngzhù wǎnhuì yě chéng le gěi Lǐ Zhé jiēfēng[a] de wǎnhuì.

Zhāng Tiānmíng hé Lìshā hěn kuài jiù yào huí Měiguó le, suǒyǐ zhè cì jùhuì yě shì gěi tāmen jiànxíng[b] de wǎnhuì.

Lái de kèren chúle Tiānmíng, Lìshā, Lǐ Zhé wài, hái yǒu Lǐ Wén hé Mǎkè.

Kē Lín qù chāoshì mǎi le hěn duō yǐnliào, língshí hé shuǐguǒ[1]. Xuěméi zhǔnbèi le yí ge huǒguō, hái cóng fùjìn de yì jiā cānguǎn jiào le wàimài[c].

Jīntiān wǒmen dàjiā jù zài yìqǐ, shì wèile gěi Lǐ Zhé jiēfēng, gěi Tiānmíng hé Lìshā jiànxíng, yě qìngzhù Xuěméi zhǎo dào gōngzuò.

Duì, dàjiā bú yào kèqi, hǎo hāo chī, hǎo hāo wánr.

Xuěméi, gōngxǐ nǐ zhǎo dào le hǎo gōngzuò. Shénme shíhou shàng bān?

Xià gè xīngqīyī, xīngqīwǔ jiù yào dào Ōuzhōu chū chāi, tuīxiāo tàiyángnéng bǎn hé jiénéng diànchí.

Tàiyángnéng bǎn hé jiénéng diànchí? Tài hǎo le! Zuìjìn gēn huánbǎo hé jiénéng yǒu guānxi de lǜsè chǎnpǐn shìchǎng shang dōu mài de hěn huǒ[d].

Āi, Mǎkè, Lǐ Wén, nǐmen guò lai, wǒ lái jièshào yí xià, zhè shì wǒmen Měiguó dàxué de xiàoyǒu, Lǐ Zhé, gāng cóng Měiguó lái.

Huānyíng lái Běijīng.

Dàjiā hǎo! Qǐng duō guānzhào[e].

Lǐ Zhé, nǐ lái Běijīng nǎ jiā gōngsī shíxí?

Wǒ yǐjīng gàosu Tiānmíng le, jiù shì nǐ yào qù de nà ge gōngsī. Tā méi bǎ zhè ge xiāoxi gàosu nǐ[2]? Nà tiān miànshì nǐ de shì wǒ gēge de hǎo péngyou.

Zhēn de? Nà wǒmen bú jiù shì tóngshì le ma? Tài hǎo le, yǐhòu wǒmen kěyǐ hùxiāng bāngzhù, hùxiāng zhàogù.

Suǒyǐ wǒ shuō qǐng duō guānzhào ma.

Hái bù zhīdào shéi guānzhào shéi ne.

Mǎkè, nǐ lái Zhōngguó duō cháng shíjiān le?

Liù nián le.

Mǎkè, nǐ zài Zhōngguó dōu zuò shénme gōngzuò?

Wǒ shì ge "zìyóu" zhíyè zhě[f], dāng guo Yīngwén jiājiào, yǎn guo diànshìjù, hái pāi guo guǎnggào, yǒu shíhou yě gǎo diǎnr fānyì.

Wǒ shuō zěnme yǒu diǎnr miànshú ne, wǒ kàn guo nǐ yǎn de diànshìjù. Nǐ yǎn de hěn búcuò.

Búguò shì sān liú yǎnyuán éryǐ.

Kàn qi lai nǐ de gōngzuò jīhuì hěn duō, hěn máng a.

Bù yídìng, yǒude shíhou hěn máng, yǒude shíhou méi shì zuò. Shuō bái le[g], shíjìshang shì gōngzuò yǒu diǎnr bù wěndìng. Búguò méi guānxi, shēnghuó méi wèntí. Zài zhèr, wǒ shēnghuó de hěn kuàilè, jiāo le hěn duō Zhōngguó péngyou.

Nánguài nǐ de Zhōngwén zhème hǎo.

Lǐ Zhé, nǐ gēge de péngyou zhēn bù jiǎndān a, zhème niánqīng jiù dāng shang zǒng jīnglǐ le.

Tā búdàn dǒng xiāoshòu, yě shì ge hěnhǎo de guǎnlǐ réncái. Tīngshuō zài tā de lǐngdǎo xià, gōngsī yuè bàn yuè hǎo.

Xiànzài zài Zhōngguó de wàiguó rén yuè lái yuè duō, nǐmen xíguàn Zhōngguó de shēnghuó ma?

Nǐ shuō ne? Wǒ zài nǐmen jiā, měitiān gēn nǐ fùmǔ dǎ tàijíquán, chī tāmen zuò de yòu hàochī, yòu jiànkāng de fàn cài, dōu bù xiǎng huí qu le.

Wǒ gèng méi wèntí le.

Nǐ hái xiě bókè ma?

Dāngrán. Zài zhèli, wǒ měi tiān dōu huì kàn dào, tīng dào xīnxian de shì, yǒngyuǎn yě xiě bù wán.

Wǒ jiù búyòng shuō le, yàobùrán zěnme huì zhù zhème jiǔ ne? Wǒ juéde zìjǐ yǐjīng róngrù zhè ge shèhuì le.

Wǒ yuánlái hái pà zìjǐ shìyìng bù liǎo zhèr de shēnghuó. Tīng le nǐmen de huà, wǒ fàngxīn duō le.

Xiànzài wàiguó rén lái Zhōngguó fāzhǎn, Zhōngguó rén dào guówài xuéxí, gōngzuò, dàjiā de liánxì duō le, guānxi jìn le, shìjiè biàn xiǎo le.

Lǐ Wén shuō de zhēn hǎo. Péngyou men, lái, dàjiā jǔ qǐ bēi lái, wèi wǒmen de yǒuyì gān bēi!

Wèi nǐmen zài Zhōngguó shìyè chénggōng gān bēi!

Zhù Tiānmíng hé Lìshā yí lù píng'ān!

Zhù dàjiā shēntǐ jiànkāng!

Gān bēi!

A | **Chinese character crossword puzzles**

Many of the new words and phrases from Lessons 16–20 share the same characters. In these puzzles, the common character is positioned in the center of the cluster of bubbles. The triangular points indicate which way you should read the words. Work with a partner and see how many association bubbles you can complete, adding more bubbles if you can think of additional words/phrases, e.g.:

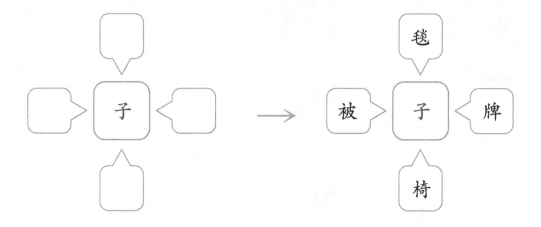

1

2

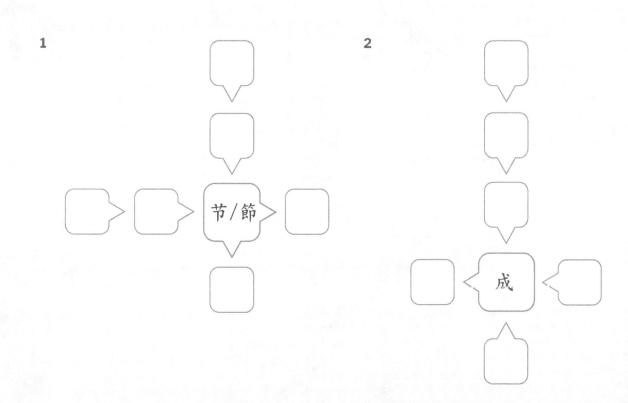

3

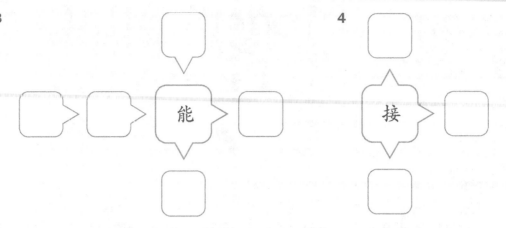

能

4

接

5

用

6

海

7

发/發

8 Create your own

Matching words

1 Draw lines to connect each verb with its proper object.

得	宫殿/宮殿
修/修	合同
打	病
赔/賠	故事
盖/蓋	麻将/麻將
讲/講	钱/錢
签/簽	房子
抵押	大楼/大樓

2 Draw lines to connect each verb with its proper object.

建立	革命
推销/推銷	思考
领导/領導	建议/建議
进行/進行	产品/產品
造成	国家/國家
享受	经济/經濟
引起/引起	污染/汙染
接受	生活
发展/發展	贸易/貿易

3 Draw lines to connect each noun with the adjective that can best serve as its predicate.

技术/技術   大

工作   郁闷/鬱悶

心里/心裡   火

生活   高

经济/經濟   先进/先進

收入   幸福

餐馆儿/餐館兒   稳定/穩定

风险/風險   发达/發達

C

To the contrary

Give the antonyms of these words, following the example below.

方便   麻烦/麻煩

1 高   _____   5 老   _____

2 长/長   _____   6 干/乾   _____

3 硬   _____   7 涨/漲   _____

4 赢/贏   _____   8 增加   _____

In other words

1   You've learned many vocabulary items that are actually abbreviations. Give the full phrase or expression for each abbreviation, following the example below.

古国/古國   古老的国家/古老的國家

古城   _____

春晚   _____

环保/環保   _____

节能/節能   _____

超市   _____

房价/房價   _____

股市   _____

男足   _____

海归/海歸   _____

那时/那時   _____

2   You've learned several Chinese set phrases and sayings. See if you can explain each of the following in Chinese with the help of your partner.

丢三拉四

望子成龙，望女成凤/望子成龍，望女成鳳

人山人海

年年有余/年年有餘

民以食为天/民以食為天

同工同酬

省吃俭用/省吃儉用

有朋自远方来，不亦乐乎/有朋自遠方來，不亦樂乎

Put your thoughts into words

1   Brainstorm with a partner and ask each other what words or phrases you can use when you want to:

- advocate for energy conservation

浪费能源　　　绿色能源　　　节约能源
浪費能源　　　綠色能源　　　節約能源

_____　　_____　　_____

_____　　_____　　_____

_____　　_____　　_____

_____　　_____　　_____

- engage in financial planning

怎么存钱/怎麼存錢　　　　　怎么投资/怎麼投資

_____　　_____

_____　　_____

_____　　_____

_____　　_____

- briefly talk about one Chinese historical figure and one Chinese dynasty

历史人物/歷史人物　　　　　　　　　朝代

_____　　　　_____

_____　　　　_____

_____　　　　_____

_____　　　　_____

- explain why China attracts people from other countries

_____

_____

_____

_____

_____

- discuss how people from other countries adapt to life in China

_____

_____

_____

_____

_____

2 Study these words/phrases with a few classmates. Using the list that follows, group the words/phrases according to their meanings and usages. Feel free to add other words/phrases if you can.

而已

其中

跟…有关系／跟…有關係

既然

好在

你说呢？／你說呢？

之一

在…下

在…方面

…吧，…吧

可不是吗？／可不是嗎？

- When you wish to cite or refer to examples: _____

- When you wish to ponder different options: _____

- When you wish to solicit someone's opinion: _____

- When you wish to downplay the importance of something: _____

- When you wish to express your relief: _____

- When you wish to point out the relevance of something: _____

- When you wish to point out the circumstances: _____

- When you wish to signal your agreement: _____

- When you wish to point out what is given: _____

- When you wish to refer to various aspects of something: _____

Present your thoughts

With a partner, give a brief presentation on your view on energy conservation, your thoughts on the best ways to save or invest money, an aspect of Chinese history, your reasons for going to China, or your expectations of studying or living in China.

First, discuss with your partner:

· which topic you will select, and why

· what aspects of the topic you want to focus on

· what words or phrases from the first part of (D) should be used in your presentation

· what should be said first, next, and last

· what transitions may be needed between parts of the presentation

· what linking devices should be used to connect your sentences

· what words or phrases from the second part of (D) can be useful in presenting your point of view

It's a good idea to jot down sentences that you wish to say, then number them in the order you think they should be presented. Consider how you can make your list into a coherent discourse. Once you've finished, present your work to the class.

G

Speak methodically

Reorganize the following sentences to compose a well-connected paragraph about Mark's life in China. Pay attention to time expressions, transitional devices, and pronouns.

平常早晨打太极拳

平常早晨打太極拳

他已经完全适应了中国的生活

他已經完全適應了中國的生活

一放假不是参观博物馆就是游览中国各地的景点

一放假不是參觀博物館就是遊覽中國各地的景點

马克在中国生活了六年了

馬克在中國生活了六年了

但担心他工作不稳定

但擔心他工作不穩定

马克回答说他热爱中国

馬克回答說他熱愛中國

都劝他早点回国

都勸他早點回國

短期内不打算回国

短期內不打算回國

中午吃盒饭

中午吃盒飯

融入了中国的社会

融入了中國的社會

另外，马克对中国的历史和少数民族文化很有兴趣，
也十分了解

另外，馬克對中國的歷史和少數民族文化很有興趣，
也十分了解

马克在德国的家人虽然知道他在中国生活得不错

馬克在德國的家人雖然知道他在中國生活得不錯

很满意自己在中国的生活

很滿意自己在中國的生活

晚上打麻将

晚上打麻將

Vocabulary Index (Chinese-English), Volumes 3–4

The Chinese-English index is alphabetized according to *pinyin*. Words containing the same Chinese characters are first grouped together. Homonyms appear in the order of their tonal pronunciation (i.e., first tones first, second tones second, third tones third, fourth tones fourth, and neutral tones last).

Simplified	Traditional	Pinyin	Part of Speech	English	Lesson
A					
哎	哎	āi	excl	(exclamatory particle to express surprise or dissatisfaction or to remind)	1
哎呀	哎呀	āiyā	interj	gosh, ah (an exclamation to express surprise)	4
爱好	愛好	àihào	n/v	hobby, interest; to love (something)	6
安排	安排	ānpái	v	to arrange	9
安全	安全	ānquán	adj	safe	1
熬夜	熬夜	áo yè	vo	to stay up late or all night	14
B					
摆	擺	bǎi	v	to put, to place	2
拜年	拜年	bài nián	vo	to wish somebody a happy Chinese New Year, to pay a Chinese New Year call	11
搬家	搬家	bān jiā	vo	to move (one's residence)	1
板	板	bǎn	n	board, plank, panel	16
帮忙	幫忙	bāng máng	vo	to help	1
帮助	幫助	bāngzhù	v/n	to help; help	7
包括	包括	bāokuò	v	to include, to consist of	13
饱	飽	bǎo	adj	full, satiated (after a meal)	14
保护	保護	bǎohù	v	to protect, to safeguard	16
保留	保留	bǎoliú	v	to remain as before, to retain	12
报名	報名	bào míng	vo	to sign up, to register	13
抱怨	抱怨	bàoyuàn	v	to complain	9

Simplified	Traditional	Pinyin	Part of Speech	English	Lesson
倍	倍	bèi	m	(measure word for times by which something is multiplied)	10
背景	背景	bèijǐng	n	background	6
被子	被子	bèizi	n	comforter, quilt	2
笔	筆	bǐ	m	(measure word for sums of money)	17
比方说	比方說	bǐfāng shuō		for example	3
比分	比分	bǐfēn	n	score	15
比较	比較	bǐjiào	adv/v	relatively, comparatively, rather; to compare	1
比如	比如	bǐrú	v	for example	16
必须	必須	bìxū	adv	must, have to, be obliged to	14
毕业	畢業	bì yè	vo	to graduate	5
鞭炮	鞭炮	biānpào	n	firecracker	11
变	變	biàn	v	to change	12
变化	變化	biànhuà	v/n	to change; change	12
标准	標準	biāozhǔn	n/adj	criterion; standard	4
表哥	表哥	biǎogē	n	older male cousin of a different surname	12
表现	表現	biǎoxiàn	v/n	to display, to manifest; performance; manifestation	15
冰灯	冰燈	bīngdēng	n	ice lantern	10
兵马俑	兵馬俑	bīngmǎyǒng	n	terracotta warriors and horses	18
菠菜	菠菜	bōcài	n	spinach	3
博客	博客	bókè	n	blog	7
博士	博士	bóshì	n	doctorate (academic degree), Dr. (academic title)	9
博物馆	博物館	bówùguǎn	n	museum	14
补充	補充	bǔchōng	v	to supplement, to replenish	14

Simplified	Traditional	Pinyin	Part of Speech	English	Lesson
部	部	*bù*	n	part, section	10
部分	部分	*bùfen*	n	portion, part	18
不必	不必	*búbì [bùbì]**	adv	need not, do not need to	14
不管	不管	*bùguǎn*	conj	no matter, regardless of	12
不见得	不見得	*bújiànde [bùjiànde]*		not necessarily	1
不是…而是…	不是…而是…	*búshì…érshì… [bùshì…érshì…]*		it's not…but…	9
不停	不停	*bùtíng*	adv	continuously, incessantly	6
不同	不同	*bù tóng*		different, not the same	6

<table>
<tr><td colspan="6" align="center">C</td></tr>
</table>

Simplified	Traditional	Pinyin	Part of Speech	English	Lesson
菜单	菜單	*càidān*	n	menu	3
参观	參觀	*cānguān*	v	to visit, to look around	18
参加	參加	*cānjiā*	v	to participate, to take part, to attend	13
餐馆儿	餐館兒	*cānguǎnr*	n	restaurant	2
餐巾	餐巾	*cānjīn*	n	napkin	3
餐具	餐具	*cānjù*	n	eating utensil, tableware	16
层	層	*céng*	m	(measure word for stories of a building)	2
曾经	曾經	*céngjīng*	adv	once; at some time in the past	18
茶馆	茶館	*cháguǎn*	n	teahouse	13
产品	產品	*chǎnpǐn*	n	product, merchandise	19
尝	嚐	*cháng*	v	to taste	12
长	長	*cháng*	adj	long	1
长江	長江	*Chángjiāng*	pn	Yangtze River	10

* For vocabulary items starting with 不 or 一, we have included the *pinyin* with the stand-alone tone of these two characters in square brackets. However, the *pinyin* listed first indicates how the characters are conventionally pronounced as a lexical unit.

Simplified	Traditional	Pinyin	Part of Speech	English	Lesson
超过	超過	*chāoguò*	v	to surpass, to exceed	15
超市	超市	*chāoshì*	n	supermarket	16
朝代	朝代	*cháodài*	n	dynasty	18
炒股	炒股	*chǎo gǔ*	vo	to flip stocks	17
吵架	吵架	*chǎo jià*	vo	to quarrel	6
车厢	車廂	*chēxiāng*	n	train carriage	13
成功	成功	*chénggōng*	v/adj	to succeed; successful	11
成绩	成績	*chéngjì*	n	performance, achievement, result, score, grade	15
成为	成為	*chéngwéi*	v	to become, to turn into	14
迟到	遲到	*chídào*	v	to arrive late	7
初	初	*chū*		first, early part of	11
出差	出差	*chū chāi*	vo	to be away on business or on a business trip	20
出汗	出汗	*chū hàn*	vo	to sweat	16
出门	出門	*chū mén*	vo	to go out, to leave home	14
出生	出生	*chūshēng*	v	to be born	1
出现	出現	*chūxiàn*	v	to appear, to arise, to emerge	15
除夕	除夕	*chúxī*	n	Chinese New Year's Eve	11
船	船	*chuán*	n	boat, ship	10
传统	傳統	*chuántǒng*	n/adj	tradition; traditional	11
春节	春節	*Chūnjié*	pn	Spring Festival, Chinese New Year	11
纯棉	純棉	*chúnmián*	adj	pure cotton, one-hundred-percent cotton	4
从来	從來	*cónglái*	adv	from past till present, always, at all times	12
存	存	*cún*	v	to deposit, to accumulate	8
存款	存款	*cúnkuǎn*	n/vo	bank savings; to deposit money at a bank	17

Simplified	Traditional	Pinyin	Part of Speech	English	Lesson
				D	
答应	答應	*dāying*	v	to agree (to do something), to promise, to answer	6
打交道	打交道	*dǎ jiāodào*	vo	to deal with	5
大多	大多	*dàduō*	adv	mostly, for the most part	10
大理	大理	*Dàlǐ*	pn	Dali	13
大人	大人	*dàren*	n	adult	8
待	待	*dāi*	v	to stay	7
代	代	*dài*	v	to replace, to substitute	11
贷款	貸款	*dàikuǎn*	n/vo	loan; to provide a loan	8
单位	單位	*dānwèi*	n	unit	15
倒	倒	*dào*	v	to turn upside down, to go backwards	11
到处	到處	*dàochù*	adv	all around, all over	10
到底	到底	*dàodǐ*	adv	what on earth, what in the world, in the end	6
道理	道理	*dàoli*	n	reason, sense	4
道歉	道歉	*dào qiàn*	vo	to apologize	6
德国	德國	*Déguó*	pn	Germany	15
灯笼	燈籠	*dēnglong*	n	lantern	13
等	等	*děng*	p	and so forth, etc.	14
等于	等於	*děngyú*	v	to equal, to be equivalent to, to amount to	14
低	低	*dī*	adj	low	8
抵押	抵押	*dǐyā*	v	to mortgage	17
地道	地道	*dìdao*	adj	authentic, genuine	2
地理	地理	*dìlǐ*	n	geography	10
地球	地球	*dìqiú*	n	the earth, the globe	16

Simplified	Traditional	Pinyin	Part of Speech	English	Lesson
地位	地位	*dìwèi*	n	position, status	15
地形	地形	*dìxíng*	n	terrain, topography	10
电池	電池	*diànchí*	n	battery	20
电视剧	電視劇	*diànshìjù*	n	TV drama, TV series	20
电影院	電影院	*diànyǐngyuàn*	n	movie theater	6
跌	跌	*diē*	v	to fall	17
丢三拉四	丢三拉四	*diū sān là sì*		scatterbrained, forgetful	6
栋	棟	*dòng*	m	(measure word for buildings)	2
动作	動作	*dòngzuò*	n	movement, action	14
读书	讀書	*dú shū*	vo	to attend school, to study, to read aloud	8
度	度	*dù*	m	(measure word for degrees of temperature, heat, hardness, humidity, etc.)	16
端午节	端午節	*Duānwǔjié*	pn	Dragon Boat Festival	11
短	短	*duǎn*	adj	short	10
短期	短期	*duǎnqī*	n	short term	19
段	段	*duàn*	m	(measure word for section, segment, or part)	16
锻炼	鍛煉	*duànliàn*	v	to exercise, to work out, to undergo physical training	14
队	隊	*duì*	n	team, a row or line of people, (measure word for teams and lines)	15
队员	隊員	*duìyuán*	n	team member	15
对面	對面	*duìmiàn*	n	opposite side	12
顿	頓	*dùn*	m	(measure word for meals)	13

		E			
而	而	*ér*	conj	(conjunction to connect two clauses)	10
而已	而已	*éryǐ*	p	and no more	20

Simplified	Traditional	Pinyin	Part of Speech	English	Lesson
		F			
发财	發財	*fā cái*	vo	to get rich, to make a fortune	11
发达	發達	*fādá*	adj	developed, flourishing	18
发电	發電	*fā diàn*	vo	to generate electricity	16
发明	發明	*fāmíng*	n/v	invention; to invent	18
发生	發生	*fāshēng*	v	to happen, to occur, to take place	6
发展	發展	*fāzhǎn*	v/n	to develop; development	18
法国	法國	*Fǎguó*	pn	France	12
番	番	*fān*	m	(measure word for type or kind)	9
翻译	翻譯	*fānyì*	v/n	to translate; interpreter, translation	7
反对	反對	*fǎnduì*	v	to oppose	9
方面	方面	*fāngmiàn*	n	aspect, respect	14
房东	房東	*fángdōng*	n	landlord	13
放心	放心	*fàng xīn*	vo	to feel relieved, to be at ease	20
非⋯不可	非⋯不可	*fēi … bù kě*		have to, nothing but … would do	4
分手	分手	*fēn shǒu*	vo	to break up, to part company	6
分享	分享	*fēnxiǎng*	v	to share (joy, happiness, benefits, etc.) (lit. to divide and enjoy)	13
坟墓	墳墓	*fénmù*	n	grave, tomb	18
风	風	*fēng*	n	wind	16
风景	風景	*fēngjǐng*	n	scenic landscape, scenery	10
风俗	風俗	*fēngsú*	n	custom	13
风险	風險	*fēngxiǎn*	n	risk, danger, hazard	17
夫妻	夫妻	*fūqī*	n	husband and wife, couple	14

Simplified	Traditional	Pinyin	Part of Speech	English	Lesson
夫子庙	夫子廟	*Fūzǐmiào*	pn	Temple of Confucius	12
福	福	*fú*	n	blessing, good fortune	11
服装	服裝	*fúzhuāng*	n	clothing, apparel	12
负担	負擔	*fùdān*	n	burden	8
妇女	婦女	*fùnǚ*	n	women	15
G					
改革开放	改革開放	*gǎigé kāifàng*	v/n	to reform and open up; Reform and Opening-Up	15
盖	蓋	*gài*	v	to build, to construct	12
干杯	乾杯	*gān bēi*	vo	to drink a toast (lit. to dry the cup)	11
干衣机	乾衣機	*gānyījī*	n	(clothes) dryer	2
敢	敢	*gǎn*	mv	to dare	7
感恩节	感恩節	*Gǎn'ēnjié*	pn	Thanksgiving	11
感觉	感覺	*gǎnjué*	n/v	feeling, sense perception; to feel, to perceive	7
干吗	幹嗎	*gànmá*	qpr	why, why on earth, whatever for	19
钢琴	鋼琴	*gāngqín*	n	piano	9
高（速）铁（路）	高（速）鐵（路）	*gāo(sù) tiě(lù)*	n	high-speed rail	12
高原	高原	*gāoyuán*	n	plateau (lit. high field)	10
高中	高中	*gāozhōng*	n	senior high school	6
搞	搞	*gǎo*	v	to do, to carry on, to be engaged in	20
革命	革命	*gémìng*	n	revolution	18
各	各	*gè*	pr	each, every	3
根本	根本	*gēnběn*	adv	at all, simply	6
弓	弓	*gōng*	n	bow (for archery)	1

Simplified	Traditional	Pinyin	Part of Speech	English	Lesson
供	供	*gōng*	v	to provide, to support financially	8
工厂	工廠	*gōngchǎng*	n	factory	15
工学院	工學院	*gōng xuéyuàn*	n	school of engineering	5
工资	工資	*gōngzī*	n	wages, pay	8
宫殿	宮殿	*gōngdiàn*	n	palace	18
公共场所	公共場所	*gōnggòng chǎngsuǒ*	n	public place or space	16
公平	公平	*gōngpíng*	adj	fair, just, impartial, equitable	15
恭喜	恭喜	*gōngxǐ*	v	to congratulate	11
贡献	貢獻	*gòngxiàn*	v/n	to contribute, to devote; contribution	18
购物	購物	*gòuwù*	vo	to shop	4
咕噜	咕嚕	*gūlū*	ono	rumbling sound	12
姑妈	姑媽	*gūmā*	n	aunt (father's sister)	17
古老	古老	*gǔlǎo*	adj	ancient, old	13
股票	股票	*gǔpiào*	n	stock, share (lit. stock certificate)	17
股市	股市	*gǔshì*	n	stock market	17
故事	故事	*gùshi*	n	story, tale	13
挂	掛	*guà*	v	to hang, to hang up	2
乖	乖	*guāi*	adj	obedient, well-behaved (of children)	8
关	關	*guān*	v	to close, to turn off	13
关系	關係	*guānxì*	n	relation, relationship, connection	18
关照	關照	*guānzhào*	v	to take care of, to look after	20
管	管	*guǎn*	v	to control, manage, to mind, to care about	5
管理学院	管理學院	*guǎnlǐ xuéyuàn*	n	school of management	5

Simplified	Traditional	Pinyin	Part of Speech	English	Lesson
冠军	冠軍	guànjūn	n	champion, first place in a competition	15
广场	廣場	guǎngchǎng	n	public square	14
广东	廣東	Guǎngdōng	pn	Guangdong	3
广州	廣州	Guǎngzhōu	pn	Guangzhou	10
规定	規定	guīdìng	v/n	to regulate, to specify; rules and regulations, provisions	16
归来	歸來	guīlái	v	to return, to come back	19
柜子	櫃子	guìzi	n	cabinet, cupboard	2
国家	國家	guójiā	n	country, nation	16
国外	國外	guówài	n	abroad	19
过几天	過幾天	guò jǐ tiān		in a few days	2
过节	過節	guò jié	vo	to celebrate a holiday	10

H

Simplified	Traditional	Pinyin	Part of Speech	English	Lesson
哈	哈	hā	ono	(sound of laughter)	12
哈尔滨	哈爾濱	Hā'ěrbīn	pn	Harbin	10
海	海	hǎi	n	sea, ocean	10
海龟	海龜	hǎiguī	n	sea turtle	19
海外	海外	hǎiwài	n	overseas	19
害	害	hài	v	to cause trouble, to harm	7
汉朝	漢朝	Hàncháo	pn	Han dynasty	18
杭州	杭州	Hángzhōu	pn	Hangzhou	3
好处	好處	hǎochu	n	advantage, benefit	1
好看	好看	hǎokàn	adj	nice-looking, attractive	4
好在	好在	hǎozài	adv	fortunately, luckily	19

Simplified	Traditional	Pinyin	Part of Speech	English	Lesson
河	河	*hé*	n	river	13
河流	河流	*héliú*	n	river	10
合	合	*hé*	v	to combine, to join	17
合同	合同	*hétong*	n	agreement, contract	17
盒饭	盒飯	*héfàn*	n	box lunch	13
红包	紅包	*hóngbāo*	n	red envelope containing gift money	11
湖南	湖南	*Húnán*	pn	Hunan	3
互相	互相	*hùxiāng*	adv	mutually, each other, reciprocally	15
画画儿	畫畫兒	*huà huàr*	vo	to draw, to paint	9
化学	化學	*huàxué*	n	chemistry	5
环境	環境	*huánjìng*	n	environment, surroundings	11
皇帝	皇帝	*huángdì*	n	emperor	18
黄河	黃河	*Huánghé*	pn	Yellow River	10
回答	回答	*huídá*	v	to reply, to answer	19
回收	回收	*huíshōu*	v	to recycle	16
活字印刷	活字印刷	*huózì yìnshuā*	n	movable-type printing, letterpress printing	18
火	火	*huǒ*	adj/n	thriving, flourishing; fire, flame	20
火车	火車	*huǒchē*	n	train	10
火锅	火鍋	*huǒguō*	n	hotpot	20
火药	火藥	*huǒyào*	n	gunpowder (lit. fire chemical)	18

J

Simplified	Traditional	Pinyin	Part of Speech	English	Lesson
鸡	雞	*jī*	n	chicken	3
机会	機會	*jīhuì*	n	opportunity	15

Simplified	Traditional	Pinyin	Part of Speech	English	Lesson
急忙	急忙	jímáng	adv	hastily, in a hurry	7
即使	即使	jíshǐ	conj	even if	14
挤	擠	jǐ	adj/v	crowded; to push against, to squeeze	10
寄	寄	jì	v	to mail, to send	19
纪念品	紀念品	jìniànpǐn	n	souvenir, keepsake, memento	13
既然	既然	jìrán	conj	since, as, now that	19
计时	計時	jì shí	vo	to count time	11
技术	技術	jìshù	n	technology, technique	18
记载	記載	jìzǎi	v/n	to put down in writing, to record; record, account	18
加	加	jiā	v	to add	4
加班	加班	jiā bān	vo	to work overtime, to work extra shifts	19
加油	加油	jiā yóu	vo	to make an extra effort, to work harder, to refuel	16
家教	家教	jiājiào	n	tutor	8
家庭	家庭	jiātíng	n	family, household	8
家务	家務	jiāwù	n	household chores, household duties	15
家乡	家鄉	jiāxiāng	n	hometown, place of family origin	10
价钱	價錢	jiàqian	n	price	4
减肥	減肥	jiǎn féi	vo	to lose weight (lit. to reduce fat)	14
减轻	減輕	jiǎnqīng	v	to lessen	8
减少	減少	jiǎnshǎo	v	to reduce, to decrease, to lessen	16
建立	建立	jiànlì	v	to build, to establish	18
建议	建議	jiànyì	n/v	suggestion; to suggest	5
建筑	建築	jiànzhù	n/v	architecture; to build	12

Simplified	Traditional	Pinyin	Part of Speech	English	Lesson
健身房	健身房	jiànshēnfáng	n	fitness center, gym	14
饯行	餞行	jiànxíng	v	to host a farewell meal	20
将来	將來	jiānglái	n	future	5
讲	講	jiǎng	v	to speak, to tell	13
奖学金	獎學金	jiǎngxuéjīn	n	scholarship money	8
交	交	jiāo	v	to hand over, to turn in	8
交朋友	交朋友	jiāo péngyou	vo	to make friends	6
交通	交通	jiāotōng	n	transportation, traffic (lit. to intersect and go through)	13
骄傲	驕傲	jiāo'ào	adj/n	proud, arrogant, full of oneself; pride	15
脚步	腳步	jiǎobù	n	footstep	12
叫	叫	jiào	v	to make (someone do something)	6
叫（菜）	叫（菜）	jiào (cài)	v (o)	to order (food)	3
叫做	叫做	jiào zuò	vc	to be called, to be known as	19
教授	教授	jiàoshòu	n	professor	5
教育	教育	jiàoyù	n/v	education; to educate	8
街	街	jiē	n	street	12
接风	接風	jiēfēng	v	to host a welcome meal for a visitor from afar	20
接受	接受	jiēshòu	v	to accept, to take on, to undertake	20
接着	接著	jiēzhe	v	to follow, to continue	19
结果	結果	jiéguǒ	conj/n	as a result; result	7
结婚	結婚	jié hūn	vo	to get married, to marry	9
节俭	節儉	jiéjiǎn	adj	thrifty, frugal	17
节日	節日	jiérì	n	holiday, festival	11
节约	節約	jiéyuē	v	to economize, to save, to conserve	16

Simplified	Traditional	Pinyin	Part of Speech	English	Lesson
解决	解決	jiějué	v	to solve, to resolve	5
解释	解釋	jiěshì	v	to explain	19
借	借	jiè	v	to borrow, to lend	8
芥兰	芥蘭	jièlán	n	Chinese broccoli	3
金融	金融	jīnróng	n	finance, banking	5
尽可能	儘可能	jǐn kěnéng		as much as possible	12
进步	進步	jìnbù	v/adj	to make progress; progressive	11
进入	進入	jìnrù	v	to enter, to get into	19
进行	進行	jìnxíng	v	to carry on, to carry out, to conduct	18
经济	經濟	jīngjì	n	economics, economy	5
经理	經理	jīnglǐ	n	manager	19
经验	經驗	jīngyàn	n/v	experience; to experience	5
景点	景點	jǐngdiǎn	n	scenic spot, tourist spot	10
酒	酒	jiǔ	n	alcohol, liquor	11
旧	舊	jiù	adj	old (of things)	2
舅舅	舅舅	jiùjiu	n	uncle (mother's brother)	11
舅妈	舅媽	jiùmā	n	aunt (mother's brother's wife)	11
举	舉	jǔ	v	to lift, to raise	11
句	句	jù	m	(measure word for sentences)	12
聚	聚	jù	v	to gather, to get together, to congregate	20
聚会	聚會	jùhuì	v/n	to get together, to congregate; party, get-together, social gathering	20
决定	決定	juédìng	v/n	to decide; decision	5

Simplified	Traditional	Pinyin	Part of Speech	English	Lesson
			K		
卡拉OK	卡拉OK	*kǎlā ōukēi*	n	karaoke	7
开朗	開朗	*kāilǎng*	adj	extroverted, open and sunny in disposition	6
开玩笑	開玩笑	*kāi wánxiào*	vo	to crack a joke, to joke	3
开学	開學	*kāi xué*	vo	to begin a new semester	1
砍	砍	*kǎn*	v	to cut, to chop	16
看法	看法	*kànfǎ*	n	point of view	9
考虑	考慮	*kǎolǜ*	v	to consider	3
柯林	柯林	*Kē Lín*	pn	(a personal name)	1
科学	科學	*kēxué*	n/adj	science; scientific	14
可靠	可靠	*kěkào*	adj	dependable	7
可怕	可怕	*kěpà*	adj	awful, terrible, fearful	19
客人	客人	*kèren*	n	guest, visitor	20
空	空	*kōng*	adj	empty	2
空气	空氣	*kōngqì*	n	air, atmosphere	16
空调	空調	*kōngtiáo*	n	air conditioning	2
恐怕	恐怕	*kǒngpà*	adv	I'm afraid that, I think perhaps, probably	2
孔子	孔子	*Kǒngzǐ*	pn	Confucius	18
口味	口味	*kǒuwèi*	n	(personal) taste	3
跨国	跨國	*kuàguó*	adj	transnational, multinational	19
快餐	快餐	*kuàicān*	n	fast food, quick meal	12
筷子	筷子	*kuàizi*	n	chopsticks	3
昆明	昆明	*Kūnmíng*	pn	Kunming (capital of Yunnan Province)	13

Simplified	Traditional	Pinyin	Part of Speech	English	Lesson
				L	
垃圾	垃圾	lājī	n	garbage, trash	7
拉	拉	là	v	to leave (something) behind inadvertently (colloq.)	1
辣	辣	là	adj	spicy	3
来不及	來不及	lái bu jí	vc	to not have enough time to do something, to be too late to do something	12
浪费	浪費	làngfèi	v/adj	to waste, to squander; wasteful	11
老百姓	老百姓	lǎobǎixìng	n	ordinary people	12
老年	老年	lǎonián	n	old age	17
老是	老是	lǎoshì	adv	always	7
老太太	老太太	lǎotàitai	n	elderly lady	17
老外	老外	lǎowài	n	foreigner (slang)	12
离开	離開	lí kāi	vc	to leave, to depart from	7
李白	李白	Lǐ Bái	pn	Li Bai (701–762 CE)	18
李文	李文	Lǐ Wén	pn	(a personal name)	14
李哲	李哲	Lǐ Zhé	pn	(a personal name)	5
理财	理財	lǐcái	vo	to manage wealth	17
理解	理解	lǐjiě	v	to understand	9
厉害	厲害	lìhai	adj	terrible, formidable	9
丽江	麗江	Lìjiāng	pn	Lijiang	13
丽莎	麗莎	Lìshā	pn	(a personal name)	3
历史	歷史	lìshǐ	n	history	5
利息	利息	lìxī	n	interest (on invested funds)	17
联系	聯繫	liánxì	v/n	to contact, to get in touch; connection, relation (lit. to combine and tie)	20

Simplified	Traditional	Pinyin	Part of Speech	English	Lesson
良好	良好	*liánghǎo*	adj	good, fine (literary)	8
亮	亮	*liàng*	adj	bright, light	16
辆	輛	*liàng*	m	(measure word for vehicles)	1
了解	了解	*liǎojiě*	v	to understand, to know about, to be informed	10
林雪梅	林雪梅	*Lín Xuěméi*	pn	(a personal name)	3
零食	零食	*língshí*	n	snack	19
零用钱	零用錢	*língyòngqián*	n	allowance, spending money	8
领导	領導	*lǐngdǎo*	v/n	to lead; leadership, leader (lit. to lead and guide)	18
流	流	*liú*	v	to flow	10
流	流	*liú*	n	class, level, rank, category	20
留（下）	留（下）	*liú (xia)*	v(c)	to leave behind, to stay behind	13
留学	留學	*liú xué*	vo	to study abroad	9
留学生	留學生	*liúxuéshēng*	n	study-abroad student	3
遛	遛	*liù*	v	to walk (an animal), to stroll	8
路线	路線	*lùxiàn*	n	route, itinerary	10
录用	錄用	*lùyòng*	v	to take someone on staff, to employ	19
旅客	旅客	*lǚkè*	n	passenger, voyager, traveler	13
旅游	旅遊	*lǚyóu*	v/n	to travel (for pleasure); (pleasure) travel	10
落伍	落伍	*luòwǔ*	v	to lag behind, to be outdated	7

M

Simplified	Traditional	Pinyin	Part of Speech	English	Lesson
麻将	麻將	*májiàng*	n	mahjong	17
马虎	馬虎	*mǎhu*	adj	careless, perfunctory, mediocre	6
马克	馬克	*Mǎkè*	pn	(a personal name)	16

Simplified	Traditional	Pinyin	Part of Speech	English	Lesson
马路	馬路	mǎlù	n	road, street	2
嘛	嘛	ma	p	(particle used to emphasize the obvious)	11
满意	滿意	mǎnyì	v	to be satisfied, to be pleased	19
猫	貓	māo	n	cat	8
矛盾	矛盾	máodùn	n/adj	contradiction, conflict; contradictory, conflicting	17
毛巾	毛巾	máojīn	n	towel	4
毛衣	毛衣	máoyī	n	woolen sweater	4
贸易	貿易	màoyì	n/v	trade; to trade	18
煤	煤	méi	n	coal	16
美	美	měi	adj	beautiful, good	13
美丽	美麗	měilì	adj	beautiful	13
门	門	mén	m	(measure word for academic courses)	5
门	門	mén	n	door	2
门口	門口	ménkǒu	n	doorway, entrance	3
门票	門票	ménpiào	n	admission ticket, admission fee	13
迷	迷	mí	n/v	fan; to be infatuated with	6
免费	免費	miǎnfèi	v/vo	free of charge (lit. exempt from paying the fee)	7
面	麵	miàn	n	noodles	13
面积	面積	miànjī	n	area (of land)	10
面熟	面熟	miànshú	adj	familiar-looking	20
民以食为天	民以食為天	mín yǐ shí wéi tiān		ordinary people consider food as important as heaven	12
民族	民族	mínzú	n	ethnic group, nationality	10

Simplified	Traditional	Pinyin	Part of Speech	English	Lesson
名牌	名牌	*míngpái*	n	famous brand, name brand	4
模范	模範	*mófàn*	adj/n	exemplary; model, fine example	15
末	末	*mò*	n	end	12
墨西哥	墨西哥	*Mòxīgē*	pn	Mexico	9

N

难怪	難怪	*nánguài*	adv	no wonder	8
南京	南京	*Nánjīng*	pn	Nanjing	10
男子	男子	*nánzǐ*	n	man, male	15
嫩	嫩	*nèn*	adj	tender	3
能力	能力	*nénglì*	n	ability, capacity, competence	19
能源	能源	*néngyuán*	n	energy, energy source	16
年轻	年輕	*niánqīng*	adj	young	20
年夜饭	年夜飯	*niányèfàn*	n	Chinese New Year's Eve dinner	11
牛仔裤	牛仔褲	*niúzǎikù*	n	jeans	4
农村	農村	*nóngcūn*	n	countryside, village, rural area	8
农历	農曆	*nónglì*	n	traditional Chinese lunar calendar (lit. agricultural calendar)	11
女性	女性	*nǚxìng*	n	female gender, woman	15
暖气	暖氣	*nuǎnqì*	n	heating (lit. warm air)	16

O

欧洲	歐洲	*Ōuzhōu*	pn	Europe	20

P

爬山	爬山	*pá shān*	vo	to hike in the mountains, to climb a mountain	16
拍	拍	*pāi*	v	to take a picture, to shoot a film	12

Simplified	Traditional	Pinyin	Part of Speech	English	Lesson
牌子	牌子	*páizi*	n	brand	4
陪	陪	*péi*	v	to accompany	6
赔	賠	*péi*	v	to lose (money, etc.), to suffer a loss in a deal	17
碰见	碰見	*pèng jiàn*	vc	to run into (a person by chance)	5
乒乓球	乒乓球	*pīngpāngqiú*	n	ping pong, table tennis	15
平等	平等	*píngděng*	adj/n	equal; equality (lit. level and equal)	15
平原	平原	*píngyuán*	n	plain (lit. flat field)	10
瓶装水	瓶裝水	*píngzhuāng shuǐ*	n	bottled water	16
		Q			
妻子	妻子	*qīzi*	n	wife	15
骑	騎	*qí*	v	to ride	12
奇怪	奇怪	*qíguài*	adj	strange, weird	11
其他	其他	*qítā*	pr	other, else	5
其中	其中	*qízhōng*		among which/whom, in which/whom, of which/whom	18
企业	企業	*qǐyè*	n	enterprise, business, company, firm	15
签	簽	*qiān*	v	to sign, to autograph	17
千万	千萬	*qiānwàn*	adv	by all means, absolutely must	13
欠	欠	*qiàn*	v	to owe	8
墙	牆	*qiáng*	n	wall	11
秦朝	秦朝	*Qíncháo*	pn	Qin dynasty	18
秦始皇	秦始皇	*Qínshǐhuáng*	pn	First Emperor of the Qin dynasty	18
清朝	清朝	*Qīngcháo*	pn	Qing dynasty	18
清淡	清淡	*qīngdàn*	adj	light in flavor	3

Simplified	Traditional	Pinyin	Part of Speech	English	Lesson
清蒸	清蒸	*qīngzhēng*	v	to steam (food without heavy sauce)	3
轻松	輕鬆	*qīngsōng*	adj	light, relaxed	5
晴	晴	*qíng*	adj	sunny	19
情况	情況	*qíngkuàng*	n	situation, condition, circumstances	15
庆祝	慶祝	*qìngzhù*	v	to celebrate	20
取得	取得	*qǔdé*	v	to obtain, to gain, to acquire	8
劝	勸	*quàn*	v	to persuade, to advise, to urge	17
缺点	缺點	*quēdiǎn*	n	shortcoming, defect, weakness	19

		R			
热闹	熱鬧	*rènao*	adj	lively, buzzing with excitement, bustling with activity (of a place or scene)	11
人材	人材	*réncái*	v	person of ability and talent	19
人口	人口	*rénkǒu*	n	populations	10
人山人海	人山人海	*rén shān rén hǎi*		huge crowds of people (lit. mountains and seas of people)	10
认为	認為	*rènwéi*	v	to think, to consider	9
扔	扔	*rēng*	v	to throw, to toss, to throw away	16
日用品	日用品	*rìyòngpǐn*	n	daily necessities	2
融入	融入	*róngrù*	v	to merge into, to meld into	12
软	軟	*ruǎn*	adj	soft	13
软件	軟件	*ruǎnjiàn*	n	software	7

		S			
散步	散步	*sàn bù*	vo	to take a walk, to go for a walk	14
嫂子	嫂子	*sǎozi*	n	older brother's wife	9

Simplified	Traditional	Pinyin	Part of Speech	English	Lesson
杀	殺	shā	v	to kill	18
沙漠	沙漠	shāmò	n	desert	10
厦	廈	shà		mansion, tall building	12
山	山	shān	n	mountain, hill	10
善于	善於	shànyú		to be good at, to be adept in	19
上班	上班	shàng bān	vo	to go to work, to start work, to be on duty	12
上衣	上衣	shàngyī	n	upper outer garment, jacket	19
上瘾	上癮	shàng yǐn	vo	to become addicted	7
烧	燒	shāo	v	to burn, to set fire to, to cook	18
少数	少數	shǎoshù	n	few, minority (lit. small number)	10
社会	社會	shèhuì	n	society	9
设计	設計	shèjì	v/n	to design; design	9
摄氏	攝氏	Shèshì	pn	Celsius, centigrade	16
深	深	shēn	adj	deep, profound dark (color)	13
深圳	深圳	Shēnzhèn	pn	Shenzhen	10
申请	申請	shēnqǐng	v	to apply (to a school or job)	5
生	生	shēng	v	to give birth to, to be born	8
生活	生活	shēnghuó	n/v	(day-to-day) life; to live	1
生气	生氣	shēng qì	vo	to get angry	6
声音	聲音	shēngyīn	n	sound, voice	12
省	省	shěng	n	province (administrative division)	10
省吃俭用	省吃儉用	shěng chī jiǎn yòng		to be frugal (with food and other living expenses)	17
省会	省會	shěnghuì	n	provincial capital	13
省钱	省錢	shěng qián	vo	to save money, to economize	1

Simplified	Traditional	Pinyin	Part of Speech	English	Lesson
省下来	省下來	shěng xia lai	vc	to save (money, time)	5
剩（下）	剩（下）	shèng (xia)	v(c)	to leave a surplus, to be left (over)	11
湿	濕	shī	adj	wet	19
诗	詩	shī	n	poetry, poem	18
诗人	詩人	shīrén	n	poet	18
时代	時代	shídài	n	era, age	7
时髦	時髦	shímáo	adj	fashionable, stylish	4
实际上	實際上	shíjìshang	adv	in fact, in reality, actually	6
石林	石林	Shílín	pn	The Stone Forest	13
石头	石頭	shítou	n	stone, rock, pebble	13
石油	石油	shíyóu	n	petroleum, oil	16
市场	市場	shìchǎng	n	market	15
适合	適合	shìhé	v	to suit	8
适应	適應	shìyìng	v	to adapt, to become accustomed to	1
世纪	世紀	shìjì	n	century	19
世界	世界	shìjiè	n	world	5
事业	事業	shìyè	n	career, undertaking	9
收入	收入	shōurù	n	income	8
受不了	受不了	shòu bu liǎo	vc	cannot take it, unable to bear	5
受到	受到	shòu dào	vc	to receive	8
输	輸	shū	v	to lose, to be defeated	15
树	樹	shù	n	tree	14
树林	樹林	shùlín	n	woods, forest	13
数字	數字	shùzì	n	numeral, figure, digit	5

Simplified	Traditional	Pinyin	Part of Speech	English	Lesson
税	稅	*shuì*	n	tax	4
睡眠	睡眠	*shuìmián*	n	sleep	14
顺利	順利	*shùnlì*	adj	smooth, successful, without a hitch	11
说不定	說不定	*shuōbudìng*	adv	perhaps, maybe	6
说服	說服	*shuōfú*	v	to persuade, to convince	17
硕士	碩士	*shuòshì*	n	master's (academic degree)	9
丝绸	絲綢	*sīchóu*	n	silk, silk fabric	18
思考	思考	*sīkǎo*	v/n	to think deeply, to ponder over; contemplation, cogitation	17
思想	思想	*sīxiǎng*	n	thinking, ideology, thoughts	18
四川	四川	*Sìchuān*	pn	Sichuan	3
四季如春	四季如春	*sìjì rú chūn*		spring-like all year round	10
宋朝	宋朝	*Sòngcháo*	pn	Song dynasty	18
塑料袋	塑料袋	*sùliào dài*	n	plastic bag	16
算	算	*suàn*	v	to count as, to be considered as	17
随便	隨便	*suíbiàn*	adj/vo	casual, careless; to do as one pleases	14
随手	隨手	*suíshǒu*	adv	without extra effort or motion, conveniently	16
孙女	孫女	*sūnnü*	n	granddaughter (son's daughter)	17
孙中山	孫中山	*Sūn Zhōngshān*	pn	Sun Yat-sen	18
孙子	孫子	*sūnzi*	n	grandson (son's son)	17

| | | | **T** | | |

Simplified	Traditional	Pinyin	Part of Speech	English	Lesson
塔	塔	*tǎ*	n	tower, pagoda	13
台	台	*tái*	m	(measure word for machines)	2
态度	態度	*tàidu*	n	attitude	6

Simplified	Traditional	Pinyin	Part of Speech	English	Lesson
太极拳	太極拳	tàijíquán	n	tai chi (a form of traditional Chinese shadowboxing)	14
太阳	太陽	tàiyáng	n	sun	16
太阳能	太陽能	tàiyángnéng	n	solar energy, solar power	16
谈	談	tán	v	to talk, to discuss	5
毯子	毯子	tǎnzi	n	blanket	2
唐朝	唐朝	Tángcháo	pn	Tang dynasty	18
讨论	討論	tǎolùn	v	to discuss	5
讨厌	討厭	tǎoyàn	v/adj	to dislike, to loathe; disgusting, disagreeable	15
套装	套裝	tàozhuāng	n	suit, a set of matching outer garments	19
特色	特色	tèsè	n	distinguishing feature or quality, characteristic	12
T恤衫	T恤衫	tīxùshān	n	T-shirt	4
提	提	tí	v	to mention, to bring up	6
天津	天津	Tiānjīn	pn	Tianjin	10
条件	條件	tiáojiàn	n	condition	10
贴	貼	tiē	v	to paste, to glue	11
通知	通知	tōngzhī	n/v	notice; to notify, to inform	19
同工同酬	同工同酬	tóng gōng tóng chóu		equal pay for equal work	15
同事	同事	tóngshì	n	colleague, coworker	20
同屋	同屋	tóngwū	n	roommate	2
同意	同意	tóngyì	v	to agree	4
童年	童年	tóngnián	n	childhood	9
筒	筒	tǒng	n	thick tube-shaped container	16

Simplified	Traditional	Pinyin	Part of Speech	English	Lesson
统一	統一	*tǒngyī*	v/adj	to unify, to unite; unified, centralized	18
投资	投資	*tóu zī*	vo/n	to invest capital; investment (financial) (lit. to throw or cast capital)	17
突然	突然	*tūrán*	adv/adj	suddenly, unexpectedly; sudden, unexpected	17
团	團	*tuán*	n	group, organization	13
团圆	團圓	*tuányuán*	v	to reunite (as a family)	11
推	推	*tuī*	v	to push, to shove	16
推销	推銷	*tuīxiāo*	v	to market, to promote the sale (of goods/ merchandise)	20
退休	退休	*tuìxiū*	v	to retire	14
W					
外卖	外賣	*wàimài*	n	takeout	7
完全	完全	*wánquán*	adv/adj	completely, fully; complete, whole	9
晚会	晚會	*wǎnhuì*	n	evening gathering, soiree	11
网络	網絡	*wǎngluò*	n	network, the Internet	7
网站	網站	*wǎngzhàn*	n	website	7
往往	往往	*wǎngwǎng*	adv	more often than not	19
望女成凤	望女成鳳	*wàng nǚ chéng fèng*		to hope that one's daughter will become successful (lit. to hope that one's daughter will become a phoenix)	9
望子成龙	望子成龍	*wàng zǐ chéng lóng*		to hope that one's son will become successful (lit. to hope that one's son will become a dragon)	9
危机	危機	*wēijī*	n	crisis	16
微信	微信	*Wēixìn*	pn	WeChat	3
伟大	偉大	*wěidà*	adj	great, outstanding, magnificent	18

Simplified	Traditional	Pinyin	Part of Speech	English	Lesson
喂	餵	wèi	v	to feed	8
味道	味道	wèidao	n	taste, flavor (of food)	3
未婚妻	未婚妻	wèihūnqī	n	fiancée	17
卫生纸	衛生紙	wèishēngzhǐ	n	toilet paper	4
温度	溫度	wēndù	n	temperature	16
文具	文具	wénjù	n	stationery, writing supplies	2
文明	文明	wénmíng	n/adj	civilization; civilized	18
文学	文學	wénxué	n	literature	5
文章	文章	wénzhāng	n	essay, article	5
文字	文字	wénzì	n	characters, written form of a language	18
稳定	穩定	wěndìng	adj/v	stable, steady; to stabilize, to be steady	20
卧铺	臥鋪	wòpù	n	sleeping bunk (on a train)	13
握手	握手	wò shǒu	vo	to shake hands, to clasp hands	19
污染	汙染	wūrǎn	v/n	to pollute, to contaminate; pollution, contamination	16
屋子	屋子	wūzi	n	room	7
无论	無論	wúlùn	conj	regardless of . . . , whether it be . . .	4
雾霾	霧霾	wùmái	n	smog	16

X

Simplified	Traditional	Pinyin	Part of Speech	English	Lesson
西班牙	西班牙	Xībānyá	pn	Spain	15
西方	西方	Xīfāng	pn	the West	18
吸烟	吸菸	xī yān	vo	to smoke a cigarette	14
吸引	吸引	xīyǐn	v	to attract, to draw, to fascinate	19
习惯	習慣	xíguàn	n/v	habit; to be accustomed to	13
洗	洗	xǐ	v	to wash	2

Simplified	Traditional	Pinyin	Part of Speech	English	Lesson
洗衣粉	洗衣粉	xǐyīfěn	n	laundry powder	4
洗衣机	洗衣機	xǐyījī	n	washing machine	2
系	系	xì	n	academic department (of a college or university)	5
吓人	嚇人	xiàrén	adj	scary, frightening	19
下载	下載	xiàzài	v	to download	7
先进	先進	xiānjìn	adj	advanced	18
咸	鹹	xián	adj	salty	3
现金	現金	xiànjīn	n	cash	4
现象	現象	xiànxiàng	n	phenomenon, appearance	15
香	香	xiāng	adj	fragrant, pleasant-smelling	3
相处	相處	xiāngchǔ	v	to get along	6
相信	相信	xiāngxìn	v	to believe, to trust	15
想法	想法	xiǎngfǎ	n	idea, opinion	17
想像	想像	xiǎngxiàng	v/n	to imagine, to visualize; imagination	12
享受	享受	xiǎngshòu	v/n	to enjoy; enjoyment, pleasure	17
像	像	xiàng	v	to resemble, to be like	4
销售	銷售	xiāoshòu	v	to sell, to market	19
消息	消息	xiāoxi	n	news, message, information	15
小吃	小吃	xiǎochī	n	small and inexpensive dishes, snacks	12
小区	小區	xiǎoqū	n	residential development, residential complex	11
小学	小學	xiǎoxué	n	elementary school	9
校内	校內	xiào nèi		on campus	1
校外	校外	xiào wài		off campus	1

Simplified	Traditional	Pinyin	Part of Speech	English	Lesson
校友	校友	xiàoyǒu	n	schoolmate, alumnus, alumna	20
心	心	xīn	n	heart, mind	6
心事	心事	xīnshì	n	something that weighs on one's mind	6
新疆	新疆	Xīnjiāng	pn	Xinjiang	10
新生	新生	xīnshēng	n	new student	1
新闻	新聞	xīnwén	n	news	7
新鲜	新鮮	xīnxian	adj	fresh	3
辛苦	辛苦	xīnkǔ	adj/v	hard, strenuous; to work hard	17
薪水	薪水	xīnshuǐ	n	salary, pay, wages	15
幸福	幸福	xìngfú	n/adj	happiness; happy	9
熊猫	熊貓	xióngmāo	n	panda	14
修	修	xiū	v	to build, to repair	18
需要	需要	xūyào	v/n	to need; needs	4
选	選	xuǎn	v	to choose	5
选择	選擇	xuǎnzé	n/v	choice; to choose	9
学分	學分	xuéfēn	n	academic credit	5
学位	學位	xuéwèi	n	academic degree	5

Y

Simplified	Traditional	Pinyin	Part of Speech	English	Lesson
压力	壓力	yālì	n	pressure	8
牙膏	牙膏	yágāo	n	toothpaste	4
研究生	研究生	yánjiūshēng	n	graduate student	1
严肃	嚴肅	yánsù	adj	stern, serious	19
严重	嚴重	yánzhòng	adj	serious, grave	7

Simplified	Traditional	Pinyin	Part of Speech	English	Lesson
演唱会	演唱會	yǎnchànghuì	n	vocal concert	6
演员	演員	yǎnyuán	n	actor, performer	20
要不是	要不是	yàobúshì [yàobùshì]	conj	if it were not for, but for	12
要么…，要么…	要麼…，要麼…	yàome…, yàome…	conj	if it's not…it's…, either…or…	5
钥匙	鑰匙	yàoshi	n	key	6
一般	一般	yìbān [yībān]	adv	generally	2
一次性	一次性	yícìxìng [yīcìxìng]	adj	one-time	16
一干二净	一乾二淨	yì gān èr jìng [yī gān èr jìng]		completely, thoroughly	6
一会儿	一會兒	yíhuìr [yīhuìr]	n+m	in a moment, a little while	4
一下子	一下子	yíxiàzi [yīxiàzi]	adv	in an instant, all of a sudden	10
衣柜	衣櫃	yīguì	n	wardrobe	2
衣食住行	衣食住行	yī shí zhù xíng		basic necessities of life (lit. food, clothing, shelter, and transportation)	7
移民	移民	yímín	n/v	immigrant; to immigrate	9
以	以	yǐ	prep	with	11
以来	以來	yǐlái	t	since	15
义工	義工	yìgōng	n	volunteer work (lit. righteous work), volunteer	17
意见	意見	yìjiàn	n	opinion	5
意思	意思	yìsi	n	meaning	11
阴	陰	yīn	adj	overcast, hidden from the sun	19
银行	銀行	yínháng	n	bank	8
引起	引起	yǐnqǐ	v	to give rise to, to lead to	17
饮食	飲食	yǐnshí	n	diet, food and drink	13

Simplified	Traditional	Pinyin	Part of Speech	English	Lesson
赢	赢	*yíng*	v	to win	15
营养	營養	*yíngyǎng*	n	nutrition, nourishment	14
影响	影響	*yǐngxiǎng*	v/n	to influence, to have an impact; influence	8
硬	硬	*yìng*	adj	hard, stiff	13
永远	永遠	*yǒngyuǎn*	adv	always, forever	20
优点	優點	*yōudiǎn*	n	merit, strong point, advantage	19
幽默	幽默	*yōumò*	adj	humorous	13
由	由	*yóu*	prep	by	15
油	油	*yóu*	n/adj	oil; oily	3
游客	遊客	*yóukè*	n	tourist	12
游览	遊覽	*yóulǎn*	v/n	to go sightseeing, to tour; excursion	13
游戏	遊戲	*yóuxì*	n	game	7
有机	有機	*yǒujī*	adj	organic	3
有益	有益	*yǒuyì*	adj	beneficial, useful	16
有用	有用	*yǒuyòng*	adj	useful	7
友谊	友誼	*yǒuyì*	n	friendship	20
余	餘	*yú*	n/v	surplus; to have a surplus	11
于	於	*yú*	prep	towards, in, on, at, (indicating comparison)	16
瑜伽	瑜伽	*yújiā*	n	yoga	14
与	與	*yǔ*	conj/prep	and; with	14
郁闷	鬱悶	*yùmèn*	adj	gloomy, depressed	17
原来	原來	*yuánlái*	adv/adj	as a matter of fact; original, former	6

Simplified	Traditional	Pinyin	Part of Speech	English	Lesson
元宵	元宵	yuánxiāo	n	night of the fifteenth of the first lunar month, sweet dumplings made of sticky-rice flour	11
元宵节	元宵節	Yuánxiāojié	pn	Lantern Festival	11
月饼	月餅	yuèbǐng	n	moon cake	11
云	雲	yún	n	cloud	19
云南	雲南	Yúnnán	pn	Yunnan	10
		Z			
杂志	雜誌	zázhì	n	magazine	7
在乎	在乎	zàihu	v	to mind, to care	4
赞成	贊成	zànchéng	v	to approve, to support	16
早晨	早晨	zǎochen	n	morning, early morning	14
造成	造成	zào chéng	vc	to cause, to give rise to	16
造纸	造紙	zào zhǐ	vo	to make paper	18
增加	增加	zēngjiā	v	to increase, to add	17
展厅	展廳	zhǎntīng	n	exhibition hall, gallery	18
张天明	張天明	Zhāng Tiānmíng	pn	(a personal name)	1
涨	漲	zhǎng	v	to rise, to surge, to go up (of water, prices, etc.)	17
丈夫	丈夫	zhàngfu	n	husband	15
着急	著急	zháojí	v	to worry	2
哲学	哲學	zhéxué	n	philosophy	5
者	者	zhě		(suffix meaning person)	20
真的	真的	zhēn de	adv	really, truly	2
正月	正月	zhēngyuè	n	first month of the lunar year	11

Simplified	Traditional	Pinyin	Part of Speech	English	Lesson
正好	正好	*zhènghǎo*	adv	coincidentally	3
整天	整天	*zhěng tiān*		all day long	5
政府	政府	*zhèngfǔ*	n	government	8
挣钱	掙錢	*zhèng qián*	vo	to earn money	5
之	之	*zhī*	p	(literary equivalent of 的)	18
只	隻	*zhī*	m	(measure word for one of certain paired things and some animals)	14
只好	只好	*zhǐhǎo*	adv	to be forced to, to have no choice but	4
只要	只要	*zhǐyào*	conj	as long as, provided	14
知识	知識	*zhīshi*	n	knowledge	9
侄女	侄女	*zhínǚ*	n	brother's daughter	9
职业	職業	*zhíyè*	n	occupation, profession, vocation	15
指南针	指南針	*zhǐnánzhēn*	n	compass	18
质量	質量	*zhìliàng*	n	quality	4
中华民国	中華民國	*Zhōnghuá Mínguó*	pn	Republic of China	18
中秋节	中秋節	*Zhōngqiūjié*	pn	Mid-Autumn Festival, Moon Festival	11
重男轻女	重男輕女	*zhòng nán qīng nǚ*		to regard males as superior to females, to privilege men over women	15
重视	重視	*zhòngshì*	v	to attach importance to	14
重要	重要	*zhòngyào*	adj	important	7
周	週	*zhōu*	n	week	20
逐渐	逐漸	*zhújiàn*	adv	gradually, little by little	15
主意	主意	*zhúyi*	n	idea	3
主要	主要	*zhǔyào*	adj	main, principal	10

Simplified	Traditional	Pinyin	Part of Speech	English	Lesson
注意	注意	zhùyì	v/n	to pay attention to; attention	14
转	轉	zhuǎn	v	to turn, to shift, to change	19
赚钱	賺錢	zhuànqián	vo	to make a profit	17
资料	資料	zīliào	n	material (reference, academic)	7
自然	自然	zìrán	n/adj	nature; natural	10
自行车	自行車	zìxíngchē	n	bicycle	12
自由	自由	zìyóu	adj	free, unconstrained	1
总	總	zǒng	adj	general, chief	19
粽子	粽子	zòngzi	n	sticky-rice dumpling wrapped in bamboo or reed leaves	11
尊重	尊重	zūnzhòng	v	to respect	9
座	座	zuò	m	(measure word for buildings and mountains)	12
做法	做法	zuòfǎ	n	way of doing things, course of action	9

The English-Chinese index is organized based on the alphabetical order of the English definitions. For ease of reference, indefinite articles and definite articles are omitted when they are the beginning of a phrase.

English	Simplified	Traditional	Pinyin	Part of Speech	Lesson
A					
ability, capacity, competence	能力	能力	nénglì	n	19
abroad	国外	國外	guówài	n	19
academic credit	学分	學分	xuéfēn	n	5
academic degree	学位	學位	xuéwèi	n	5
academic department (of a college or university)	系	系	xì	n	5
accept, take on, undertake	接受	接受	jiēshòu	v	20
accompany	陪	陪	péi	v	6
actor, performer	演员	演員	yǎnyuán	n	20
adapt, become accustomed to	适应	適應	shìyìng	v	1
add	加	加	jiā	v	4
admission ticket, admission fee	门票	門票	ménpiào	n	13
adult	大人	大人	dàren	n	8
advanced	先进	先進	xiānjìn	adj	18
advantage, benefit	好处	好處	hǎochu	n	1
agree	同意	同意	tóngyì	v	4
agree (to do something), promise, answer	答应	答應	dāying	v	6
agreement, contract	合同	合同	hétong	n	17
air, atmosphere	空气	空氣	kōngqì	n	16
air conditioning	空调	空調	kōngtiáo	n	2
alcohol, liquor	酒	酒	jiǔ	n	11

English	Simplified	Traditional	Pinyin	Part of Speech	Lesson
all around, all over	到处	到處	dàochù	adv	10
all day long	整天	整天	zhěng tiān		5
allowance, spending money	零用钱	零用錢	língyòngqián	n	8
always	老是	老是	lǎoshì	adv	7
always, forever	永远	永遠	yǒngyuǎn	adv	20
among which/whom, in which/whom, of which/whom	其中	其中	qízhōng		18
ancient, old	古老	古老	gǔlǎo	adj	13
and no more	而已	而已	éryǐ	p	20
and so forth, etc.	等	等	děng	p	14
and; with	与	與	yǔ	conj/prep	14
apologize	道歉	道歉	dào qiàn	vo	6
appear, arise, emerge	出现	出現	chūxiàn	v	15
apply (to a school or job)	申请	申請	shēnqǐng	v	5
approve, support	赞成	贊成	zànchéng	v	16
architecture; build	建筑	建築	jiànzhù	n/v	12
area (of land)	面积	面積	miànjī	n	10
arrange	安排	安排	ānpái	v	9
arrive late	迟到	遲到	chídào	v	7
as a matter of fact; original, former	原来	原來	yuánlái	adv/adj	6
as a result; result	结果	結果	jiéguǒ	conj/n	7
as long as, provided	只要	只要	zhǐyào	conj	14
as much as possible	尽可能	儘可能	jǐn kěnéng		12
aspect, respect	方面	方面	fāngmiàn	n	14

English	Simplified	Traditional	Pinyin	Part of Speech	Lesson
at all, simply	根本	根本	gēnběn	adv	6
attach importance to	重视	重視	zhòngshì	v	14
attend school, study, read aloud	读书	讀書	dú shū	vo	8
attitude	态度	態度	tàidu	n	6
attract, draw, fascinate	吸引	吸引	xīyǐn	v	19
aunt (father's sister)	姑妈	姑媽	gūmā	n	17
aunt (mother's brother's wife)	舅妈	舅媽	jiùmā	n	11
authentic, genuine	地道	地道	dìdao	adj	2
awful, terrible, fearful	可怕	可怕	kěpà	adj	19

		B			
background	背景	背景	bèijǐng	n	6
bank	银行	銀行	yínháng	n	8
bank savings; deposit money at a bank	存款	存款	cúnkuǎn	n/vo	17
basic necessities of life (lit. food, clothing, shelter, and transportation)	衣食住行	衣食住行	yī shí zhù xíng		7
battery	电池	電池	diànchí	n	20
be away on business or on a business trip	出差	出差	chū chāi	vo	20
be born	出生	出生	chūshēng	v	1
be called, be known as	叫做	叫做	jiào zuò	vc	19
be forced to, have no choice but	只好	只好	zhǐhǎo	adv	4
be frugal (with food and other living expenses)	省吃俭用	省吃儉用	shěng chī jiǎn yòng		17
be good at, be adept in	善于	善於	shànyú		19
be satisfied, be pleased	满意	滿意	mǎnyì	v	19
beautiful	美丽	美麗	měilì	adj	13

English	Simplified	Traditional	Pinyin	Part of Speech	Lesson
beautiful, good	美	美	měi	adj	13
become addicted	上瘾	上癮	shàng yǐn	vo	7
become, turn into	成为	成為	chéngwéi	v	14
begin a new semester	开学	開學	kāi xué	vo	1
believe, trust	相信	相信	xiāngxìn	v	15
beneficial, useful	有益	有益	yǒuyì	adj	16
bicycle	自行车	自行車	zìxíngchē	n	12
blanket	毯子	毯子	tǎnzi	n	2
blessing, good fortune	福	福	fú	n	11
blog	博客	博客	bókè	n	7
board, plank, panel	板	板	bǎn	n	16
boat, ship	船	船	chuán	n	10
borrow, lend	借	借	jiè	v	8
bottled water	瓶装水	瓶裝水	píngzhuāng shuǐ	n	16
bow (for archery)	弓	弓	gōng	n	1
box lunch	盒饭	盒飯	héfàn	n	13
brand	牌子	牌子	páizi	n	4
break up, part company	分手	分手	fēn shǒu	vo	6
bright, light	亮	亮	liàng	adj	16
brother's daughter	侄女	侄女	zhínǚ	n	9
build, construct	盖	蓋	gài	v	12
build, establish	建立	建立	jiànlì	v	18
build, repair	修	修	xiū	v	18
burden	负担	負擔	fùdān	n	8

English	Simplified	Traditional	Pinyin	Part of Speech	Lesson
burn, set fire to, cook	烧	燒	shāo	v	18
by	由	由	yóu	prep	15
by all means, absolutely must	千万	千萬	qiānwàn	adv	13

C

English	Simplified	Traditional	Pinyin	Part of Speech	Lesson
cabinet, cupboard	柜子	櫃子	guìzi	n	2
cannot take it, unable to bear	受不了	受不了	shòu bu liǎo	vc	5
career, undertaking	事业	事業	shìyè	n	9
careless, perfunctory, mediocre	马虎	馬虎	mǎhu	adj	6
carry on, carry out, conduct	进行	進行	jìnxíng	v	18
cash	现金	現金	xiànjīn	n	4
casual, careless; do as one pleases	随便	隨便	suíbiàn	adj/vo	14
cat	猫	貓	māo	n	8
cause, give rise to	造成	造成	zào chéng	vc	16
cause trouble, harm	害	害	hài	v	7
celebrate	庆祝	慶祝	qìngzhù	v	20
celebrate a holiday	过节	過節	guò jié	vo	10
Celsius, centigrade	摄氏	攝氏	Shèshì	pn	16
century	世纪	世紀	shìjì	n	19
champion, first place in a competition	冠军	冠軍	guànjūn	n	15
change	变	變	biàn	v	12
change; change	变化	變化	biànhuà	v/n	12
characters, written form of a language	文字	文字	wénzì	n	18
chemistry	化学	化學	huàxué	n	5

English	Simplified	Traditional	Pinyin	Part of Speech	Lesson
chicken	鸡	雞	jī	n	3
childhood	童年	童年	tóngnián	n	9
Chinese broccoli	芥兰	芥蘭	jièlán	n	3
Chinese New Year's Eve	除夕	除夕	chúxī	n	11
Chinese New Year's Eve dinner	年夜饭	年夜飯	niányèfàn	n	11
choice; choose	选择	選擇	xuǎnzé	n/v	9
choose	选	選	xuǎn	v	5
chopsticks	筷子	筷子	kuàizi	n	3
civilization; civilized	文明	文明	wénmíng	n/adj	18
class, level, rank, category	流	流	liú	n	20
close, turn off	关	關	guān	v	13
(clothes) dryer	干衣机	乾衣機	gānyījī	n	2
clothing, apparel	服装	服裝	fúzhuāng	n	12
cloud	云	雲	yún	n	19
coal	煤	煤	méi	n	16
coincidentally	正好	正好	zhènghǎo	adv	3
colleague, coworker	同事	同事	tóngshì	n	20
combine, join	合	合	hé	v	17
comforter, quilt	被子	被子	bèizi	n	2
compass	指南针	指南針	zhǐnánzhēn	n	18
complain	抱怨	抱怨	bàoyuàn	v	9
completely, fully; complete, whole	完全	完全	wánquán	adv/adj	9
completely, thoroughly	一干二净	一乾二淨	yì gān èr jìng		6
condition	条件	條件	tiáojiàn	n	10

English	Simplified	Traditional	Pinyin	Part of Speech	Lesson
Confucius	孔子	孔子	*Kǒngzǐ*	pn	18
congratulate	恭喜	恭喜	*gōngxǐ*	v	11
(conjunction to connect two clauses)	而	而	*ér*	conj	10
consider	考虑	考慮	*kǎolǜ*	v	3
contact, get in touch; connection, relation (lit. combine and tie)	联系	聯繫	*liánxì*	v/n	20
continuously, incessantly	不停	不停	*bùtíng*	adv	6
contradiction, conflict; contradictory, conflicting	矛盾	矛盾	*máodùn*	n/adj	17
contribute, devote; contribution	贡献	貢獻	*gòngxiàn*	v/n	18
control, manage, mind, care about	管	管	*guǎn*	v	5
count as, be considered as	算	算	*suàn*	v	17
count time	计时	計時	*jì shí*	vo	11
country, nation	国家	國家	*guójiā*	n	16
countryside, village, rural area	农村	農村	*nóngcūn*	n	8
crack a joke, joke	开玩笑	開玩笑	*kāi wánxiào*	vo	3
crisis	危机	危機	*wēijī*	n	16
criterion; standard	标准	標準	*biāozhǔn*	n/adj	4
crowded; push against, squeeze	挤	擠	*jǐ*	adj/v	10
custom	风俗	風俗	*fēngsú*	n	13
cut, chop	砍	砍	*kǎn*	v	16

D

English	Simplified	Traditional	Pinyin	Part of Speech	Lesson
daily necessities	日用品	日用品	*rìyòngpǐn*	n	2
Dali	大理	大理	*Dàlǐ*	pn	13
dare	敢	敢	*gǎn*	mv	7

English	Simplified	Traditional	Pinyin	Part of Speech	Lesson
(day-to-day) life; live	生活	生活	shēnghuó	n/v	1
deal with	打交道	打交道	dǎ jiāodào	vo	5
decide; decision	决定	決定	juédìng	v/n	5
deep, profound, dark (color)	深	深	shēn	adj	13
dependable	可靠	可靠	kěkào	adj	7
deposit, accumulate	存	存	cún	v	8
desert	沙漠	沙漠	shāmò	n	10
design; design	设计	設計	shèjì	v/n	9
develop; development	发展	發展	fāzhǎn	v/n	18
developed, flourishing	发达	發達	fādá	adj	18
diet, food and drink	饮食	飲食	yǐnshí	n	13
different, not the same	不同	不同	bù tóng		6
discuss	讨论	討論	tǎolùn	v	5
dislike, loathe; disgusting, disagreeable	讨厌	討厭	tǎoyàn	v/adj	15
display, manifest; performance; manifestation	表现	表現	biǎoxiàn	v/n	15
distinguishing feature or quality, characteristic	特色	特色	tèsè	n	12
do, carry on, be engaged in	搞	搞	gǎo	v	20
doctorate (academic degree), Dr. (academic title)	博士	博士	bóshì	n	9
door	门	門	mén	n	2
doorway, entrance	门口	門口	ménkǒu	n	3
download	下载	下載	xiàzài	v	7
Dragon Boat Festival	端午节	端午節	Duānwǔjié	pn	11
draw, paint	画画儿	畫畫兒	huà huàr	vo	9
drink a toast (lit. dry the cup)	干杯	乾杯	gān bēi	vo	11

English	Simplified	Traditional	Pinyin	Part of Speech	Lesson
dynasty	朝代	朝代	*cháodài*	n	18

E

English	Simplified	Traditional	Pinyin	Part of Speech	Lesson
each, every	各	各	*gè*	pr	3
earn money	挣钱	掙錢	*zhèng qián*	vo	5
earth, the globe	地球	地球	*dìqiú*	n	16
eating utensil, tableware	餐具	餐具	*cānjù*	n	16
economics, economy	经济	經濟	*jīngjì*	n	5
economize, save, conserve	节约	節約	*jiéyuē*	v	16
education; educate	教育	教育	*jiàoyù*	n/v	8
elderly lady	老太太	老太太	*lǎotàitai*	n	17
elementary school	小学	小學	*xiǎoxué*	n	9
emperor	皇帝	皇帝	*huángdì*	n	18
empty	空	空	*kōng*	adj	2
end	末	末	*mò*	n	12
energy, energy source	能源	能源	*néngyuán*	n	16
enjoy; enjoyment, pleasure	享受	享受	*xiǎngshòu*	v/n	17
enter, get into	进入	進入	*jìnrù*	v	19
enterprise, business, company, firm	企业	企業	*qǐyè*	n	15
environment, surroundings	环境	環境	*huánjìng*	n	11
equal; equality (lit. level and equal)	平等	平等	*píngděng*	adj/n	15
equal pay for equal work	同工同酬	同工同酬	*tóng gōng tóng chóu*		15
equal, be equivalent to, amount to	等于	等於	*děngyú*	v	14
era, age	时代	時代	*shídài*	n	7

English	Simplified	Traditional	Pinyin	Part of Speech	Lesson
essay, article	文章	文章	wénzhāng	n	5
ethnic group, nationality	民族	民族	mínzú	n	10
Europe	欧洲	歐洲	Ōuzhōu	pn	20
even if	即使	即使	jíshǐ	conj	14
evening gathering, soiree	晚会	晚會	wǎnhuì	n	11
(exclamatory particle to express surprise or dissatisfaction or to remind)	哎	哎	āi	excl	1
exemplary; model, fine example	模范	模範	mófàn	adj/n	15
exercise, work out, undergo physical training	锻炼	鍛煉	duànliàn	v	14
exhibition hall, gallery	展厅	展廳	zhǎntīng	n	18
experience; experience	经验	經驗	jīngyàn	n/v	5
explain	解释	解釋	jiěshì	v	19
extroverted, open and sunny in disposition	开朗	開朗	kāilǎng	adj	6

		F			
factory	工厂	工廠	gōngchǎng	n	15
fair, just, impartial, equitable	公平	公平	gōngpíng	adj	15
fall	跌	跌	diē	v	17
familiar-looking	面熟	面熟	miànshú	adj	20
family, household	家庭	家庭	jiātíng	n	8
famous brand, name brand	名牌	名牌	míngpái	n	4
fan; be infatuated with	迷	迷	mí	n/v	6
fashionable, stylish	时髦	時髦	shímáo	adj	4
fast food, quick meal	快餐	快餐	kuàicān	n	12
feed	喂	餵	wèi	v	8

English	Simplified	Traditional	Pinyin	Part of Speech	Lesson
feel relieved, be at ease	放心	放心	*fàng xīn*	vo	20
feeling, sense perception; feel, perceive	感觉	感覺	*gǎnjué*	n/v	7
female gender, woman	女性	女性	*nǚxìng*	n	15
few, minority (lit. small number)	少数	少數	*shǎoshù*	n	10
fiancée	未婚妻	未婚妻	*wèihūnqī*	n	17
finance, banking	金融	金融	*jīnróng*	n	5
firecracker	鞭炮	鞭炮	*biānpào*	n	11
first, early part of	初	初	*chū*		11
First Emperor of the Qin dynasty	秦始皇	秦始皇	*Qínshǐhuáng*	pn	18
first month of the lunar year	正月	正月	*zhēngyuè*	n	11
fitness center, gym	健身房	健身房	*jiànshēnfáng*	n	14
flip stocks	炒股	炒股	*chǎo gǔ*	vo	17
flow	流	流	*liú*	v	10
follow, continue	接着	接著	*jiēzhe*	v	19
footstep	脚步	腳步	*jiǎobù*	n	12
for example	比方说	比方說	*bǐfāng shuō*		3
for example	比如	比如	*bǐrú*	v	16
foreigner (slang)	老外	老外	*lǎowài*	n	12
fortunately, luckily	好在	好在	*hǎozài*	adv	19
fragrant, pleasant-smelling	香	香	*xiāng*	adj	3
France	法国	法國	*Fǎguó*	pn	12
free of charge (lit. exempt from paying the fee)	免费	免費	*miǎnfèi*	v/vo	7
free, unconstrained	自由	自由	*zìyóu*	adj	1
fresh	新鲜	新鮮	*xīnxian*	adj	3

English	Simplified	Traditional	Pinyin	Part of Speech	Lesson
friendship	友谊	友誼	yǒuyì	n	20
from past till present, always, at all times	从来	從來	cónglái	adv	12
full, satiated (after a meal)	饱	飽	bǎo	adj	14
future	将来	將來	jiānglái	n	5
G					
game	游戏	遊戲	yóuxì	n	7
garbage, trash	垃圾	垃圾	lājī	n	7
gather, get together, congregate	聚	聚	jù	v	20
general, chief	总	總	zǒng	adj	19
generally	一般	一般	yìbān	adv	2
generate electricity	发电	發電	fā diàn	vo	16
geography	地理	地理	dìlǐ	n	10
Germany	德国	德國	Déguó	pn	15
get along	相处	相處	xiāngchǔ	v	6
get angry	生气	生氣	shēng qì	vo	6
get married, marry	结婚	結婚	jié hūn	vo	9
get rich, make a fortune	发财	發財	fā cái	vo	11
get together, to congregate; party, get-together, social gathering	聚会	聚會	jùhuì	v/n	20
give birth to, be born	生	生	shēng	v	8
give rise to, lead to	引起	引起	yǐnqǐ	v	17
gloomy, depressed	郁闷	鬱悶	yùmèn	adj	17
go out, leave home	出门	出門	chū mén	vo	14
go sightseeing, tour; excursion	游览	遊覽	yóulǎn	v/n	13

English	Simplified	Traditional	Pinyin	Part of Speech	Lesson
go to work, start work, be on duty	上班	上班	shàng bān	vo	12
good, fine (literary)	良好	良好	liánghǎo	adj	8
gosh, ah (an exclamation to express surprise)	哎呀	哎呀	āiyā	interj	4
government	政府	政府	zhèngfǔ	n	8
gradually, little by little	逐渐	逐漸	zhújiàn	adv	15
graduate	毕业	畢業	bì yè	vo	5
graduate student	研究生	研究生	yánjiūshēng	n	1
granddaughter (son's daughter)	孙女	孫女	sūnnü	n	17
grandson (son's son)	孙子	孫子	sūnzi	n	17
grave, tomb	坟墓	墳墓	fénmù	n	18
great, outstanding, magnificent	伟大	偉大	wěidà	adj	18
group, organization	团	團	tuán	n	13
Guangdong	广东	廣東	Guǎngdōng	pn	3
Guangzhou	广州	廣州	Guǎngzhōu	pn	10
guest, visitor	客人	客人	kèren	n	20
gunpowder (lit. fire chemical)	火药	火藥	huǒyào	n	18

H

English	Simplified	Traditional	Pinyin	Part of Speech	Lesson
habit; be accustomed to	习惯	習慣	xíguàn	n/v	13
Han dynasty	汉朝	漢朝	Hàncháo	pn	18
hand over, turn in	交	交	jiāo	v	8
hang, hang up	挂	掛	guà	v	2
Hangzhou	杭州	杭州	Hángzhōu	pn	3
happen, occur, take place	发生	發生	fāshēng	v	6
happiness; happy	幸福	幸福	xìngfú	n/adj	9

English	Simplified	Traditional	Pinyin	Part of Speech	Lesson
Harbin	哈尔滨	哈爾濱	Hā'ěrbīn	pn	10
hard, stiff	硬	硬	yìng	adj	13
hard, strenuous; work hard	辛苦	辛苦	xīnkǔ	adj/v	17
hastily, in a hurry	急忙	急忙	jímáng	adv	7
have to, nothing but … would do	非…不可	非…不可	fēi … bù kě		4
heart, mind	心	心	xīn	n	6
heating	暖气	暖氣	nuǎnqì	n	16
help	帮忙	幫忙	bāng máng	vo	1
help; help	帮助	幫助	bāngzhù	v/n	7
high-speed rail	高（速）铁（路）	高（速）鐵（路）	gāo(sù) tiě(lù)	n	12
hike in the mountains, climb a mountain	爬山	爬山	pá shān	vo	16
history	历史	歷史	lìshǐ	n	5
hobby, interest; love (something)	爱好	愛好	àihào	n/v	6
holiday, festival	节日	節日	jiérì	n	11
hometown, place of family origin	家乡	家鄉	jiāxiāng	n	10
hope that one's daughter will become successful (lit. hope that one's daughter will become a phoenix)	望女成凤	望女成鳳	wàng nǚ chéng fèng		9
hope that one's son will become successful (lit. hope that one's son will become a dragon)	望子成龙	望子成龍	wàng zǐ chéng lóng		9
host a farewell meal	饯行	餞行	jiànxíng	v	20
host a welcome meal for a visitor from afar	接风	接風	jiēfēng	v	20
hotpot	火锅	火鍋	huǒguō	n	20
household chores, household duties	家务	家務	jiāwù	n	15

English	Simplified	Traditional	Pinyin	Part of Speech	Lesson
huge crowds of people (lit. mountains and seas of people)	人山人海	人山人海	rén shān rén hǎi		10
humorous	幽默	幽默	yōumò	adj	13
Hunan	湖南	湖南	Húnán	pn	3
husband	丈夫	丈夫	zhàngfu	n	15
husband and wife, couple	夫妻	夫妻	fūqī	n	14

I

English	Simplified	Traditional	Pinyin	Part of Speech	Lesson
ice lantern	冰灯	冰燈	bīngdēng	n	10
idea	主意	主意	zhúyi	n	3
idea, opinion	想法	想法	xiǎngfǎ	n	17
if it were not for, but for	要不是	要不是	yàobúshì	conj	12
if it's not … it's …, either … or …	要么…, 要么…	要麼…, 要麼…	yàome …, yàome …	conj	5
I'm afraid that, I think perhaps, probably	恐怕	恐怕	kǒngpà	adv	2
imagine, visualize; imagination	想像	想像	xiǎngxiàng	v/n	12
immigrant; immigrate	移民	移民	yímín	n/v	9
important	重要	重要	zhòngyào	adj	7
in a few days	过几天	過幾天	guò jǐ tiān		2
in a moment, a little while	一会儿	一會兒	yíhuìr	n+m	4
in an instant, all of a sudden	一下子	一下子	yíxiàzi	adv	10
in fact, in reality, actually	实际上	實際上	shíjìshang	adv	6
include, consist of	包括	包括	bāokuò	v	13
income	收入	收入	shōurù	n	8
increase, add	增加	增加	zēngjiā	v	17

English	Simplified	Traditional	Pinyin	Part of Speech	Lesson
influence, have an impact; influence	影响	影響	*yǐngxiǎng*	v/n	8
interest (on invested funds)	利息	利息	*lìxī*	n	17
invention; invent	发明	發明	*fāmíng*	n/v	18
invest capital; investment (financial) (lit. throw or cast capital)	投资	投資	*tóu zī*	vo/n	17
it's not … but …	不是…而是…	不是…而是…	*búshì … érshì …*		9
J					
jeans	牛仔裤	牛仔褲	*niúzǎikù*	n	4
K					
karaoke	卡拉OK	卡拉OK	*kǎlā ōukēi*	n	7
Ke Lin (a personal name)	柯林	柯林	*Kē Lín*	pn	1
key	钥匙	鑰匙	*yàoshi*	n	6
kill	杀	殺	*shā*	v	18
knowledge	知识	知識	*zhīshi*	n	9
Kunming (capital of Yunnan Province)	昆明	昆明	*Kūnmíng*	pn	13
L					
lag behind, be outdated	落伍	落伍	*luòwǔ*	v	7
landlord	房东	房東	*fángdōng*	n	13
lantern	灯笼	燈籠	*dēnglong*	n	13
Lantern Festival	元宵节	元宵節	*Yuánxiāojié*	pn	11
laundry powder	洗衣粉	洗衣粉	*xǐyīfěn*	n	4
lead; leadership, leader (lit. lead and guide)	领导	領導	*lǐngdǎo*	v/n	18
leave a surplus, be left (over)	剩（下）	剩（下）	*shèng (xia)*	v(c)	11
leave behind, stay behind	留（下）	留（下）	*liú (xia)*	v(c)	13

English	Simplified	Traditional	Pinyin	Part of Speech	Lesson
leave (something) behind inadvertently (colloq.)	拉	拉	*là*	v	1
leave, depart from	离开	離開	*lí kāi*	vc	7
lessen	减轻	減輕	*jiǎnqīng*	v	8
Li Bai	李白	李白	*Lǐ Bái*	pn	18
Li Wen (a personal name)	李文	李文	*Lǐ Wén*	pn	14
Li Zhe (a personal name)	李哲	李哲	*Lǐ Zhé*	pn	5
lift, raise	举	舉	*jǔ*	v	11
light, relaxed	轻松	輕鬆	*qīngsōng*	adj	5
light in flavor	清淡	清淡	*qīngdàn*	adj	3
Lijiang	丽江	麗江	*Lìjiāng*	pn	13
Lin Xuemei (a personal name)	林雪梅	林雪梅	*Lín Xuěméi*	pn	3
Lisha (a personal name)	丽莎	麗莎	*Lìshā*	pn	3
(literary equivalent of 的)	之	之	*zhī*	p	18
literature	文学	文學	*wénxué*	n	5
lively, buzzing with excitement, bustling with activity (of a place or scene)	热闹	熱鬧	*rènao*	adj	11
loan; provide a loan	贷款	貸款	*dàikuǎn*	n/vo	8
long	长	長	*cháng*	adj	1
lose, be defeated	输	輸	*shū*	v	15
lose (money, etc.), suffer a loss in a deal	赔	賠	*péi*	v	17
lose weight (lit. reduce fat)	减肥	減肥	*jiǎn féi*	vo	14
low	低	低	*dī*	adj	8

M

| magazine | 杂志 | 雜誌 | *zázhì* | n | 7 |

English	Simplified	Traditional	Pinyin	Part of Speech	Lesson
mahjong	麻将	麻將	*májiàng*	n	17
mail, send	寄	寄	*jì*	v	19
main, principal	主要	主要	*zhǔyào*	adj	10
make (someone do something)	叫	叫	*jiào*	v	6
make a profit	赚钱	賺錢	*zhuànqián*	vo	17
make an extra effort, work harder, refuel	加油	加油	*jiā yóu*	vo	16
make friends	交朋友	交朋友	*jiāo péngyou*	vo	6
make paper	造纸	造紙	*zào zhǐ*	vo	18
make progress; progressive	进步	進步	*jìnbù*	v/adj	11
man, male	男子	男子	*nánzǐ*	n	15
manage wealth	理财	理財	*lǐcái*	vo	17
manager	经理	經理	*jīnglǐ*	n	19
mansion, tall building	厦	廈	*shà*		12
Mark (a personal name)	马克	馬克	*Mǎkè*	pn	16
market	市场	市場	*shìchǎng*	n	15
market, promote the sale (of goods/merchandise)	推销	推銷	*tuīxiāo*	v	20
master's (academic degree)	硕士	碩士	*shuòshì*	n	9
material (reference, academic)	资料	資料	*zīliào*	n	7
meaning	意思	意思	*yìsi*	n	11
(measure word for academic courses)	门	門	*mén*	m	5
(measure word for buildings)	栋	棟	*dòng*	m	2
(measure word for buildings and mountains)	座	座	*zuò*	m	12
(measure word for degrees of temperature, heat, hardness, humidity, etc.)	度	度	*dù*	m	16

English	Simplified	Traditional	Pinyin	Part of Speech	Lesson
(measure word for machines)	台	台	tái	m	2
(measure word for meals)	顿	頓	dùn	m	13
(measure word for one of certain paired things and some animals)	只	隻	zhī	m	14
(measure word for section, segment, or part)	段	段	duàn	m	16
(measure word for sentences)	句	句	jù	m	12
(measure word for stories of a building)	层	層	céng	m	2
(measure word for sums of money)	笔	筆	bǐ	m	17
(measure word for times by which something is multiplied)	倍	倍	bèi	m	10
(measure word for type or kind)	番	番	fān	m	9
(measure word for vehicles)	辆	輛	liàng	m	1
mention, bring up	提	提	tí	v	6
menu	菜单	菜單	càidān	n	3
merge into, meld into	融入	融入	róngrù	v	12
merit, strong point, advantage	优点	優點	yōudiǎn	n	19
Mexico	墨西哥	墨西哥	Mòxīgē	pn	9
Mid-Autumn Festival, Moon Festival	中秋节	中秋節	Zhōngqiūjié	pn	11
mind, care	在乎	在乎	zàihu	v	4
moon cake	月饼	月餅	yuèbǐng	n	11
more often than not	往往	往往	wǎngwǎng	adv	19
morning, early morning	早晨	早晨	zǎochen	n	14
mortgage	抵押	抵押	dǐyā	v	17
mostly, for the most part	大多	大多	dàduō	adv	10
mountain, hill	山	山	shān	n	10

English	Simplified	Traditional	Pinyin	Part of Speech	Lesson
move (one's residence)	搬家	搬家	bān jiā	vo	1
movable-type printing, letterpress printing	活字印刷	活字印刷	huózì yìnshuā	n	18
movement, action	动作	動作	dòngzuò	n	14
movie theater	电影院	電影院	diànyǐngyuàn	n	6
museum	博物馆	博物館	bówùguǎn	n	14
must, have to, be obliged to	必须	必須	bìxū	adv	14
mutually, each other, reciprocally	互相	互相	hùxiāng	adv	15
N					
Nanjing	南京	南京	Nánjīng	pn	10
napkin	餐巾	餐巾	cānjīn	n	3
nature; natural	自然	自然	zìrán	n/adj	10
need; needs	需要	需要	xūyào	v/n	4
need not, do not need to	不必	不必	búbì	adv	14
network, the Internet	网络	網絡	wǎngluò	n	7
new student	新生	新生	xīnshēng	n	1
news	新闻	新聞	xīnwén	n	7
news, message, information	消息	消息	xiāoxi	n	15
nice-looking, attractive	好看	好看	hǎokàn	adj	4
night of the fifteenth of the first lunar month, sweet dumplings made of sticky-rice flour	元宵	元宵	yuánxiāo	n	11
no matter, regardless of	不管	不管	bùguǎn	conj	12
no wonder	难怪	難怪	nánguài	adv	8
noodles	面	麵	miàn	n	13

English	Simplified	Traditional	Pinyin	Part of Speech	Lesson
not have enough time to do something, to be too late to do something	来不及	來不及	*lái bu jí*	vc	12
not necessarily	不见得	不見得	*bújiànde*		1
notice; notify, inform	通知	通知	*tōngzhī*	n/v	19
numeral, figure, digit	数字	數字	*shùzì*	n	5
nutrition, nourishment	营养	營養	*yíngyǎng*	n	14

O

English	Simplified	Traditional	Pinyin	Part of Speech	Lesson
obedient, well-behaved (of children)	乖	乖	*guāi*	adj	8
obtain, gain, acquire	取得	取得	*qǔdé*	v	8
occupation, profession, vocation	职业	職業	*zhíyè*	n	15
off campus	校外	校外	*xiào wài*		1
oil; oily	油	油	*yóu*	n/adj	3
old (of things)	旧	舊	*jiù*	adj	2
old age	老年	老年	*lǎonián*	n	17
older brother's wife	嫂子	嫂子	*sǎozi*	n	9
older male cousin of a different surname	表哥	表哥	*biǎogē*	n	12
on campus	校内	校內	*xiào nèi*		1
once; at some time in the past	曾经	曾經	*céngjīng*	adv	18
one-time	一次性	一次性	*yícìxìng*	adj	16
opinion	意见	意見	*yìjiàn*	n	5
opportunity	机会	機會	*jīhuì*	n	15
oppose	反对	反對	*fǎnduì*	v	9
opposite side	对面	對面	*duìmiàn*	n	12

English	Simplified	Traditional	Pinyin	Part of Speech	Lesson
order (food)	叫（菜）	叫（菜）	jiào (cài)	v (o)	3
ordinary people	老百姓	老百姓	lǎobǎixìng	n	12
ordinary people consider food as important as heaven	民以食为天	民以食為天	mín yǐ shí wéi tiān		12
organic	有机	有機	yǒujī	adj	3
other, else	其他	其他	qítā	pr	5
overcast, hidden from the sun	阴	陰	yīn	adj	19
overseas	海外	海外	hǎiwài	n	19
owe	欠	欠	qiàn	v	8
		P			
palace	宫殿	宮殿	gōngdiàn	n	18
panda	熊猫	熊貓	xióngmāo	n	14
part, section	部	部	bù	n	10
participate, take part, attend	参加	參加	cānjiā	v	13
(particle used to emphasize the obvious)	嘛	嘛	ma	p	11
passenger, voyager, traveler	旅客	旅客	lǚkè	n	13
paste, glue	贴	貼	tiē	v	11
pay attention to; attention	注意	注意	zhùyì	v/n	14
performance, achievement, result, score, grade	成绩	成績	chéngjì	n	15
perhaps, maybe	说不定	說不定	shuōbudìng	adv	6
person of ability and talent	人材	人材	réncái	v	19
(personal) taste	口味	口味	kǒuwèi	n	3
persuade, advise, urge	劝	勸	quàn	v	17

English	Simplified	Traditional	Pinyin	Part of Speech	Lesson
persuade, convince	说服	說服	*shuōfú*	v	17
petroleum, oil	石油	石油	*shíyóu*	n	16
phenomenon, appearance	现象	現象	*xiànxiàng*	n	15
philosophy	哲学	哲學	*zhéxué*	n	5
piano	钢琴	鋼琴	*gāngqín*	n	9
ping pong, table tennis	乒乓球	乒乓球	*pīngpāngqiú*	n	15
plain (lit. flat field)	平原	平原	*píngyuán*	n	10
plastic bag	塑料袋	塑料袋	*sùliào dài*	n	16
plateau (lit. high field)	高原	高原	*gāoyuán*	n	10
poet	诗人	詩人	*shīrén*	n	18
poetry, poem	诗	詩	*shī*	n	18
point of view	看法	看法	*kànfǎ*	n	9
pollute, contaminate; pollution, contamination	污染	汙染	*wūrǎn*	v/n	16
population	人口	人口	*rénkǒu*	n	10
portion, part	部分	部分	*bùfen*	n	18
position, status	地位	地位	*dìwèi*	n	15
pressure	压力	壓力	*yālì*	n	8
price	价钱	價錢	*jiàqian*	n	4
product, merchandise	产品	產品	*chǎnpǐn*	n	19
professor	教授	教授	*jiàoshòu*	n	5
protect, safeguard	保护	保護	*bǎohù*	v	16
proud, arrogant, full of oneself; pride	骄傲	驕傲	*jiāo'ào*	adj/n	15

English	Simplified	Traditional	Pinyin	Part of Speech	Lesson
provide, support financially	供	供	gōng	v	8
province (administrative division)	省	省	shěng	n	10
provincial capital	省会	省會	shěnghuì	n	13
public place or space	公共场所	公共場所	gōnggòng chǎngsuǒ	n	16
public square	广场	廣場	guǎngchǎng	n	14
pure cotton, one-hundred-percent cotton	纯棉	純棉	chúnmián	adj	4
push, shove	推	推	tuī	v	16
put down in writing, record; record, account	记载	記載	jìzǎi	v/n	18
put, place	摆	擺	bǎi	v	2
Q					
Qin dynasty	秦朝	秦朝	Qíncháo	pn	18
Qing dynasty	清朝	清朝	Qīngcháo	pn	18
quality	质量	質量	zhìliàng	n	4
quarrel	吵架	吵架	chǎo jià	vo	6
R					
really, truly	真的	真的	zhēn de	adv	2
reason, sense	道理	道理	dàoli	n	4
receive	受到	受到	shòu dào	vc	8
recycle	回收	回收	huíshōu	v	16
red envelope containing gift money	红包	紅包	hóngbāo	n	11
reduce, decrease, lessen	减少	減少	jiǎnshǎo	v	16
reform and open up; Reform and Opening-Up	改革开放	改革開放	gǎigé kāifàng	v/n	15

English	Simplified	Traditional	Pinyin	Part of Speech	Lesson
regard males as superior to females, privilege men over women	重男轻女	重男輕女	*zhòng nán qīng nǚ*		15
regardless of . . . , whether it be . . .	无论	無論	*wúlùn*	conj	4
regulate, specify; rules and regulations, provisions	规定	規定	*guīdìng*	v/n	16
relation, relationship, connection	关系	關係	*guānxì*	n	18
relatively, comparatively, rather; compare	比较	比較	*bǐjiào*	adv/v	1
remain as before, retain	保留	保留	*bǎoliú*	v	12
replace, substitute	代	代	*dài*	v	11
reply, answer	回答	回答	*huídá*	v	19
Republic of China	中华民国	中華民國	*Zhōnghuá Mínguó*	pn	18
resemble, be like	像	像	*xiàng*	v	4
residential development, residential complex	小区	小區	*xiǎoqū*	n	11
respect	尊重	尊重	*zūnzhòng*	v	9
restaurant	餐馆儿	餐館兒	*cānguǎnr*	n	2
retire	退休	退休	*tuìxiū*	v	14
return, come back	归来	歸來	*guīlái*	v	19
reunite (as a family)	团圆	團圓	*tuányuán*	v	11
revolution	革命	革命	*gémìng*	n	18
ride	骑	騎	*qí*	v	12
rise, surge, go up (of water, prices, etc.)	涨	漲	*zhǎng*	v	17
risk, danger, hazard	风险	風險	*fēngxiǎn*	n	17
river	河	河	*hé*	n	13
river	河流	河流	*héliú*	n	10

English	Simplified	Traditional	Pinyin	Part of Speech	Lesson
road, street	马路	馬路	*mǎlù*	n	2
room	屋子	屋子	*wūzi*	n	7
roommate	同屋	同屋	*tóngwū*	n	2
route, itinerary	路线	路線	*lùxiàn*	n	10
rumbling sound	咕噜	咕嚕	*gūlū*	ono	12
run into (a person by chance)	碰见	碰見	*pèng jiàn*	vc	5

S

English	Simplified	Traditional	Pinyin	Part of Speech	Lesson
safe	安全	安全	*ānquán*	adj	1
salary, pay, wages	薪水	薪水	*xīnshuǐ*	n	15
salty	咸	鹹	*xián*	adj	3
save (money, time)	省下来	省下來	*shěng xia lai*	vc	5
save money, economize	省钱	省錢	*shěng qián*	vo	1
scary, frightening	吓人	嚇人	*xiàrén*	adj	19
scatterbrained, forgetful	丢三拉四	丢三拉四	*diū sān là sì*		6
scenic landscape, scenery	风景	風景	*fēngjǐng*	n	10
scenic spot, tourist spot	景点	景點	*jǐngdiǎn*	n	10
scholarship money	奖学金	獎學金	*jiǎngxuéjīn*	n	8
school of engineering	工学院	工學院	*gōng xuéyuàn*	n	5
school of management	管理学院	管理學院	*guǎnlǐ xuéyuàn*	n	5
schoolmate, alumnus, alumna	校友	校友	*xiàoyǒu*	n	20
science; scientific	科学	科學	*kēxué*	n/adj	14
score	比分	比分	*bǐfēn*	n	15
sea, ocean	海	海	*hǎi*	n	10
sea turtle	海龟	海龜	*hǎiguī*	n	19

English	Simplified	Traditional	Pinyin	Part of Speech	Lesson
sell, market	销售	銷售	xiāoshòu	v	19
senior high school	高中	高中	gāozhōng	n	6
serious, grave	严重	嚴重	yánzhòng	adj	7
shake hands, clasp hands	握手	握手	wò shǒu	vo	19
share (joy, happiness, benefits, etc.) (lit. divide and enjoy)	分享	分享	fēnxiǎng	v	13
Shenzhen	深圳	深圳	Shēnzhèn	pn	10
shop	购物	購物	gòuwù	vo	4
short	短	短	duǎn	adj	10
short term	短期	短期	duǎnqī	n	19
shortcoming, defect, weakness	缺点	缺點	quēdiǎn	n	19
Sichuan	四川	四川	Sìchuān	pn	3
sign, autograph	签	簽	qiān	v	17
sign up, register	报名	報名	bào míng	vo	13
silk, silk fabric	丝绸	絲綢	sīchóu	n	18
since	以来	以來	yǐlái	t	15
since, as, now that	既然	既然	jìrán	conj	19
situation, condition, circumstances	情况	情況	qíngkuàng	n	15
sleep	睡眠	睡眠	shuìmián	n	14
sleeping bunk (on a train)	卧铺	臥鋪	wòpù	n	13
small and inexpensive dishes, snacks	小吃	小吃	xiǎochī	n	12
smog	雾霾	霧霾	wùmái	n	16
smoke a cigarette	吸烟	吸菸	xī yān	vo	14
smooth, successful, without a hitch	顺利	順利	shùnlì	adj	11

English	Simplified	Traditional	Pinyin	Part of Speech	Lesson
snack	零食	零食	*língshí*	n	19
society	社会	社會	*shèhuì*	n	9
soft	软	軟	*ruǎn*	adj	13
software	软件	軟件	*ruǎnjiàn*	n	7
solar energy, solar power	太阳能	太陽能	*tàiyángnéng*	n	16
solve, resolve	解决	解決	*jiějué*	v	5
something that weighs on one's mind	心事	心事	*xīnshì*	n	6
Song dynasty	宋朝	宋朝	*Sòngcháo*	pn	18
(sound of laughter)	哈	哈	*hā*	ono	12
sound, voice	声音	聲音	*shēngyīn*	n	12
souvenir, keepsake, memento	纪念品	紀念品	*jìniànpǐn*	n	13
Spain	西班牙	西班牙	*Xībānyá*	pn	15
speak, tell	讲	講	*jiǎng*	v	13
spicy	辣	辣	*là*	adj	3
spinach	菠菜	菠菜	*bōcài*	n	3
Spring Festival, Chinese New Year	春节	春節	*Chūnjié*	pn	11
spring-like all year round	四季如春	四季如春	*sìjì rú chūn*		10
stable, steady; stabilize, be steady	稳定	穩定	*wěndìng*	adj/v	20
stationery, writing supplies	文具	文具	*wénjù*	n	2
stay	待	待	*dāi*	v	7
stay up late or all night	熬夜	熬夜	*áo yè*	vo	14
steam (food without heavy sauce)	清蒸	清蒸	*qīngzhēng*	v	3
stern, serious	严肃	嚴肅	*yánsù*	adj	19

English	Simplified	Traditional	Pinyin	Part of Speech	Lesson
sticky-rice dumpling wrapped in bamboo or reed leaves	粽子	粽子	zòngzi	n	11
stock, share (lit. stock certificate)	股票	股票	gǔpiào	n	17
stock market	股市	股市	gǔshì	n	17
stone, rock, pebble	石头	石頭	shítou	n	13
Stone Forest	石林	石林	Shílín	pn	13
story, tale	故事	故事	gùshi	n	13
strange, weird	奇怪	奇怪	qíguài	adj	11
street	街	街	jiē	n	12
study abroad	留学	留學	liú xué	vo	9
study-abroad student	留学生	留學生	liúxuéshēng	n	3
succeed; successful	成功	成功	chénggōng	v/adj	11
suddenly, unexpectedly; sudden, unexpected	突然	突然	tūrán	adv/adj	17
(suffix meaning person)	者	者	zhě		20
suggestion; suggest	建议	建議	jiànyì	n/v	5
suit	适合	適合	shìhé	v	8
suit, a set of matching outer garments	套装	套裝	tàozhuāng	n	19
sun	太阳	太陽	tàiyáng	n	16
Sun Yat-sen	孙中山	孫中山	Sūn Zhōngshān	pn	18
sunny	晴	晴	qíng	adj	19
supermarket	超市	超市	chāoshì	n	16
supplement, replenish	补充	補充	bǔchōng	v	14
surpass, exceed	超过	超過	chāoguò	v	15

English	Simplified	Traditional	Pinyin	Part of Speech	Lesson
surplus; have a surplus	余	餘	*yú*	n/v	11
sweat	出汗	出汗	*chū hàn*	vo	16

		T			
T-shirt	T恤衫	T恤衫	*tīxùshān*	n	4
tai chi (a form of traditional Chinese shadowboxing)	太极拳	太極拳	*tàijíquán*	n	14
take a picture, shoot a film	拍	拍	*pāi*	v	12
take a walk, go for a walk	散步	散步	*sàn bù*	vo	14
take care of, look after	关照	關照	*guānzhào*	v	20
take someone on staff, employ	录用	錄用	*lùyòng*	v	19
takeout	外卖	外賣	*wàimài*	n	7
talk, discuss	谈	談	*tán*	v	5
Tang dynasty	唐朝	唐朝	*Tángcháo*	pn	18
taste	尝	嚐	*cháng*	v	12
taste, flavor (of food)	味道	味道	*wèidao*	n	3
tax	税	税	*shuì*	n	4
teahouse	茶馆	茶館	*cháguǎn*	n	13
team, a row or line of people, (measure word for teams and lines)	队	隊	*duì*	n	15
team member	队员	隊員	*duìyuán*	n	15
technology, technique	技术	技術	*jìshù*	n	18
temperature	温度	溫度	*wēndù*	n	16
Temple of Confucius	夫子庙	夫子廟	*Fūzǐmiào*	pn	12
tender	嫩	嫩	*nèn*	adj	3
terracotta warriors and horses	兵马俑	兵馬俑	*bīngmǎyǒng*	n	18

English	Simplified	Traditional	Pinyin	Part of Speech	Lesson
terrain, topography	地形	地形	dìxíng	n	10
terrible, formidable	厉害	厲害	lìhai	adj	9
Thanksgiving	感恩节	感恩節	Gǎn'ēnjié	pn	11
thick tube-shaped container	筒	筒	tǒng	n	16
think, consider	认为	認為	rènwéi	v	9
think deeply, ponder over; contemplation, cogitation	思考	思考	sīkǎo	v/n	17
thinking, ideology, thoughts	思想	思想	sīxiǎng	n	18
thrifty, frugal	节俭	節儉	jiéjiǎn	adj	17
thriving, flourishing; fire, flame	火	火	huǒ	adj/n	20
throw, toss, throw away	扔	扔	rēng	v	16
Tianjin	天津	天津	Tiānjīn	pn	10
toilet paper	卫生纸	衛生紙	wèishēngzhǐ	n	4
toothpaste	牙膏	牙膏	yágāo	n	4
tourist	游客	遊客	yóukè	n	12
towards, in, on, at, (indicating comparison)	于	於	yú	prep	16
towel	毛巾	毛巾	máojīn	n	4
tower, pagoda	塔	塔	tǎ	n	13
trade; trade	贸易	貿易	màoyì	n/v	18
tradition; traditional	传统	傳統	chuántǒng	n/adj	11
traditional Chinese lunar calendar (lit. agricultural calendar)	农历	農曆	nónglì	n	11
train	火车	火車	huǒchē	n	10
train carriage	车厢	車廂	chēxiāng	n	13
translate; interpreter, translation	翻译	翻譯	fānyì	v/n	7

English	Simplified	Traditional	Pinyin	Part of Speech	Lesson
transnational, multinational	跨国	跨國	kuàguó	adj	19
transportation, traffic (lit. intersect and go through)	交通	交通	jiāotōng	n	13
travel (for pleasure); (pleasure) travel	旅游	旅遊	lǚyóu	v/n	10
tree	树	樹	shù	n	14
turn, shift, change	转	轉	zhuǎn	v	19
turn upside down, go backwards	倒	倒	dào	v	11
tutor	家教	家教	jiājiào	n	8
TV drama, TV series	电视剧	電視劇	diànshìjù	n	20
U					
uncle (mother's brother)	舅舅	舅舅	jiùjiu	n	11
understand	理解	理解	lǐjiě	v	9
understand, know about, be informed	了解	了解	liǎojiě	v	10
unify, unite; unified, centralized	统一	統一	tǒngyī	v/adj	18
unit	单位	單位	dānwèi	n	15
upper outer garment, jacket	上衣	上衣	shàngyī	n	19
useful	有用	有用	yǒuyòng	adj	7
V					
visit, look around	参观	參觀	cānguān	v	18
vocal concert	演唱会	演唱會	yǎnchànghuì	n	6
volunteer work (lit. righteous work), volunteer	义工	義工	yìgōng	n	17
W					
wages, pay	工资	工資	gōngzī	n	8
walk (an animal), stroll	遛	遛	liù	v	8

English	Simplified	Traditional	Pinyin	Part of Speech	Lesson
wall	墙	牆	qiáng	n	11
wardrobe	衣柜	衣櫃	yīguì	n	2
wash	洗	洗	xǐ	v	2
washing machine	洗衣机	洗衣機	xǐyījī	n	2
waste, squander; wasteful	浪费	浪費	làngfèi	v/adj	11
way of doing things, course of action	做法	做法	zuòfǎ	n	9
website	网站	網站	wǎngzhàn	n	7
WeChat	微信	微信	Wēixìn	pn	3
week	周	週	zhōu	n	20
West	西方	西方	Xīfāng	pn	18
wet	湿	濕	shī	adj	19
what on earth, what in the world, in the end	到底	到底	dàodǐ	adv	6
why, why on earth, whatever for	干吗	幹嗎	gànmá	qpr	19
wife	妻子	妻子	qīzi	n	15
win	赢	贏	yíng	v	15
wind	风	風	fēng	n	16
wish somebody a happy Chinese New Year, pay a Chinese New Year call	拜年	拜年	bài nián	vo	11
with	以	以	yǐ	prep	11
without extra effort or motion, conveniently	随手	隨手	suíshǒu	adv	16
women	妇女	婦女	fùnǚ	n	15
woods, forest	树林	樹林	shùlín	n	13
woolen sweater	毛衣	毛衣	máoyī	n	4
work overtime, work extra shifts	加班	加班	jiā bān	vo	19

English	Simplified	Traditional	Pinyin	Part of Speech	Lesson
world	世界	世界	shìjiè	n	5
worry	着急	著急	zháojí	v	2
X					
Xinjiang	新疆	新疆	Xīnjiāng	pn	10
Y					
Yangtze River	长江	長江	Chángjiāng	pn	10
Yellow River	黄河	黃河	Huánghé	pn	10
yoga	瑜伽	瑜伽	yújiā	n	14
young	年轻	年輕	niánqīng	adj	20
Yunnan	云南	雲南	Yúnnán	pn	10
Z					
Zhang Tianming (a personal name)	张天明	張天明	Zhāng Tiānmíng	pn	1

Lesson 11 (Text)

Winter break has begun. Ke Lin has decided to go to Beijing to study Chinese while Lin Xuemei would like to intern and look for a job in Beijing. They arrive at Xuemei's uncle's home in Beijing.

Xuemei's uncle is a lawyer, and her uncle's wife is a university professor. The surroundings of their residential complex are very nice. Their apartment has three bedrooms, a living room and a dining room, and two bathrooms. The furniture is all new and very beautiful. Every room is very clean and comfortable to live in.

Today is New Year's Eve—that is, the day before the Spring Festival. Xuemei's aunt is busy making New Year Eve's Dinner. Xuemei's uncle is at her side helping.

Ke Lin sees a medium-sized piece of red paper pasted on the wall. On the paper is a Chinese character. He recognizes it as the 福 in the word 幸福 (fortune), but it is pasted upside down.

Ke Lin:	How strange, Xuemei. How come this 福 character is pasted incorrectly? 福 is upside down.
Lin Xuemei:	It isn't pasted incorrectly. 福倒了 (fortune is upside down), 福到了 (fortune has arrived). Think how great that pun is!
Ke Lin:	I get it, I get it. How interesting!
Uncle:	Xuemei, Ke Lin, come, come, please sit down. Time to eat . . . None of us drinks alcohol. Come, let's have tea instead. Let's raise our cups to welcome you to Beijing!
Aunt:	Let's toast to your smooth job search and academic progress in the new year!
Lin Xuemei:	Here's to Uncle and Auntie's professional success!
Ke Lin:	To Uncle and Auntie's health!
Uncle:	Look, the Spring Festival Evening Gala has started on TV. Let's eat and watch.
Lin Xuemei:	Ke Lin, right now many, many Chinese families are like us, having New Year's Eve dinner and watching the Spring Festival Evening Gala.
Ke Lin:	Is that so? There's good TV to watch and delicious food to eat. Couldn't be any better! Auntie's steamed fish is both tender and fragrant. It's simply delicious.
Lin Xuemei:	Ke Lin, did you know? Fish is a must for New Year's Eve dinner, but you can't eat all of it. You have to leave some of it uneaten.
Ke Lin:	Why? Isn't that wasteful?
Uncle:	"When you have fish every year, you'll have a surplus every year." "Fish" and "surplus" are pronounced the same. "Surplus" means "excess left over from what is needed."
Ke Lin:	"When you have fish every year, you'll have a surplus every year." Does that mean "having money left over"? Chinese is really interesting. Hey, China has quite a few other traditional holidays, and the food associated with them is all different, right?
Aunt:	That's right. On the fifth day of the fifth month of the lunar year during the Dragon Boat Festival . . .

Ke Lin:	People eat *zongzi*.
Uncle:	On the fifteenth day of the eighth month of the lunar calendar during the Mid-Autumn Festival . . .
Ke Lin:	People eat moon cakes.
Lin Xuemei:	The Mid-Autumn Festival is a bit like Thanksgiving in the U.S. It is a holiday for family reunions. There is also the Lantern Festival on the fifteenth day of the first month on the lunar calendar when . . .
Ke Lin:	People eat those round, white things . . .
Lin Xuemei:	During the Lantern Festival (元宵节/元宵節) you eat dumplings of the same name (元宵).
Ke Lin:	Right, right. I remember now—元宵.
Aunt:	Look, the countdown on TV is starting. "Ten, nine, eight, seven, six, five, four, three, two, one." It's twelve o'clock. The new year has started!
Lin Xuemei:	Uncle, Auntie, we wish you a Happy New Year!
Uncle:	Happy New Year, everybody!
Ke Lin:	Uncle, Auntie, Happy New Year! Best wishes for a prosperous new year!
Uncle:	A prosperous new year for everyone. It's New Year. Uncle and Auntie have some red envelopes for you.
Ke Lin:	Thanks, thank you very much . . . How come it's so lively outside?
Uncle:	Setting off firecrackers to celebrate the New Year is a must. We've also bought many [firecrackers]. Go out and set them off.
Ke Lin:	Xuemei, why don't you send Tianming [and Lisha] a New Year text message?
Lin Xuemei:	OK, I'd like to first call Mom and Dad on my cell phone to wish them a happy Chinese New Year and then send Tianming and Lisha a New Year WeChat message.
Ke Lin:	OK. Uncle and Auntie, let's go light firecrackers.
Aunt:	Ke Lin, you and Uncle go. I'll do some preparation and we'll have dumplings together when you are back from lighting the firecrackers.
Ke Lin:	What, more food?

Lesson 12 (Text)

At the end of last semester, Zhang Tianming and Lisha applied to go to China to study Chinese. They had originally thought that it might be too late. To their surprise, the school very quickly agreed. The two of them could study and live in China for three or four months. This made them very happy.

Zhang Tianming and Lisha arrived in Shanghai first, and then took a high-speed train to Nanjing. The train was very fast, reaching their destination in over one hour. Tianming's cousin drove to the train station to pick them up. Tianming's cousin was happy to see them and said that he'd be willing to be their tour guide, taking them around on the streets to let them get a good look at Nanjing.

Zhang Tianming:	My dad often says that Nanjing is a very quiet city. I never imagined it would be so lively! Look, there are new high-rises all along the streets, and there are cars everywhere.
Cousin:	Over the last few years the changes in Nanjing have indeed been great. I used to bike to work. Now I've started driving, too.
Lisha:	This is completely different from the China I imagined. When we were in Shanghai, if it hadn't been for the Chinese characters everywhere, I'd have thought that I was in America.
Zhang Tianming:	My dad says that when he was little, Nanjing saw very few foreigners, but now you see foreign tourists everywhere!
Lisha:	Aren't the two of us foreigners, too? Haha! Look, on the other side of the street, there's American fast food, a Japanese bank, a French clothing store . . .
Cousin:	Other places in China are the same. The changes have really been immense.
Zhang Tianming:	China has melded into the world. This is a good thing.
Lisha:	But I worry that if it continues like this, won't there be fewer and fewer distinctly Chinese things?
Cousin:	That won't happen. Nanjing has preserved many things with distinct Chinese characteristics. Take architecture, for example—what is most distinctly Chinese in Nanjing is the Temple of Confucius. There is also food, drinks, entertainment . . .
Zhang Tianming:	Then let's go to the Temple of Confucius now and try Nanjing's local snacks.
Cousin:	Sure! No matter how much China changes, no matter how much Nanjing changes, when you are hungry, you've got to eat. That hasn't changed. You've heard the saying, "Ordinary people consider food as important as heaven," right?
Lisha:	Huh? What? Never heard of it.

Zhang Tianming:	The meaning of this saying, to put it simply, is that the most important thing in ordinary people's lives is food.
Lisha:	Hey, Tianming, look, what place is that? There are so many people there. It looks like there's food and entertainment nearby, too. It's so colorful. Really beautiful and lively!
Cousin:	That's the Temple of Confucius.
Lisha:	It seems that Nanjingers really want to preserve old Nanjing's character and tradition as much as possible.
Zhang Tianming:	Nanjing has, on the one hand, row after row of tall buildings, and row upon row of traditional buildings on the other. Standing here, I seem to hear a sound.
Lisha:	What sound?
Zhang Tianming:	The footsteps of history. Before I came to China, my dad asked me to find his middle school. I'll send him a WeChat message in a minute to tell him that the changes Nanjing has gone through are too great, and that his middle school is nowhere to be found. I'll also send him the pictures that I took today for him to look at.
Cousin:	I've also heard a sound.
Lisha and Zhang Tianming:	What sound?
Cousin:	The rumbling of my stomach. We've walked such a long way, but neither of you seems tired or hungry. But, as your tour guide, I am both thirsty and hungry. Don't forget, "Ordinary people consider food as important as heaven!" Let's go and eat!

Text

Before the new semester started, Zhang Tianming, Lisha, Ke Lin, and Xuemei went on a trip to Yunnan. They agreed to meet up in Kunming on Sunday and then tour Yunnan for a week.

On this trip, China's trains, tour guides, and Yunnan's beautiful scenery all made a deep impression on Tianming.

Zhang Tianming posted on WeChat every day to share his pleasant experience with his friends:

Before we went to Yunnan, we signed up online to join a tour group. The fees for the tour group included transportation, hotels, three meals [a day], and admission tickets to the scenic spots.

We went to Yunnan by train. In order to practice speaking Chinese with the other passengers, we bought tickets for a hard sleeper because the "rooms" in the hard-sleeper cars don't have doors, so it's easier to find people to chat with. I had the upper bunk. The upper bunk was quieter than the middle and lower bunks, so I could get a good night's sleep.

I also went to the soft-sleeper car to have a look. There, each compartment had two upper bunks and two lower bunks. The bunks were softer and also bigger, and the doors could be closed.

At night, we ate in the dining car. I thought the food was expensive and not so tasty. It's better to get a box lunch or instant noodles.

After Lisha and I got off the train in Kunming, we waited for more than two hours for Xuemei and Ke Lin's train to arrive. We walked out of the train station together and saw our tour guide holding a sign looking for us. Our names were written on the sign. Our tour guide was very humorous, but sometimes the three of us didn't understand him, so Xuemei had to be our interpreter.

Our tour guide told us that Yunnan is a province in southwestern China. The provincial capital is Kunming. The natural landscape of Yunnan is very beautiful, with mountains and rivers. Many ethnic minority groups live here. If you take a trip to Yunnan, you can see the architecture, clothing, and food and drink of the different ethnic groups and understand the customs of each ethnic group.

On the first day we visited the Stone Forest. This is a picture of the Stone Forest. There are many dark-colored rocks in the Stone Forest which, when viewed from a distance, look like a forest of trees. The rocks appear in all kinds of strange shapes. We walked around in the Stone Forest and listened to the guide tell stories about the rocks, which were very interesting.

These are the Three Pagodas of Dali. The buildings are very ancient and very famous. There are many stores that sell souvenirs in Dali. The guide took us there and hoped that we would buy lots of things. Xuemei and Lisha were very glad and bought many souvenirs, but Ke Lin and I couldn't stand it and complained that it was a waste of time. Next time when you are in China looking for a tour group, make sure that you don't join a "shopping" tour group. You can travel on your own. That way you'll have more freedom.

On the third day we arrived in the famous old town of Lijiang. We

Text

really liked it here. This old town is not very large, and it takes only a couple of hours to walk from the east to the west side. The most unusual thing [about the old town] is that there is a very clean small river that runs through it. The two sides of the river are lined with many stores, teahouses, and small restaurants. That night we drank tea in a distinctly Yunnanese teahouse while looking at the river, the red lanterns beside the doors, and tourists from all over the world. We didn't even want to go back to the hotel to sleep.

In Lijiang we stayed in a family-run hotel for two days. The rooms were small, but they were very clean, and we could also access the Internet. The landlord made us some home-style dishes that were spicy and very tasty.

Each region of Yunnan has a different landscape, and there are also many fun places. Tomorrow we will visit the Great Snow Mountain. In a few days I'll post photos taken there on my blog.

Text

After Lisha arrived in Beijing, she didn't stay in the international students' dorm. To learn more about the lives of Chinese people, she moved in with a Chinese family. The landlord and his wife are both retired. Their daughter Li Wen works at a museum and lives with her parents. Li Wen would very much like to go to America to study, so she asked Lisha to be her English tutor. This way Lisha won't have to pay rent. Because Lisha speaks Chinese with Li Wen's parents every day, her Chinese has improved very quickly.

Every morning Lisha goes out for a walk. In the residential area where she lives, on the street corners and in the parks you can see many people, especially older people, exercising. Some of them dance in public squares, and some practice tai chi. These people who exercise every morning have become a special part of the Beijing "landscape." This morning Lisha is about to go out when Li Wen comes out from her room.

Li Wen:	Lisha, today is Saturday. How come you are up so early?
Lisha:	I wanted to learn tai chi with Uncle and Auntie, but didn't expect them to go out so early.
Li Wen:	I thought you only liked to do yoga. How come you are interested in tai chi, too?
Lisha:	Tai chi and yoga are alike. Not only are they good for you, the movements are also very beautiful.
Li Wen:	Lisha, look, under the big trees my mom and dad are practicing tai chi with those retirees. Go look for them.
Lisha:	OK. I'll leave in a moment. They practice so well. Every morning I go out for a walk and see people exercising everywhere. Chinese people really take exercising very seriously!
Li Wen:	That's right. Nowadays people pay more and more attention to health. Lisha, how do Americans usually exercise?
Lisha:	Generally, they jog, swim, play ball, and so on. Some people also go to the gym. I normally do yoga, and sometimes jog, too.
Li Wen:	No wonder you are so healthy.
Lisha:	I think if you want to be healthy, besides getting plenty of exercise, you also have to pay attention to your diet.
Li Wen:	You don't have one ounce of fat on you. Do you still need to pay attention to your diet?
Lisha:	Paying attention to your diet is not the same as losing weight. I think as long as you are healthy then you're fine. Weight isn't so important.
Li Wen:	I'm busy with work and don't have time to eat well. I often just eat whatever I can find. How do you pay attention to your diet?
Lisha:	I drink lots of water and eat lots of vegetables and fruit. Besides, even if you are very busy, you must have breakfast, and it must be nutritious. Have a big lunch because you have to study and work in the afternoon. Have a small dinner. Otherwise you'll put on more and more weight, because it's too close to bedtime.

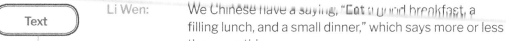
Li Wen:	We Chinese have a saying, "Eat a good breakfast, a filling lunch, and a small dinner," which says more or less the same thing.
Lisha:	Really? Everybody says that. Perhaps there's a scientific basis to it.
Li Wen:	I think if you want to be healthy, you have to pay attention to other areas, too.
Lisha:	You mean you have to have a good lifestyle, right?
Li Wen:	Right. Don't smoke, don't drink. Go to bed early and get up early. It's best not to stay up late. I can do them all except for not staying up late. I often have to burn the midnight oil to prepare for the graduate admissions exam.
Lisha:	Then you must find time to make up for your sleep deficit as much as possible.
Li Wen:	You're right. I do have to pay attention, or my two eyes will soon turn into panda eyes.

Historically, China was a society that favored men over women. Women's status in the family and in society was much lower than that of men. After 1950 the situation changed gradually. Especially in the cities, girls and boys had equal opportunities in education and employment. Women's social status also improved substantially. However, since the Reform and Opening-Up, in certain for-profit and nonprofit enterprises, the phenomenon of gender inequality has resurfaced. For example, when looking for work, women tend to have more difficulty than men. Some factories and companies haven't implemented equal pay for equal work. Of course, there are some women who have surpassed men not only in terms of professional accomplishments but also income, although their number among women is still few and far between.

Nowadays, in Chinese households, many couples are considerate to each other. Therefore, within the family is perhaps where men and women are most equal in Chinese society. Take Xuemei's uncle for example—he is a big soccer fan. The only time when he won't do any housework is when there is a soccer game on TV. However, as soon as the game is over, he will be busy helping [Xuemei's] aunt cook and wash dishes, turning back into a "model husband."

Lin Xuemei:	Uncle, how come you are doing the dishes today?
Uncle:	Haha, because I wash the dishes cleaner than your aunt.
Lin Xuemei:	I'll wash them. I do a great job washing dishes too.
Aunt:	No, no, no. You just got back from Yunnan and have been busy looking for work and going on job interviews. You haven't had a chance to rest and recover yet. Besides, last night your uncle watched a ball game until one o'clock. Today he'd better be on his best behavior, hadn't he?
Lin Xuemei:	Uncle, what game was on last night?
Uncle:	Men's soccer, Beijing vs. Shanghai.
Aunt:	What's there to watch? I really detest those men's soccer players. They are so arrogant. But come game time, they always lose. That's why I only watch the Chinese women's soccer team. They are so much better than the men's soccer team.
Lin Xuemei:	That's right. The women's soccer team has a much better record than the men, but I hear that women soccer players make only one tenth of what the men make. How unfair.
Ke Lin:	Don't forget, their income is determined by the market. The American women's professional basketball players' salaries are also much lower than the men's players' salaries.
Uncle:	Hey, don't keep talking about the Chinese men's soccer team losing. I just saw a news story on the Internet. Yesterday the Chinese men's soccer team defeated the world champions.
Aunt:	I don't believe it. That must have been made up on the Internet.

Uncle:	It seems it's true. It says online that this time the Chinese men's soccer team played quite well. The score was 0 to 0 until the last minute, when the Chinese men's team scored a goal and won 1 to 0.
Ke Lin:	Who knew! I would have never guessed it. That's fantastic! Then was their opponent the German team or the Spanish team?
Uncle:	The Chinese women's ping-pong team.
Everyone:	Huh?
Aunt:	Someone must be making fun of the men's soccer team!

Text

Zhang Tianming and his three friends have been in Beijing for two or three months now. The weather has also gradually warmed up. Every day they are busy either with classes or job-hunting. They haven't seen one another for half a month now. Today is Saturday, and everybody wants to relax a little. Tianming suggests they go hiking. Lisha and Xuemei don't object, and Ke Lin feels that it is a pretty good idea, too. He says that his German friend Make would like to go, too. But how should they get there? Taking a cab would be too expensive, and boring, too. Public transportation has too many people, and is too crowded. Ke Lin comes up with an idea—biking! Everyone agrees at once. They all feel that biking is not only good exercise but also saves money. On top of that, it is beneficial to protecting the environment.

They set out very early in the morning. After riding a long way, they feel a little hot and a little tired, too. So they get off their bikes and push them along as they start chatting.

Zhang Tianming:	The air here is better than in the city, and the smog isn't as severe!
Lisha:	It's green everywhere—so nice to look at!
Ke Lin:	Oh my, I'm parched . . . Look, I've finished this entire bottle of water! Are there any recycling bins here? We're not supposed to litter.
Lin Xuemei:	Right. We should do our part to protect the environment. Look, there's a recycling bin under the tree.
Lisha:	I haven't bought any bottled water in a long time. Some of my classmates suggested that to protect the earth we should bring [our own] water instead of buying bottled water.
Lin Xuemei:	That's a good suggestion. Oh look, those houses over there have shiny things on top of them. What are those?
Ke Lin:	Those are solar panels, I think. I've seen them in the U.S., too.
Lin Xuemei:	Using solar power to generate electricity—that's great!
Make:	If bikes could also use solar energy to generate electricity, how cool would that be!
Lin Xuemei:	Today many countries in the world are having an energy crisis. If the whole world could use solar and wind energy, think of how much that would save on petroleum and coal! And how . . .
The other four:	It would protect the environment! Haha . . .
Lisha:	I hear that the Chinese government stipulates that offices and other public spaces shouldn't set the heaters above 20 degrees Celsius in winter or set the air conditioning below 26 degrees Celsius in summer.
Ke Lin:	I raise both hands to support this stipulation. Do you remember? In the U.S. in winter, in the classroom you'd be sweating wearing a shirt and in summer you'd still feel very cold wearing a sweater.

Lin Xuemei:	I couldn't agree more. It's too wasteful.
Lisha:	I hear that nowadays many people bring their own utensils to restaurants instead of using disposable ones.
Zhang Tianming:	I think that's a great idea. Otherwise, every year, how many trees get cut down?
Make:	Besides bringing our own chopsticks, we have to bring our own bags when we go shopping.
Lisha:	That's correct. Nowadays Chinese supermarkets don't give away plastic bags. You have to buy your own. That's why many people bring their own bags. Think of how much white pollution can be reduced every year this way!
Lin Xuemei:	Then there are cars, which not only consume lots of energy, but also cause serious air pollution.
Ke Lin:	Everybody should be like us, drive less, bike more and walk more. It'd be better for the environment and better for our health, too.
Zhang Tianming:	That's right. The earth is our home. We should protect it well!
Lin Xuemei:	We should start small. For example, we should turn off the lights [whenever we don't need them] and conserve water.
The other four:	OK. Agreed!
Lisha:	Look, we've come to the foot of the mountain already. Let's start climbing. Let's see who gets to the top of the mountain first! Come on, let's go!

Lesson 17 (Text)

Ordinary Chinese people are generally very frugal. That's why many families have savings in the bank. After the start of the Reform and Opening-Up, many people began to think about how to invest and manage their money.

In recent years China's housing prices have risen rapidly. Buying real estate has become an investment choice for some people. There are also people who see others "flipping stocks," so they begin to flip stocks, too. There are still others who prefer to spend their money on their children's education. They feel that letting their children receive the best education [possible so that they] will have a successful career and a happy life in the future is the best investment.

Zhang Tianming ordinarily doesn't give much thought to investment and money management. Today his cousin chatted with him on the Internet about this question for a long time, and only then did he start to think about it. After dinner, he had a chat with Lisha.

Zhang Tianming:	Recently, my aunt and cousin started to clash with each other. My cousin seemed a little depressed.
Lisha:	Why [did they clash with each other]?
Zhang Tianming:	Before retiring, my aunt scraped and saved some money and planned to leave it for her future grandson or granddaughter's college education.
Lisha:	Your cousin isn't even married yet! Seems the money will have to stay in the bank for twenty years.
Zhang Tianming:	Exactly. That's what my cousin said. Then my aunt came up with an idea to spend the money.
Lisha:	What idea?
Zhang Tianming:	[You know how] my cousin is planning to get married next year, right? My aunt wanted to buy my cousin's fiancée a new car as a wedding gift.
Lisha:	That's really kind of your aunt.
Zhang Tianming:	But my cousin and his fiancée wouldn't agree to her buying a car. Their workplaces are so close to each other that they could share a car. They urged my aunt to buy an apartment. They said that my aunt had worked hard for years. She should live in a bigger apartment and enjoy her retired life in comfort.
Lisha:	They're right! Besides, buying an apartment is a pretty good investment.
Zhang Tianming:	But my aunt said that she didn't have enough money to buy an apartment. My cousin said that he could take out a loan for her. He also told my aunt a story about two elderly ladies buying apartments.
Lisha:	I've also heard the story before. It's about an old lady who saved her money for thirty years. The interest rate was low; her money increased very slowly. It wasn't until she was very old

413

	that she bought an apartment and moved in. However, the other old lady took out a loan and bought a house and moved in thirty years earlier. If you compare them, which old lady knows how to live better?
Zhang Tianming:	That's right. My cousin used this story to persuade my aunt to finally buy an apartment.
Lisha:	That's great. Problem solved.
Zhang Tianming:	That wasn't the end of it. Two weeks ago, there was an apartment with three bedrooms, a living room and two bathrooms that they liked. Originally, they were going to sign the purchase agreement the day after tomorrow. Who could have imagined it? My aunt suddenly changed her mind.
Lisha:	What happened?
Zhang Tianming:	Since she retired, my aunt often gets together with her volunteer friends to play mahjong and chat. A few days ago my aunt heard that some of them had made money every time they flipped stocks. So she changed her mind, and doesn't want to buy an apartment anymore.
Lisha:	Does she want to invest in the stock market?
Zhang Tianming:	Exactly.
Lisha:	But doesn't your aunt know that flipping stocks is risky? An old gentleman who practices tai chi with Li Wen's parents mortgaged his house to the bank and used all of the money to buy stocks. But who would have imagined that the stock market would keep falling. Within three months he lost half [of the money].
Zhang Tianming:	Is buying an apartment risk-free?
Lisha:	Buying an apartment when housing prices are too high is naturally risky.
Zhang Tianming:	It seems that investment isn't a simple matter. I don't know in the end what my aunt will decide to do.

Text

This semester, besides Chinese, Lisha is also taking an elective course in Chinese history. China is one of the world's ancient civilizations, with a recorded history of more than four thousand years. In order to know more about Chinese history, she asks Li Wen to take her to the National Museum of China for a visit. Zhang Tianming and Ke Lin are also interested in Chinese history. When they hear that Lisha is going to visit the museum, they want to go as well. Li Wen very happily agrees.

The National Museum of China is very big. Chinese history is only one part of it. Li Wen suggests that they concentrate on just a few dynasties today. They could visit the museum again later at a more leisurely pace. Lisha and her friends think that that is an excellent suggestion.

Li Wen:	You are all students. I'll first tell you about the most important educator in Chinese history. Do you know who he is?
Lisha:	Is it Confucius?
Li Wen:	Correct. Confucius was the greatest educator and thinker in Chinese history. Even today he has a great impact on Chinese education.
Ke Lin:	My T-shirt has a saying by Confucius on it: "Having friends from afar—isn't that a great joy?"
Li Wen:	We are now in the Qin dynasty gallery. The First Emperor of the Qin dynasty was the first emperor of China.
Lisha:	My history teacher said that the First Emperor made a great contribution to the unification of China.
Li Wen:	Correct. He also unified the script.
Ke Lin:	And he made the people build the Great Wall.
Li Wen:	Was everything he did right?
Zhang Tianming:	He killed several hundred scholars and burned many classics. Is that right?
Lisha:	And he made many many people build palaces and a tomb for him.
Li Wen:	You are all correct. Look, these are the First Emperor's terracotta warriors. Even in death, he made so many "warriors" protect him.
	. . .
Li Wen:	The Qin dynasty didn't last long. The next important dynasty is the Han dynasty. The Han made great strides politically and economically. The term "Han" [for the Han ethnicity] originated with the Han dynasty.
Lisha:	The Silk Road also has to do with the Han dynasty, right?
Li Wen:	Right. Trade with the West started in the Han dynasty.
Zhang Tianming:	Look, we've come to the Tang [gallery]. My dad often says that Chinese Tang poetry is very famous.
Li Wen:	Correct. Many great poets emerged during the Tang dynasty. Whose poems have you studied?

Zhang Tianming:	I've studied Li Bai's poems.
Li Wen:	Li Bai is one of the most famous poets from the Tang dynasty. Also, at that time, because of the Tang dynasty's flourishing economy and culture, many international students came [to China] to study.
Ke Lin:	Just like us.
Li Wen:	Did you know? Historically, China's science and technology was quite advanced.
Lisha:	Are you talking about the Four Great Inventions?
Zhang Tianming:	I know. They are paper, gunpowder, the compass, and movable-type printing.
Li Wen:	Yes, paper and gunpowder were invented early. Movable-type printing was invented during the Song dynasty. The compass also reached a sophisticated level of development during the Song.
	. . .
Li Wen:	We've now come to China's last dynasty, the Qing dynasty.
Ke Lin:	Why was it the last dynasty?
Lisha:	Because Sun Yat-sen led the Revolution of 1911. With the establishment of the Republic of China in 1912, there were no more emperors.
Zhang Tianming:	We covered several thousand years of history in a couple of hours. That's no small feat.
Lisha:	I seem to be hearing a sound.
Li Wen:	What sound?
Lisha:	The sound of history marching.
Zhang Tianming:	I'm also hearing a sound.
Lisha:	You mean the sound of your stomach . . .
Zhang Tianming:	Correct.
Li Wen:	What are you talking about?

Lesson 19 (Text)

Since the beginning of the twenty-first century, China's economy has seen significant development. Many multinational companies have entered China. These big corporations have attracted talent from all over the world, including some Chinese students who have studied and graduated abroad. They have since returned from overseas, and they are called "overseas returnees." Some people jokingly call them "sea turtles." Lin Xuemei has now become one of the new sea turtles. Soon after Xuemei returned to China, she went on the Internet to look for information about jobs. She interned at several companies, but she wasn't quite happy with them. Yesterday a big company that she likes a lot asked her to go there for an interview for a marketing and sales manager position this morning. After the interview was over, she received a call from Lisha just as she got home.

Lisha: Miss Sea Turtle, how was today's interview?

Lin Xuemei: At the beginning I was a little nervous and was sweating quite a bit. My suit jacket almost got wet.

Lisha: But that was not your first time being interviewed. Why were you so nervous?

Lin Xuemei: The person who interviewed me is the general manager of the company. He was very serious. His first question was, "Did you come back to China because you couldn't find a job in America?"

Lisha: This general manager really does sound scary. No wonder you were nervous.

Lin Xuemei: The more nervous I got, the more incoherent my explanation became. An idea flashed across my mind. Without saying anything, I took out two pieces of paper and laid them in front of him. He took a look and his face immediately went from overcast to partly cloudy.

Lisha: What paper? I should get some just in case.

Lin Xuemei: They were offer letters from two companies in California from May. After reading them, the general manager asked, "Since you found a job in America, why did you still want to come back to China to work?"

Lisha: That question isn't difficult to answer. Your boyfriend is studying in China!

Lin Xuemei: If I had said that, he very likely would have thought that it was merely a short-term plan for me to look for a job in China. Luckily, I was no longer nervous at that point. I began with China's economic development and went on to talk about the company's products and product sales. Then I explained why I hoped to work at the company. As the general manager listened to me, his face brightened.

Lisha: The interview was over?

Lin Xuemei: Not yet! At that point, all of a sudden the general manager asked me with a smile, "What do you think your biggest weakness is?"

Lisha: I think that your biggest weakness is that you like to snack.

Lin Xuemei: Then wouldn't he have thought that I was like a little girl?

Lisha: So how did you answer?

Lin Xuemei: I said that an outstanding marketing and management talent should be able to arrange her time scientifically. People who work well also rest well. I still have a way to go in this respect. When I interned, whenever I had pressure I would stay up late, so not knowing how to rest well was probably my biggest weakness.

Lisha: Xuemei, were you talking about your weakness or strength?

Lin Xuemei: Then I said that so long as we can turn our weaknesses into our strengths then our weaknesses wouldn't be something to be afraid of. After I said that, the general manager stood up. While shaking my hand, he said with a smile that he believed in my abilities and asked me to wait for their good news.

Lisha: Fantastic. Congratulations, Manager Lin!

After Xuemei's interview, the company told her to report for work next week. Xuemei and Ke Lin are both very happy. They decide to invite their friends for a get-together at Xuemei's place to celebrate.

Zhang Tianming's good friend Li Zhe has also come to China. He had accepted Tianming's suggestion to intern at a multinational company. As a result, the celebration party has also become a welcoming party for Li Zhe.

Zhang Tianming and Lisha will soon return to America, so this gathering is also a farewell party for them.

The other guests, besides Tianming, Lisha, and Li Zhe, are Li Wen and Make.

Ke Lin went to the supermarket and bought a lot of beverages, snacks, and fruit. Xuemei prepared a hotpot and ordered takeout from a nearby restaurant.

Ke Lin:	Today we get together here to welcome Li Zhe and say goodbye to Tianming and Lisha, but also to celebrate Xuemei finding a job.
Lin Xuemei:	That's right. Don't be shy. Have a lot of food and have fun.
Make:	Xuemei, congratulations on finding a great job. When do you start working?
Lin Xuemei:	Next Monday. Next Friday I'll be in Europe on a business trip promoting solar panels and energy-efficient batteries.
Make:	Solar panels and energy-efficient batteries? That's excellent! Lately, green products having to do with environmental protection and energy conservation have been selling like hot-cakes.
Zhang Tianming:	Hey, Make, Li Wen, come over here. Let me introduce our schoolmate in the United States, Li Zhe, who has just arrived from America.
Li Wen and Make:	Welcome to Beijing.
Li Zhe:	Hello everyone! I [hope I can] count on your help and guidance [since I'm new here].
Lin Xuemei:	Li Zhe, which company in Beijing will you be interning at?
Li Zhe:	I've told Tianming. It's the same company where you'll be working. He didn't tell you the news? The person who interviewed you the other day is my older brother's good friend.
Lin Xuemei:	Really? Then won't that make us colleagues? That's great! We can help each other out.
Li Zhe:	That's why I said I'll be counting on your help.
Lin Xuemei:	Who knows who'll be helping whom?
Li Zhe:	Make, how long have you been in China?
Make:	Six years.
Lisha:	Make, what jobs have you had in China?
Make:	I am a freelancer. I've been an English tutor. I've acted in TV dramas and commercials. Sometimes I also do some translating.
Li Wen:	No wonder you looked so familiar! I've seen your TV dramas. Your acting is quite good.

Make:	I'm just a third-rate actor.
Lisha:	It seems like there are many work opportunities for you. You seem to be very busy.
Make:	Not necessarily. Sometimes I'm very busy. But sometimes I don't have anything to do at all. To be frank, the work is not steady. But it doesn't matter. I can survive without a problem. I'm very happy here. I have made lots of Chinese friends.
Ke Lin:	No wonder your Chinese is so good.
Lin Xuemei:	Li Zhe, your brother's friend is extraordinary, becoming a general manager at such a young age.
Li Zhe:	He not only understands sales but is also a great manager. I hear, under his leadership, the company is getting stronger and stronger.
Li Wen:	Nowadays there are more and more foreign nationals in China. Are you used to life in China?
Lisha:	What do you think? I stay at your house. Every morning I practice tai chi with your parents and eat their delicious and healthy food every day. I don't even want to go back.
Zhang Tianming:	Even less of a problem for me.
Ke Lin:	Do you still update your blog?
Zhang Tianming:	Of course. Here, every day I see and hear something new. I have endless things to write about.
Make:	It goes without saying for me, or I wouldn't have lived here for so long. I think I've become a part of society here.
Li Zhe:	I was worried that I wouldn't be able to adapt to life here. After listening to you, I feel much more at ease.
Li Wen:	Nowadays foreigners come to China for opportunities. Chinese people go abroad to study and work. We are in more frequent and closer contact with one another. The world is getting smaller.
Lin Xuemei:	Li Wen put it well. Friends, let's raise our glasses and have a toast to our friendship!
Zhang Tianming:	To your successful careers in China!
Ke Lin:	To a safe journey for Tianming and Lisha.
Lisha:	To everyone's health!
All:	Cheers!